UNDERSTANDING GLOBALIZATION

UNDERSTANDING GLOBALIZATION

The Social Consequences of Political, Economic, and Environmental Change

Robert K. Schaeffer

ROWMAN & LITTLEFIELD PUBLISHERS, INC.
Lanham • New York • Boulder • Oxford

ROWMAN & LITTLEFIELD PUBLISHERS, INC.

Published in the United States of America
by Rowman & Littlefield Publishers, Inc.
4720 Boston Way, Lanham, Maryland 20706

12 Hid's Copse Road
Cummor Hill, Oxford OX2 9JJ, England

British Library Cataloguing in Publication Information Available

Library of Congress Cataloging-in-Publication Data
Schaeffer, Robert K.
    Understanding globalization: the social consequences of
political, economic, and environmental change / Robert K. Schaeffer.
        p.   cm.
    Includes bibliographical references and index.
    ISBN 0-8476-8351-6 (cloth : alk. paper).—ISBN 0-8476-8352-4
(pbk. : alk. paper)
    1. Social history—1945- 2. Social change.   3. Economic
history—1945-   4. Environmental indicators.   5. World
politics—1945-   I. Title.
HN17.5.S327   1997
306'.09—dc21   96-54822
                                                            CIP

ISBN 0-8476-8351-6 (cloth : alk. paper)
ISBN 0-8476-8352-4 (pbk : alk. paper)

Printed in the United States of America

∞ ™The paper used in this publication meets the minimum requirements of
American National Standard for Information Sciences—Permanence of Paper for
Printed Library Materials, ANSI Z39.48–1984.

To Torry, Jazz, and Jeffree

Contents

uted to rising homelessness in U.S. cities. And it triggered a debt crisis in the third world.

chapter explores the debate about contemporary climate change and examines ways that heat-trapping gases might be reduced.

Acknowledgments

The students, staff, and faculty at San Jose State University deserve my thanks. The students tested the ideas presented in this book, the staff provided important resources, and the faculty gave me the opportunity to develop this project. Department secretary Joan Block, Sociology Department Chair Bob Gliner, and the Inter-Library Loan staff—Shirley Miguel, Cathy Perez, and Hjordis Madsen—deserve special mention for their labors on my behalf.

The research for this book was also assisted by grants provided by the San Jose State University Foundation, the California State University, the Lottery Grants fund, and a sabbatical.

Outside the university, a number of people and organizations contributed to the development of different chapters. My colleagues at Friends of the Earth and Greenpeace supported initial work on dollar devaluations, free trade agreements, population growth, global climate change, and separatism. The Office of Appropriate Technology sponsored my initial work on housing and homelessness. Bill Friedland and participants in the globalization of the fresh fruit and vegetable industry working group helped me develop my ideas about food and hunger. My colleagues in Pugwash Conferences on Science and World Affairs, particularly Metta Spencer and Joseph Rotblat, encouraged my research on separatism. And participants in meetings sponsored by the American Sociological Association and the Political Economy of the World-System reviewed and commented on papers on separatism, democratization, free trade agreements, and job loss. Immanuel Wallerstein, Phil McMichael, Ravi Palat, Giovanni Arrighi, and Metta Spencer have my thanks for their work as organizers and editors.

Dean Birkenkamp provided crucial support for this book. His editorial suggestions and advice were important and welcome.

Torry Dickinson, my friend, colleague, and collaborator deserves special mention for her intellectual contribution to my work. Her interest in history and her appreciation of the social consequences of global change helped shape my ideas and direct my research.

To all of you, my sincere thanks.

1

Change and the Modern World

We live in a time of global change. By that I mean that people around the world are affected by common developments: increased competition, fluctuating exchange rates, the introduction of new technologies, a changing climate, a growing population, the fall of communism. But people often experience change in different ways. Global change is not ubiquitous, nor is it a uniform process. It affects some people more than others and can have very different consequences for people in different settings.

This book will examine global economic, environmental, and political change in much the way that television journalists analyze the weather. TV journalists display satellite images of the earth to identify the global systems that shape the weather in particular regions, then track the movement of weather-system fronts across the landscape. As a low-pressure system moves across the continent, it can have very different consequences for people living along its path. The same storm may bring rain to people living in the plains, snow to people in the mountains, and clear skies to people in the valleys beyond. And while some weather patterns can easily be predicted, some cannot. The storm might unexpectedly inflict flood, hail, avalanche, or drought upon people living along its path. As a result, people visited by the same weather system may experience changing weather in very different ways.

Like a weatherman following a storm, I will narrate the history of contemporary global problems as they track across the economic, environmental, and political landscape. These accounts will pay particular attention to the different and sometimes unexpected social consequences of change.

Global change often results from efforts to solve particular problems. During the 1970s, '80s, and '90s, a series of economic, environmental, and

1

political problems emerged around the world. To solve these problems, state officials, business managers, and social movements adopted policies, practices, or protests that resulted in dramatic social change. These efforts, of course, did not always succeed in addressing the problems people originally confronted. And they frequently produced new problems that demanded further attention. So, as we will see, U.S. policy makers successfully used high interest rates to slow galloping inflation, but this also led to the collapse of the savings and loan industry and contributed to rising homelessness. Farmers used new technologies to increase food production, but burgeoning food supplies led to falling prices that ruined many small farmers. Political movements overthrew dictators in countries around the world, but the new governments were then forced to wrestle with problems inherited from their predecessors. This book will measure the success and assess the failure of efforts to address contemporary problems and the changes associated with them.

Of course, the global changes examined here are interconnected. But the stories about change will be told separately. The idea is to provide accounts of change that can be studied individually or read collectively. Where the story lines intersect, reference will be made to related developments in other chapters. Many of the early chapters focus on changes that originated in the United States. This is done because the United States is a central actor in the world and initiatives taken here are widely felt. And it is done to help U.S. readers appreciate from the outset their relation to global change.

This book is about change in the contemporary world. We can imagine change on a global scale because we share a global conception of time and of space. Our shared conception of time and space is the product of a history, just like many of the other changes examined in this book. In this introductory chapter, I want to trace the history of time and space by describing the emergence of a global system of time keeping, symbolized by the adoption of the Greenwich meridian as the world's time standard in 1884, and the history of a global sense of place, which was perhaps symbolically introduced in the 1494 Treaty of Tordesillas and found full expression in photos of the Earth taken from space in the 1960s. By discussing the history of modern time and a global place, I want to help readers imagine change as both modern and global.

In the first section of this book, we will examine some of the important economic changes that affect people in different worlds around the globe. Chapter 2 examines the changing relations among first, second, and third worlds during the postwar period. In the first world, the wide economic gap that separated the United States from other first world countries after

World War II narrowed substantially by 1970. This narrowing (the relative rise of Europe and Japan and the relative decline of the United States) was the product both of U.S. policies and of European and Japanese strategies. In the second world, efforts to catch up with the first world generally failed, though the poor in the socialist countries did see their economic fortunes improve somewhat. And the economic gap between the third world and the first grew wider during the postwar period, with the exception of a few East Asian countries and oil-rich states.

The narrowing economic gap between the United States and other first world countries created a series of problems for the United States in the early 1970s. To deal with declining U.S. competitiveness and rising inflation, President Richard Nixon devalued the dollar and used wage and price controls to fight inflation. Chapter 3 examines the government's two-decade effort to improve U.S. competitiveness by devaluing the dollar, first in 1972 and again in 1985. Chapter 4 examines government efforts to use wage and price controls in the early 1970s and then high interest rates at decade's end to curb inflation. We will see how dollar devaluation led to unemployment in the northwest timber industry and how high interest rates contributed to rising homelessness.

One of the global problems that high interest rates created in other countries was a deep debt crisis. Chapter 5 explains how Latin American and other third world countries got into debt and examines the steps they had to take to pay back first world lenders. Of course, third world countries were not the only ones to go deeply into debt. During the 1980s, the United States became the world's largest debtor as a result of massive annual budget deficits. Chapter 6 explains why the U.S. debt quadrupled between 1980 and 1992. And chapter 7 shows how stock price inflation led to job losses for American workers.

We then turn to global environmental change. Chapter 8 examines the agricultural revolutions that enabled farmers to increase world food supplies. We will show how burgeoning food supplies drove down commodity prices and ruined many farmers in the United States, and how both food supplies and hunger can grow in the third world. Chapter 9 describes how free trade agreements can expand trade, but how they might also adversely affect agriculture and the environment in poor countries. Global population growth is the focus of chapter 10. It shows why rapid population growth did not produce problems that many people anticipated, but why it nonetheless remains an ongoing problem. And chapter 11 examines global climate change and the problems associated with the production of different greenhouse gases.

In the last three chapters, we will examine political and social change.

Chapter 12 looks at the fall of dictatorship and the emergence of democracy in more than thirty countries since the mid-1970s. Chapter 13 examines problems associated with the partition of nation-states and the emergence of ethnic independence movements in countries around the world. And we conclude, in chapter 14, with an examination of the globalization of regional mafias and the expansion of the world drug trade.

Modern Time

The time we keep is not our own. Instead of setting our alarm clocks and wristwatches to the time of the place we inhabit, we fix our watches to a time set by a global system of timekeeping, a system developed over several centuries by the British and finally adopted by international convention in 1884. As a practical matter, this means that the time kept by our Timex or Seiko watch may err as much as thirty minutes from the "natural" time of the place we live. The amount of error depends on where we live within our assigned "time zones." We keep the "wrong" time because we use a modern, global time, not traditional solar time.

Before the British system of timekeeping was adopted around the world, people used the high point of the sun at noon to set their clocks and mark time. Because the earth rotates past the sun, people standing around the world at the Equator would each keep a slightly different time. And if they set their watches as the sun passed overhead, each would be keeping the correct "solar time" for the place where they stood. But the adoption of a global system of timekeeping means that only people standing at one-hour intervals, measured from Greenwich, a British seaport at the mouth of the Thames River, would keep the correct solar time. Everyone else would set their watches to the time kept by people standing at one-hour intervals, at the "meridian" or center of each time zone. And their watches would err as much as thirty minutes from the watches kept by people standing at the various meridians.

So, for example, the meridian of the Pacific Standard Time Zone, where I live, runs on a north-south axis through Yakima, Washington; Reno, Nevada; and Santa Barbara, California. If you live in these cities, or between them on a straight north-south line, the time you keep is "solar time." That is, when the sun is at its highest, your clock says 12:00 "noon." But if you live on the eastern edge of the time zone, say Ely, Nevada or Yuma, Arizona, the time you keep is nearly one-half hour *behind* solar time. The sun will have already begun to set before your watch says noon. And if you live west of the meridian, in Prince Rupert,

British Columbia, the time you keep is nearly thirty minutes fast: the sun will still be rising in the sky when your watch says noon. Our watches are kept in error because we use a modern global kind of time developed by the British.

Modern global time has a history. It emerged slowly, over several centuries. And it was developed in response to a serious problem: how to find one's way at sea.

When European sailors began sailing across the Atlantic, Indian, and Pacific Oceans in the late fifteenth and early sixteenth centuries, they possessed stout ships with formidable cannons. But they had only rudimentary navigational aids. Sailors could use a compass to determine north and south, east and west. And they could use a backstaff, and later a sextant, to measure the angle between the sun and the horizon and thereby determine their "latitude," or their distance north or south of the Equator. But they could not determine how far they had traveled east or west. They had no way to fix their "longitude."

Sailors' inability to determine their longitude at sea was a serious handicap because once land disappeared from view, they could not tell whether their ship was off the coast of Africa or Brazil. And if they could not fix their position with accuracy, they risked shipwreck or missing their landfall altogether, which meant they could run out of food and starve before they reached shore. In the years between 1550 and 1680, the Portuguese lost 20 percent of their ships to shipwreck, disasters that lead to the deaths of one hundred thousand sailors.[1] And in 1707, the British Mediterranean fleet was wrecked in the approaches to the English Channel, a tragedy that was "conspicuous among the many disasters which a means to find longitude at sea might have avoided."[2]

To prevent such tragedies, mariners and government officials in western Europe tried to find a way to determine longitude at sea. They financed the construction of observatories, where astronomers could use the stars to determine the circumference of the Earth (an important first step in determining longitude), established mapmaking offices, and offered huge prizes—the Spanish offered 6,000 ducats, the Dutch 30,000 scudi, and the British 20,000 pounds—to the inventor who could discover a means of finding longitude at sea. Government investment in this research, on a scale perhaps comparable in our own time to the race to land an astronaut on the moon, placed the problem of longitude high on the scientific agenda.

Scientists already knew a simple way to determine longitude at sea. Once they knew the circumference of the Earth, which astronomers at different observatories had discovered with considerable accuracy by

1670, they could measure longitude by time. Assuming the world is a sphere divided into 360 degrees, one degree of longitude at the Equator would equal four minutes of time, or about 68 miles. So if sailors set their watches when the sun reached its high point at noon, traveled east for one day and looked at their watches when the sun reached its height the following day, if the watch now said 12:04 P.M., they would know they had traveled 68 miles west of where they began.

But theory was not easy to put into practice because clocks and watches in this period were extremely unreliable. Craft workers made watches individually. Their handmade watches did not run at the same speed or keep the same time. Because temperature changes and motion, such as the rocking of a ship at sea, affected the movement of their internal gears, they ran fast, then slow, keeping time erratically. Watchmakers had developed some very accurate pendulum clocks, but these were useless on ships. It was so difficult to make watches that could keep accurate time over long periods at sea (a voyage across the Atlantic took about six weeks) that the huge prizes offered by governments for watches that could determine longitude went unclaimed for decades. The 20,000-pound British prize, first offered in 1714, was not claimed until 1761, by the watchmaker John Harrison.

Harrison's watch had to be accurate to within one-half a degree, or 38 miles, during a six-week voyage out of sight of land. This meant the watch could not gain or lose more than two minutes in forty-two days, or three seconds a day. The Board of Longitude chose this standard of accuracy because they wanted to see British ships safely to Barbados, a Caribbean island that historian Eric Williams called "the hub of the British Empire."[3] Barbados was important to Britain because, as economic historian Ralph Davis explained, the value of the sugar produced on its slave plantations "exceeded the combined exports of all other colonial produce."[4] The Board of Longitude might just as easily have tested Harrison's watch on a run to New England, a voyage of similar distance and duration, but they tested his watch on a trial run to the Caribbean because "little Barbados with its 166 square miles was worth more to British capitalism than New England, New York and Pennsylvania combined."[5]

Watches that met the Board of Longitude's standard of accuracy were then described as "chronometers." And today, watches using the word chronometer must meet this same standard.

As it happened, British and French watchmakers almost simultaneously developed watches that could keep accurate time at sea. Pierre Le Roy's watch, which won the French prize in 1767, was of comparable accuracy. But its design was superior because it could be mass produced. Harrison,

a woodworker by trade, took the ordinary watch of his day and, with superb craft skill and the use of jewels to reduce friction in the mechanism, created an accurate, largely wooden watch. Harrison advanced the art, but not its state. Le Roy, on the other hand, by eliminating the defects and simplifying the mechanism of the ordinary watch, changed the state of the art. And using Le Roy's designs, not Harrison's, the British watchmaking industry grew rapidly in the eighteenth century.

Having discovered the means of determining longitude at sea, the French and British set out to make the watches, survey the world, and then use surveys to draw the maps needed by mariners. Naturally, the French and the British engraved their maps with Parisian or Greenwich "prime meridians" (where 0 degrees longitude is marked on the map) and set their watches to correspond with Parisian or Greenwich time. Although the French possessed state of the art watches that could be more readily mass produced, a considerable technological advantage, the British persuaded sailors around the world to accept a British conception of time and space because they were better able to survey oceans and draw superior, more extensive maps for mariners than the French. The world eventually adopted a British system of time and space, symbolized by the adoption of the Greenwich meridian as 0 degrees longitude.

War played an important role in the rise of the British system of global timekeeping. Harrison and Le Roy invented their chronometers during the Seven Years War, the first in a series of wars between Britain and France that continued, with brief interruptions, from 1767 to the end of the Napoleonic Wars in 1815. During these conflicts, British naval blockades kept French fleets bottled up in port, which made it difficult for the French to test their new watches at sea or conduct the surveys necessary to prepare maps drawn to a French prime meridian. Meanwhile, the British government financed the exploration of the uncharted world. Aided by the new chronometers, Captain James Cook sailed to the Pacific Ocean and drew accurate charts of New Zealand, Australia, the Hawaiian Islands, and the western coast of North America. As Cook wrote, the new watches have "exceeded the expectations of [their] most zealous advocates and . . . [have] been our faithful guide through all the vicissitudes of climates."[6]

When British surveyors returned from overseas voyages, they gave their charts to the British Hydrographic Office, established in 1795 as an arm of the navy, which then produced maps in great quantities and soon "became one of the chief sources of supply for the maritime world. . . ."[7] The government took responsibility for global mapmaking because the once-thriving private mapmaking industry had been unable to profit by selling

charts of faraway places. War and government policy gave the British meridian a tremendous boost. By 1862, the British printed 140,000 charts annually, sold half of them to foreign governments, and provided charts free to private mariners. And by 1883, 72 percent of the world's mariners used maps drawn to the Greenwich meridian. Only 8 percent used maps drawn to a Parisian meridian. The British naval almanac sold twenty thousand copies annually, while its French rival, *Connaissance des Temps*, sold only three thousand copies. Mariners everywhere had come to depend on British charts, drawn to a Greenwich meridian, and likely as not, took British chronometers with them on their voyages.

Although the British system of timekeeping was widely used, it had not yet become recognized as a global standard. But support for a single global system of time and space was growing in the late nineteenth century, largely because it could help solve problems associated with the construction of transcontinental railways.

During the nineteenth century, railroad companies in the United States and Europe each kept their own time. Railway stations often had many clocks, each set to the time used by different companies. In the United States, this meant that "a traveler from East Port, Maine, going to San Francisco, was obliged, if anxious to have correct railroad time, to change his watch some 20 times during the journey."[8] Not only was this inconvenient (imagine today each airline keeping its own time), it was a real hazard for trains traveling on the same stretch of track. To end confusion and risk, a convention was held to adopt a single, global system of timekeeping, which would use the same prime meridian. Given British supremacy in this field, it is not surprising that the twenty-five countries attending the conference, which opened in Washington, D.C., on October 22, 1884, chose a British system of timekeeping over French objections. Delegates fixed the prime meridian in Greenwich, set the International Dateline in the Pacific, and began introducing a global system of time zones.

What did the British gain by securing the means of determining longitude and establishing the prime meridian at Greenwich? Chronometers enabled mariners to navigate more safely, which cut losses to the British shipping industry. This reduced their insurance costs, which enabled Lloyd's of London to become the world's leading insurance broker. The development of the marine chronometer stimulated the British watchmaking industry, creating thousands of skilled, high-paying jobs, while the development of the Hydrographic Office provided considerable government employment. The government's sizable investment in the research necessary for the discovery of longitude—the construction of observatories, for instance—aided scientific inquiry in math and astron-

omy and lent prestige and monetary support to the country's scientific community. Improvements in cartography made it possible to draw accurate sea charts but also more detailed land surveys, which were essential to the subsequent development of railroads. And the British navy gained important military advantages from all this activity. For example, the admiralty's survey of the eastern seaboard of North America was completed just in time to aid British naval forces during the American War of Independence. In the end, the ascension of "British time" was the culmination of century-long efforts by the British government, its navy, its scientists, and industry. And their collective success in this endeavor enabled them to succeed in other fields.

Although a global system of timekeeping has been used for more than a century, it is not used by people everywhere. Indeed, many people objected to the imposition of British time. In Kentucky, editors of the Louisville *Courier-Journal* called the new time, which set back the time in the city almost eighteen minutes from solar time, "a compulsory lie," a "monstrous fraud" and "a swindle." Editors asked readers, "Why should we concede to John Bull's [Great Britain's] dull Greenwich the position of time dictator? Now what is Greenwich to us? A dingy London suburb."[9]

These objections persist today. China, for example, does not use "British time." Instead it uses a single time for the whole country, a time set in Beijing. In practice this means that a person living in the western corner of China keeps time that is three hours ahead of local solar time, and 6 A.M. feels like 3 A.M. And in the United States, Indiana has refused to adopt uniformly the time assigned to it. According to the *New York Times*:

> Every spring, clocks in 47 states spring forward to daylight savings time. But in Indiana, clocks spring in all directions. The capital, Indianapolis, spends five months a year on New York time and seven months on Chicago time—and that's the *official* practice. Life gets even more confusing in the Ohio River town of Levay, where some downtown businesses remain on Eastern standard time the year-round and others turn their clocks ahead one hour every spring (in defiance of Federal law) to synchronize with nearby Cincinnati, a daylight saver.[10]

An attempt to eliminate time differences in the state legislature was defeated by farmers. "It's mainly a matter of tradition," explained William Marvel, an opponent of the bill. "I think Hoosiers basically don't like change."[11] Or people telling them to keep a time not their own. So while a global system of time keeping has emerged, not everyone observes it.

A Global Place

Just as it took a long time for a global system of timekeeping to emerge, it took a long time for people to imagine their "world" as a "global" place. And like the development of time, the idea that the world was a global place, a spherical planet, emerged in response to economic, political, and military problems. Two dates—1494 and 1969—stand out as important moments in the history of the world as a global place.

The first Europeans to explore the overseas world were Portuguese. In the fifteenth century they sailed south to Africa and then made their way across the Indian Ocean to India. They claimed many of the places they landed as the property of their king, taking claim to land that others already possessed. When Columbus set out to find a route to India in 1492, he headed west and came across a "New World" that had not yet been claimed by the Portuguese. Columbus claimed these territories on behalf of the Spanish monarchy.

The overseas voyages immediately created a problem because the Portuguese and Spanish contested each other's right to claim and possess distant lands. To avert war between Portugal and Spain, in 1494 Pope Alexander VI divided the non-European world between rival Iberian kings, assigning each the right to rule overseas territories in their half of the globe.[12]

The Treaty of Tordesillas, as the arbitration agreement was called, is remarkable because it assumed, for the first time, that the world was a global place. The treaty assigned half of the world west of the Azores to Spain and the other hemisphere east of the Azores to Portugal. Because Europeans had not yet circumnavigated the globe, and had not yet found a way to determine longitude accurately, it was difficult to determine exactly where the boundary between Spain and Portugal fell on the *other* side of the world. As it turned out, this division permitted Spain to claim most of the Americas, with the exception of Brazil, which fell on the Portuguese side of the line. Brazil was subsequently colonized by Portugal, and Portuguese, not Spanish, became the language there. Portugal claimed territories in Africa, India, Indonesia, and China. Spain also claimed the Philippines, though it was actually located in the Portuguese sphere according to the treaty. But this error was not discovered until much later, long after the Spanish had colonized the islands.

To avoid conflict between two Catholic kings, Pope Alexander was forced to imagine the world as a global place. But while the Church itself contributed to a global conception of the world for political and military purposes, it was not yet willing to think about the world as a global place in theological terms. Indeed, more than a century after the Treaty of Tord-

esillas was ratified, the Catholic Church in 1633 prosecuted the Italian astronomer Galileo Galilei for heresy because he violated Church doctrine by arguing that the world was a spherical planet orbiting the sun, a view the Church regarded as dangerous.

Since the fifteenth century, people have slowly come to think of the world as a global place. This process was aided by the widespread use of maps and globes in schoolrooms (maps drawn after 1884 to a Greenwich meridian). And the development of ocean transport, railways, and then telecommunications took people to distant parts of the world or brought them closer together. But while education, travel, and electronic communication contributed in different ways to a global conception of place, it remained an abstraction for many people. It was given greater substance when U.S. astronaut Neil Armstrong landed on the moon in 1969 and announced that he was taking "one small step for man, one giant leap for mankind." The astronauts' photographs of the Earth, spinning in space, gave currency to the idea of the world as a global place. After we saw these pictures, it became difficult not to imagine the world as Columbus, Pope Alexander, or Neil Armstrong did.

Of course, some people today do not imagine the world as a global place. A journalist traveling to Sarawak, Malaysia, in 1990 was asked by indigenous people living in the rain forest, "Why are there so many moons?" Puzzled by the question, he asked what they meant. They told him that they wondered why a slightly different moon appeared in the sky each night. Evidently, the Penans do not imagine their world as a globe with an orbiting moon that waxes and wanes.

Where people do imagine the world as a global place, they do not necessarily think of it as a singular place. Instead, they see themselves as belonging to different social "worlds."

Although European voyagers began creating a singular global place, they also began dividing it. The binary division of the world by the pope was soon challenged by other Europeans who began claiming overseas territories for their own royal families. During the four hundred years between the Treaty of Tordesillas and the Conference of Berlin, which divided Africa among European empires in 1884–85, around the same time they adopted the British system of timekeeping, the world was divided and redivided by Portuguese and Spanish, then Dutch, British, and French empires, and later by Belgian, German, Italian, Japanese, Russian, and American states. These divisions created about fifty different political entities called empires or states. In the century since then, world war, revolution, and decolonization have doubled the number of political entities, now called "nation-states" to about one hundred in 1960 and to more than one hundred eighty by 1993. These divisions of the world have

created different political "worlds" for people inhabiting the globe. These political worlds are different from the worlds that preceded them: people now living in India have a republican form of government; prior to 1948 they were a colony of Great Britain, and before the seventeenth century they lived in one of many kingdoms. And they are different from the contemporary political worlds of people living in other parts of the globe.

Not only is the globe divided along political lines, it is also divided economically. Although economists and politicians have used different terms to describe the economic division of the planet, most divide it into three parts. The rich capitalist countries in Western Europe, North America, and Japan are said to belong to the "first world." The not-so-rich communist countries in Eastern Europe and Asia were, until 1990, said to belong to the "second world." The poor countries in southern Asia, Africa, and Latin America were counted as members of the "third world." (See chapter 2.)

It is important to imagine the global features that we share with other people and to recognize that some people may experience time and place in different ways. So when we examine contemporary global issues, analyzing events that are shared by many people around the world, we should recognize that the same global events may be experienced and understood in very different ways.

Notes

1. Schaeffer, Robert. "The Standardization of Time and Space," in Edward Friedman, ed., *Ascent and Decline in the World-System*. Beverly Hills, Calif.: Sage, 1982, pp. 71–72.

2. May, W. E. *Four Steps to Longitude*. Greenwich: National Maritime Museum, 1962, p. 5.

3. Williams, Eric. *Capitalism and Slavery*. New York: Putnam, 1944, p. 74.

4. Davis, Ralph. *The Rise of the Atlantic Economies*. Ithaca: Cornell University Press, 1973, p. 251.

5. Williams, 1944, p. 54.

6. Howse, D. *Greenwich Time and the Discovery of Longitude*. Oxford: Oxford University Press, 1980, p. 71.

7. Brown, L. A. *The Story of Maps*. Boston: Little, Brown, 1949, p. 282.

8. Howse, 1980, pp. 120–21.

9. O'Malley, Michael. *Keeping Watch: A History of American Time*. New York: Penguin Books, 1990, p. 134.

10. *New York Times*, February 28, 1993.

11. Ibid.

12. Parry, J. H. *Europe and a Wider World 1415–1715*. London: Hutchinson University Library, 1961, pp. 50–59.

2

The World after World War II

The contemporary world was shaped by decisions made during and after World War II. In their effort to solve some of the problems that had contributed to global conflict, leaders of the great powers decided in the mid–1940s to create a new world order that would "decolonize" European and Japanese empires and promote economic "development" in countries around the world. But political disagreements among the great powers—the United States, the Soviet Union, Great Britain, France, and China—led to a division of the world into three parts, which are commonly referred to as the first, second, and third worlds. And policies designed to promote economic growth and development have had mixed results for people living in these different worlds.

Since 1945, people in the first world have generally experienced rapid economic growth and increased wealth. Economic differences between people living in various first world countries have narrowed. Although people in the second and third worlds have also realized some economic development, their wealth has not increased as fast as that of people in the first world. The result is that the gap between rich and poor countries has grown wider in the past fifty years. This chapter will explain how different "worlds" emerged and why their economic fortunes diverged in the postwar period. These developments contributed to some of the problems people around the world experience today, problems that will be explored in subsequent chapters.

Different Worlds

At summit conferences in Newfoundland, Tehran, Cairo, Yalta, and Potsdam during and after World War II, leaders of the great powers discussed

13

how to prevent the recurrence of global war and solve the political and economic problems that had triggered war. U.S. officials argued that the seizure of colonies, first by western European countries in the eighteenth and nineteenth centuries and then by Germany, Italy, and Japan in the early and mid-twentieth century, had contributed to the outbreak of war. U.S. President Franklin Roosevelt told British Prime Minister Winston Churchill during the war: "I can't believe we can fight a war against fascist slavery and at the same time not work to free people all over the world from a backward colonial policy."[1] And Soviet leader Joseph Stalin agreed, arguing that neither victorious Allied countries nor defeated Axis powers should be allowed to keep their colonial possessions after the war. Together, U.S. and Soviet leaders insisted that "empires" should be broken up and independent countries established in their colonies, a process known as "decolonization."

Although British, French, Dutch, and Belgian empires had been allied with the victors, they were not in a position to refuse. Two world wars (1914–18 and 1939–45) and the Great Depression (1929–39) had greatly weakened them. As French leader Charles de Gaulle said of World War II, "All the nations of Europe lost. Two were defeated."[2] European empires agreed to decolonization because they relied on U.S. economic assistance to rebuild their shattered economies and because they were increasingly besieged by nationalist movements demanding independence in their colonies. So European countries agreed to begin the process of decolonization, slowly granting independence to countries in Africa, the Middle East, and Asia.

U.S. leaders were also determined to prevent a recurrence of world war by decolonizing European and Asian empires. In addition, they wanted to prevent the return of global economic depression. They believed that the Great Depression in the 1930s had fueled the rise of fascism and expansionary nationalism, so they promoted economic growth, not just in Europe but in newly independent countries around the world, to avert depression and deter war. To accomplish this, the great powers organized new global institutions like the United Nations and the World Bank to promote political decolonization and economic development as "solutions" to the problems that had led to war.

But while the victors agreed on the outlines of the postwar world, they soon disagreed about its particular contours. U.S. and Soviet officials disagreed about whether occupied Germany should be partitioned and whether a divided Germany should be allowed to develop economically. They disagreed about the kind of political parties that should take power in Eastern European and East Asian countries, and the kind of economic

policies that newly created governments would pursue. The series of U.S. and Soviet disagreements and conflicts that emerged in the late 1940s and early 1950s, collectively known as the "Cold War," began dividing the world into two political and economic parts, one with a democratic political system and capitalist economy, the other with a communist political system and a socialist economy. Over time, Japan, Australia, and the democratic-capitalist countries in Western Europe that allied themselves with the United States became known as the first world, while the communist-socialist countries in Eastern Europe and East Asia that aligned with the Soviet Union became known as the second world.

Like the Treaty of Tordesillas, the Cold War divided the world between two great powers. And the experience of people living in capitalist and socialist worlds began to diverge. But while the Cold War divided much of the world, it did not bisect all of it.

While Cold War disagreements sharpened in the 1940s and 1950s, Western European states began granting independence to countries in Asia, Africa, and the Middle East. The leaders of these new countries all wanted decolonization to spread and tried to promote economic development in their own countries. And many did not want to end up on either side of the emerging Cold War divide. They argued that they should be allowed to become "nonaligned" countries, adopting political institutions and economic policies of their own choosing. The leaders of the nonaligned countries—among them China, Indonesia, India, Yugoslavia, and Egypt—met in April 1955 at a conference in Bandung, Indonesia. European writers described the nonaligned movement as an attempt to create a third world that would provide an alternative to the policies and practices of first and second world countries. Now, forty years later, the term third world is used to describe countries that are desperately poor. The changed meaning of the term illustrates how much the political and economic fortunes of people living in this world have changed.

Each of the three worlds that emerged after World War II has experienced dramatic change. For some, change has been a positive development, while for others it has been a negative experience. By examining the postwar experience of people living in each of these worlds we can see how their economic circumstances have changed.

Worlds of Difference: The First World

World War II destroyed the economic wealth of countries in Europe and East Asia, reducing both victorious and defeated people to poverty. But

it greatly increased economic activity in the United States, lifting the country out of the Depression. By war's end, the United States produced half of the manufactured goods in the world, and Americans enjoyed a much higher standard of living than other first world people. Although the economic gap between the United States and other first world countries loomed large in 1950, it narrowed slowly and eventually closed during the next thirty to forty years. And while no other single country produced as much as the United States in 1990, many people in other first world countries enjoyed a higher standard of living.

Western European countries and Japan made a remarkable recovery and achieved rapid economic growth in the postwar period. They were able to narrow economic differences because they received substantial U.S. aid and because they undertook successful initiatives designed to improve their economic position in the world.

Today it might seem odd that the United States would provide substantial economic assistance to its wartime allies *and* its enemies, enabling them to become formidable economic competitors decades later. But at war's end, U.S. officials had compelling economic and political reasons for assisting the threadbare or shredded economies of their friends and adversaries.

In economic terms, U.S. officials worried that a slow recovery from war in Europe and Japan would mean people could not afford to buy U.S. goods, which would force U.S. industry to scale back production and lay off workers who had recently returned from military service. U.S. leaders were determined to prevent a return to prewar economic depression, not just in the United States, but also in Europe and Japan, where continuing economic misfortune might give rise to communist movements. So the United States offered in 1948 to provide substantial economic assistance to Western European countries through the European Recovery Plan (ERP). Developed by U.S. Secretary of State George C. Marshall, the "Marshall Plan," as the ERP became known, provided about $13 billion to needy European countries over the next four years.[3] Large sums of money were also given to Japan through similar programs. In addition to U.S. government aid, private corporations invested heavily in Western European countries. U.S. investments grew from $1.7 billion in 1950 to $6.6 billion in 1960, then to $25 billion in 1970 and $96 billion by 1980.[4] This investment provided capital, which created jobs, and provided U.S. currency to other first world countries, which they could use to buy imported U.S. goods. The infusion of money provided by U.S. taxpayers and private investors greatly assisted economic recovery in Europe and Japan.

U.S. officials also had political reasons to assist their friends and former foes. As U.S.-Soviet disagreements sharpened during the Cold War, U.S. leaders sought to consolidate support for democratic political institutions and capitalist economic policies in Western Europe and Japan. So when war broke out between communist North Korea and capitalist South Korea in 1950, U.S. officials began providing substantial military aid to their allies. Because the United States stationed large numbers of soldiers in allied countries and purchased military supplies and equipment from them, U.S. military spending helped spur their economies. And because the United States assumed the lion's share of military spending in regional defense organizations like the North Atlantic Treaty Organization (NATO), countries in Europe and Japan could rebuild their economies without diverting money to the military. Between 1950 and 1970, U.S. military spending was three to four times greater than the *combined* military spending of its five principal allies: the United Kingdom, France, West Germany, Italy, and Japan.[5]

For their part, European countries and Japan adopted different economic strategies that improved their economic position vis-à-vis the United States. Although European leaders were reluctant to grant independence to their colonies because they feared that the loss of colonial revenues and resources would impoverish them, they nonetheless moved ahead with decolonization.

As it turned out, their fears were unjustified. The former imperial countries quickly established commercial relations with their former colonies, providing revenue and resources while reducing the cost of maintaining expensive overseas bureaucracies and military establishments. And having dispensed with their colonies, they could turn their attention to domestic matters.

On the domestic front, European countries and Japan deployed different economic strategies. Western European countries abandoned the rivalries that had led them to successive world wars and began to collaborate, agreeing to create joint military forces in NATO in 1949, developing a common market in 1958, and eventually establishing a pan-European institutions called the European Community in 1967, which became the European Union in 1992.

These collective economic and political institutions enabled participating countries to eliminate economic barriers that hampered the emergence of large-scale businesses that could compete with large U.S. firms and to develop policies that could assist each other's economic development. For instance, political and economic cooperation led to the creation of Airbus Industries, a pan-European company whose aircraft now compete effec-

tively with U.S. aircraft manufacturers like Boeing and McDonnell Douglas. And the European space rocket consortium Arianespace has captured more than half of the world market for commercial space launch vehicles, an industry pioneered by the United States.[6]

The Japanese took a different approach. They did not attempt to create economic or political institutions with their Asian neighbors. Rather than develop a common market with Korea or Taiwan, the Japanese sought close economic ties with the United States, gearing their industry to produce goods for export to U.S. markets. And because the government discouraged competition among Japanese firms, kept wages relatively low, and encouraged workers to save their money, which could then be invested in the domestic economy, they were able to build their economy by exporting goods to the United States. The U.S. government assisted this process by setting favorable exchange rates between the U.S. dollar and the Japanese yen, which made it easier for Japan to export goods to the United States (see chapter 3).

Since World War II, timely U.S. aid and successful independent initiatives by European countries and Japan enabled them to become more competitive with the United States. And as they became more competitive, they recovered wealth lost during the war and narrowed the economic gap that once distanced them from the United States.

In 1948, the United States produced 56.7 percent of the world's manufacturing, while the United Kingdom, France, West Germany, Italy, and Japan produced 15 to 20 percent. But by 1973, the U.S. total had declined to 21.9 percent while the others collectively increased to 33.2 percent.[7] Other indicators tell a similar story.

In the thirty years between 1945 and 1974, the United States maintained a "trade surplus," meaning that it sold more goods abroad than it imported. But after 1975, the United States began to run a persistent "trade deficit," which grew from about $2 billion in 1975 to $122 billion in 1990.[8] And the domination of markets by U.S. companies has also declined. Of the world's largest 200 firms in 1960, 127 were American and they accounted for 72 percent of the sales in this league. But by 1980, only half of the world's biggest firms were based in the United States, and they made only half of all sales.[9] As European countries and Japan became more competitive, the economic differences between first world countries narrowed and their standards of living became more alike.

But it is important to remember that first world people experienced *increasing economic equality* in different ways. For people living in Western Europe and Japan, increasing economic equality with the United States meant greater wealth and a higher standard of living. But many people living in the United States experienced this in a different way.

Initially, North Americans viewed economic recovery in Europe and Japan as a good thing because the sale and export of U.S. goods to these regions created U.S. jobs. Because nearly one-third of the U.S. workforce was unionized and because U.S. firms were very profitable, U.S. workers received high wages in the 1950s and '60s. This enabled them to purchase cars and buy houses, which made the economy grow and helped most Americans prosper. The booming postwar economy and a tax structure that provided the government with money that enabled it to assist poor Americans created a higher standard of living and greater economic equality. The number of people living in poverty declined in the United States in the 1950s and '60s, and the gap between rich and poor narrowed.

But as Europe and Japan revived, it became more difficult to sell U.S. goods abroad. U.S. companies and their workers began to experience first world economic equality as a problem because it became more difficult for them to maintain high profits and wages in this new, more competitive environment.

Widening Gaps in the United States

The 1970s were a turning point for the United States. Before 1970, people in the United States benefited from the economic reconstruction and recovery of other first world countries. And U.S. military spending provided jobs and stimulated economic growth in the United States and in countries overseas. But after 1970, first world recovery led to increasing first world competition, which led to falling profits, lost jobs, and a decline of some U.S. industries.

In the early 1970s, U.S. government officials introduced policies designed to address the problems associated with growing first world competition. To improve U.S. competitiveness, the Nixon administration began by devaluing the dollar in August 1972. By reducing the official value of the dollar, which increased the value of other first world currencies, officials hoped it would be easier for firms to sell goods overseas and harder for first world countries to sell their products in the United States. By making U.S. firms more competitive, officials hoped to eliminate the trade deficit and end the decline of U.S. industries (see chapter 3).

But the OPEC oil embargo, which began after the Arab-Israeli Yom Kippur War in 1973, made it difficult to achieve these goals. Rising oil prices renewed inflation and increased the cost of imported oil, which led to larger U.S. trade deficits.

In the 1970s, U.S. government officials and industrial leaders developed two other kinds of policies to increase their ability to compete with other

first world countries. First, they believed that if U.S. wages, which were then higher than wages in Europe and Japan, could be reduced, they could better compete with other first world countries. And if profits could be increased, they believed that firms could invest in new technologies that would modernize U.S. industry and make it more competitive with first world rivals.

During the 1970s and '80s, government and private industry took numerous steps to reduce labor costs in U.S. industries. In 1973, the Nixon administration introduced wage and price controls through the Economic Stabilization Act to restrain wages. To reduce labor costs after wage and price controls expired in 1974, U.S. businesses moved factories to lower-wage settings in the United States or overseas. And they sought to reduce or eliminate unions. Government policy assisted this process. The Reagan administration disbanded the air traffic controllers union during a strike and subsequently made it more difficult for unions to organize workers or strike successfully. As a result, union membership in the United States declined from 31 percent of the workforce in 1970 to only 17 percent in 1990.[10]

These developments weakened the bargaining power of U.S. workers and wages fell. From a 1973 high of $327.45, real weekly earnings declined nearly 20 percent to $264.76 by 1990.[11] And where industries declined, migrated overseas, or introduced new technologies to replace workers, unemployment also rose. In 1971, 5.8 percent of the workforce was unemployed. But during the 1982 recession, unemployment reached 9.5 percent.[12]

At the same time, tax policies were changed to increase the profitability of U.S. businesses and the earnings of wealthy individuals (see chapter 6). Corporate tax cuts raised profits and increased the value of stocks. Because the wealthiest 10 percent of U.S. families owns 90 percent of corporate stocks and 95 percent of government bonds, and because their taxes were cut sharply in the 1980s, wealthy individuals earned more (see chapter 7).

These two developments—declining wages for poor and working people, but higher profits for corporations and rising incomes for wealthy individuals—created increasing economic inequality in the United States between 1970 and 1990.[13] After shrinking during the 1950s and '60s, the gap between rich and poor widened in the 1970s and '80s.[14]

This growing gap meant different things for different people. On the one hand, the number of millionaires nearly tripled, and billionaires quadrupled during the 1980s.[15] The pay of corporate executives increased from forty times greater than that of the average factory worker in 1980

to ninety-three times greater in 1989. Kevin Phillips, a former Reagan administration official, said of these developments, "No parallel upsurge of riches has been seen since the late 19th century, the era of the Vanderbilts, Morgans and Rockefellers."[16]

On the other hand, incomes for middle-class Americans stagnated and more family members needed to work to keep the household afloat, much less get ahead. In 1993, nearly thirty-seven million people lived in poverty, more than any year since 1962.[17]

One way to understand the way people experience different economic circumstances is to compare the monthly household budgets of poor, middle-class, and wealthy Americans.

Sonja Blutgarten, an unemployed woman raising two children in San Francisco, lives on income provided by the state of California through the Aid to Families with Dependent Children program. Each month she receives $663 in welfare and $168 worth of food stamps, totaling $831. The *New York Times* reported that she spent $400 for rent, $60 for utilities, $218 for food, $35 for a transit pass, $40 for laundry, $30 for household supplies, $20 for personal supplies, $5 for a checking account, and $20 to pay for old bills, for a total of $828. If she keeps to this budget, she can save $3 a month.[18]

Reynell Tyndall, his wife, Margaret, and their daughter live in Brooklyn. He works as a mechanic at a tool and die company, she works as a bank teller, and their combined monthly income is $2,643, just above the median family income. They pay $265 for rent, $20 for gas, $40 for electricity, $347 for food, $87 for transportation, $200 for day care, $300 for telephone (they call family in Jamaica regularly), $217 for baby supplies, $170 for life insurance, and $200 for medical bills, totaling $1,846. By living in a low-rent and high-crime neighborhood, they can save nearly $800 a month, which they hope to use for a down payment on a house.[19]

Donald Trump, a real estate developer who builds and owns hotels and casinos in New York and Atlantic City, is listed as a billionaire. He owns three homes, including a fifty-room penthouse overlooking Central Park. When he lost money in some real estate deals, bankers put him on a restricted *monthly* budget, allowing him $450,000 for personal spending, $246,000 for maintaining his Boeing 727 jet, $841,000 for keeping up his 282-foot yacht, $2,138,000 to pay interest on personal lines of credit, and $382,000 for business, legal, and charitable spending.[20]

As a result of these developments, many people in the United States have experienced the "narrowing" of economic differences between first world countries as a problem because it has led to the decline of U.S. competitiveness. And because efforts to increase U.S. competitiveness

have resulted in falling incomes and lost jobs, many Americans have experienced the widening of economic differences in the United States as a problem.

Although U.S. officials and business leaders developed policies designed to slow U.S. economic decline and improve U.S. competitiveness, which increased the gap between rich and poor in the United States, they did little to prevent first world differences from narrowing further. Indeed, between 1970 and 1990, Europe and Japan became even more competitive with the United States. U.S. trade deficits have continued to rise, and the per capita wealth of other first world countries continues to increase and even surpass per capita U.S. wealth: Switzerland, Luxembourg, Japan, Iceland, and Norway all have a higher gross domestic product per capita than the United States, while Sweden, Finland, Germany, Denmark, Canada, and France are approaching that of the United States.[21] And today, most of the world's billionaires are residents of other first world countries. Of the top twenty-five billionaires in 1989, only four were American.

During the past fifty years, economic differences among first world countries have greatly narrowed, though this has led to widening economic differences within the United States.

Worlds of Difference: The Second World

In the late 1940s, political disputes between the United States and the Soviet Union led to Cold War divisions and the emergence of a second world, which consisted of communist countries in Eastern Europe and East Asia. Although first world leaders often viewed the second world as a single political entity, with its member states acting in concert, political differences within the communist world quickly surfaced. Yugoslavia's Marshal Josip Broz Tito successfully broke away from the Soviet Union. Leaders in Hungary also tried, unsuccessfully, to do so in 1956. China broke with the Soviet Union and began pursuing independent foreign and economic policies in the mid–1950s. And representatives from Yugoslavia, China, and Vietnam attended the Bandung Conference in 1955, a meeting of poor and nonaligned countries that led to the emergence of a third world.

After World War II, the economic differences between second world countries in Eastern Europe and first world countries in Western Europe were relatively small. World war had leveled economies throughout Europe and East Asia, and countries on both sides of the emerging political

divide struggled to recover lost wealth and improve their economic circumstances. But while first world countries in Western Europe and Asia quickly recovered lost wealth and drew nearer to the United States in economic terms, second world states did not. They were able to rebuild their economies but could not forge ahead or close the widening economic gap between first and second world countries. Indeed, when communist regimes collapsed in Eastern Europe and the Soviet Union in 1989 and 1990, it became evident that the economic differences between second and first world countries had widened considerably during the Cold War (1950–90). One 1990 *Wall Street Journal* survey estimated that per capita income in the Soviet Union stood at $1,780.[22] If accurate, this meant that Soviet citizens earned, on average, a little less than people living in Algeria ($2,645), Argentina ($2,331), Mexico ($2,082), and Chile ($1,950), and slightly more than people in Costa Rica ($1,584) or Brazil ($1,523), countries regarded by most economists as belonging to the third world.

Another way of looking at the declining economic fortunes of second world countries would be to compare them with Japan. As the Italian economist Giovanni Arrighi noted, "In 1938, Japan's GNP per capita was about one-half that of Yugoslavia, about four-fifths that of Hungary and Poland, and about five times that of China. In 1988, by contrast, it was more than eight times that of Yugoslavia, more than 10 times that of Hungary and Poland, and more than 65 times that of China."[23]

Economic differences between second and first world countries grew wider during the Cold War for a variety of reasons. First, postwar reconstruction in communist countries proceeded without the generous financial assistance or investment given by the United States to allied first world countries. U.S. officials initially offered Marshall Plan funds to communist countries in Eastern Europe, but the Soviet Union would not allow them to accept the conditions that accompanied the U.S. offer. The Soviet Union tried, like Western European countries, to develop common economic policies with its Eastern European allies, but it offered them little economic assistance and often established economic relations that worked to their allies' disadvantage. Lacking both an infusion of external wealth and an effective way to collaborate with other second world countries, some of whom refused to cooperate in joint economic programs (Yugoslavia, China), second world countries recovered slowly from the war.

What is more, as political differences sharpened during the Cold War, second world countries spent heavily on military expenditures, which absorbed much of the wealth they produced in agriculture and industry.[24] Estimates vary, but the Soviet Union spent about $4.6 trillion between

1960 and 1987, between 15 and 30 percent of its GNP, on military expenditures, two to four times as much as the United States spent in the same period.[25]

Heavy military spending absorbed scarce supplies of capital, skilled labor, and natural resources, which retarded economic growth and contributed to economic stagnation and decline. For second world consumers, these problems meant crowded housing, long lines, and empty shelves. By the mid-1980s, Soviet leader Mikhail Gorbachev wrote, "the country found itself in a state of severe crisis which embraced all spheres of life." And he attributed many of these problems to military spending, which he said had "exhausted our economy."[26] (See chapter 13.)

Although a large military enabled Soviet leaders to exercise political power and assist neighboring communist countries and socialist movements overseas, Soviet military hardware proved ineffective against U.S. arms in the Middle East and Afghanistan. During a 1982 air battle over Lebanon for example, Israeli pilots flying U.S. planes shot down eighty Soviet aircraft flown by Syrian pilots while losing none of their own. And during the 1991 Gulf War, Allied forces destroyed four thousand Soviet-made Iraqi tanks, prompting many Soviet leaders to conclude that the entire Soviet military model had become "obsolete."[27]

Although economic differences between second and first world countries grew wider during the Cold War, leading to the political collapse of communist governments in Eastern Europe, their poor economic performance should also be compared with capitalist countries in the third world. Communist countries performed badly relative to first world countries, but so too did many capitalist and nonaligned countries in the third world.

During the postwar period, Eastern European countries fared about as well economically as capitalist countries in Latin America. Arrighi notes that between 1938 and 1988, Yugoslavia did worse than Latin America as a whole, about the same as Turkey and Egypt, but better than southern and central Africa. Hungary and Poland did better than Turkey and Egypt, and about the same as countries in Latin America. And the Soviet Union did about as well as Mexico or Chile, which is to say not very well, though better than countries in Africa. According to Arrighi,

> The U.S.S.R. has probably done no better (and may have done worse) than Latin America in the "race" to catch up with the standards of wealth set by the West. Yet the lower strata of its population have done incomparably better than the lower social strata of the population in Latin America in improving their nutritional, health and education standards. And the improvement

has been even greater for the lower strata in China in comparison with those of South Asia or Southeast Asia.[28]

There is, however, one important difference between the economic performance of communist countries in Europe and Asia and capitalist countries in Latin America. Generally speaking, income differences within the communist countries remained small, while income differences between rich and poor in capitalist Latin American countries remained quite large. That is, poor people living in Poland or the Soviet Union received a better education and health care, access to efficient public transit, greater employment opportunities, and higher wages than poor rural or urban people in most Latin American countries. In this regard, communist countries were more like Western European countries and Japan, with relatively narrow domestic gaps between rich and poor, and less like the United States, which, like Latin American countries, had relatively large domestic gaps between rich and poor.

But this may be changing. The income equality characteristic of communist countries during the Cold War may be a thing of the past. In former communist countries, and in China (which is still communist), the adoption of capitalist economic policies has significantly widened the gap between rich and poor in just a few years. Some economists, like Simon Kuznets, have long argued that the "initial" phase of capitalist development is accompanied by increasing differences between rich and poor, but that these differences will shrink over time. While this was true of many Western European and North American countries in the nineteenth century, economic differences have grown and persisted in many poor countries during the postwar period. It is to these other countries, the third world, that we now turn.

Worlds of Difference: The Third World

When the term was coined in the 1950s, the third world referred to countries that were politically nonaligned. Today, it simply means countries that are poor or underdeveloped.

Initially, the third world was created by the decolonization of empires based in Europe, Japan, and North America. The United States participated in the decolonization process when it gave independence to the Philippines in 1946. And when colonies in Asia, Africa, and the Middle East won their independence, most of them in the 1950s and early 1960s, they resisted being assigned to one of two emerging Cold War worlds.

Instead they tried to create an alternative political world of their own. But while they were fairly successful at pursuing independent, nonaligned foreign policies, they found it difficult to develop economically. And during the decades that followed, the economic differences between third and first world countries grew larger.

There are different ways of describing the economic differences, or gap, between third and first worlds. The third world, with about 75 percent of the world's population, has about 15 percent of its income and wealth. The 25 percent of the world's population living in the first world has 85 percent of all wealth.[29]

Most economists believe that economic differences have been growing since the end of World War II. One way to measure this is to compare the average per capita incomes of third world countries with those of first world countries. In 1950, the per capita income of people living in the third world was $164, while per capita income of first world people was $3,841, a difference of $3,677. Thirty years later, in 1980, people in the third world earned more, $245, but people in the first world increased their incomes to $9,648. Using this measure, one could say that the difference or gap between third and first world incomes was three times greater in 1980 than it was in 1950.[30]

Throughout much of the postwar period, many third world economies grew at a faster *rate* than First World countries. But because they were so much poorer to begin with, they did not catch up. If they could maintain higher rates of growth, which would be difficult, they might eventually catch up.[31] If, for example, South Korea could grow at the rapid 7.3 percent annual rate it achieved between 1960 and 1975, it could catch up with the first world in 69 years. But it would take Brazil (4.2 percent annual growth) 362 years, Turkey (4 percent) 675 years, Panama (3.8 percent) 1,866 years, and China (3.8 percent) 2,900 years to catch up with the first world.[32]

In a 1986 report, Louis Emmery, head of the Organization for Economic Cooperation and Development (OECD), said, "If per capita growth rates in both Asia and OECD remain at their rates of the past 15 years, Asia will not reach the OECD per capita income average until more than two *centuries* from now."[33]

Economists have made the same point by looking backward instead of forward. The level of economic development "reached by Afro-Asian countries in 1970 is very low, close to that of the western countries . . . in the 1770s. Latin America's level . . . is nearer to that of France in 1880–90 . . . [while] Argentina and Chile nearer to what France achieved by 1900–10," said Paul Bairoch, author of *The Economic Development of the Third World Since 1900*.[34]

Some economists have gone even further, arguing that

> most of the people in the two million villages of the Third World do not have the technical knowledge (particularly of mechanics) that European villagers of the 12th and 13th century had. They are thus not one industrial revolution behind but two, because they do not know about machines driven by vertical wheels or methods of lifting water that were invented or updated in the "First Industrial Revolution" of the Middle Ages.[35]

With these economic and temporal differences between third and first worlds in mind, Nigerian President Olusegun Obasanjo observed, "It is difficult to believe that we [in the third world] inhabit the same historical time [as that of the first world]."[36]

The gap between third and first world economic fortunes has increased for a variety of reasons. After World War II, people throughout the third world increased their production of agricultural goods, raw materials, and industrial products. By selling their goods to the first world, they expected to make money that could improve their standard of living. According to Bairoch, third world countries doubled their production of agricultural goods and increased their production of raw materials eightfold between 1934–38 and 1963–65.[37] But the increasing supply of third world goods led to falling prices and lower earnings.

In addition, third world countries sold their goods to large transnational companies based in the first world. Some of these firms have annual sales figures that are larger than the gross national product of many third world countries. For example, in 1991 Unilever, the British transnational that trades in food and natural resources, had sales of $40 billion, making it as large in economic terms as Pakistan or Venezuela. In real terms, Unilever was the economic equal of—combined—Angola (GNP $4.5 billion), Bolivia ($3.7 billion), Chad ($0.8 billion), Congo ($2 billion), Gambia ($0.18 billion), Jordan ($4.3 billion), Laos ($0.5 billion), Nicaragua ($4.3 billion), Panama ($5.1 billion), Senegal ($3.8 billion), Uganda ($3.2 billion), and Zambia ($2.1 billion).

Large first world transnationals often control world markets in the goods that third world countries produce, making it difficult for third world producers to earn the kind of money they might in more competitive markets. Unilever, for example, dominated the world trade in palm oil, while just four companies controlled 60 to 80 percent of world cocoa sales: Cadbury-Schweppes, Nestlé, Gill and Diffus, and Rowntree.[38]

Because there are many third world suppliers but few first world buyers, third world countries earned less than they might. Economists describe declining earnings for third world countries as "falling terms of

trade." Bairoch estimates that the terms of trade for third world goods fell nearly 20 percent between 1952 and 1970.[39] And since 1970, the terms of trade have declined even more. Between 1970 and 1990, prices for agricultural products declined 40 percent, for fats and oils 60 percent, for metals and minerals nearly 80 percent.[40] At the same time, however, the price third world countries paid for imported first world goods increased. The declining terms of trade meant that a ton of African copper could buy 115 barrels of oil in 1975, but only 58 barrels in 1980; a ton of coffee could buy 148 barrels of oil in 1975 but only 82 barrels in 1980.[41] And if the African coffee grower wanted to buy a 16–ton truck, he would need 66 bags of coffee in 1969 but 123 bags of coffee to buy the same truck in 1979.[42]

There were other reasons why the gap increased. Rapid population increases in many third world countries meant that the economic wealth of a country (GNP) was divided by an increasing number of mouths, so that per capita income fell (GNP divided by population equals per capita income). And much of the wealth that was produced was captured by government officials, bureaucrats, or dictators. In Congo's Brazzaville, the Africa historian Basil Davidson notes,

> the bureaucracy grew by 636 percent or from 3,000 to 21,000 persons [between 1960 and 1972], after which it continued to grow at an even faster rate, totalling by 1987 some 73,000 effectives. . . . By the end of the 1960s, this relatively immense and useless civil and military service was eating up about three-fourths of the national budget. . . . [43]

In East Africa, citizens called their soldiers, businessmen, and civil servants the *Wabenzi*, a Swahili word meaning "tribe of the Mercedes Benz."[44] By capturing much of the wealth, the gap between rich and poor people living in third world countries grew or remained high throughout the postwar period. In Mexico, for instance, the richest 20 percent of the population received 54 percent of the country's wealth, while the poorest 20 percent received only 3 percent of all income, a difference of eighteen to one.[45] And in Brazil, Turkey, Peru, the Philippines, Zambia, and Kenya, the top 20 percent of the population received 50 to 60 percent of the wealth, while the bottom 20 percent received between 2 and 4 percent.[46]

For third world people, economic differences have important social and individual consequences. According to the World Bank, one billion people (one-fifth of the world) live in "poverty," which means they earn less than $370 a year.[47] Poverty of this sort means that people have poor diets.[48] And with poor diets, it is common for children in rural Africa to

be ill one hundred forty days a year. "The typical pattern is 3 or 4 bouts of diarrhea, four or five respiratory coughs or colds, an attack of measles or malaria, all complicated by internal parasites and inadequate protein."[49]

With the spread of AIDS, the World Bank expects the average African, who now lives to the age of 52, to live only to the age of 47 by the year 2000.[50] And the poor will receive little education. People in the third world go to school, on average, only 3.5 years in all, the equivalent of a second-grade education in the United States. Typically, girls receive even less schooling.

Although most third world countries grew increasingly distant from first world countries during the postwar period, there were some important exceptions. Two groups of third world countries—oil producers and fast-growing East Asian "tigers" as they are often called—managed to improve their economic standing in the world.

In the postwar period, the prices that third world countries received for their agricultural products and natural resources fell. And this contributed to deteriorating "terms of trade" with first world countries and to increasing economic inequality. But oil turned out to be an important exception to this general rule, at least for a time.

Between 1950 and 1970, the price of oil, like the price of cocoa or cotton, declined (see chapters 3 and 4). First world countries that used the oil to promote their economic recovery and development paid, in constant 1973 dollars, $5.38 for a barrel of oil in 1951, but only $2.09 in 1970 ($1.71 in 1950 in real dollars, $1.30 in 1970).[51] Determined to prevent the continued fall in the price of this important commodity, the leaders of some oil-producing countries decided to band together in an organization that could control the supply of oil and increase its price. Led by Venezuelan oil officials, a number of countries joined the Organization of Petroleum Exporting Countries (OPEC), which was formed in 1960 in response to price cuts by the major Western oil companies.

OPEC members first tried to cut off oil supplies to the first world during the 1967 Arab-Israeli Six Day War. But Indonesia and the United States, then still one of the world's largest oil producers, increased their production so that declining OPEC production would not increase oil prices. Although the first OPEC oil embargo failed, a second one in 1973 succeeded. During the Arab-Israeli Yom Kippur War in 1973, OPEC again cut supplies of oil to the first world. OPEC countries were able to cut supplies and increase prices because the United States was already producing as much oil as it could and because the thirty- to forty-year contracts between first world oil companies and oil-producing countries, which were first signed in the 1930s and 1940s, had expired. These devel-

opments and a third oil embargo in 1978–79 made it possible for OPEC countries to demand and receive better deals and higher prices. By 1980, the price of oil increased to $16.48 a barrel, eight times the 1970 price, and consumers in the United States saw gasoline prices rise from 39 cents a gallon in 1973 to $1.38 a gallon in 1981.[52]

Higher oil prices transferred first world wealth to third world oil-producing countries. The United States, for instance, paid about $1 trillion to OPEC countries between 1970 and 1990.[53] But it also transferred wealth from third world countries that did not produce oil to OPEC countries. To pay for oil, many of these poor countries borrowed money from first world countries or from oil producers themselves, which led to massive debts. In the 1980s, these debts would lead to a crisis that would increase the economic differences between first and third world countries (see chapter 5).[54]

Although the oil-producing countries grew rich, many of them found it difficult to sustain the kind of wealth and economic growth they achieved in the 1970s.[55]

Faced with higher oil prices, first world countries began to conserve energy and search for new oil supplies. They found new oil in the North Sea and encouraged countries that were not members of OPEC, like Mexico, to produce more oil. And OPEC members began to quarrel over production levels and prices. Bitter disputes led to open warfare, first between Iraq and Iran and then between Iraq and Kuwait. These destructive wars in the 1980s and early '90s led to the collapse of OPEC's political unity at a time when non-OPEC countries emerged as important suppliers. As a result, the price of oil fell during the 1980s, particularly after 1985. And today the real price of oil is about what it was in 1973. The "real" price of oil depends on whether it is calculated in "1970s dollars" or "inflation-adjusted 1993 dollars." In 1970 dollars, the "real" price of oil increased from $2.10 per barrel to $4.69 a barrel in 1989, while in 1993 dollars, the price of a gallon of gas fell from $1.25 in 1973 to $1.12 in 1993.[56] In either case, the gains OPEC countries achieved in the 1970s have eroded. And while oil-producing countries with small populations have done well, countries with large populations have seen their oil wealth slip away. So, for example, countries like Indonesia, Nigeria, and Mexico have found that oil has not made them "rich" like Saudi Arabia or Libya, or enabled them to become like first world countries, though oil revenues kept them from falling as far as third world countries without oil.

In East Asia, another small group of third world countries dramatically improved their economic circumstances in the postwar period. The newly industrializing economies (NIEs) or "tigers"—as South Korea, Taiwan,

Hong Kong, and Singapore are called—all recorded rapid rates of growth and substantial increases in per capita income. Paul Kennedy notes that South Korea, for example, had a per capita GNP equal to that of Ghana ($230) in 1960, but in 1993 it had become "10 to 12 times more prosperous."[57] And the economic development of the newly industrializing economies in Asia has been hailed as a model for the rest of the third world.

These economic tigers were able to succeed, where other third world countries did not, for a variety of reasons. South Korea and Taiwan had special relations in the postwar period with both the United States and Japan (Japan had occupied both of them as colonies during the first half of the century). Because U.S. officials viewed them as "front line" states abutting communist countries in Asia, they received economic assistance, which helped them buy the imported goods they needed, and gave them privileged access to U.S. markets, while the Japanese made substantial investments in both countries. The $6 billion in U.S. economic aid to South Korea between 1945 and 1978 was "as much as the total aid provided to all African countries during the same period."[58] Meanwhile, Great Britain treated Hong Kong, still a colony, and Singapore, a former colony, in much the same way. Later, as economic competition between first world countries sharpened in the 1970s and '80s, first world businesses seeking low-wage suppliers for industrial goods migrated to or invested in these countries.

For their part, governments in these countries used immigration from neighboring countries and labor-control laws to keep wages low, they encouraged (or forced) people to save their money so that it could be used for investment in the domestic economy by erecting trade barriers that made it difficult for them to purchase foreign consumer goods, and they established monopolies so that businesses would not face domestic competition and so they could compete effectively with large transnational corporations based in the first world. The authoritarian governments that ruled these countries for most of the postwar period also benefited from the fact that they ruled relatively small populations. South Korea and Taiwan are small countries, while Hong Kong and Singapore are really just big cities. Because they had been detached from large, populous neighbors (Taiwan and Hong Kong from China, South Korea from North Korea, Singapore from Malaysia), they did not have to share their increased economic wealth with poor, populous hinterlands—as they might have if they were joined with neighboring countries—and could concentrate on building the infrastructure and providing widespread education that could provide productive, skilled, *and* low-cost workers that could assist their economic development.

Some third world countries have closed the gap between themselves and the first world. But they have been few in number and small in population. Their economic success will be difficult for others to emulate because they relied on unique commodities (oil) or exceptional circumstances (first world aid) that was not widely available to others. The vast majority of third world countries are increasingly distant from the first world. And many of these, particularly in Africa, have become so poor by comparison that some economists speak of a "fourth world" emerging in some continents.

Because the first, second, and third worlds are being knit together by migration and tourism, by global communications and interdependent industry, the "relative" relations between these worlds are becoming increasingly apparent to people living in them. Today people experience economic reality in referential terms and they measure their standard of living, their economic wealth and progress, in relation to people living in other parts of the world. As they do, economic similarities (in the case of first world peoples) and economic differences (in the case of third world peoples) appear in sharp relief.

Measuring the Wealth of Nations

For most of the postwar period, economists have monitored the economic circumstances of people around the world by measuring their gross national product. They calculate the GNP of a country by adding up all the wealth produced by a country—how much individuals spend on consumption, how much money they invest, how much money the government spends, and how much they receive for goods they sell abroad—and then subtracting the money they spend on imported goods and the money "used up" or consumed in this process (the depreciation of equipment and factories).[59] By comparing the GNP of a country from one year to the next, economists can determine whether a country has grown and, if so, by how much.

Economists also take the GNP and divide it by the number of people living in a country. The result, per capita income, shows how much wealth would be available to each person if it were divided equally. Both GNP and per capita income figures are usually expressed in U.S. dollars to provide a uniform measure of wealth. Most of the figures used in this chapter are based on this method of measuring wealth because it is the most commonly used and consistently collected information for most countries around the world.

The data on second world countries are less reliable because their governments often do not provide accurate information or express their wealth in their own currencies. They sometimes overstate their wealth because their currencies are usually worth less than the official rate of exchange with the U.S. dollar.

But while GNP is typically used to assess and compare wealth, some economists believe that the wealth of nations should be measured in different ways. Environmental economists, for instance, have developed a different method, what they call a "Green GNP," to measure a country's wealth.[60] Like other economists, they add up the wealth produced by a country. But instead of subtracting only the value of imports and the value of goods used up in the process of producing wealth, they also subtract the value of natural resources—oil, timber, topsoil—that were pumped up, cut down, or blown away to create wealth. The idea is that when oil is pumped up, trees are cut down, and topsoil is blown away, a country is poorer, not richer, as a result. Conventional economists place the value of oil pumped and trees felled on the assets part of the ledger. Green economists say they should be put on the debit side of the balance sheet. Using this kind of measure, it is likely that many third world countries that export food, fuel, and natural resources are poorer than economists using conventional measures of GNP now assume. This would mean that the gap between rich and poor countries is probably wider than is considered using conventional measures. Using this method, Robert Repetto, an economist for the World Resources Institute, found that Indonesia grew only 4 percent annually between 1970 and 1974, not the 7 percent recorded by conventional measurements.[61]

Other economists have argued that a country's wealth should be measured not simply in economic terms but in terms of its ability to provide education, health, and a clean environment. Mahub ul-Haq, a Pakistani economist working for the United Nations, developed a "Quality of Life Index" or "Human Development Index" (HDI) that uses a variety of indicators, both economic and noneconomic, to assess the circumstances of particular countries. Using this system, the average Costa Rican is better off than the average Brazilian, even though Brazil has a higher per capita GNP ($4,718 for a Brazilian, $4,542 for a Costa Rican) because a Costa Rican lives longer, attends more years of school, and has cleaner water and better sanitation. Although this method is more comprehensive in many respects, some economists claim it is sometimes misleading. In a review of the index, *The Economist* wrote, "The strength of the HDI is reminding those who cannot see beyond the end of their statistics that there is more to life than GNP." But it adds, "Oddities become absurdi-

ties in the case of communist and new ex-communist countries, whose underlying GNP figures are worthless. Hands up for everybody who thinks that North Korea has reached a higher plane of development than Brazil, or the Soviet Union than Portugal?"[62]

While some economists debate the best way to measure wealth, others argue that the wealth of a country should not be expressed in U.S. dollars but in "purchasing power parity" (PPP). They are unhappy with expressing wealth in dollars because the value of the dollar and of other currencies has changed during the postwar period. So instead of using variable currencies, some economists argue that wealth should be calculated by measuring how much people can buy in their own country, using their own currency. This is then compared to what people in other countries can buy, using their own money. A simple way to do this is to see how much they have to pay in their own currencies to buy a Big Mac. At the newly opened McDonald's in Beijing, Chinese patrons paid 6.30 yuan for a Big Mac, which sells for $2.19 in the United States. Based on the Big Mac Standard, the Chinese yuan was actually worth 2.88 to the dollar, not the 5.44 to the dollar that is the official rate.[63] If this theory is extended to the rest of the economy, the Chinese earn more and have greater wealth than conventional GNP dollar-based statistics would suggest. When it used the new PPP method, the International Monetary Fund estimated that China's economy was four times larger than previously reported, making China the third largest economy in the world, not the tenth. And instead of earning $370 per capita, under the conventional method, the average Chinese citizen earned $1,600. If this method applied widely, it might suggest that some third world countries are not as poor as economists now report because their money goes further at home than it would abroad. But while this method would "upgrade" China, it would not necessarily do the same for others. It would reshuffle the ranking of poor countries within the third world, as it would in the first, but it would not substantially close the gap or erase differences between first and third worlds. And until this method or any of the other methods (HDI, Green GNP) are widely adopted and historically applied, it will be difficult to know how they would change the general picture presented here.

Gender Gaps

There are vast economic differences between first and third world countries, and important differences between rich and poor within individual countries. There are also significant differences between women and men,

whether they are rich or poor, whether they live in first or third world countries. Economic differences based on gender, what economists call the "gender gap," exist in virtually every country in the world. According to the U.N.'s Human Development Index, "women's standard of living lagged behind [that of] men in every country for which data were available."[64] They had lower incomes, shorter education, and poorer access to health care.

But while the gender gap is a universal phenomenon, it is not everywhere the same. In many Western European countries, for instance, working women earn 80 percent as much as men, a relatively small gender-based gap.[65] In many third world countries, they may earn only 40 percent as much, a huge difference.

A century ago, women in the United States earned only 45 percent as much as men, a figure comparable to much of the third world today. The gender gap closed during the first half of the century, so that women in 1950 earned about 63 cents to a man's dollar. But it widened again after 1950, falling to about 56 cents to the dollar in 1973. With the rise of the women's movement and widespread entry into the labor force, women's earnings increased slowly, returning to the 1950 level in 1984. Women's wages continued rising, reaching 72 cents to the dollar in 1990. But they have since fallen to about 70 cents. Overall, the gap between women and men has narrowed, though a substantial difference remains.[66]

There are also important differences among women from different ethnic backgrounds. Chinese-, Filipina-, and Japanese-American women earned somewhat more than the average, while Native American, African-American, and Hispanic women earned considerably less. In 1980 for example, African-American women earned only 53 cents on the average man's dollar, Native American women only 51 cents, Hispanic women only 47 cents, and women in Puerto Rico only 36 cents.[67]

In the third world, women typically earn less than half the amount men do for the same work. They also work longer hours—twelve to eighteen hours a day compared to eight to twelve hours for men—and devote a greater share of their earnings to the household. Economists have found that women in Mexico contribute 100 percent of their earnings to the family budget, while men contributed only 75 percent of theirs. As a result, reported the World Bank, "It is not uncommon for children's nutrition to deteriorate while wrist watches, radios and bicycles are acquired by the adult male household members."[68]

In general, the gender gap has narrowed in first world countries, some more than others, and for some women, not all, while it has remained persistently wide in most third world countries. And in countries where

religious political parties have come to power, the existing gender gap may have widened considerably.

Summary

After World War II, the world was divided politically and economically into three distinct "worlds." Since 1945, first world countries have grown closer together in economic and political terms. At the same time, these first world countries have distanced themselves in economic terms from the second and third worlds, though democratization in some second and third world countries has recently made them more like first world countries in political terms (see chapter 13).

Although U.S. officials helped Japan and its allies in Western Europe improve their economies after World War II, they began to see the narrowing economic gap as a problem in the 1970s. And they took steps to address this problem, using successive dollar devaluations to improve the competitiveness of U.S. industries and shrink growing trade deficits with its first world partners.

Notes

1. Louis, Roger W. *Imperialism at Bay.* New York: Oxford University Press, 1978, p. 226.

2. Nixon, Richard M. *RN: The Memoirs of Richard Nixon.* New York: Warner Books, 1978, p. 461.

3. Vadney, T. E. *The World Since 1945.* London: Penguin Books, 1992, p. 73.

4. Berberoglu, Berch. *The Legacy of Empire: Economic Decline and Class Polarization in the United States.* New York: Praeger, 1992, p. 22.

5. Kennedy, Paul. *The Rise and Fall of the Great Powers: Economic Change and Military Conflict from 1500 to 2000.* New York: Random House, 1987, p. 384.

6. Stevenson, Richard W. "Way Ahead in the Space Race," *New York Times,* April 5, 1995.

7. Bellon, Bertrand, and Niosi, Jorge. *The Decline of the American Economy.* Montreal: Black Rose Books, 1988, p. 29.

8. Orr, Bill. *The Global Economy in the 90s: A User's Guide.* New York: New York University Press, 1992, p. 92.

9. Hedley, Alan R. *Making a Living: Technology and Change.* New York: HarperCollins, 1992, p. 226.

10. Ibid., p. 290.

11. Peterson, Wallace C. "The Silent Depression," *Challenge,* July–August 1991, p. 32.

12. Berberoglu, 1992, pp. 55–57.

13. Phillips, Kevin. *The Politics of Rich and Poor: Wealth and the American Electorate in the Reagan Aftermath.* New York: Random House, 1990, p. 13.

14. Rauch, Jonathan. "Downsizing the Dream," *National Journal,* August 12, 1989, p. 2039.

15. Phillips, 1990, p. 157.

16. Ibid., p. 10.

17. Pear, Robert. "Poverty in U.S. Grew Faster Than Population Last Year," *New York Times,* October 5, 1993. Pear, Robert. "Ranks of U.S. Poor Reach 35.7 Million, the Most Since 1964," *New York Times,* September 4, 1992.

18. Gross, Jane. "On the Edge of Poverty in California: A Welfare Mother Fears Deeper Cuts," *New York Times,* August 11, 1992.

19. Chira, Susan. "Working Class Families Losing Middle-Class Dreams," *New York Times,* October 3, 1989.

20. Hylton, Richard D. "Bridge Loan for Trump Is Expected," *New York Times,* June 20, 1990.

21. Phillips, 1990, p. 249.

22. Kennedy, Paul. *Preparing for the 21st Century.* New York: Random House, p. 234.

23. Arrighi, Giovanni. "World Income Inequalities and the Future of Socialism," *New Left Review,* 189, September-October 1991, pp. 53–54.

24. Rowen, Henry S., and Wolf, Charles, Jr. *The Impoverished Superpower: Perestroika and the Military Burden.* San Francisco: Institute for Contemporary Studies Press, 1990, p. 232.

25. Sivard, Ruth. *World Military and Social Expenditures, 1987–88.* Washington, D.C.: World Priorities, 1987, pp. 54–55, 174.

26. Schmemann, Serge. "The Sun Has Trouble Setting on the Soviet Empire," *New York Times,* March 10, 1991.

27. Ibid.

28. Arrighi, 1991, p. 57.

29. Singer, Hans W., and Ansar, Javed A. *Rich and Poor Countries.* London: George Allen and Unwin, 1982, p. 23. Seligson, Mitchell A. *The Gap Between Rich and Poor: Contending Perspectives on the Political Economy of Development.* Boulder, Colo.: Westview, 1984, p. 7. Orr, 1992, p. 29. Escobar, Arturo. *Encountering Development: The Making and Unmaking of the Third World.* Princeton: Princeton University Press, 1995, p. 213.

30. Seligson, 1984, p. 3.

31. Ibid., pp. 9–10.

32. Ibid., p. 10.

33. Salomon, Jean-Jacques, and Lebeau, Andre. *Mirages of Development: Science and Technology for the Third Worlds.* Boulder, Colo.: Rienner, 1993, pp. 147–48.

34. Bairoch, Paul. *The Economic Development of the Third World Since 1900.* London: Methuen, 1975, p. 198.

35. Salomon and Lebeau, 1993, p. 156.

36. Kennedy, 1993, p. 211.

37. Bairoch, 1975, p. 133.

38. Dinham, Barbara, and Hines, Colin. *Agribusiness in Africa*. London: Earth Resources Research, 1983, p. 34.

39. Bairoch, 1975, p. 128.

40. Orr, 1992, p. 263.

41. Davidson, Basil. *The Black Man's Burden: Africa and the Curse of the Nation-State*. New York: Times Books, 1992, p. 220.

42. Dinham and Hines, 1983, p. 69.

43. Davidson, 1992, p. 235.

44. Timberlake, Lloyd. *Africa in Crisis: The Causes, the Cures of Environmental Bankruptcy*. London: International Institute for Environment and Development, 1985, p. 9.

45. Brown, Lester. *State of the World 1990*. New York: Norton, 1987, p. 138.

46. Adriaansen, W. L. M., and Waardenburg, J. G. *A Dual World Economy: Forty Years of Development Experience*. Center for Development Planning, Erasmus University, Rotterdam. Association of Post-Keynesian Economists: Wolters-Noordhof, 1989, p. 18.

47. Farnsworth, Clyde H. "Report by World Bank Sees Poverty Lessening by 2000 Except in Africa," *New York Times*, July 16, 1990. Brown, 1990, p. 137.

48. Brown, Lester. *State of the World 1992*. New York: Norton, 1992, p. 68.

49. Ibid., p. 48.

50. Scroggins, Deborah. "Screams of a Continent," *Syracuse Herald American*, April 18, 1993. Orr, 1992, p. 319.

51. Brown, Lester. *State of the World 1984*. New York: Norton, 1984, p. 73.

52. Ibid., pp. 43–44.

53. Ibid., p. 43.

54. Krasner, Stephen D. *Structural Conflict: The Third World Against Global Liberalism*. Berkeley: University of California Press, 1985, p. 47.

55. Ibid., pp. 106–7.

56. Orr, 1992, p. 261. Wald, Matthew L. "After 20 Years, America's Foot Is Still on the Gas," *New York Times*, October 17, 1993.

57. Kennedy, 1993, p. 193.

58. Bello, Walden. "Dragons in Distress," *World Policy Journal*, 7, 3, 1990, p. 434.

59. Carnes, W. Stansbury, and Slifer, Stephen D. *The Atlas of Economic Indicators*. New York: HarperBusiness, 1991, pp. 28–35.

60. Passel, Peter. "The Wealth of Nations: A 'Greener' Approach Turns List Upside Down," *New York Times*, September 19, 1995.

61. Brown, 1990, pp. 7–8. Passell, Peter. "Rebel Economists Add Ecological Cost to Price of Progress," *New York Times*, November 27, 1990. Shabecoff, Philip. "The Environment," *New York Times*, June 29, 1989. "Getting Physical," *The Economist*, August 26, 1989.

62. Lewis, Paul. "New UN Index Measures Wealth and Quality of Life," *New York Times*, May 20, 1993. "Development Brief: The Human Condition," *The Economist*, May 26, 1990. Greenhouse, Steven. "New Talley of World's Economies Catapults China into 3rd Place," *New York Times*, May 20, 1993.

63. Smil, Vaclav. "How Rich Is China?" *Current History*, September 1993, p. 266.

64. Brown, Lester. *State of the World 1993*. New York: Norton, 1993, p. 63.

65. Amott, Teresa, and Matthaei, Julie. *Race, Gender and Work: A Multicultural Economic History of Women in the United States*. Boston: South End Press, 1991, p. 19.

66. Nasar, Sylvia. "Women's Progress Stalled? Just Not So," *New York Times*, October 18, 1992.

67. Brown, 1993, pp. 64, 66.

68. Ibid., p. 64.

3

Dollar Devaluations

At the beginning of the 1970s, Americans faced two economic problems: declining competitiveness and rising inflation. The postwar economic recovery of Western Europe and Japan had enabled businesses there to become more competitive with U.S. firms. As a result, U.S. businesses found it increasingly difficult to sell their goods in foreign and domestic markets. In 1971, for the first time in the twentieth century, the United States posted a trade deficit, meaning that Americans purchased more goods from other countries than they sold to people living in those countries. U.S. policy makers took this as a signal that U.S. competitiveness had declined.

At the same time, U.S. military spending on the war in Vietnam had pushed up wages and prices at a rapid rate, leading to inflation. The trouble with inflation was that some people were better able to negotiate higher salaries or wages than others. And when managers or union members received higher wages, private and public employers tried to pay higher salaries by raising prices, charging consumers more for their goods. This led to declining real incomes for nonunionized workers or people living on fixed incomes, who could not raise their wages as easily or as fast. It also led to declining profits for businesses that could not easily pass on higher prices to their customers. Instead of paying more for some goods, some consumers simply buy less, which means that producers of these goods earn less. U.S. policy makers worried that continued inflation would create serious problems for some social groups and undermine the U.S. economy as a whole.

On August 15, 1971, President Richard Nixon confronted both problems simultaneously. To improve U.S. competitiveness, he took steps to devalue the dollar in relation to currencies in other first world countries. And to fight inflation, he introduced wage and price controls, which were

designed to limit wage raises and price increases. The "Nixon Shocks,"
or *shokku* (shocks) as these were called in Japan, marked the beginning of
U.S. efforts to solve two serious economic problems.[1] As we will see, the
economic "solutions" devised by Nixon and subsequent U.S. presidents
had mixed success. Dollar devaluations in 1971 and again in 1985 did not
greatly improve the competitiveness of U.S. firms in domestic and foreign
markets, and they led to some serious, unanticipated economic problems.
In the United States, dollar devaluations led to the purchase of U.S. businesses, real estate, and natural resources by foreigners, with important
consequences for U.S. workers. And dollar devaluations contributed to
declining incomes for oil-producing countries, which contributed, some
years later, to war in the Persian Gulf.

Wage and price controls did not curb inflation, which continued to be
a problem in the United States for the next decade. During the 1980s,
government economists successfully used high interest rates to curb inflation. But high interest rates contributed to a host of other economic
problems. In Latin America high U.S. interest rates triggered a massive
debt crisis, and in the United States they crippled the savings and loan
industry and led to increasing homelessness, which remains a problem
today.

To explain these developments in detail, we will look first at currency
devaluations and at efforts to improve U.S. competitiveness. In the next
chapter we will examine efforts to curb inflation. Both stories begin in
1971 with Nixon's August 15 speech. And both stories have two parts.
The dollar is devalued twice, first in 1971 and again in 1985. And there
are two anti-inflationary campaigns, the first in 1971 and the second beginning in 1979. By focusing on successive "solutions" to economic problems, we will discuss the problems with macroeconomic management.
U.S. attempts to improve competitiveness and fight inflation are important because the United States has been the world's leading economic
power during the postwar period. Furthermore, its decisions have had
significant consequences for people in other countries.

Although the story of government efforts to improve U.S. competitiveness and the story about the government's fight against inflation will be
told separately, they are joined in important ways. For example, high interest rates in the early 1980s strengthened the value of the dollar, creating
problems that led to a second, deeper devaluation of the dollar in 1985.
We will note these connections as the stories unfold. And both stories are
about the social "costs" and unanticipated "problems" associated with
macroeconomic management. In this regard, it is useful to describe how
powerful political institutions can affect people's lives. The Group of Five,

for instance, played an important role in the 1985 decision to devalue the dollar; the Federal Reserve System was a central actor in the anti-inflationary policies of the early 1980s. These institutions are relatively obscure to most people, even though their decisions have important impacts on people living in different parts of the world.

1971 Dollar Devaluations

"At the end of World War II, the economies of the major industrial nations of Europe and Asia were shattered," President Nixon told his television audience on August 15, 1971. "Today, largely with our help, they have regained their vitality. They have become our strong competitors. . . . But now that [they] have become economically strong . . . the time has come for exchange rates to be set straight, and for the major nations to compete as equals."[2]

In this speech, Nixon recognized that the ability of U.S. firms to compete with businesses in Western Europe and Japan had declined during the postwar period. To address this problem and improve U.S. competitiveness, he sought to devalue the dollar and alter the relation between first world currencies. Nixon's devaluation of the dollar opened a two-decade campaign to improve the competitiveness of U.S. firms by changing global monetary relations. But the monetary policies of Nixon and, later, President Ronald Reagan did not greatly improve the ability of U.S. firms to compete with other first world businesses. And successive dollar devaluations, the first in 1971 and a second in 1985, created problems that policy makers did not expect.

As Nixon noted, businesses in Western Europe and Japan became "strong competitors" during the postwar period for a variety of reasons. They "regained their vitality" because they adopted policies designed to develop economically and received substantial U.S. economic aid amounting to $14.3 billion, according to Nixon's calculations. They also benefited from favorable exchange rates that were set by the Bretton Woods agreement, an international monetary treaty named after the New Hampshire town where negotiations were held in 1944.

The Bretton Woods agreement made the U.S. dollar the world's monetary standard and fixed the value of other currencies in relation to the dollar. Like the global system of timekeeping the dollar became the monetary prime meridian. And other currencies were assigned a fixed value in relation to it.

For example, the value of the yen, Japan's currency, was fixed at a rate

of 360 yen to the dollar between 1949 and 1971. This low rate made it easy for Japanese firms to sell their "cheap" goods in the United States, while making it difficult for Japanese consumers to buy "expensive" American goods in Japan. In effect, exchange rates set at Bretton Woods helped Japanese and Western European businesses sell their goods at home (where U.S. goods were relatively expensive) and abroad, particularly in the United States (where their goods were relatively cheap). The exchange rates fixed after World War II acted somewhat like a golfer's handicap, making the price or "score" of Japanese and Western European firms lower than they would be otherwise. And the handicap remained the same even though they improved their own economy or "game" throughout this period.[3]

The sale of Volkswagen Beetles and Sony transistor radios to U.S. consumers in the 1960s helped West German and Japanese economies recover and grow. While they grew stronger, producing goods that were of increasing quality, the exchange rates did not change, which kept their products cheap. By the late 1960s, they had begun to compete successfully with American firms in both domestic and U.S. markets, where consumers purchased their goods in increasing volume. And in 1971, the United States imported more goods than it exported, posting a $2.3 billion trade deficit, the first in decades.[4]

Government officials viewed the trade deficit as a sign that the ability of U.S. firms to compete with other *first* world businesses had declined. And they blamed it on the monetary system, which assigned favorable exchange rates to U.S. competitors. But it was difficult for officials to alter long-standing exchange rates because the values of other currencies were fixed in relation to the dollar. In effect, they could not alter exchange rates unless they were prepared to abandon the dollar's role as the monetary prime meridian for currencies around the world.

By 1971, officials decided to eliminate the dollar as a monetary standard and destroy the system based on it for two reasons. First, the value of the dollar was weakening. When the dollar became the global monetary standard, the United States agreed to supply dollars to people around the world so they could pay for the imports they needed to rebuild their shattered economies. The United States used the Marshall Plan, foreign aid, and military spending on overseas bases and war in Korea to provide dollars to countries that needed "hard currency" to pay for imports. By providing liquidity and easing cash flow problems, the dollars supplied by the United States helped first world countries grow and prosper. But while U.S. overseas spending helped provide much-needed cash, continued military spending on NATO and the war in Vietnam pumped too

many dollars into the world economy. Dollars piled up in central banks around the world. To reduce their stocks of dollars, which they found increasingly difficult to use, some governments decided to return them to the United States and cash them in for gold, at the rate of $35 to the ounce, a rate set by the Bretton Woods agreement.

By the late 1960s and early 1970s, it became clear that the number of dollars in global circulation far outstripped the amount of gold stored at Fort Knox. If too many countries had asked to redeem dollars for gold, the U.S. government would soon exhaust its gold reserves and the dollar would lose its value as a standard.

The fact that the world economy needed the United States to pump dollars into the monetary system to maintain liquidity, but that doing so undermined the value of the dollar and its role as a global monetary standard, was known to economists as the Trifflin Dilemma because it was first identified by Robert Trifflin, an economist who published a book on this subject, *Gold and the Dollar Crisis*, in 1960.[5]

To address this problem, Nixon administration officials decided to stop redeeming gold for dollars and force a devaluation of the dollar vis-à-vis other first world currencies. By lowering the value of the dollar and raising the value of other first world currencies, U.S. firms could sell more of the (now cheaper) goods overseas, and U.S. consumers would be discouraged from buying (now more expensive) products from Western Europe and Japan. By exporting more and importing less, Nixon administration officials reasoned that they could eliminate the trade deficit and restore the competitiveness of U.S. firms. By abandoning the Bretton Woods system of fixed exchange rates (and the promise to convert dollars for gold at $35 an ounce) and devaluing the dollar, by making "exchange rates to be set straight" as Nixon put it, U.S. businesses could again "compete as equals."

Although Nixon's 1971 policy was designed to devalue the dollar, he was reluctant to describe it that way. He argued that his actions would not result in "the bugaboo of . . . what is called 'devaluation.' " And he told viewers that "if you want to buy a foreign car or take a trip abroad, market conditions may cause your dollar to buy slightly less. But if . . . you buy American-made products, in America, your dollar will be worth just as much tomorrow as it is today." Nixon and Treasury Secretary John Connally argued that this new policy was not a "devaluation" because Nixon administration officials in previous months had proclaimed they would not devalue the dollar to improve U.S. competitiveness or impose wage and price controls to curb inflation.[6]

But this, and Connally's subsequent press conference statement that

the dollar had not been devalued "by Presidential action," was misleading. As Paul Volcker, a Treasury Department official who helped draft Nixon's speech, later recalled, a dollar devaluation "was exactly what we had decided was essential."[7] Nixon was reluctant to call it a devaluation because this term was politically charged. But if one looks at his own example, Nixon describes precisely what a devaluation is all about. A dollar devaluation did not mean that a dollar could buy fewer American goods. But it would mean that Americans could not purchase as many *foreign* goods, either in the United States or abroad, as they could previously. As a result of changing exchange rates, which weakened the dollar and strengthened first world currencies (franc, yen, deutsche mark), an American tourist in Paris could buy fewer croissants and a shopper in Des Moines could buy fewer Christmas toys labeled "Made in Japan."

As a result of Nixon's 1971 policy, the dollar's value fell and other first world currencies rose during the next few months. By December 1971, the dollar had fallen between 8 and 17 percent, depending on the currency. The yen, for example, rose 16.9 percent, to 308 yen to the dollar.[8] After this initial change, the dollar overall slowly declined to about 20 percent of its August 1971 value by the end of the decade. And in 1980, the yen stood at 275 to the dollar, a decline of about 25 percent.

One might have expected Nixon's dollar devaluation, and the collapse of the Bretton Woods system (the values of different currencies were no longer fixed and instead began to float in relation to the dollar and to other currencies), to improve U.S. competitiveness and reduce its trade deficit. After all, that was the administration's intent. But it did not. The modest $2.3 billion trade deficit in 1971 grew to $25.5 billion by 1980, a tenfold increase.[9]

U.S. trade deficits increased in part because Americans spent more on imported oil and on foreign cars that got better mileage than U.S. cars. Rising oil prices, which tripled between 1973 and 1974, also increased the cost of imported oil.[10] In 1973, for instance, the United States spent $23.9 billion for imported oil.[11]

As gas prices climbed as a result of the OPEC oil embargo and price hikes of 1973, U.S. consumers turned to high-mileage Toyotas and Hondas. It was during the 1970s, for example, that U.S. demand for reliable high-mileage Japanese cars grew dramatically. In 1970, Japanese auto makers sold about four million cars in the United States. By 1975 Nissan had surpassed Volkswagen as the leading foreign car manufacturer, and by the end of the decade, Japanese manufacturers sold nearly twelve million cars, a threefold increase from 1970.[12]

Rising oil prices contributed to a growing U.S. trade deficit in two

ways, first by increasing the cost of imported oil and second by increasing U.S. demand for foreign autos. Another oil embargo in 1978 tripled prices again. As a result, whatever gains in U.S. competitiveness that might have been achieved by devaluing the dollar were undermined by rising oil prices and increasing consumer demand for imported goods.

While the value of the dollar fell during the 1970s as a result of Nixon's policies, the dollar actually increased in value during the first half of the 1980s, largely as a result of efforts to curb inflation. As we will see in the next chapter, former Nixon aide Paul Volcker, who became head of the Federal Reserve System in 1979, took steps to raise interest rates as a way to slow inflation. As a result, interest rates on government bonds (savings bonds, Treasury bills) rose to very high levels, as high as 20 percent. Attracted by rates that were higher than they could earn on their savings in other countries, investors from around the world bought U.S. bonds. By 1986, the Japanese had purchased $186 billion in U.S. Treasury Bonds.[13]

This massive purchase of U.S. bonds, stimulated by high interest rates, increased the value of the dollar. The increasing value of the dollar undermined whatever gains had been achieved by Nixon's devaluation. Volcker observed that by the end of 1984, "the yen and the mark, relative to the dollar, had been driven back . . . to their 1973 levels or below, and their car, machinery, and electronics manufacturers were finding the lush American market easy pickings."[14]

U.S. firms found it more difficult to sell their (now more expensive) goods abroad, while (now cheaper) foreign products flooded U.S. markets. As a result, U.S. trade deficits exploded from $25.3 billion in 1980 to $122 billion in 1985.[15] And nearly one-third of this deficit, $50 billion, was with Japan.[16] Princeton economist Robert Gilpin observed, "In the first part of 1986, the United States had achieved the impossible: it had a deficit with almost every one of its trading partners. Not since 1864 had the U.S. trade balance been so negative."[17]

Whereas a $2.3 billion trade deficit had seemed a major problem requiring dramatic solutions in 1971, U.S. officials in 1985 faced a trade deficit sixty times bigger. To deal with declining competitiveness and soaring trade deficits, officials again turned to a dollar devaluation as the cure for economic ills.

1985 Devaluation: The Plaza Accords

As U.S. trade deficits rose to unprecedented levels in the mid-1980s, government officials once again sought to devalue the dollar to improve the

competitiveness of U.S. firms in foreign and domestic markets. But this time, they could not act alone, as they had in 1971. Because exchange rates were no longer fixed and world currency markets played a larger role in setting the value of different currencies, the Reagan administration had to secure the cooperation of other first world countries to successfully devalue the dollar. In September 1985, the Reagan administration asked the financial representatives of the five leading economic powers, then known as the Group of Five (G-5), to meet at the Plaza Hotel in New York City and hammer out an agreement to devalue the dollar in relation to other first world currencies.

When they convened in the White and Gold Room of the Plaza Hotel on September 22, representatives from the United States, Japan, West Germany, France, and the United Kingdom agreed to devalue the dollar. They issued an innocuous statement saying that "some orderly appreciation of the main non-dollar currencies against the dollar is desirable. They [the Group of Five] stand ready to cooperate more closely to encourage this when to do so would be helpful."[18]

Reagan administration officials, like Nixon, were reluctant to describe their decision as a "dollar devaluation." Instead they called it an "appreciation" of "non-dollar currencies," which is the same thing. And they insisted that "it does not represent a fundamental change in the exchange rate intervention policy," though that is exactly what it was, since the agreement made by G-5 members specified interventionary steps to be taken. As one Reagan official later said, "No country ever likes to say that their currency will depreciate. . . . A government does not make statements that imply weakness."[19]

Although the G–5 ministers said they wanted to see the dollar depreciate, they refused to say how much it should be devalued. They kept this decision secret from the public.

In private, G-5 ministers agreed to devalue the dollar substantially. Over the next two years, the dollar would fall to one-half its 1985 value against the yen and the deutsche mark. And it would continue to fall, to only one-third its 1985 value by the early 1990s. So in 1993, for example, the yen traded for 105 to the dollar, down from 250 in 1985.[20]

The decision to devalue the dollar was made by an institution—the G-5—that was largely unknown to the public prior to its 1985 meeting in New York. But the decisions made by this secretive and select group had important global consequences.

Summits and Sherpas

Although the 1985 Plaza accords would have profound consequences for people around the world, the meeting was not widely noticed. On the

day it was announced, the *New York Times* gave more attention to an earthquake in Mexico City. Except for financial experts, the economic tremors produced by the Plaza accords went unregistered by the public. This was because first world economic summits were typically secret and select. As Volcker, one of two U.S. representatives at the meeting, said, "Until that day, [the G-5] had been a secret organization. Nobody outside a very tight official circle knew exactly where and when the five ministers met, what they discussed, and what they agreed. This was the first time a G-5 meeting was announced in advance [it was announced the day before] and a communique was issued afterward."[21]

The meeting was so secret that Japanese Finance Minister Noboru Takeshita "arranged to play golf at a course near Narita airport . . . but then, without playing the back nine," he slipped off to the airport and boarded a Pan Am jet to New York so that the press would not notice his departure from Japan.[22]

The secretive G-5 grew out of a meeting first held in the White House library in April 1973. The "Library Group" consisted of the finance ministers and sometimes central bank governors of the United States, West Germany, France, and the United Kingdom. They added the minister from Japan the following year.[23] In 1975, French President Valery Giscard d'Estaing called a summit meeting of the leading first world countries (the United States, France, West Germany, Japan, the United Kingdom, and Italy). They added Canada the following year. At these Group of Seven (G-7) summits, the G-5 finance ministers played important roles, crafting the economic agenda for political leaders. Because they worked to prepare presidents and prime ministers for these "summits," insiders referred to them as sherpas. A British official is said to have coined the phrase because sherpas are the native porters who help mountaineers scale summits in the Himalayas.[24]

After the Plaza accords were announced, Canadian and Italian officials complained that they were excluded, and the following year they were added, so that in 1986 the G-5 and G-7 had become one group known as G-7.[25]

Not only has the G-5/7 been *secretive*, it has been a selective group. Most of the world's 180-plus countries have been excluded from its meetings. Some of them have since formed the Group of 77, which has 120 members and convenes an "alternative economic summit" when the G-7 holds its annual meeting. G-7 members have not opened the door to participation by others because, as West German Prime Minister Helmut Schmidt explained, "We want a private, informal meeting of those who really matter in the world."[26]

The first world countries had other reasons for maintaining secrecy among a select group. If they had announced how much they intended to devalue the dollar after the Plaza meeting, people would have rushed to sell dollars and buy other currencies, which could have caused financial chaos. Because they did not disclose their plans, currency traders reacted "cautiously" to the announcement, according to the *New York Times*.[27]

Impact of the Plaza Accords

Although the Plaza accords initiated a substantial devaluation of the dollar, they created a host of new problems. First and foremost, the dollar devaluation did not reduce the U.S. trade deficit. In 1985, the United States recorded a $122 billion trade deficit. By raising the prices of imported goods from first world countries, G-5 ministers expected U.S. consumers to buy fewer imports; by lowering the value of the dollar, they expected U.S. manufacturers to sell more of their goods abroad. But despite a substantial devaluation, the U.S. trade deficit actually *increased* to $155 billion in 1986 and $170 billion in 1987. It then decreased slowly, though it remained at pre-1985 levels in 1988 ($137 billion) and 1989 ($129 billion), before falling to $122 billion in 1990.[28] Volcker said of this development,

> One of the ironies of [this] story . . . is that, after repeated depreciation of the dollar since 1971 to the point where it is 60 percent lower against the yen and 53 percent lower against the deutsche mark, the American trade and current account deficits are nonetheless much higher than anything imagined in the 1960s.[29]

What went wrong? Why didn't the dollar devaluation accomplish the goals of U.S. policy makers? The reason is that manufacturers and consumers did not respond to macroeconomic changes in the way policy makers expected.

The devaluation of the dollar and the appreciation of the yen should have doubled the price of Japanese imports. But Japanese auto makers did not double their prices after the Plaza accords. As economist Daniel Burstein explained, "A Nissan automobile that sold in the United States for $9,000 in 1984, and should have sold for $18,000 in 1987 according to changes in yen/dollar exchange rates, actually sold for only $11,000. If it had really sold for $18,000, it might well have been priced out of the market. At $11,000 . . . it was still highly competitive. In fact, Nissan's total U.S. car sales for 1987 fell only 3 percent from the prior year."[30]

Rather than raise prices to conform with post-Plaza exchange rates, Japanese firms kept price increases modest, squeezed costs, and accepted lower profits to retain their share of U.S. markets. U.S. manufacturers, meanwhile, actually increased their prices to keep up with Japanese price increases. "Studies by auto market research firm J. D. Power confirm that while Japanese manufacturers were raising U.S. prices an average of 9–13 percent from 1985 to 1988, General Motors, Ford and Chrysler were raising prices by . . . 12–15 percent."[31]

Rather than keep prices steady, which would have given them a price advantage vis-à-vis foreign car makers, U.S. firms raised their prices so they could make more money per car (rather than expand their production of cars) and swell profits, not increase their market share. U.S. firms emphasized short-term profits rather than increased market share because they wanted to increase stock prices and shareholder dividends. They did this because the U.S. stock market plays a much greater role in corporate decision making than it does in Japan, where firms do not seek to reward stockholders with dividends and instead concentrate on long-term investment strategies.

Faced with only modest price differentials between imported and domestic goods, differences that often disappeared when quality and brand loyalty were considered, U.S. consumers kept purchasing imported goods from Western Europe and Japan. Given a choice between a Honda Accord and a Chrysler K-car, cars close in price despite the dollar devaluation, American consumers kept buying Accords.

Because foreign and domestic producers and U.S. consumers did not behave as policy makers expected, U.S. trade deficits increased and the Plaza accords did not achieve their objectives. As this became apparent in the years after 1985, economists sought to explain the failure of macroeconomic policy. They use the term "hysteresis," which means a "resistance to change" according to economist Dilip Das, to describe the unwillingness of producers and consumers to act as economic theory predicted.[32] But this abstract term, which is drawn from physics, is simply a way of saying that people don't always act as economic theory says they should.

The Plaza accords resulted in problems in the United States and other countries that G-5 representatives did not anticipate. In the United States, the decline of the dollar reduced the value of U.S. assets, while the appreciation of other first world currencies provided Western European and Japanese investors with the means to purchase U.S. assets at bargain prices. "In 1974, the three largest banks in the world were American while only two of the top ten were Japanese," notes one economist. But by

1988, largely as a result of devaluation, "of the 25 largest banks in the world . . . 17 were Japanese (nine of them were in the top ten), 7 were Western European and 1 was from the United States."[33]

The growth of Japanese and Western European banks was due in part to the dollar devaluation, which increased their assets. Assets rose because Japanese and European banks are larger, on average, than their U.S. counterparts, so they were able to use size to their advantage. Japan has only 158 commercial banks; the United States has 14,000.[34]

As a result of the dollar devaluation, Japanese and Western European investors could buy U.S. banks and businesses, real estate, and natural resources for half price. At post-Plaza prices, foreign businesses rushed to invest in the United States. In the three years after 1985, Japanese firms invested $235 billion in the United States, purchasing government bonds ($30 billion in 1988), U.S. corporations (Sony purchased Columbia Records in 1988), real estate (Rockefeller Center in New York City and Pebble Beach in California), and natural resources (timber from the Pacific Northwest).[35] (After 1988, however, Japanese investment in the United States slowed and many of the real estate deals made during the late 1980s proved to be poor investments for their Japanese buyers.)

Because the dollar devaluation made Japan richer, some Americans even asked the Japanese government to give them money. Noting that Japan's post-Plaza economy was growing at the equivalent of one South Korea every year, or one France every five years, that its per capita income ($23,000) rose above that of the United States, and that its government was providing $9 billion in development assistance to third world countries, the health department of Summers County, West Virginia, which in 1990 faced substantial debts with only $13 in its bank account, asked the Japanese government for foreign aid.[36]

While Japanese investors found bargain prices in the United States, American tourists in Japan discovered unbelievable prices. In a Tokyo supermarket, a box of cherries cost $185 and a can of Spam $648. A three-bedroom apartment in Tokyo could easily rent for one million yen or $9,345.79 per month (108 yen to the dollar), and the tab for one beer at a bar would run $29.90. The *New York Times* correspondent who reported this story noted that the cost of a copy of the Sunday *Times*, delivered three days late, set him back $42.91.[37]

Historically, firms from the United Kingdom and Western Europe have been the biggest foreign investors in the United States. But Japanese investment has been the focus of increasing attention for two reasons. First, the dollar devaluation gave the Japanese a better price for U.S. assets than it did for Western European investors. Second, Japanese investment grew

more rapidly than European investment. Some economists expect Japan to overtake the United Kingdom as the largest investor in the United States sometime in the 1990s. While media attention focused on Japanese investment in the United States, little attention was paid to British Petroleum's $7.6 billion purchase of Standard of Ohio or Nestlé's $3 billion buyout of Carnation or the fact that Western European chemical companies now own one-third of the chemical industry in the United States or that foreign investors own 46 percent of the office space in Los Angeles.[38]

The Debate Over Foreign Investment

Although the dollar devaluation greatly increased the purchase of U.S. assets by investors from Japan *and* Western Europe, the impact of these sales has been fiercely debated.

Some Americans welcome foreign investment. Georgia Governor Joe Harris argued that foreign firms were "replacing jobs that had been lost from American manufacturing operations."[39] And Reagan's ambassador to the European Community, J. William Middendorf, said of foreign investors, "Send us your tired. Send us your poor. Send us your money."[40]

Some economists argue that Japanese real estate investments "shored up a nearly crippled real estate industry [in the late 1980s]. Japanese . . . investors took up the slack in real estate lending in the wake of the S&L crisis."[41] And more recently, Robert Reich, Labor secretary in the Clinton administration and author of *The Work of Nations*, argued that the United States should "draw no distinctions based on the nationality of a firm's shareholders or top executives."[42]

Other economists disagree. Laura D'Andrea Tyson, head of President Bill Clinton's Council of Economic Advisers, argued, "If foreign investment knocks out one or more domestic competitors, either by buying them out directly or by squeezing them out gradually, the result may be a concentrated industry both nationally and globally, with the remaining firms able to exercise significant market power."[43]

The debate over foreign investment turns on how foreign firms act in U.S. and world markets. But it is difficult to determine in advance how they will act. As we have seen with the dollar devaluation and hysteresis, economic theory does not always anticipate how people will behave. Jobs are a related issue. There economists disagree whether foreign investment creates jobs. Reich argues that it does. In 1986, for instance, foreign companies "employed nearly 3 million U.S. workers, paying them $87 billion in compensation."[44]

But other economists argue that foreign investors both create and eliminate jobs. "Like American companies," Norman Glickman and Douglas Woodward write, "foreigners close plants and lay off workers. . . . In fact, we find that foreigners eliminated approximately 56,000 more jobs than they created [between 1982 and 1986]."[45] And they noted that even when foreign companies build new factories and create jobs in the United States, the cost to taxpayers is high because local and state governments provide substantial subsidies and tax abatements to foreign investors. Officials in Scott County, Kentucky, for example, provided Toyota with incentives worth $325 million to locate a factory there, a cost to taxpayers of about $108,333 for each of the three thousand jobs at the plant.[46]

Of course, the sale of U.S. assets to foreign investors may have little or no impact on jobs. Japanese investors did not fire Hollywood actors and filmmakers when they purchased entertainment companies, nor did their purchase of the Pebble Beach golf course or Heavenly Valley ski resort result in the layoffs of caddies or ski instructors. The impact of investment on jobs varies from industry to industry. In one industry, however, the dollar devaluation and increased foreign investment did contribute to substantial job loss: the Pacific Northwest timber industry.

Falling Dollar, Falling Trees

The Plaza accords had a dramatic impact on timber and jobs in the Pacific Northwest, the heavily forested region west of the Cascade Mountains in Washington, Oregon, and northern California. The dollar devaluation combined with long-standing forestry practices to cut timber, send much of it to Japan, and lay off workers in U.S. mills.

During the postwar period, the federal government, which owns 191 million acres of timber in the United States, adopted policies to make cheap timber available to the logging and housing industry, providing jobs for the most job-intensive industry in America and inexpensive housing for would-be homeowners (see chapter 4).

The Forest Service, which oversees public forests, made cheap timber available to private industry in two ways. First, it sold timber for less than it cost the government to hire forest rangers and build access roads to timber stands. The Forest Service built and maintained 340,000 miles of heavy-duty roads, a network eight times longer than the interstate highway system, able to span the globe thirteen times. Instead of charging buyers for the full cost of its roads and other timber services, the Forest Service, and taxpayers, assumed much of the cost. For example, it amor-

tizes the cost of road building over many years, hundreds of years in some cases, so that buyers only have to cover artificially low annual costs. Between 1980 and 1991, the Forest Service lost $5.6 billion dollars from below-cost timber sales.

Second, the Forest Service greatly increased the amount of public timber cut in the postwar period. It increased timber sales from 3.5 billion board feet (1 board foot is 12 by 12 inches square by 1 inch thick) in 1950 to 8.3 billion board feet in 1960 and to 12 billion board feet in the late 1960s, a fourfold increase.[47] The infusion of large public timber supplies into the market kept prices low. Forest managers were encouraged to sell as much timber as possible by laws that based their operating budgets on the volume of timber sales from their districts. In many parts of the country, they did not practice sustained-yield harvesting but cut trees faster than they grew back. Wilderness Society economist Jeffrey Olson estimated that from 1980 to 1985, the Forest Service overcut Northwest woods by 61 percent, and private industry overcut their woods by 126 percent.[48] Over time, this practice led to declining timber supplies and rising prices. The timber sold by the Forest Service in the Pacific Northwest declined by 75 percent, from 8 billion board feet in 1986 to 2.5 billion board feet in 1992.[49] It was in this context that the 1985 dollar devaluation made its appearance in the Pacific Northwest.

The dollar devaluation made Northwest timber available to foreign buyers at bargain-basement prices. For Japanese buyers, it represented a two-for-one sale. (The Japanese were the principal purchasers, though buyers in China, Taiwan, and South Korea also bought heavily.) As the dollar fell, Japanese purchases of Northwest timber increased from 3 billion board feet in 1986 to 4.2 billion board feet in 1988. By 1988, one of every four trees cut in the Northwest was shipped to Japan. In Washington State, 40 percent of the harvest was exported. George Leonard, associate chief of the U.S. Forest Service, admitted that log exports affected the supply of timber in the Northwest. "But if we want to buy Sonys and Toyotas from Japan, we've got to sell them something they want," he said.[50]

Increased U.S. timber exports led to two problems: higher timber prices and fewer jobs. First, the sale of large quantities of timber to overseas buyers reduced domestic supplies and competition between domestic and foreign buyers, who could offer more. This competition led to higher timber prices in the United States. Timber prices increased from about $250 per thousand board feet in the mid-1980s to $350 in 1992 ($474 in 1993), a 30 percent increase.[51] Because a 2,050-square-foot house uses 14,350 board feet of wood, a 30 percent increase in timber prices adds

$3,000 to the cost of the house. And higher costs made it more difficult for U.S. consumers to purchase a home (see chapter 4).

Second, foreign buyers insisted on buying and shipping whole, raw logs. Japanese buyers did not want U.S. lumber mills to cut the wood before shipping it overseas. Instead they wanted to provide timber to the workers in Japanese mills, where they cut timber into the metric equivalent of two-by-fours. (U.S. mills do not use the metric system and do not cut timber to suit the Japanese construction industry.) Because the United States exported raw logs, not milled wood, employment in U.S. mills declined. Although estimates vary, between three and five jobs are lost for every million board feet of raw timber exported. Oregon Representative Peter DeFazio calculated that the export of 4.3 billion board feet in 1988 resulted in the loss of between 13,800 and 23,000 jobs.[52] And between 1986 and 1991, 163 mills were closed.[53] "Decks at Japanese mills are piled high as Mount Fuji with logs from the Northwest, while mills here at home are scrapping for leftovers," said DeFazio. "We're facing the greatest timber supply crisis in our history while Japanese mills are running around the clock."[54]

In addition to export-related unemployment, lumber jacks and mill workers were laid off as the industry automated production, moved some mills to lower-wage countries like Mexico, and ran out of wood to cut in this part of the country. The Forest Service estimated in 1990 that technological change alone would displace 13 percent of the workforce by the end of the century.[55] And Forest Service plans to set aside timber for the protection of spotted owls, a bird threatened by timber cutting in old-growth forests, and salmon, whose streams are threatened by soil erosion from heavily logged forests, will also reduce timber supplies and affect jobs. Although no one at the Plaza meeting considered or anticipated the impact of a dollar devaluation on U.S. natural resources, the one-two punch of Forest Service policy and dollar devaluation resulted in declining timber supplies, higher prices, and growing unemployment in the Pacific Northwest.

Plaza Accords and the World

South Korea, the United Nations, Panama, and oil-producing countries around the world all felt the impact of the Plaza accords, though it affected each in different ways.

After 1985, South Korea saw its currency increase in value by 40 percent between 1986 and 1989.[56] The increasing value of its currency and

rising wages, which were the product of strikes, made it difficult for South Korea to sell its goods overseas or compete with lower-wage Southeast Asian countries like China and Thailand. As one South Korean executive explained, "We can absorb [domestic] wage demands, but we can't take any more [currency] appreciation." As Walden Bello noted, "The one-two punch of a 60 percent rise in wage costs and a 30 percent appreciation of the won . . . wiped out the Korean advantage."[57] And government officials worried about South Korea becoming an "Argentina, a country that manages to climb up to the ridge marking the transition to 'developed country' status, only to slip and fall back to the third world."[58]

The Plaza accords had a different effect on the United Nations, reducing its operating budget. Because the world body uses dollars as its currency, "the sharp decline in its value . . . resulted in an $83 million loss in 1986–87 alone."[59] This, coupled with cutbacks in U.S. contributions in the mid-1980s and the unwillingness or inability of other members to make timely contributions, pushed the United Nations to the "brink of insolvency," making it difficult to perform its peacekeeping responsibilities around the world.[60]

Like the United Nations, Panama uses the U.S. dollar as its national currency, the result of U.S. expenditures on the Panama Canal and its military forces based there. After 1985, Panamanians watched helplessly as the value of the dollar fell, making it more difficult for them to import goods from other countries. As a result, "they consumed more [domestic] rum and less [imported] whiskey. 'I used to eat caviar,' one wealthy Panamanian put it, 'Now I eat ham.' "[61]

The devaluation of the dollar came at a time of rising indebtedness and deteriorating relations between Panama and the United States. The U.S. government wanted to oust or arrest Panama's ruler, General Manuel Noriega, on drug trafficking charges, and applied economic sanctions on the country to force him to surrender power. The combination of intentional sanctions and unintentional devaluation crippled the economy, leading to a 17 percent decline in gross domestic product and 25 percent unemployment by 1989.[62] When Noriega refused to surrender power and observe the results of an election, and began attacking U.S. military personnel, the United States invaded the country on December 20, 1989. Noriega was captured and deported for trial in Miami. Although civilian democrats assumed power after Noreiga was deposed, the economy remained in difficult circumstances as a result of debt, devaluation, embargo, and invasion.

While the Plaza accords had some negative consequences for South Korea, Panama, and the United Nations, it had a serious impact on oil-

producing countries around the world, contributing to falling revenues and war in the Persian Gulf.

Because the dollar was the world's monetary standard for many years, the world oil trade was and still is conducted in dollars. As a result, dollar devaluations have played an important role in the contemporary history of oil. The 1971 dollar devaluation lowered revenues of oil-producing countries. Determined to regain lost revenues and to increase the price of oil in real terms, the members of OPEC responded in 1973 with an oil embargo during the Yom Kippur War between Egypt and Israel. This embargo, and a subsequent embargo during the Iranian revolution in 1979, increased oil prices to more than $35 a barrel. During the 1970s, then, the dollar devaluation helped trigger rising oil prices, which spurred inflation in the United States and around the world.

While the first dollar devaluation in 1971 contributed to oil-price hikes and increased the power of OPEC, the 1985 devaluation had the opposite effect, leading instead to falling oil prices, declining revenues, and the collapse of OPEC as an arbiter of world oil prices.

Between 1980 and 1985, the price of oil declined slowly from $35 to just under $30 a barrel (still, a tenfold increase over the 1970 price of $3 a barrel). Prices fell because countries discovered new oil in the North Sea or expanded production to take advantage of high prices. Increased supplies undermined the price of oil. But it didn't fall below $30 because the Saudi Arabian government was determined to keep the price up on behalf of OPEC. They were willing to cut back their production so that an oil glut, and lower prices, did not materialize. But by 1985, increasing production by OPEC and non-OPEC countries exhausted the patience of the Saudi Arabians, who had seen their oil revenues decline from $119 billion in 1981 to $26 billion in 1985.[63] In that year, to Saudi embarrassment, the British were producing more oil than Saudi Arabia. After a December 9, 1985, OPEC meeting, less than three months after the Plaza meeting, the Saudi Arabians abandoned their low-production, price-support policy and increased their production to recapture lost market share. Within a few months the price of oil had collapsed to $10.[64]

Although U.S. consumers welcomed lower oil prices, the domestic U.S. oil industry did not because it could not make money at that level. In response to low prices, U.S. firms quit drilling and pumping oil and laid off workers. The recession in the oil industry depressed the price of real estate in the Southwest, which contributed to the collapse of savings and loan organizations that had invested heavily in office buildings in the region (see chapter 4). "Moreover," explained Daniel Yergin, "if prices stayed down, U.S. oil demand would shoot up [as consumers drove

more], domestic production would plummet, and imports would start flooding in again, as they had in the 1970s."[65]

To head this off, Vice President George Bush flew to the Middle East to persuade the Saudi Arabian government to *increase* oil prices. He later explained:

> I think it is essential that we talk about stability and that we not just have a continued free fall [in prices] like a parachutist jumping out without a parachute.... I'm absolutely sure ... that *low* prices would cripple the domestic American energy industries, with serious consequences for the nation [emphasis added].[66]

To provide *higher* prices to U.S. and Saudi Arabian oil producers, the United States, Saudi Arabia, and some OPEC countries reached a consensus that oil prices should stabilize at $18, a considerable rise from $10. And their combined efforts eventually established new OPEC quotas, bringing OPEC and nonOPEC producers into line by 1987.

Of course the decline in oil prices, measured in dollars, was accompanied in this same period by a devaluation of the dollar. In effect, the price of oil fell twice, first when rising oil supplies drove down prices and second when devaluation forced down the *dollar* price of oil. In real terms, the price of oil had returned to about what it had been in 1973. As a result, the price of a gallon of gas, in inflation-adjusted 1993 dollars, was $1.12 in 1993 compared to $1.25 in 1973.[67]

But falling oil prices had different consequences for different countries. The United States did well, the Japanese and Europeans better, and the oil-producing countries did badly.

The United States saved money because the price of oil was cheaper. This helped reduce the U.S. trade deficit. And consumers were pleased with lower gas prices at the pump. But while the United States saved money, the Japanese and Europeans saved money twice. They benefited from the falling *price* of oil and from the *devaluation* of the dollar, which further lowered its cost to them. So while the United States saw its bill for imported oil fall by about 30 percent, Japan saw its bill fall by 50 percent and West Germany by 57 percent in this period.[68] As James Sterngold noted, "The stronger yen also slashed Japan's import bills, since oil is paid for in dollars."[69] Because Japan worked hard to improve its energy efficiency and promote conservation during this period, while the United States did little, Japan actually reduced its dependence on foreign oil.

Japan and West Germany also captured other benefits. In the late 1980s, the U.S. government spent about $50 billion providing military and naval

protection to Kuwait and Saudi Arabia, equal to about $100 per barrel of oil imported from the Persian Gulf. Energy economist Amory Lovins notes that "since Germany and Japan depend heavily on Persian Gulf oil (without suffering these tremendous annual military costs) America in effect subsidizes the economies of its two major trading competitors."[70]

For oil-exporting countries, the price decline and dollar devaluation drastically reduced revenues. Despite organizing collectively in OPEC and waging a two-decade campaign to increase oil price and use the revenue to promote economic development, oil-producing countries in the late 1980s found themselves back where they began in 1973. As a result of falling prices and heavy spending, "The $121 billion in financial reserves amassed by Saudi Arabia [in the early 1980s] have almost vanished," the *New York Times* reported in 1993. " 'The Saudis have been drawing down reserves for 10 years,' an American official said. 'They're a mere shadow of their former selves.' "[71]

Although oil-producing countries with small populations (Saudi Arabia, Kuwait, Libya) were still relatively prosperous, the heavily populated oil-producing countries like Nigeria, Iraq, and Iran saw their economic fortunes decline. For instance, Iraq, the second largest oil-producing country in OPEC, saw its oil revenues decline from $26 billion in 1980 to $12 billion in 1988, at a time when it was engaged in a costly war with Iran. Iraqi leader Saddam Hussein waged war with Iran to capture its oil fields so that he could control enough of world oil production to raise prices and recapture revenues lost to price cuts and then dollar devaluation. Having failed in the attempt to capture Iran's oil during a decade-long war, Saddam Hussein then invaded Kuwait in 1990. Iraqi forces were driven out of Kuwait by a multinational U.N. force led by the United States in 1991.

While the 1985 dollar devaluation contributed to lower world oil prices, which benefited first world countries at the expense of third world states, it also contributed, in part, to war in the Middle East, which led to military intervention by first world countries. It turned out that the Plaza accords had consequences and repercussions that policy makers did not intend, anticipate, or fully appreciate.

While the 1971 dollar devaluations marked the beginning of a two-decade effort to improve U.S. competitiveness, which continues to this day, it also marked the beginning of a long campaign against inflation. The fight against inflation was more successful, though it created a crisis for the savings and loan industry in the United States and for borrowers in the third world.

Notes

1. Volcker, Paul A., and Gyohten, Toyoo. *Changing Fortunes: The World's Money and the Threat to American Leadership*. New York: Times Books, 1992.

2. "Transcript of President Nixon's Address on Moves to Deal with Economic Problems," *New York Times*, August 16, 1971.

3. Tsuru, Shigeto. *The Mainsprings of Japanese Growth: A Turning Point*. Paris: Atlantic Institute for International Economics, 1989, p. 18.

4. Berberoglu, Berch. *The Legacy of Empire: Economic Decline and Class Polarization in the US*. New York: Praeger, 1992, p. 56.

5. Volcker and Gyohten, 1992, pp. 38–39.

6. Ibid., pp. 79–80.

7. Ibid., p. 81.

8. Ibid., p. 346.

9. Berberoglu, 1992, p. 56.

10. Orr, Bill. *The Global Economy in the 90s: A User's Guide*. New York: New York University Press, 1992, p. 261.

11. Wald, 1993.

12. Pollack, Andrew. "A Lower Gear for Japan's Auto Makers," *New York Times*, August 30, 1992.

13. Gilpin, Robert. *The Political Economy of International Relations*. Princeton: Princeton University Press, 1987, p. 331.

14. Volcker and Gyohten, 1992, p. 229.

15. Berberoglu, 1992, p. 56. Gilpin, 1987, p. 157.

16. Gilpin, 1987, p. 194.

17. Ibid.

18. Funabashi, Yoichi. *Managing the Dollar: From the Plaza to the Louvre*. Washington, D.C.: Institute for International Economics, 1989, p. 263.

19. Ibid., p. 231.

20. Burstein, Daniel. *Yen! Japan's New Financial Empire and Its Threat to America*. New York: Simon and Schuster, 1988, p. 142. Orr, 1992, p. 167.

21. Volcker and Gyohten, 1992, p. 256.

22. Ibid., p. 252.

23. Putnam, Robert D., and Bayne, Nicholas. *Hanging Together: The Seven-Power Summits*. Cambridge: Harvard University Press, 1984, p. 18. Volcker and Gyohten, 1992, pp. 329–30.

24. Putnam, 1984, pp. 45–46, 48, 237. Hajnal, Peter I. *The Seven-Power Summit: Documents from the Summits of Industrialized Countries, 1975–1989*. Millwood, N.Y.: Kraus International, 1989, pp. xxiii, xxiv.

25. Volcker and Gyohten, 1992, pp. 329–30.

26. Putnam, 1984, p. 17.

27. Kilborn, Peter T. "U.S. and 4 Allies Plan Move to Cut Value of Dollar," *New York Times*, September 23, 1985.

28. Orr, 1992, p. 91.

29. Volcker and Gyohten, 1992, p. 294.

30. Burstein, 1988, p. 147.

31. Ibid., p. 148.

32. Volcker and Gyohten, 1992, p. 270. Das, Dilip K. *The Yen Appreciation and the International Economy.* New York: New York University Press, 1993, pp. 25–28.

33. Berberoglu, 1992, pp. 42–43.

34. Das, 1993, p. 77.

35. Sterngold, James. "Intractable Trade Issues With Japan," *New York Times*, December 4, 1991. Sterngold, James. "Japan Shifting Investment Flow Back Toward Home," *New York Times*, March 22, 1992.

36. Stokes, Bruce. "Help From Japan," *National Journal*, February 10, 1990, p. 357.

37. Sanger, David E. "Tokyo, Outrageously Costly, Gets More So for Americans," *New York Times*, May 28, 1993.

38. Zysman, John, and Tyson, Laura. *American Industry in International Competition: Government Policies and Corporate Strategies.* Ithaca: Cornell University Press, 1983, pp. 7, 46, 63.

39. Ibid., p. 11.

40. Ibid.

41. Das, 1993, p. 130.

42. Judis, John. "Foreign Investment: Up for Grabs," *In These Times*, January 25, 1993, p. 6.

43. Ibid.

44. Glickman, Norman J., and Woodward, Douglas P. *The New Competitors: How Foreign Investors Are Changing the U.S. Economy.* New York: Basic Books, 1989, p. 7.

45. Ibid., p. 128.

46. Ibid., table 8.1.

47. "The Forest Service: Time for a Little Perestroika," *The Economist*, March 10, 1988.

48. Olson, Jeffrey T. *National Forests: Policies for the Future. Volume 4. Pacific Northwest Lumber and Wood Products: An Industry in Transition.* Washington, D.C.: Wilderness Society, 1988, p. 10.

49. Pelline, Jeff. "Timber Shortage Chops Industry," *San Francisco Chronicle*, July 13, 1992.

50. Egan, Timothy. "With Fate of the Forests at Stake, Power Saws and Arguments Echo," *New York Times*, March 20, 1989.

51. Egan, Timothy. "Export Boom Dividing Pacific Timber Country," *New York Times*, April 23, 1988.

52. Ibid.

53. Pelline, 1992.

54. Egan, 1988.

55. Gup, Ted. "Owl vs. Man," *Time*, June 25, 1990.

56. Bello, Walden, and Rosenfeld, Stephanie. "Dragons in Distress," *World Policy Journal*, VII, 3, Summer 1990, p. 439.

57. Ibid., p. 450.

58. Ibid., p. 433.

59. Karns, Margaret P., and Mingst, Karen A. "Multilateral Institutions and International Security," in Michael T. Klare and Daniel C. Thomas, eds., *World Security: Trends and Challenges at Century's End*. New York: St. Martin's Press, 1991, p. 286.

60. Ibid., pp. 285–86.

61. Ropp, Steve C. "Military Retrenchment and Decay in Panama," *Current History*, January 1990, p. 39.

62. Ropp, Steve C. "Panama: The United States Invasion and Its Aftermath," *Current History*, March 1991, p. 116.

63. Yergin, Daniel. *The Prize: The Epic Quest for Oil, Money and Power*. New York: Simon and Schuster, 1991, p. 747.

64. Ibid., p. 750.

65. Ibid., p. 755.

66. Ibid., pp. 756–57.

67. Orr, 1992, p. 261. Wald, 1993.

68. Orr, 1992, pp. 302–3. Das, 1993, p. 18.

69. Sterngold, James. "Leaders Come and Go, But the Japanese Boom Seems to Last Forever," *New York Times*, October 6, 1991.

70. Lovins, Amory B., and Romm, Joseph J. "Fueling a Competitive Economy," *Foreign Affairs*, Winter 1992–93, p. 49.

71. Engelberg, Stephen, Gerth, Jeff, and Weiner, Tim. "Saudi Stability Hit by Heavy Spending Over the Last Decade," *New York Times*, August 22, 1993.

4

Fighting Inflation

When President Nixon devalued the dollar to improve U.S. competitiveness, he also introduced wage and price controls to fight inflation. "The time has come for decisive action," he said in his August 15, 1971, speech, "action that will break the vicious circle of spiraling prices and costs."[1] His orders to "freeze . . . all prices and wages throughout the United States for a period of 90 days" opened the government's attack on inflation.

During the following decade, the government would wage two major campaigns to slow inflation. The first, in 1971, proved to be a failure. The second, which began in 1979, succeeded in curbing inflation. But the cost of victory was high. The policies used to fight inflation prompted a debt crisis in the third world and contributed to the collapse of the savings and loan industry in the United States, and this led to rising homelessness in America.

In his speech, Nixon blamed inflation on the war in Vietnam. "One of the cruelest legacies of the artificial prosperity produced by the [Vietnam] war is inflation," he argued. "For example, in the four war years between 1965 and 1969, your wage increases were completely eaten up by price increases. Your paychecks were higher but you were not better off."[2]

Economists agree that government spending on the war in Vietnam contributed to rising inflation. But they argue that other factors also contributed to it. In the postwar period, most first world countries experienced modest inflation. This inflation was caused by government policies designed to keep unemployment low and to prevent the recurrence of prewar depression. During the 1930s, businesses had responded to recession by laying off workers to cut costs. But high levels of unemployment reduced the demand for goods. Without consumers to buy their goods,

businesses could not increase production, rehire workers, and begin the steps to economic recovery.

After the war, first world governments developed programs designed to maintain demand and prevent widespread unemployment when normal business-cycle recessions occurred. They did this by pumping money into the economy, either through defense, social service, or public works programs. These policies, generally described as "Keynesian" after the British economist John Maynard Keynes who developed them, helped avert depression. But by pumping money into the economy, they also produced modest rates of inflation. When money was plentiful and demand high, businesses could raise prices. And because unemployment rates were low, and labor was relatively scarce, workers could demand and get higher wages. These developments, and the fact that the United States was pumping dollars into first world countries to promote economic recovery, (see chapter 2), produced modest rates of inflation in most first world countries during the 1950s and '60s.[3]

When the United States began waging the Vietnam War in earnest in 1965, U.S. military spending in the United States *and* overseas soared. But U.S. officials were unwilling to raise taxes to pay for the war. If they had, taxes would have taken away some of the money the government was putting into the hands of businesses and into the pockets of workers, which would have lowered *their* demand for goods. But because taxes stayed low, demand remained high. And when demand stayed high, businesses could raise prices and workers could ask for higher wages. As a result, inflation rose sharply.

If prices and wages rose in tandem, for everyone, inflation would not be regarded as a terrible social problem. But inflation is a discriminatory economic process, hurting some people more than others. Some businesses, for example, were better able to raise their prices than others, usually because what they produced was *more* of a necessity than other products. Oil, for example, was something that homeowners in wintry New England or drivers in suburban Los Angeles could not do without. It was more of a necessity than lawn chairs or vintage wine. By the same token, some workers were better able to demand and get higher wages, usually because they were organized in unions or performed services regarded as essential to others. So workers who belonged to the United Auto Workers Union or worked for the local fire department or collected garbage were better able to bargain for pay raises than restaurant waiters or office workers employed by insurance companies.

Other groups were also disadvantaged by inflation. People living on fixed incomes or pensions—some twenty million Americans in 1971 ac-

cording to Nixon—found it difficult to increase their incomes to keep pace with inflation. And people who derived their income from savings accounts and government bonds found that inflation eroded the value of their assets because the interest they received was fixed at fairly low levels (often below the rate of inflation) or set for long periods of time. So, for example, if the rate of inflation was 6 percent annually, a savings account offering 4 percent was losing value and a ten-year savings bond that provided a 6 percent return was not earning a dime.

Because inflation is discriminatory, affecting businesses, workers, pensioners, and investors in different ways, government officials regarded it as a social problem. Although people adversely affected by inflation despair of its consequences, *even* those who kept up with inflation complained about it. As economist Anthony Compagna notes,

> If someone's income increased by $1,000 (which he or she regards as due to merit, conveniently forgetting that inflation boosts other people's income as well) and rising prices take away $500 of the $1,000, the person is still better off but *feels cheated anyway* [because] $1,000 at the old prices would have meant a [more] significant increase in living standards.[4]

For these reasons, Nixon introduced wage and price controls to curb inflation, then increasing at about 4 percent annually. When inflation rises 7 percent annually, as it did during the rest of the decade, consumer prices and monthly wages double in just ten years.[5] This is what occurred in the 1970s.

Nixon's wage and price controls, which remained in effect until April 1973, briefly slowed but did not curb inflation.[6] As journalist William Greider observed,

> The inflation rate subsided for a time, but still remained about 3 percent. By 1973, prices were escalating rapidly again and the consumer price index rose by a new postwar record, 8.89 percent. The following year, 1974, OPEC pushed up oil and the price level rose 12.2 percent.[7]

Several developments frustrated the Nixon administration's efforts to slow inflation. Many economists believe that the wage-and price control program was not effectively managed, allowing exemptions to some businesses and workers but not others. And when the controls ended, everyone scrambled to recover lost gains.[8] Soviet crop failures in 1973 and 1974 increased the demand for grain and sent food prices soaring (see chapter 7). At the same time, dramatically increased oil prices followed successive oil crises—the first in 1974 following the Yom Kippur War, and the sec-

ond during the 1979 revolution that overthrew the Shah of Iran and resulted in the capture of hostages at the U.S. embassy in Tehran. The simultaneous rise of food and oil prices pushed inflation to record, first world heights. After each oil crisis, inflation in the United States hit double-digit figures, 12 percent in 1974, 13.3 percent in 1979, and 12.4 percent in 1980.[9]

The burst of inflation at the end of the 1970s prompted government officials to launch a second campaign against inflation. But instead of using wage and price controls administered by the federal government, officials used high interest rates and the Federal Reserve, a semipublic agency, to curb inflation.

1979: The Second Battle Against Inflation

At the beginning of 1979, inflation was running at a rapid 11 percent annual rate. "In a year's time, a dollar would buy only 89 cents' worth of goods. A $6,000 car would soon cost $660 more. And every wage earner would need a pay raise of more than 10 percent simply to stay even," noted Greider.[10] By the summer of 1979, OPEC price increases began to kick in, pushing the inflation rate to 14 percent. Rising inflation and lengthening lines at gas stations drove down President Jimmy Carter's popularity. By July, "barely a fourth of the voters approved of his performance as President."[11]

Faced with rising inflation and declining popularity, Carter took two steps. First, he made a stern speech criticizing American materialism:

> In a nation that was proud of hard work, strong families, close-knit communities and our faith in God, too many of us now tend to worship self-indulgence and consumption. Human identity is no longer defined by what one does, but by what one owns. But . . . owning things and consuming things does not satisfy our longing for meaning. We have learned that piling up material goods cannot fill the emptiness of our lives which have no confidence or purpose.[12]

Overnight, this speech boosted Carter's popularity by 10 percent, and "75 percent of voters agreed with the President's warning of spiritual crisis."[13] His increased popularity proved to be only temporary. After Iranian students seized hostages at the U.S. embassy in Tehran on November 4, 1979, his popularity again began to decline.

In addition to his speech, Carter took another step. On July 25, he appointed Paul Volcker, who had helped shape the Nixon administra-

tion's 1971 dollar devaluation and introduce wage and price controls, (see chapter 3) to head the Federal Reserve System.[14] Volcker's subsequent decision to raise interest rates to curb inflation would have a long and lasting impact on U.S. economic fortunes. Although his high interest rate policies succeeded in bringing down inflation, they created other problems for the United States and other countries around the world. One important problem was an economic recession during an election year. This and the hostage crisis in Iran led to Carter's electoral defeat by Ronald Reagan one year later.

The Federal Reserve System and High Interest Rates

The Federal Reserve System, established in 1913, acts as the central bank for the United States, controlling the supply of money and credit to private banks and financial institutions, supervising the industry, and managing the sale of U.S. bonds, which are used (along with taxes and fees) to raise money for the government so that it can pay its bills.[15] Its governors are appointed by the president, subject to Senate confirmation, to serve fourteen-year terms. As a result, the Federal Reserve System has considerable autonomy to shape economic policy.

In general, the "Fed" can use its control over money and credit to affect U.S. economic fortunes. If it increases the supply of government money and credit going to private banks, investors, and businesses, the "stimulated" economy usually grows. And if it decreases the money supply, making it harder to get, then the "price" or interest rates that banks, investors, and businesses have to pay for money rises. The higher the price of money, and the higher the interest rate, the harder it is to borrow money, invest, or build new factories. As a result, the economy usually slows and unemployment increases.

After he was appointed to the Fed, Volcker adopted an anti-inflationary strategy. By tightening the supply of money and credit, he hoped to force up interest rates, slow economic growth, and curb inflation. Although he knew this would trigger an economic recession and increase unemployment, Volcker thought it necessary to act. "After years of inflation," he told an audience in the autumn of 1979, "the long run has caught up with us."[16]

So on October 6, 1979, Volcker announced that he would fight inflation by restricting the supply of money and credit and raising interest rates. "Appropriate restraint of the supply of money and credit is an essential part of any program to achieve the needed reduction in inflationary mo-

mentum and in inflationary expectations," he announced. "Such restraint
. . . will help to restore a stable base for financial, foreign exchange and
commodity prices."[17]

During the next six months, interest rates nearly doubled, rising from
about 11 percent when Volcker became chairman to 20 percent in the
summer of 1980.[18] But when the Fed eased off, inflation resumed, so Volcker pushed interest rates back up. And during the next two years, until
the summer of 1982, interest rates rocketed up and down as the Fed used
interest rates to wrestle with the tag team of inflation and recession.[19] In
the end, the high interest rate policy pinned inflation, though recession
remained standing. As Greider noted,

> The Gross National Product contracted in real terms by more than $82 bil-
> lion from its peak and, since 1979, the country had accumulated as much as
> $600 billion in lost economic output. The excess supply of goods, the declin-
> ing incomes, the surplus labor—all had worked to force down wages and
> prices. Price inflation fell dramatically: from above 13 percent [in 1979] to
> less than 4 percent [in 1983].[20]

In a sense, Volcker's high interest rate policies, which triggered the
deepest recession in the postwar period, had returned the U.S. economy
to the kind of modest inflation that had first triggered Nixon's wage and
price controls in 1971.[21] Recall that Nixon took action to curb inflation
when it was running at about 4 percent. After 1982, inflation remained at
this level, running about 4 percent for the rest of the decade.[22]

In addition to a deep recession, the Fed's high interest rate policies
also affected the fortunes of different social groups in the United States.
Although everyone complained about its effect, inflation had been good
for some groups—middle-income homeowners, for instance—and bad
for others. Wealthy investors, for instance, had seen the value of their
assets, particularly bonds, decline sharply in the 1970s. As New York
University economist Edward N. Wolf reported, "Inflation acted like a
progressive tax, leading to greater equality in the distribution of wealth."[23]

But high interest rates and falling inflation changed that. High interest
rates rewarded the wealthy, primarily because the top 10 percent of the
population "owned 72 percent of corporate and federal bonds . . . plus 86
percent of state and local bonds."[24] As interest rates rose to record highs,
and inflation fell to modest lows, their assets increased. "According to the
U.S. Census, only families in the top 20 percent of the economic ladder
enjoyed real increases in their after-tax household incomes from 1980 to
1983. The others, the bottom 80 percent, actually lost."[25]

Volcker anticipated this development. When farm representatives asked him to lower interest rates, Volcker responded, "Look, your constituents are unhappy, mine [banks and bond holders] aren't."[26]

By squeezing the supply of money and credit and raising interest rates, the Federal Reserve triggered a deep recession and curbed inflation. But while high interest rates curbed inflation, they also contributed to a third world debt crisis, rising U.S. budget deficits, and declining U.S. competitiveness.

Debt, Deficits, and Devaluation

When the Fed raised interest rates to record highs in the early 1980s, foreign and domestic investors rushed to buy U.S. bonds or "securities." They did so because they viewed them as "safe"—nothing is safer than U.S. government-backed securities—and profitable: a 15 to 20 percent annual return was higher than more risky investments in stock markets or real estate. High U.S. interest rates, which were substantially higher than what other governments offered in this period, acted like a magnet, attracting monies from around the world. The magnetism created by high U.S. interest rates had important consequences for different countries.

In Latin America, high U.S. interest rates resulted in increased debt and "capital flight." During the 1970s, businesses and governments borrowed money from the United States and other first world countries and spent it on economic development projects (see chapter 5). The interest rate they paid on borrowed money was tied to U.S. interest rates. So when the Fed pushed up U.S. interest rates, borrowers in Latin America saw their interest payments soar, which made it more difficult for them to repay their debts.

High U.S. interest rates also attracted Latin American investors, who spent their money on U.S. bonds rather than on development projects in their own countries. In 1978, before U.S. interest rates rose, Latin American investors sent about $7 billion overseas. But in 1980, Latin Americans invested nearly $25 billion overseas, most of it in the United States.[27] "Capital flight" as it is called by economists, was a problem for Latin American countries because it reduced domestic investment, which resulted in unemployment, and deprived governments of the currency they needed to run their countries and repay debts. In August 1982, the Mexican government ran out of money to manage its affairs or repay its $80 billion debt to foreign countries, and the Federal Reserve had to take emergency measures to prevent it from defaulting on its loans. If Mexico

had declared bankruptcy, major U.S. banks would also have been forced into bankruptcy and a global financial crisis would have ensued.[28] In subsequent years, the Fed and the U.S. government had to address a series of financial crises in Latin American countries, known collectively as the debt crisis, which was partly a product of the Fed's high interest rate policies.

High U.S. interest rates also acted like a magnet for other first world investors, drawing huge sums of money from Western Europe and Japan. Although these countries did not have foreign debts, like Latin American countries, U.S. economists thought that the flight or migration of capital from other first world countries would deprive them of money to invest in public works or new factories in their countries, causing increased unemployment and reducing their ability to compete with the United States. But despite massive purchases of U.S. securities, these problems did not materialize in Western Europe and Japan because the U.S. government gave back to them through military spending what the Federal Reserve took away from them in capital flight.

When President Reagan took office, he promised to increase military spending and to cut taxes. As foreign capital flooded into U.S. securities markets as a result of high U.S. interest rates, the administration found that it could deliver on both its promises. With high interest rates, the Reagan administration could sell bonds and raise the money it needed to increase military spending without raising the taxes to pay for it. By using the sale of U.S. bonds to borrow money from foreigners, the government increased military spending 50 percent, from $201 billion a year in 1980 to $311 billion in 1987.[29] And it could do this without raising taxes to pay for it. In fact, the Reagan administration cut taxes during much of this period (see chapter 6).

Put another way, in 1985, the U.S. government spent about $79 billion more on defense than it had in 1980. And it received $71.4 billion from foreign investors. Thus the increases in military spending were almost entirely paid for by foreigners, which meant that the government did not have to use domestic taxes to raise this money.

This policy—increased military spending and lower taxes—had several important consequences for first world countries in Western Europe and Japan, and for the United States as well.

Western Europe and Japan have been U.S. military allies since World War II. To protect them from invasion by communist countries, the U.S. government had stationed troops and spent money on defense in these countries throughout the postwar period. Economists estimate that between 60 and 70 percent of *all* U.S. military spending is devoted to the

North Atlantic Treaty Organization (NATO), which defends Western Europe.[30] The United States spends a smaller though still large amount defending U.S. allies in East Asia, Japan among them. As U.S. military spending increased under the Reagan administration, its spending in Western Europe and Japan also increased. By purchasing equipment and supplies from its allies, by paying the salaries of about 351,000 U.S. soldiers in Europe, and by providing military aid to its allies, the U.S. government injected huge sums of money into the economies of its first world allies.[31]

In 1985, for example, foreigners (mostly from Western Europe and Japan but also from Latin America) purchased $71.4 billion in U.S. securities.[32] That year, the United States spent $278.9 billion on the military.[33] If the United States spent 60 percent of its military budget for the defense of its first world allies (a low figure since some estimates of U.S. spending on NATO are higher and this figure does not include U.S. spending on Japan), then about $167.34 billion was spent on U.S. allies. This means that the United States "took in" less capital from first world allies than it "gave back" to them in military spending. Total U.S. "giving" to first world allies in that year amounted to $95.94 billion, a kind of massive military "rebate." So while the Federal Reserve's high interest rate policy pulled money out of European and Japanese economies, the Reagan administration's defense spending policies put much of it back. And the high U.S. interest rates, which U.S. economists expected to hurt other first world economies, did not result in recession or high unemployment in either Europe or Japan.

High U.S. interest rates did not greatly reduce the availability of capital in Western Europe and Japan for another reason. Workers in these countries save more of their money than Americans. They are more thrifty because high tariffs often make imported goods expensive, because their governments and banks do not make consumer credit as easily available as they do in the United States, and because they are more reluctant to go into debt than Americans. Because they put a higher percentage of their income in their savings accounts, their banks have more money available to invest. As a result, Japan substantially increased its domestic investments—building new roads and factories and creating more jobs—while *also* increasing its purchases of U.S. government securities in this period (see chapter 6).[34]

As a result of U.S. defense spending and their own thriftiness, Western Europe and Japan were able to benefit three times from high U.S. interest rates. First, they profited from interest rates that were higher than they could obtain at home. Second, they benefited from increased U.S. military

spending in their countries. And third, the flood of foreign currency into the United States increased the value of the dollar, which had declined throughout the 1970s. During the early 1980s, the stronger dollar made it more difficult for U.S. firms to sell their goods abroad, while making it easier for Western European and Japanese businesses to sell their products in the United States. Propped up by high U.S. interest rates, the stronger dollar undermined U.S. competitiveness with first world countries and led, in 1985, to a second devaluation of the dollar through the Plaza accords.

These developments were the product of two sets of policies. It was the combination of the Fed's *monetary* policy, which used high interest rates to fight inflation, and the Reagan administration's *fiscal* policy, which borrowed money from abroad to increase military spending while cutting taxes, that contributed to these different *global* developments: debt in the Third World and increasing competitiveness in first world countries.

For the U.S. economy, the combination of the Fed's high interest rate policy and the Reagan administration's policy of increased military spending but lower taxes had important consequences. By increasing its spending and cutting taxes, the Reagan administration created large and growing budget deficits that contributed to a rapidly growing national debt. And because it borrowed money to cover annual budget deficits at high rates of interest, the government's interest payments grew, which also contributed to the size of total debt (see chapter 6).

High interest rates also contributed to the collapse of the domestic savings and loan (S&L) industry. Widespread bankruptcies in this industry reduced investment in the housing industry. This led to a housing shortage and to rising home prices and rents. And this led, by decade's end, to rising homelessness in America.

Housing and Homelessness

During the thirty years before 1979, the housing industry built millions of inexpensive homes and apartments, making it possible for two-thirds of all Americans to purchase and own their homes. But in the ten years after 1979, the savings and loan organizations that provided money to the construction industry and to home buyers collapsed. Home building slowed, prices and rents rose, and homelessness increased. The Federal Reserve's 1979 decision to raise interest rates marked a turning point and played an important role in reversing the housing industry's fortunes.

High U.S. interest rates not only attracted money from Latin America

and first world investors, they also drew money out of domestic savings accounts. The flight of capital from the passbook savings accounts of domestic S&Ls created problems that led to the collapse of the industry, which had long been a mainstay of the housing industry. Although capital flight from the domestic S&L industry had been a minor problem since 1965, it became a major ongoing problem after 1979.

During the postwar period, S&Ls provided much of the money used by private construction companies and independent contractors to build homes and apartments. S&Ls differed from commercial banks in several important respects. Unlike commercial banks, they did not offer checking accounts or provide services to merchants or loans to businesses. Instead they offered passbook savings accounts to local depositors and attracted customers by paying interest rates that were slightly higher than those offered by banks. (The federal government set these rates and made sure they were higher than those offered by commercial banks.) The S&Ls then took the money deposited in savings accounts and lent the money to contractors and home buyers at a slightly higher rate so they could build and buy homes and so S&Ls could profit from the loans. The income they received from construction loans and mortgage payments enabled the fifty-five hundred S&Ls in the United States to pay their depositors interest on their savings account and make a small profit, which they used to pay salaries, rent, and dividends to shareholders.

Between 1950 and 1970, "31 million housing units were built, including 20 million single-family homes."[35] The large supply of inexpensive housing and the availability of cheap, low-interest, thirty-year home loans made it possible for most Americans to purchase homes. Although only 43.6 percent of Americans owned homes in 1940, 64.4 percent owned homes in 1980, a 50 percent increase.[36] By collecting the savings of small depositors and lending it out to builders and buyers, the S&Ls played an important role in postwar prosperity.

The industry's first real problems began in the mid-1960s. To fight the war in Vietnam, President Lyndon Johnson needed to increase military spending. But he was reluctant to increase taxes to pay for the war because he worried that tax increases would make the war more unpopular. To raise the money, Johnson persuaded the Fed to raise interest rates on government securities, much as Volcker did fifteen years later. Interest rose to a rate that was slightly higher than the rate S&Ls offered depositors on passbook savings accounts. In 1966, for example, the government's three-month Treasury bills (T-bills) paid 5.28 percent interest, while S&Ls provided only 4.75 percent interest on savings accounts (and commercial banks offered only 4 percent).[37]

As a result, some depositors began withdrawing their money from S&
L savings accounts and investing it in government securities that offered
a higher rate of return. When investors withdraw money from a financial
institution, they reduce its assets and weaken its ability to make loans.
The technical term for this process is "disintermediation," but it might
also be called a "slow run on the bank" or "capital flight," which undermines the ability of financial institutions to operate as "intermediaries"
between investors and borrowers.

Initially, investors drawn by higher U.S. interest rates withdrew only
modest amounts of money from S&Ls, only $2.5 billion in 1966, a small
sum compared to the more than $500 billion held by S&Ls. But disinter-
mediation continued, growing to $4 billion in 1969. The federal govern-
ment responded to this slow flight of capital by raising the interest rates
S&Ls could offer on savings accounts to 5 percent in 1970 and 5.25 percent in 1973. They also made it more difficult to purchase T-bills by setting a $10,000 minimum on purchases, which was more than most small
savers could afford.[38] But because the government's interest rates also increased, remaining one or two percentage points higher than S&L rates
for much of the 1970s, the flow of money out of S&Ls continued at a
moderate pace.

But in 1979, the Federal Reserve raised interest rates, and the return on
three-month T-bills reached 12.07 percent in 1979, 15.66 percent in 1980,
and 16.30 percent in 1981.[39] As a result, money flooded out of S&Ls offering depositors only one-half or one-third as much. In 1981, investors
withdrew $21.5 billion from S&Ls, five times as much as they had in 1969.
To stop this massive capital flight and to prevent the wholesale disintermediation of the S&L industry, government officials took two steps that
would have fateful consequences.

As its first step, Congress in 1980 passed and President Carter signed
the Depository Institutions Deregulation and Monetary Control Act.
This bill allowed S&Ls to increase their interest rates on savings accounts
(the federal government had previously limited interest rates) so they
could win back runaway investors, and it increased the government's insurance on investors' deposits from $40,000 to $100,000.

Although higher interest rates prompted some investors to redeposit
their money in S&L accounts, they created another problem. Recall that
payments on home mortgages provided the income for S&Ls. If they
took in money from borrowers at 8 percent and they paid depositors 5
percent on their savings accounts, the S&Ls earned 3 percent. But when
they raised interest rates on savings accounts, to say 10 percent, which
increased their expenditures, they could not easily raise their *income* from

mortgage payments because they had made home loans at fixed rates for long periods of time. In the 1980s, S&Ls' income came from people who had borrowed money at 8 percent in the 1960s. Because they could not raise the mortgage payments of long-term borrowers to increase their income, the S&Ls began paying depositors (10 percent) more than they earned from borrowers (8 percent). As a result, they began to *lose* money, about $4.6 billion in 1981. And bankruptcies began to mount: 17 S&Ls failed in 1980, 65 in 1981, 201 in 1982. The assets of insolvent S&Ls grew from one-tenth of a billion dollars in 1980 to $49 billion in 1982, a 500 percent increase.[40]

Although disintermediation had been slowed, government policy had contributed to increasing bankruptcy. To address this problem, the Garn-St. Germain Depository Institutions Act was passed in 1982. This bill allowed S&Ls to offer checking accounts, issue credit cards, loan money to consumers for autos and personal purchases, make commercial loans to businesses, and invest in stocks and bonds. By allowing S&Ls to offer these services and become more like commercial banks, government officials expected S&Ls to increase their income. For example, the interest rates on credit cards or business or auto loans are much higher than interest rates on home loans. So if the S&Ls could make 15 percent from their credit card customers, government officials thought, they could pay depositors 10 percent and still make money. For a time it worked. S&Ls loaned money in new ways, at higher rates of interest, and paid depositors higher rates on their savings accounts. For a brief time they attracted investors and turned a profit. But two problems soon emerged.

First, increased commercial lending led to the widespread construction of office buildings, golf courses, and resort developments, particularly in the Southwest, where high oil prices in the early 1980s encouraged the expansion of the domestic oil industry and created a booming market for commercial real estate in cities like Dallas (site of a famous TV show depicting these developments in the mid-1980s). But the massive construction of office towers and shopping malls created a glut of commercial properties, and the fall of oil prices after 1985 led to the collapse of the domestic oil industry, which crippled the real estate market. The value of commercial real estate in the Southwest fell by nearly one-half between 1984 and 1989.[41] As the value of real estate fell, builders and developers found it difficult to repay their loans and many went bankrupt. And when the S&Ls could not recover their loans from bankrupt borrowers, they too went bankrupt. As bankruptcy threatened, depositors began withdrawing their money, which led to renewed disintermediation. Profits plummeted, and the S&L industry began to collapse wholesale.

It did not help matters that the Reagan administration cut the budget for bank examiners during this period, which actually reduced the number of field agents and cut the number of federal examinations by 50 percent between 1980 and 1984.[42] Nor did it help that regulators ignored a 1983 government report warning that

> the deregulation of the past few years . . . has substantially reduced the ability of regulatory agencies to constrain the risk-taking of insured institutions. . . . In light of the competitive pressures the industry will face in the next few years, this deregulation could result in substantial losses.[43]

When S&Ls went bankrupt, the Federal Reserve and U.S. government agencies seized control and paid off depositors, who were insured up to $100,000 (as a result of changes in the 1980 law). Investors who owned shares of bank stock were not covered by government insurance, and many lost their investments. The cost of repaying depositors in failed S&Ls will be high. In 1990, Treasury Secretary Nicholas Brady testified to Congress that one thousand S&Ls, or 40 percent of the industry, would have to be seized and depositors repaid. He estimated that this would cost the government between $89 billion and $130 billion. Taxpayers will eventually cover this cost, amounting to $1,300 for each American household.[44] Other cost estimates are higher. Some economists calculate that the bailout will cost between $159 billion and $203 billion. And if one includes the interest payments on this debt, the cost could climb to between $325 billion and $500 billion, or about $5,000 for each American household.[45]

The government can try to recover some of these costs by selling off the assets of seized S&Ls. By 1992 it had sold off assets worth $144 billion. But the sale of 2,300 square miles of real estate, an area twice the size of Rhode Island, has been difficult in a sluggish market.[46]

Second, the S&Ls' changed lending practices reduced the amount of money going to the housing industry. In the early 1970s, S&Ls loaned 60 percent of their assets to home builders and buyers. But as they shifted their emphasis to consumer and commercial loans, at higher rates of interest, they made only 40 percent of the money available to home buyers in 1984 and only 30 percent in 1988.[47] As money for the housing industry dried up, and the money that was available cost more (because of higher interest rates), fewer homes were built and fewer people could borrow money to purchase homes.

In 1972, the housing industry built 2.4 million new homes. But in 1984, when the population was larger and the demand for housing had grown, the industry built only 1.7 million homes.[48]

During the 1970s, inflation had pushed up the cost of housing. In the 1980s, inflation abated, but a shrinking supply of houses and a growing demand for houses continued to push prices up. As the price of housing and the cost of money to purchase a home rose in the early 1980s, fewer people could afford to buy a home and the percentage of homeowners began to decline for the first time since 1940.

The people who might have bought a home in previous decades kept on renting apartments. This development, and the decline in the construction of apartment units, increased the demand for rental units. The Joint Center for Housing Studies at Harvard University reported in 1989 that the number of poor renters had grown, but rental housing stock had declined, and this helped drive up rents. As a result, rents began to rise sharply after 1980, increasing from about $350 a month in the Northeast in 1980 to $420 a month in 1986, and from $380 a month in the West in 1980 to $480 by 1986.[49]

While rents rose, federal housing assistance to the poor declined. The Reagan administration cut housing assistance from $27 billion in 1980 to less than $8 billion in 1987, and the number of federally subsidized housing units declined from 200,000 to 15,000.[50]

As a result, the demand for rental housing outstripped the supply and rents rose. "In 1978 there were 370,000 more low-cost units (renting for $250 a month) than there were low-income renter households, but by 1985, there were 3.7 million fewer low-cost units than there were low-income renter households."[51] Government cuts in housing assistance and stagnant wages made it difficult for poor people to pay higher rents or compete for the available housing. And poor people who could not devote 70 or 80 percent of their income to housing were forced out of the housing market. Many of them became homeless.

By 1990, there were between six hundred thousand and three million homeless people in the United States.[52] Of course, they were not all forced to wander the streets of American cities by high interest rates and the collapse of the S&L industry. A small homeless population had long existed in the United States, and its number increased as a result of personal choice or misfortune, economic recession or government policies, such as the de-institutionalization of mentally disabled patients from state hospitals in the 1970s. But the growing percentage of homeless *families*, about 40 percent of the homeless population in 1993, indicates that economic developments of the past decade played an important role in increased homelessness.[53]

Compared to the third world, where between 30 and 75 percent of the urban population is homeless, homelessness in first world countries rep-

resents a small but visible proportion of urban populations. But homeless people in third world countries have an important advantage over the homeless in first world cities. They typically build shantytowns or illegal settlements on public or private land. Although their constructions of corrugated tin and cardboard boxes and packing crates are rude and crude to begin with, as shantytown dwellers improve and rebuild their homes, they eventually develop the appearance of legal and permanent residential neighborhoods. In the United States, by contrast, homeless populations are generally prevented from establishing encampments or building structures on public or private land. Local authorities typically raze or bulldoze homeless camps, though some, like the "Mole People," as they are called, have built housing and live illegally in New York City's extensive railway tunnels or build shanties under the closed Westside Highway.

Although the Federal Reserve's high interest rate policy successfully curbed inflation, the victory was costly. The collapse of the S&L industry and the rise of homelessness have become major and continuing problems in the United States. And although interest rates have descended in the 1990s, it has been difficult to revive the housing industry, increase the supply of homes and apartments, and increase homeownership or rental levels to the point that homelessness can be reduced.

While the battle against inflation was won in the early 1980s, inflation continued at a modest rate, about 2 percent for the next decade. In 1994, the Federal Reserve, led by Alan Greenspan, began to raise interest rates to battle inflation once again. But this move was controversial because inflation, then running at about 3 percent, was modest by 1980 standards (then 12 percent), though it was comparable to inflation rates that triggered Nixon's wage and price controls in 1971 (about 4 percent). Economists opposed to higher interest rates warned that it could lead to recession, unemployment, and many of the problems that emerged after interest rates rose in the 1980s.[54]

Notes

1. "Transcript of President's Address on Moves to Deal with Economic Problems," *New York Times*, August 16, 1971.

2. Ibid.

3. Smith, Michael R. *Power, Norms and Inflation: A Skeptical Treatment*. New York: Aldine de Gruyter, 1992.

4. Campagna, Anthony S. *The Economic Consequences of the Vietnam War*. New York: Praeger, 1991, p. 122.

5. Berberoglu, Berch. *The Legacy of Empire: Economic Decline and Class Polarization in the United States*. New York: Praeger, 1992, p. 61.

6. Campagna, 1991, p. 89.

7. Greider, William. *Secrets of the Temple: How the Federal Reserve Runs the Country*. New York: Touchstone, 1987, p. 91.

8. Campagna, 1991, p. 114.

9. Volcker, Paul A., and Gyohten, Toyoo. *Changing Fortunes: The World's Money and the Threat to American Leadership*. New York: Times Books, 1992, p. 115. Berberoglu, 1992, p. 61.

10. Greider, 1987, p. 14.

11. Ibid.

12. Ibid.

13. Ibid., p. 15.

14. Ibid., pp. 46–47.

15. *The World Almanac and Book of Facts 1990*. New York: Pharos Books, 1990, p. 83. Greider, 1987, pp. 32–33.

16. Greider, 1987, p. 104.

17. "Test of Fed's Announcement on Measures to Curb Inflation," *New York Times*, October 8, 1979. Rattner, Steven. "Anti-Inflation Plan by Federal Reserve Increases Key Rate," *New York Times*, October 7, 1979.

18. Greider, 1987, pp. 148–49.

19. Ibid., p. 219.

20. Ibid., p. 507.

21. Orr, Bill. *The Global Economy in the 90s: A User's Guide*. New York: New York University Press, 1992, p. 257.

22. Ibid., p. 258.

23. Greider, 1987, p. 44.

24. Ibid., p. 372.

25. Ibid., p. 577.

26. Ibid., p. 676.

27. Pastor, Manuel Jr. *Capital Flight and the Latin American Debt Crisis*. Washington, D.C.: Economic Policy Institute, 1989, p. 9.

28. Greider, 1987, p. 517.

29. Orr, 1992, p. 287.

30. Sivard, Ruth. *World Military and Social Expenditures, 1987–88*. Washington, D.C.: World Priorities, 1987, p. 37.

31. "U.S. Official Affirms a 40% Cut in Troops Based in Europe by '96," *New York Times*, March 29, 1992.

32. Glickman, Norman J., and Woodward, Douglas P. *The New Competitors: How Foreign Investors Are Changing the U.S. Economy*. New York: Basic Books, 1989, p. 116.

33. Orr, 1992, p. 287.

34. Sanger, David E. "Japan Keeps Up the Big Spending to Maintain Its Industrial Might," *New York Times*, April 11, 1990.

35. Kotz, David. "S&L Hell: Loan Wolves Howl All the Way to the Bank," *In These Times*, August 8, 1989, p. 20.

36. Ibid.

37. White, Lawrence J. *The S&L Debacle: Public Policy Lessons for Bank and Thrift Regulation.* New York: Oxford University Press, 1991, p. 63.

38. Ibid., pp. 62, 64.

39. Ibid., p. 68.

40. Kotz, 1989, p. 21.

41. White, 1991, p. 111.

42. Ibid., pp. 88–89.

43. Ibid., p. 92.

44. Rosenbaum, David E. "How Capital Ignored Alarms on Savings," *New York Times*, June 6, 1990.

45. Ibid.

46. Wayne, Leslie. "The Great American Land Sale," *New York Times*, November 30, 1992.

47. Kotz, 1989, p. 21.

48. Greider, 1987, p. 654.

49. Mariano, Ann. "Fewer Can Buy Homes, Study Finds: Poor Seen Trapped in Rent Cost Squeeze," *Washington Post*, June 24, 1989.

50. Phillips, 1990, Appendix 1.1. Sweeney, Richard. *Out of Place: Homelessness in America.* New York: HarperCollins, 1993, p. 89.

51. Dionne, E. J., Jr. "Poor Paying More for Their Shelter," *New York Times*, April 18, 1989.

52. Levitas, Michael. "Homelessness in America," *New York Times Magazine*, June 10, 1990.

53. Clairborne, William. "Big Increase in Homeless Families," *San Francisco Chronicle*, December 22, 1993.

54. Marshall, Jonathan. "Fed Criticized for Boost in Rates," *San Francisco Chronicle*, April 19, 1994. Pinder, Jeanne B. "Building Slump Is Seen as Brake on Recovery," *New York Times*, August 22, 1993.

5

Debt and Taxes in the Third World

On March 27, 1981, Polish government officials in London told representatives of five hundred Western banks that Poland could not repay the $27 billion it had borrowed from them. In July, the Romanian government followed suit, suspending payments on its more modest $7 billion debt to Western banks.[1] The financial problems created by these defaults were dwarfed a year later, in August 1982, when Mexico's finance secretary, Jesus Silva Herzog, announced that Mexico could no longer make payments on its $90 billion foreign debt. And during the next year, more than forty other countries, most of them in Latin America, ran out of money and announced they could no longer repay the interest or principal on huge debts owed to private banks and government lending agencies in first world countries. Collectively, third world countries owed $810 billion in 1983, a twelvefold increase from the $64 billion they owed in 1970.[2] "Never in history have so many nations owed so much money with so little promise of repayment," *Time* magazine observed.[3]

The sudden inability of so many countries to repay their debts created a "debt crisis" that threatened first and third world countries alike. If countries like Poland, Mexico, and Brazil could not repay loans made by first world banks, then major Western banks could fail, creating widespread bankruptcy, financial chaos, and possibly, global economic depression. And if third world countries defaulted on their loans and declared bankruptcy, they could no longer obtain the money they needed to pay for essential food and oil imports, or develop the industry they needed to provide jobs for growing populations.

Although the debt crisis, which became acute in the early 1980s, threatened first and third world countries alike, measures taken to address the crisis had different consequences for first world creditors and third world debtors. The threat of bankruptcy for first world lenders has receded. In

1994, the *New York Times* even announced that the debt crisis was "officially" over. But while the crisis may have ended for first world lenders, it continues for third world debtors. Third world debtors now find themselves deeper in debt, despite having made every effort to repay debts accumulated in the 1970s.

But how did a collective crisis produce such different outcomes? As we will see, third world debts increased rapidly during the 1970s, both because first world countries wanted to lend and third world countries wanted to borrow large sums of money. While the transfer of money from first to third world countries proved beneficial to both in the 1970s, it proved troublesome in the early 1980s as a result of two developments. First, rising interest rates, which were designed to fight inflation in first world countries, increased the amount that third world borrowers were expected to pay first world lenders. Second, falling commodity prices for the goods third world countries exported to the first world decreased third world incomes, making it more difficult for them to repay first world lenders. Increasing costs and falling incomes made it difficult for third world borrowers to repay their debts, and a debt crisis ensued. To solve this crisis, first world creditors demanded that third world borrowers adopt strenuous economic measures to repay their debts. These steps provided money to first world creditors, which enabled them to avert a financial crisis. But they caused enormous economic hardship for third world countries and left them, a decade later, deeper in debt. Since the onset of the crisis, third world debt has doubled from $639 billion in 1980 to $1,341 billion in 1990.[4] In Latin America, the region with the largest share of debt, "total indebtedness . . . now equals about $1,000 for every man, woman and child" in the continent, this in a region where $1,000 is more than most families earn in a year.[5]

Although countries around the world experienced a debt crisis, Latin America will be the focus of the discussion because the third world countries with the largest outstanding foreign debts (Mexico and Brazil with $90 billion each, Argentina with $38 billion) are in Latin America and because the continent owes more than half of the total third world debt.[6] By contrast, for example, Eastern European countries collectively owed $92.8 billion in 1981, equal to Mexico's debt,[7] and African countries together owed $82 billion in 1985, less than either Mexico or Brazil.[8]

Getting Into Debt

In the 1970s, the amount of first world money loaned to Latin American and other third world countries increased dramatically. Between 1970 and

1973, first world countries lent $23.4 billion to Latin America, more money than had been loaned in the previous thirty years.[9] During the next decade, Latin America multiplied its debts more than twelve times. Third world debt expanded rapidly in the 1970s because first world lenders had large supplies of money that they were eager to lend and because third world countries had great demand for borrowed money. "Indebtedness is a two-sided relationship," New York investment banker Richard Weinert observed. "It depends not only on a willing borrower, but equally on a willing lender. [Third world] indebtedness results as much from the need of [first world] lenders to lend as from the need of borrowers to borrow."[10] But conditions that in the 1970s encouraged first world countries to lend, and third world countries to borrow, changed dramatically in the 1980s.

First World Lenders

After World War II, government agencies and institutions like the International Monetary Fund (IMF) and the World Bank made the majority of the loans to third world countries. They did not lend large amounts (about $20 billion to Latin America between 1950 and 1970), they attached strict conditions to the loans, and they loaned money primarily to promote financial stability or to finance large-scale development projects like dams and ports. During the 1970s, private first world banks began lending increasing amounts of money, increasing their share of total lending from about one-third to more than one-half of all loans by the end of the decade.[11] Private banks lent large sums of money to Latin American countries because they saw it as a way to invest profitably the growing pool of money available to them in Eurodollar or European currency markets.

During the 1970s, governments and private investors from around the world deposited U.S. dollars and other "hard currencies" they had earned in trade with the United States in Western European banks and in U.S. banks with subsidiaries in Europe. Some of the first dollar deposits were made by the Soviet Union. They were joined by investors in Latin America, Japan, and other countries around the world, who deposited dollars in these accounts because they regarded them as safe and because they were not subject to the same kind of government regulations that applied to currencies deposited in the accounts of domestic banks.[12]

The money available in this Eurodollar banking pool grew from about $10 billion in 1960 to $110 billion in 1970.[13] Then, in the 1970s, money from another source began to deepen and expand this monetary pool.

After the 1973 OPEC oil embargo sent oil prices soaring, OPEC countries received huge amounts of dollars from first world countries in payment for their oil, as much as $100 billion a year. "Since $100 billion a year is hard to spend," one writer observed, "even on Cadillacs, private 747s, and sophisticated missiles," the OPEC countries deposited much of their money in Western European and U.S. banks, and this money found its way into the Eurodollar market.[14] OPEC countries did this because they wanted to earn interest on their newfound wealth and because they regarded first world banks as safe havens for their money. With the influx of dollars from oil-producing countries, often called Petrodollars because they were dollars used to pay for OPEC oil, the pool of money in the Eurodollar market grew to $1,525 billion by the 1980s.[15] (Precise estimates vary enormously because government regulatory agencies have a difficult time monitoring or tracking this money. Still, the rate of increase during the 1970s is the same regardless of the figures used.)[16]

As the money available to Western banks grew, bank officials searched for profitable ways to invest or loan it. Large U.S. banks became particularly active in Latin America, where banks had numerous subsidiaries and a fairly long history of involvement in local economies. "The nine largest U.S. banks, whose total capital is $27 billion, have lent over $30 billion (or more than their net worth) to private and government borrowers in just three countries: Mexico, Brazil and Argentina," the *Wall Street Journal* wrote in 1984.[17] The banks loaned money from Eurodollar pools, from U.S. depositors in their branch banks, and from smaller banks that joined loan syndicates.

Public and private lenders in the first world lent money to third world countries for a variety of reasons. Mainly, first world countries made loans so that third world countries could purchase first world goods. In the 1970s, for example, "42 percent of [Britain's] construction equipment, 33 percent of new aircraft and 32 percent of British textile machinery went to third world markets. In the United States, by 1980, the third world market accounted for . . . 20 percent of U.S. industrial product and about one-quarter of gross farm income."[18]

The U.S. government's Export-Import Bank, for example, loaned money to Latin American governments so they could purchase U.S. airplanes. As Boeing Aircraft President Malcolm Stamper explained, "the Ex-Im Bank . . . was created to help promote exports . . . to help foreign firms and their nations to buy big-ticket goods that would be of social and economic benefit. Airplanes certainly meet this description. . . . Airplane exports are also very good business for this country's own economy, by the way."[19]

Private lenders also discovered that they could make more money loaning money to third world borrowers than to domestic borrowers.

> While the ten largest U.S. banks had a phenomenal expansion of international earnings [from third world loans] in 1970 to 1976, profitability in the domestic market ran generally flat. By the mid-1970s, most of the large banks had 50 percent or more of their earnings from abroad. In the case of Citicorp . . . by 1970 over 80 percent of their earnings came from their international operations.[20]

U.S. bankers in the 1970s did not worry greatly about the risks associated with third world loans for several reasons. First, most of their money was loaned to Latin American dictatorships, which maintained close and friendly ties to first world countries and seemed unlikely to renege on their debts (see chapter 9).[21] Second, they observed that the prices of some third world commodities, particularly oil, were rising in the 1970s, which helped third world economies grow. This suggested that as their incomes grew, third world countries would be able to repay old debts and shoulder new ones without difficulty. And third, because governments had the authority to raise money by taxing their citizens, they could still repay loans should economic problems develop. Explaining why his bank was bullish on third world loans, Citicorp Chairman Walter Wriston told the *New York Times* in 1982, "A country does not go bankrupt."[22]

Not everyone was so optimistic. *Euromoney* observed in 1975 that "a purely technical analysis of the current financial position [of many third world countries] would suggest that defaults are inevitable; yet many experts feel this is not likely to happen [because] the World Bank, the IMF and the governments of major industrialized nations . . . would step in rather than watch any default seriously disrupt the entire Euromarket apparatus."[23]

Despite their enthusiasm for third world loans, first world banks worried about the risks associated with mounting debt. So they hedged their bets, insisting in the late 1970s that borrowers agree to readjust interest rates on new *and old* loans every six months and bring interest rates into line with current market rates.[24] And by 1983, nearly 70 percent of all loans in Latin America were subject to floating interest rates, which would rise or fall depending on the interest rates set in *first* world countries.[25] Although interest rates were then stable, which meant that borrowers did not worry greatly about accepting this new condition, first world insistence on floating interest rates would have important consequence for both lenders and borrowers in the early 1980s.

Third World Borrowers

Not only were first world countries and bankers willing to lend, third world countries and corporations were eager to borrow money in the 1970s. Public and private borrowers had substantial and diverse needs for first world loans. Much of the money they borrowed was simply used to repay first world lenders. "Between 1976 and 1981," Sue Branford and Bernardo Kucinski wrote,

> Latin America borrowed an enormous $272.9 billion. But over 60 percent of this, $170.5 billion, was immediately paid back to the banks as debt repayments or interest. Another $22.9 billion remained with [first world] banks as reserves [against potential losses], which were a kind of additional guarantee for the debt itself. And an estimated $56.6 billion was quickly sent abroad as capital flight. Only $22.9 billion effectively entered the continent to be used (or not) in productive investment.[26]

Of the $88 billion Mexicans borrowed between 1977 and 1979, only $14.3 billion was actually available for use in the country.[27]

Although estimates of the amount of borrowed money actually available for use in any given country vary considerably, the money that remained was put to different uses by public and private borrowers.

In their effort to promote economic growth, governments borrowed money to pay for "essential" imported goods like oil, food, and machinery. Rising oil prices in the 1970s forced third world countries without oil to pay more for imported oil. U.S. economist William Cline estimated that oil price increases cost third world countries an extra $260 billion in the years between 1974 and 1982, a figure comparable to the $299 billion acquired by these same countries during this period.[28]

Of course, some third world countries like Mexico had large oil supplies of their own. But while Mexico did not pay more for imported oil, it borrowed heavily to develop its oil fields and become a major producer, expecting that increasing oil prices would enable it to pay off mounting debts. As we will see, this expectation did not materialize, and falling oil prices after 1980 helped trigger Mexico's debt crisis.[29]

The cost of imported food also rose in the 1970s. Rising oil prices increased the cost of growing food because farmers rely heavily on gasoline-powered tractors and petroleum-based fertilizers and pesticides. And poor harvests in the Soviet Union during the mid-1970s increased the demand and therefore the price of food on world markets (see chapter 7). "For low-income countries, the increased cost in these years . . . of food

imports from [first world] countries far exceeded the increased cost of oil imports," argued Shahid Burki.[30]

As we have seen, with money provided by first world lenders, governments also purchased tractors and textile machines to expand commodity production in fields and factories and built roads, ports, and airports—and the aircraft to use them—to facilitate the transport of commodities, business managers, and bankers. Many of these activities provided jobs to first world manufacturers of imported goods and employment for domestic third world users of these products. By building huge mining, hydroelectric, irrigation, and industrial projects, governments could put people to work and increase their income from project revenues and worker taxes.

In addition to paying for essential imports, governments used borrowed money to build up hard currency reserves and stabilize their currencies, to subsidize or lower the cost of fuel, food, and transportation so that domestic consumers would not be adversely affected by rising oil and food prices, and sometimes to balance their budgets.[31] As one Latin American finance minister recalled, "I remember how the bankers tried to corner me at conferences to offer me loans. If you are trying to balance your budget, it's terribly tempting to borrow money instead of raising taxes."[32] (As we will see in chapter 6, this was also a temptation for the U.S. government in the 1980s.)

Of course, not all the money was used for essential or legitimate government purposes. Some of it was used to increase military expenditures, wasted on boondoggle development projects, or siphoned off for personal gain. Military spending by Latin American countries doubled during the 1970s, despite the fact that they faced no external threats. Military spending in Africa increased by one-third.[33] Many development projects proved to be boondoggles. A huge development project providing electricity from the Inga dam on the Zaire River to a copper-cobalt mining complex in Shaba province cost nearly $1 billion, but when it was finished, the electricity it delivered was no longer needed at the mines.[34] And in some countries, government corruption was widespread. In Zaire, a country described by some writers as an "absolutist kleptocracy," President Mobutu Sese Seko stashed away about $5 billion in personal Swiss bank accounts, a sum equal to his country's total foreign debt.[35] In Brazil, President Fernando Collor de Mello was impeached for corruption in 1992.

Governments were not the only borrowers. Private borrowers acquired a substantial portion of Latin American debt. In Latin America, "private debt rose from $15 billion in 1972 to $58 billion in 1981," accounting for

about 20 percent of the total ($272.9 billion in 1981).[36] During the 1970s, domestic owners of Latin American farms and factories, often "the principal national monopolistic groups of the country," borrowed heavily to finance the expansion of their businesses.[37] In Mexico these groups acquired one-quarter of the country's total debt.

Alongside private domestic borrowers, subsidiaries of first world countries also borrowed money, and when they did, they increased the debt of third world countries. So, for example, General Motors, Ford, Union Carbide, Pepsico, and Volkswagen were all important borrowers in Mexico, adding $750 million of debt to Mexico's total.[38]

Like first world lenders, third world borrowers were confident they could repay mounting debts. Inflation in first world countries meant that real interest rates were fairly low and stable in the 1970s, commodity prices for the raw materials and goods they produced were rising, and their economies were growing. But these favorable conditions, which encouraged both lenders and borrowers in the 1970s, did not last. And changed conditions—rising interest rates and falling commodity prices—in the 1980s triggered a crisis that proved earlier assumptions wrong.

The Crisis: Rising Interest Rates, Falling Commodity Prices

When Paul Volcker, head of the Federal Reserve, raised U.S. interest rates in 1979 to fight inflation in the United States, he did not intend to create a third world debt crisis. But rising U.S. interest rates, and the rising London Interbank Offered Rate (LIBOR), which set interest rates for Eurodollar lending, greatly increased the cost of third world loans, most of them now tied to floating rates set by the United States or LIBOR.[39]

Rising interest rates had two important consequences. First, they increased interest payments on accumulated debt. "Mexico's interest bill tripled from $2.3 billion in 1979 to $6.1 billion in 1982 . . . for the region as a whole, interest payments more than doubled, from $14.4 billion in 1979 to $36.1 billion in 1982."[40] High interest rates made it harder for borrowers to pay back their debts. U.S. economist William Cline estimated that high interest rates in the 1980s cost third world countries $41 billion more than they would have paid had interest rates remained at the average level between 1961 and 1980.[41] Other economists have estimated that Latin American countries paid out more than $100 billion in "excessive" interest between 1976 and 1985.[42]

A second problem was that high U.S. interest rates acted like a magnet,

attracting money from around the world. U.S. officials understood that capital flight from other countries would reduce investment abroad and undermine the competitiveness of other countries. As we have seen, it did not greatly weaken Western Europe and Japan because they had higher savings rates, which meant they had more capital available to them, and because the U.S. government returned some of this capital to them in the form of U.S. military spending. Unfortunately, Latin American and other third world countries did not have these advantages, since they had low savings rates and a huge demand for capital (which is why they had been borrowing money from abroad). And except for Panama, where the United States stationed a large military force, the United States returned little of the money it acquired from Latin American investors in the form of military spending. As Volcker observed, "In many [third world countries], their excessive debt burdens can be traced in large part to a flight of capital by their own citizens discouraged from investing at home."[43] He might have added that U.S. policies also encouraged them to invest their capital in the United States.

High interest rates attracted $150 billion in capital from Latin America between 1973 and 1987, the bulk of it after 1979, when as much as $25 billion annually "flew" to the United States to purchase Treasury bonds.[44] Massive capital flight created several problems for Latin American countries: it deprived them of money they might have used to invest in their own countries, pay for imports, or repay debt, and it eroded their country's tax base as investors withdrew taxable savings from Latin American banks and placed them in tax-free deposits in U.S. banks.[45] During the height of Mexico's debt crisis, "a Mexico City newspaper published the names of 537 Mexicans each with over a million dollars on deposit with foreign banks."[46] As a result, capital flight deprived third world countries of money at a time when they needed it most.

Just as interest rates increased, commodity prices began to fall. During the 1970s, the price of commodities typically exported by third world countries—metals, raw materials, and foodstuffs—generally rose. They could then use the hard currencies they earned by selling these goods to first world countries to repay their loans, which had to be repaid in hard, first world currencies. First world lenders insisted on repayment in dollars or other hard currencies, not in pesos, astrals, or local currencies, because they worried that indebted governments would simply print more money and use inflation to repay loans in worthless, depreciated currency.

Generally speaking, the prices third world countries could get for their commodities fell slowly between 1950 and the mid-1970s, when the OPEC embargo and weather-related food shortages began to increase

commodity prices, particularly of oil and food. Commodities then began to fall dramatically in the 1980s.[47] Between 1980 and 1982, world commodity prices fell by more than one-third, "to their lowest level in 30 years, a disastrous development for countries that expected commodity exports to pay their way," noted sociologist John Walton.[48] "The beef that Argentina [exported] fell from $2.25 a kilogram . . . in 1980 to $1.60 by the end of 1981. Sugar from Brazil and the Caribbean fell from 79 cents a kilo to 27 cents by 1982. And copper, a big-ticket item for the likes of Chile and Zaire, fell from $2.61 a kilo to $1.66," one writer observed.[49]

Falling prices reduced the ability of third world countries to repay debts then being pushed up by higher interest rates. And prices continued to fall during the rest of the 1980s. A World Bank index of raw material prices, which started at 168.2 in 1980, fell to 100 by 1990, and 86.1 in 1992, the lowest prices in real terms since 1948.[50]

The price of oil also fell, slowly after 1980 and then sharply after 1985. Mexico, which borrowed heavily to become a major oil producer because it believed oil prices would continue to climb, found itself with mounting debt and declining revenues.[51] "Given the deterioration in the terms of trade, Latin Americans sell more and get less," observed Mexico's finance minister, Jesus Silva Herzog.[52]

Why did commodity prices fall so dramatically in the 1980s, crippling the ability of third world borrowers to repay their debts? They did so because high U.S. interest rates triggered a global recession that reduced demand for their goods. And they fell because first world countries had begun to develop new supplies or to substitute materials for third world commodities. In the case of oil, the discovery of new oil fields in the North Sea increased the supply and helped lower global prices, while energy conservation measures reduced demand. In a way, fiberglass insulation in American attics provided a substitute for imported oil and contributed to falling oil prices. And commodity prices fell because third world countries collectively produced *more* of these goods in the 1980s. Remember that in the 1970s third world borrowers used first world money to expand their production of oil (Mexico), coffee (Colombia), frozen orange juice (Brazil), beef (Argentina), copper (Chile, Zaire), and tin (Bolivia). With money and hard work, they succeeded in producing more of these goods. But as production expanded, supplies increased and prices fell. The irony is that as they worked harder, they earned less and fell deeper into debt.

Crisis Management: First World Lenders Pull Together

Mounting third world debt and a growing inability to repay loans threatened to bankrupt the major U.S. and Western European banks. If that

occurred, financial chaos and a global economic crisis would have ensued. To avert such a catastrophe, first world lenders acted quickly to manage the crisis. Led by the Federal Reserve and international lending agencies like the World Bank and the International Monetary Fund, first world lenders joined together to manage the debt crisis of individual countries, insisting that these countries take steps to ensure full repayment of all their debts, both public and private. As Princeton economist Robert Gilpin observed, "Interest payments on the debt would not be decreased across the board nor world commodity prices received by debtors be increased. The burden of solving the problem would continue to rest squarely on the debtors. . . ."[53]

If they had not acted in concert, if each bank had attempted to collect debts or seize assets individually, chaos would have ensued and third world debtors might have been able to play lenders against each other. Instead, by forming what Gilpin calls a "creditor's cartel," first world lenders could practice a "divide and conquer strategy" and "impose their will on the debtors."[54] They were able to do this because private lenders could speak with one voice, through powerful public institutions like the World Bank, in negotiations with foreign borrowers. In negotiations they also possessed two important advantages: they alone could lend borrowers the money they needed to make ends meet and they alone possessed accurate information on the debts and economic conditions of third world borrowers (most debtor governments lacked key financial information on private debt in their country).[55] First world unity, financial resources, and economic information enabled them to bargain with third world debtors from a position of strength.

While Federal Reserve and World Bank officials managed the debt crisis in dozens of countries, private first world lenders moved to protect themselves from the consequences of the crisis by reducing credit and shifting the burden of financing new loans to public agencies and making taxpayers assume some losses.

During previous Latin American debt crises, first world lenders simply stopped lending to third world borrowers, sometimes for decades. During the 1980s, private banks greatly reduced their lending, though they did not cut off credit entirely. Capital flows to Latin America fell by one-third between 1980 and 1984 as private lenders began to cut and run.[56] The problem was that third world borrowers desperately needed new loans, at least in the short term, so they could get their finances in order and take steps that would eventually enable them to repay debts. Public lending agencies urged private bankers to continue lending money. U.S. Treasury Secretary James Baker, whose 1985 Baker Plan attempted to advance a comprehensive settlement of the debt crisis, argued that "increased lend-

ing by the private banks in support of comprehensive economic adjustment programs" was essential in order to make it possible for borrowers
to repay their debts. As Baker told bankers, "I would like to see the banking community make a pledge to provide these amounts" ($20 billion
over the next three years) on a "voluntary basis."[57]

Because private banks did not respond to Baker's invitation the Baker
Plan failed.[58] So the U.S. government and international lending agencies
had to pick up the slack, which meant that first world taxpayers had to
shoulder increasing responsibilities for debt crisis management.

Private lenders also protected themselves by declaring "losses" on third
world loans, which enabled them to reduce their taxes. But while they
claimed losses, they could still demand full repayment from borrowers,
so they could declare losses, receive tax breaks, *and* recover their original
investment.[59] Although the tax laws that allow banks to take "provisions," or make "loan-loss reserves" as they are called, differ from country to country, the savings to banks can be substantial. One economist
estimated that between 1987 and 1990, "over $20 billion of U.S. bank debt
on the third world was charged off and provisioned under federal man-
date. Since the corporate tax rate on U.S. banks is 34 percent, this sum
would give rise to tax credits of at least $6.8 billion."[60] British banks re-
ceived about $7 billion, German banks $10 billion, and French banks
$10.9 billion as a result of similar laws.[61] Altogether, private first world
banks probably received between $44 billion and $50.8 billion in tax credits in this period.[62]

Again, taxpayers had to assume responsibility for revenues lost in this
fashion. And if governments agree to provide debt relief to third world
borrowers, as they did occasionally—for example when the U.S. government discharged $7 billion of Egypt's debt for agreeing to participate as
an ally in the 1990–91 Persian Gulf War—taxpayers have to cover these
loses.[63]

Although the stockholders of some first world banks experienced
losses when it became apparent that their banks had lent heavily to third
world debtors and the value of their stocks declined, private banks
emerged from a potentially devastating crisis relatively unscathed. No
major first world bank failed as a result of the third world debt crisis
(though many savings and loans in the United States failed as a result of
higher interest rates). But while first world lenders averted serious problems, third world borrowers did not.

Third World Debtors Fall Apart

Third world borrowers who ran out of money to repay their debts faced
serious problems. Without foreign currency, they could not pay for im-

ported fuel or food, and owners of domestic capital began to send it abroad. Without imported or domestic capital, agricultural and industrial businesses would grind to a halt and lay off workers, and the economy would collapse. To avert these economic disasters, third world governments, under the direction of first world lenders, took steps to get the hard, first-world currency they needed to purchase imported goods and repay first world lenders.

As a condition for receiving a continued influx of money, third world governments were asked to assume responsibility for repaying private debts that they did not themselves incur. In Venezuela and Argentina, nearly 60 percent of the total debt had been acquired by private businesses, domestic *and* foreign.[64] Although private borrowing in Latin America as a whole accounted for 20 percent of the outstanding debt, about $58 billion, governments and taxpayers were asked to repay this debt as if it were their own. According to Harvard economist Jeffrey Sachs,

> In country after country, governments took over the private debt on favorable terms for the private sector firms, or subsidized the private debt service payments, in order to bail out the private firms. This "socialization" of the private debt resulted in a significant increase in the *fiscal* burden of the nation's foreign debt.[65]

Not only did governments bail out private sector firms in their own country, many of them subsidiaries of first world corporations, they effectively bailed out private first world banks because these banks would not otherwise have been able to recover private debts in foreign countries. Once they knew potential losses were averted and private debt responsibilities assumed by third world governments, private first world lenders agreed to continue making loans during the debt crisis, though, as we have seen, they reduced their share of new loans.

With the money they needed to avert the immediate crisis, third world governments then began adopting the painful economic policies that would allow them to repay debts in the long term. Although the specific policies adopted by third world countries varied, most third world borrowers implemented similar "structural adjustment programs" as they were called by the World Bank officials who directed them, trying to create "trade surpluses" and government "budget surpluses" to raise the money they needed to repay their debts.

Third world governments first took steps to increase their trade surpluses. If they could export more goods than they imported, they could acquire a larger amount of first world currency, which they could then

use to repay old debts and reduce their need to borrow money to pay for imported goods. To create trade surpluses they tried simultaneously to increase exports and reduce imports. To increase exports, governments urged agricultural and industrial businesses to expand production and export more of their goods. They assisted this process by devaluing their currencies. When the United States devalued the dollar, government officials hoped that this would make U.S. exports cheaper abroad and make Japanese goods more expensive in America. They expected the devaluation to increase U.S. exports and discourage U.S. consumers from buying imported Japanese goods, thereby reducing the U.S. trade deficit. Latin American governments hoped their own currency devaluations would have the same effect, helping them create a trade surplus that would provide them with much-needed currency.

Latin American countries did export more goods, though falling prices for those commodities, global recession, which reduced demand, and first world restrictions or tariffs on many third world goods meant they had a difficult time keeping exports at 1980 levels. From 1980 to 1985, Latin American countries increased the volume of goods they exported by 23 percent, but the value of these exports remained about the same.[66] Latin American countries exported between $90 billion and $100 billion worth of goods between 1980 and 1984. Exports then fell to about $78 billion from 1984 to 1986, mostly as a result of falling oil prices, before recovering to the $100 billion level by 1988.[67]

With exports holding steady (despite increased efforts), the only way Latin American governments managed to create trade surpluses in the 1980s was by cutting back on imported goods. Whereas Latin American countries imported between $90 billion and $100 billion worth of goods in 1980, they imported only $60 billion by 1982, staying at this level throughout much of the mid–1980s.[68] By slashing imports, they created a trade surplus that gave them between $30 billion and $40 billion, which they used to repay first world lenders. As Mexican Finance Minister Silva Herzog observed, "The much heralded improvement in Latin America's current accounts therefore is attributable mostly to import reduction, rather than to export increase."[69] As we will see, this development would have important consequences for first world countries.

Because third world governments were responsible for repaying public and private debts, they also had to find ways of raising money to repay first world lenders. They did so by selling off state assets to foreign or domestic buyers and by creating budget surpluses.

During the 1960s and 1970s, many third world governments created state-run business to promote economic development. Governments

could borrow money for them and derive revenue from their operations. These businesses—the government-owned phone, airline, bank, oil, or cement company, the state coffee board—often enjoyed monopoly status, either because they provided services that private businesses could not profitably provide or because monopoly eliminated "wasteful" domestic competition and allowed these firms to compete with large first world corporations. In debt crisis negotiations, first world lenders insisted that third world governments sell off or "privatize" state-owned businesses, both to increase "competition" and to raise money to pay off debts. They also insisted that governments change their laws so that first world businesses could purchase these assets when they were offered for sale. Many third world governments had long restricted foreign investment because they worried that key sectors of the economy would fall under the control of foreign owners. (Some U.S. economists now worry about this too, see chapter 3.)

Under these conditions, Latin American governments began selling off state-owned businesses. By 1990, for example, the Mexican government sold off 875 of the 1,155 enterprises that it had owned all or part of in 1982.[70] And this pattern was repeated around the continent, with governments selling off airlines, port facilities, phone companies, and chemical plants. Of course, currency devaluations played an important role in this process.

As in the United States, where the 1985 dollar devaluation made U.S. assets available for sale to Japanese investors at one-half their previous price, currency devaluations in Latin America enabled first world investors to purchase important economic assets at bargain-basement prices. Privatization and currency devaluations worked more to the advantage of first world investors, though Latin American investors who had placed their money in the dollar accounts of first world banks during the great capital flights of the early 1980s could also acquire state assets at advantageous prices. So, for example, Mexico sold Teléfonos de México, the government's telephone company, for $1.76 billion to a French, American, and Mexican communications consortium.[71] And because the government had devalued the peso, the price they paid for it was a bargain.

Although governments could raise money to repay debts by selling public assets, this was a one-time way to raise money. To raise the money they needed, governments had to create continuing budget surpluses. They did this by increasing taxes and cutting public spending. And the burden of tax increases and spending cuts typically fell on poor and middle-income taxpayers.

During the 1970s, many third world governments used borrowed

money to keep oil and food prices low so that transportation, cooking fuel (kerosene), and basic foodstuffs would remain affordable for poor and working people at a time when world oil and grain prices were climbing. But to create budget surpluses, they were forced in the 1970s to eliminate these "subsidies," which accounted for a considerable proportion of government spending, and to increase taxes. Generally speaking, taxes on corporations and the rich were reduced (as they were in the United States in this same period), while excise and sales taxes, which fell most heavily on the poor, and income taxes on middle-income groups increased. "A 1986 study of 94 [IMF]-supported adjustment programs implemented between 1980 and 1984 found [that] 63 percent . . . contained wage and salary restraints; 61 percent included transfer payment [for Social Security and unemployment programs] and subsidy [for food and fuel] restraints; . . . and 46 percent included personal income tax measures," writes economist Howard Lehman.[72]

The Consequences

The steps taken by first world lenders and third world borrowers to address the debt crisis had important economic, social, and political consequences for third world countries.

In economic terms, third world countries succeeded in repaying their debts, but found themselves deeper in debt. And their strenuous efforts to repay debt exhausted their economies, prompting some economists to describe the 1980s as a "lost decade." As Volcker said, "Even a decade later, the wounds in Latin America itself have not fully healed. For some of those countries (and for those similarly affected in Africa), the 1980s was a lost decade in terms of growth and price stability."[73]

How could third world countries "repay" their debts, yet end up deeper in debt? Between 1982 and 1990, first world lenders sent $927 billion to third world countries. In the same period, third world borrowers paid first world lenders $1,345 billion in principal and interest. As a result, third world countries paid $418 billion more than they received. British economist Susan George argues that this sum is six times greater in real terms than the amount of money the U.S. transferred to postwar Europe through the Marshall Plan.[74] Despite these payments, third world borrowers found themselves "61 percent more in debt than they were in 1982."[75]

Mexico, for example, paid lenders $100 billion in debt service between 1982 and 1988, $10 billion more than it owed when the crisis struck in

1982. But while it repaid vast sums to first world lenders, it owed even more: $112 billion in 1988. How could this happen? It is similar to what happens when people buy a house. Home buyers understand that if they borrow $100,000 at 10 percent interest for a thirty-year period, they will actually pay $300,000 in all, two-thirds of it as interest and one-third as the principal (the amount of the original loan). The bank, of course, insists that the borrower repay the interest first. After ten years, the borrower has repaid $100,000, but still owes $200,000, which is still larger than the original loan. In the same way, Mexico had made substantial payments, but still had a lot left to repay.

Latin American debt has increased from about $280 billion in 1982 to $435 billion in 1993, and total third world debt climbed from $639 billion in 1980 to $1,341 billion in 1990. And third world borrowers will continue to repay debt into the foreseeable future.

Third world governments' successful efforts to repay lenders in the 1980s drained their economies. Instead of growing, most Latin American and third world economies actually shrank by about 10 percent while their populations continued to grow.[76] In Mexico, the real incomes of average workers fell 40 percent between 1981 and 1988, while the incomes of government employees fell even more, nearly 50 percent.[77] In most Latin American and third world countries, wages fell, while unemployment rose, prices and taxes increased, and hunger grew. In 1986, twenty million more people in Latin America were living below the poverty line than in 1981, one hundred fifty million people in all.[78] Not surprisingly, declining incomes and rising unemployment persuaded many Latin Americans to emigrate to the United States in search of jobs. According to Sachs, "As for the debtor countries, many have fallen into the deepest economic crisis in their histories. . . . Many countries' living standards have fallen to levels of the 1950s and 1960s. A decade of development has been wiped out throughout the debtor world."[79]

Governments also increased the rate of deforestation so they could export hardwood timber or beef raised on cleared rainforests. Brazil and Mexico, the two largest debtors, are also major deforesters. Brazil is ranked number one and Mexico number six in the world. In Mexico, much of this deforestation has occurred in Chiapas, the southern state where Zapatista peasants revolted in 1994. And both have increased deforestation rates dramatically in the past two decades: Brazil up 245 percent, Mexico up 15 percent.[80]

These social and environmental problems frequently led to social conflict, what some scholars have called "IMF riots," when people protested government "structural adjustment" policies. University of California so-

ciologist John Walton recorded fifty major "protest events" in thirteen countries between 1976 and 1986. He found that when governments cut subsidies for food and basic necessities, increased fares on public transportation, or eliminated government jobs, riots sometimes resulted. In September 1985, for example, "hundreds of Panamanian workers invaded their legislature chanting: 'I won't pay the debt! Let the ones who stole the money pay!' "[81]

While the debt crisis had disastrous economic and social consequences for third world countries, it had some important and positive political consequences. The debt crisis and structural adjustment programs imposed by first world lenders discredited the dictators who had borrowed and ruled most Latin American countries. When debt crises struck, civilian democrats demanded and received political power in return for their support for arduous debt crisis management programs. As we will see (chapter 12), debt crisis contributed to the democratization of much of Latin America in the 1980s.

While third world countries experienced great difficulties as a result of debt crisis, first world countries also experienced debt-related problems. As we have seen, Latin American borrowers increased trade surpluses, which provided them with much-needed cash, by reducing their imports. Because many of these imports were goods made or grown in first world countries, import reductions led to first world unemployment.

Between 1980 and 1986, U.S. exports to Latin America fell by $10 billion. One economist estimated that this resulted in the loss of 930,000 jobs in the United States.[82] And U.S. Trade Representative William Brock calculated that 240,000 U.S. jobs were lost as a result of the Mexican debt crisis alone.[83] Senator Bill Bradley observed that Latin American debtors had made a "Herculean effort" to service their debts. But he noted, "The price the United States has paid for Latin America's ability to meet its new debt schedules has been the collapse of Latin American markets for U.S. products . . . and the loss of more than one million [U.S.] jobs."[84]

So while private first world lenders have managed to cover their assets through effective debt crisis management, debt crisis has also led to job loss for first world workers and increased tax liabilities for first world taxpayers.

Although first world lenders have averted a global economic crisis, third world borrowers continue to wrestle with the consequences of the debt crisis. From the perspective of first world lenders, third world borrowers still owe them a great deal. But from the perspective of third world borrowers, they have already paid a high price. Some first world economists have suggested that remaining debts could be forgiven or reduced without

great harm to first world lenders. And they note that continued indebtedness undermines the ability of third world countries to purchase first world goods, which is essential for the health of first world economies. Former World Bank President Robert McNamara argued, "The evidence that growth and progress in the developing countries now has a measurable impact on the economy of the United States reflects the importance of the developing countries to the United States as export markets and as customers of U.S. commercial banks."[85]

The continued insistence on full repayment of third world debt, the objective of first world lenders, conflicts in the long run with the sale of first world goods in third world markets, the objective of first world farmers and manufacturers. The problem in coming years will be how to resolve the conflicting objectives and needs of different groups in the first and third worlds.

One solution, advanced by the World Bank and International Monetary Fund in 1996, would be to provide $5.6 billion to $7.7 billion in debt relief to the poorest countries. The money would come in part from the sale of gold reserves held by the IMF.[86] For extremely poor countries like Uganda, which "spends $3 per inhabitant on health annually, and about $17 a person on debt repayment," debt relief would be extremely welcome.[87] But German, Japanese, and other officials in the Group of Seven have objected to the plan, arguing that the IMF should not sell off even a small part of its $40 billion in gold.[88]

During the 1980s, the debt crisis created serious problems for people in the third world. But they were not the only ones to go deep into debt. The United States also became deeply indebted in the 1980s, when its debt grew from $1 trillion to nearly $4 trillion, a sum twice as big as all third world debt combined. It is to the U.S. debt crisis that we now turn.

Notes

1. Zloch-Christy, Iliana. *Debt Problems of Eastern Europe*. Cambridge: Cambridge University Press, 1987, pp. 29, 34. Kojm, Christopher A. *The Problem of International Debt: The Reference Shelf,* vol. 56, no. 1. New York: Wilson, 1984, p. 8.

2. Walton, John. "Debt, Protest and the State in Latin America," in Susan Eckstein, *Power and Popular Protest: Latin America Social Movements.* Berkeley: University of California Press, 1989, p. 301.

3. Gilpin, Robert. *The Political Economy of International Relations.* Princeton: Princeton University, 1987, p. 317.

4. Greenhouse, Steven. "Third World Markets Gain Favor," *New York Times*, December 17, 1993.

5. Kennedy, Paul. *Preparing for the 21st Century*. New York: Random House, 1987, p. 204.

6. Kojm, 1984, p. 10.

7. Zloch-Christy, 1987, p. xiii.

8. Parfitt, Trevor W., and Riley, Stephen P. *The African Debt Crisis*. London: Routledge, 1989, pp. 16, 17.

9. Branford, Sue, and Kucinski, Bernardo. *The Debt Squads: The US, the Banks and Latin America*. London: Zed Books, 1988, p. 47.

10. Moffitt, Michael. *The World's Money: International Banking from Bretton Woods to the Brink of Insolvency*. New York: Simon and Schuster, 1983, p. 98.

11. Branford and Kucinski, 1988, p. 47. Schatan, Jacobo. *World Debt: Who Is To Pay?* London: Zed Books, 1987, p. 9.

12. Branford and Kucinski, 1988, p. 58.

13. Ibid., p. 58. See Griffith-Jones, Stephany, and Sunkel, Osvaldo. *Debt and Development Crises in Latin America: The End of an Illusion*. Oxford: Clarendon Press, 1986, p. 72.

14. Kojm, 1984, p. 36.

15. Branford and Kucinski, 1987, p. 58.

16. Cherry, Robert. *The Imperiled Economy. Book 1: Macroeconomics from a Left Perspective*. New York: Union for Radical Political Economics, 1987, p. 202. Gilpin, 1987, p. 315.

17. Kojm, 1984, p. 18.

18. Lombardi, Richard W. *Debt Trap: Rethinking the Logic of Development*. New York: Praeger, 1985, p. 91.

19. Ibid., p. 90.

20. Devlin, Robert. *Debt and Crisis in Latin America: The Supply Side of the Story*. Princeton: Princeton University Press, 1989, pp. 36, 38.

21. Lombardi, 1985, pp. 76–77.

22. Ibid., p. 74.

23. Cherry, 1987, p. 201.

24. Branford and Kucinski, 1987, p. 59. Schatan, 1987, p. 7.

25. Branford and Kucinski, 1987, p. 56.

26. Ibid., p. xiv. Cherry, 1987, p. 200.

27. Branford and Kucinski, 1987, p. 78. Griffith-Jones and Sunkel, 1986, p. 107.

28. Branford and Kucinski, 1987, p. 64. Ferraro, Vincent. "Global Debt and Third World Development," in Michael T. Klare and Daniel C. Thomas, eds., *World Security: Trends and Challenges at Century's End*. New York: St. Martin's Press, 1991, p. 329.

29. Lustig, Nora. *Mexico: The Remaking of an Economy*. Washington D.C.: Brookings Institution, 1992, p. 20.

30. Burki, Shahid Javed. "The Prospects for the Developing World: A Review of Recent Forecasts," *Finance and Development*, 18, 1, March 1981, p. 21.

31. Walton, 1989, p. 305.

32. Ibid., p. 305.

33. Branford and Kucinski, 1987, p. 75.

34. Schatan, 1987, p. 83.

35. Lombardi, 1985, p. 86.

36. Parfitt and Riley, 1989, p. 79.

37. Guillen, Arturo R. "Crisis, the Burden of Foreign Debt and Structural Dependence," in *Latin American Perspectives*, Issue 60, 16, 1, Winter 1989, p. 38.

38. Ibid.

39. Ibid., p. 40.

40. Sachs, Jeffrey D. *Developing Country Debt and the World Economy*. Chicago: University of Chicago Press, 1989, p. 302. Devlin, 1989, p. 50. Roddick, Jackie. *Dance of the Millions: Latin America and the Debt Crisis*. London: Latin America Bureau, 1988, p. 35.

41. Branford and Kucinski, 1987, p. 95. Kojm, 1984, p. 15. Schatan, 1987, p. 10.

42. Ferraro, 1991, p. 329.

43. Schatan, 1987, p. 110. Branford and Kucinski, 1988, p. 96.

44. Morris, Frank E. "Disinflation and the Third World Debt Crisis," in Michael P. Claudon, *World Debt Crisis*. New York: Ballinger, 1986, p. 83.

45. Pastor, Manuel, Jr. *Capital Flight and the Latin America Debt Crisis*. Washington, D.C.: Economic Policy Institute, 1989, pp. 8–9.

46. Ibid., pp. 11–12.

47. Roddick, 1988, p. 65.

48. Orr, 1992, p. 262. Sachs, 1989, pp. 303, 309–10.

49. Walton, 1989, p. 306. Griffith-Jones and Sunkel, 1986, p. 13. Lehman, Howard P. *Indebted Development: Strategic Bargaining and Economic Adjustment in the Third World*. New York: St. Martin's Press, 1993, p. 15. Parfitt and Riley, 1989, pp. 2–3.

50. Delamaide, Darrell. *Debt Shock: The Full Story of the World Credit Crisis*. New York: Doubleday, 1984, p. 28. Schatan, 1987, p. 41.

51. Lombardi, 1985, p. 10. Ortiz de Zevallos, Filipe. "Manana Has Arrived: Latin America Recovers from the Lost Decade," *The World Paper*. October 1993, p. 5.

52. Kojm, 1984, pp. 16–17. Pastor, Robert A. *Latin America's Debt Crisis: Adjusting to the Past or Planning for the Future?* Boulder, Colo.: Rienner, 1987, p. 13. Lustig, 1992, pp. 24–25, 39.

53. Pastor, 1987, p. 35.

54. Gilpin, 1987, p. 326.

55. Ibid., pp. 319–20.

56. Roddick, 1988, p. 10.

57. Branford and Kucinski, 1987, p. 8. Gilpin, 1987, p. 327.

58. Pastor, 1987, pp. 151–52.

59. Branford and Kucinski, 1987, pp. 120–21.

60. George, Susan. *The Debt Boomerang: How Third World Debt Harms Us All*. Boulder, Colo.: Westview, 1992, pp. 65–66.

61. Ibid., p. 74.

62. Ibid., pp. 79–81.

63. Ibid., p. 82.

64. Ibid., p. 156.

65. Roddick, 1988, pp. 71, 110–11.

66. Sachs, 1989, p. 13.

67. Branford and Kucinski, 1987, p. 5.

68. Pastor, 1987, pp. 35–36. Farnsworth, Clyde H. "Latin America Records Some Economic Gains," *New York Times*, September 11, 1989.

69. Farnsworth, 1989.

70. Pastor, 1987, p. 36.

71. Lustig, 1992, p. 105.

72. Ibid., p. 106.

73. Lehman, 1993, pp. 44–45.

74. Volcker, Paul A., and Gyohten, Toyoo. *Changing Fortunes: The World's Money and the Threat to American Leadership*. New York: Times Books, 1992, p. 187.

75. George, 1992, p. xv.

76. Ibid., p. xvi.

77. Griffith-Jones and Sunkel, 1986, p. 6.

78. Lustig, 1992, p. 69.

79. Branford and Kucinski, 1988, p. 24.

80. Ferraro, 1991, p. 333.

81. George, 1992, pp. 10–11.

82. Walton, 1989, pp. 200, 316.

83. Ferraro, 1991, p. 335.

84. Lombardi, 1985, p. 91. Delamaide, 1984, p. 12.

85. Pastor, 1987, p. 70.

86. Lewis, Paul. "Debt-Relief Cost for the Poorest Nations," *New York Times*, June 10, 1996.

87. Lewis, Paul. "World Bank Moves to Cut Poorest Nations' Debts," *New York Times*, March 16, 1996.

88. Lewis, June 10, 1996.

6

Debt and Taxes in the United States

When President Ronald Reagan took office in 1981, the federal government's debt stood at nearly $1 trillion. Although he described this figure as "incomprehensible," Reagan told Congress in his 1981 State of the Union message, "I've been trying . . . to think of a way to illustrate how big a trillion is. The best I could come up with is that if you had a stack of $1,000 bills in your hand only four inches high, you would be a millionaire. A trillion dollars would be a stack of $1,000 bills 67 miles high."[1]

Reagan was determined to reduce the annual federal deficit, which in 1980 amounted to about $80 billion, balance the budget, and prevent the $1 trillion national debt from growing.[2] "Starting next year," he told Congress, "the deficits will get smaller until in just a few years the budget can be balanced. And we hope we can begin whittling at the $1 trillion debt that hangs over the future of our children."[3]

Although he wanted to balance the budget and reduce the national debt, Reagan also wanted to cut taxes and increase defense spending. He outlined this program during a 1980 campaign speech in Chicago, where he told the crowd, "We can do it. We must do it. We must do all three things together: balance the budget, cut taxes and build our defenses."[4]

But subsequent efforts to do all three things proved incompatible. During the next twelve years, the Reagan and Bush administrations cut taxes and increased defense spending from 1980 levels, but annual budget deficits increased and the national debt skyrocketed. By 1992, the debt had quadrupled from $1 trillion to nearly $4 trillion. The stack of $1,000 bills representing the debt reached 268 miles high. Put another way, the debt owed by every person living in the United States increased from $4,000 in 1980 to $16,000 in 1992.[5]

Since then, budget deficits have remained high, $331 billion in 1993 and

$268 billion in 1994.[6] At this rate, the debt will increase by an additional $1 trillion every three or four years.

Because debts incurred by governments must be repaid, taxpayers must eventually shoulder these burdens in coming years. The question is when? And how?

President Herbert Hoover once remarked, "Blessed are the young, for they shall inherit the debt."[7] Unless some effort is soon made to address large deficits and growing indebtedness, the burden of paying off the debt will fall on the young in the next century. Boston University economist Laurence J. Kotlikoff argued that the "lifetime tax rate for Americans born in 1900 was 21.5 percent." But he predicted that "for Americans born in 1990, the lifetime tax rate will be 33.5 percent," 50 percent higher. He said this was the "natural outgrowth of four decades of Government pursuing a variety of policies . . . to expropriate the young and future generations for the benefit of older generations."[8] If this is true, then Reagan's promise to whittle away the "debt that hangs over the future of [American] children" will have been an empty dream.

As in Latin America, rising debt may lead to difficult social and economic problems. As interest payments, which amounted to $200 billion in 1992, consume a greater percentage of the budget (about 13.4 percent in 1993), less money will be available to spend on other things.[9] Government may have to spend less and taxpayers pay more. But while indebtedness can create problems for governments and taxpayers, the debt crisis in the United States differs from the third world debt crisis in four important respects. First, the United States is bigger and richer than third world borrowers, so it has a greater capacity to repay its debts, which are more than twice as large as all third world borrowers combined (U.S. debt = $4 trillion; third world debt = $1.6 trillion in 1992).

Second, the United States owes little of this debt to foreigners. In 1989, public agencies and private businesses in the United States "owed" foreigners between $361 billion and $664 billion, depending on how the calculation is made, and only part of this was in the form of "loans" or government securities owned by foreigners.[10] Most of the U.S. government's debt is owed to U.S. citizens, who purchase the bulk of savings bonds, T-bills, and securities.

Third, the U.S. debt is a product of decisions made by government officials and elected representatives during the past forty years. U.S. debt is not the product of foreign initiative—first world bankers eager to lend money to third world borrowers—but of domestic fiscal policy choices.

And fourth, the debt crisis in the United States will be managed, at least in the foreseeable future, by officials of U.S. institutions, not by the World Bank and other first world countries.

Although the U.S. government's debt quadrupled between 1980 and 1992, it had grown substantially during the 1960s and '70s to nearly $1 trillion. During the 1950s, miniscule budget deficits—$6.5 billion in 1953—were offset by tiny budget surpluses. The U.S. debt crisis has to be understood as a long-term process, some thirty years in the making, a process in which Republican *and* Democratic presidents and Congresses played important roles. The decisions they made about revenue and spending policies created deficits that slowly accumulated debt in the 1960s and '70s, then accelerated rapidly in the 1980s, leading to mounting deficits and skyrocketing debt. The debt itself was a product of two developments that affected the government's income and spending.

First, taxes that provided income for the government were reduced, without being effectively "replaced" by new taxes. Both Democratic and Republican administrations reduced taxes on corporation and on wealthy individuals, modestly during the 1960s and '70s, then dramatically in the 1980s. Although economists fiercely debate their merits, these cuts eroded the government's tax base, made the tax structure less "progressive," and shifted the tax burden to middle-income taxpayers. The trouble with this tax shift was that in the 1970s and '80s, the ability of middle-income groups to pay taxes and make up tax revenues lost to cuts for corporations and wealthy individuals was weakened by stagnant incomes and impaired by high unemployment. If this group had increased their incomes, as they had during the 1950s and '60s, then government revenues would have expanded and the revenue lost as a result of tax cuts on corporations and wealthy individuals could have been replaced. If, for example, the government had the same tax structure today as it had in the mid-1970s, it could maintain current spending levels *and* still balance the budget. But it did not. As the tax base has eroded, budget deficits have grown and debt has mounted.

Second, throughout this period, government spending increased. Two major programs are responsible for most of the increase. During the 1970s, Social Security and other entitlement programs increased federal spending, and the government spent more than it took in, particularly when inflation and cost of living adjustments pushed up the cost of entitlement programs. In the 1980s, however, higher Social Security taxes began to "cover" increased costs and provide "surplus revenues" that were supposed to be invested to cover future costs, which were expected to rise as the population aged. But these surplus revenues were actually used to cover other debts. The result is that taxpayer liabilities for Social Security and other programs are growing.

Military spending also increased dramatically in the late 1970s and

throughout the 1980s. The Reagan administration increased defense spending 50 percent from 1980 levels. Increased military spending, together with the higher cost of borrowing money, which was a product of Volcker's anti-inflationary, high interest rate policies, and the unexpected costs associated with bailing out the savings and loan industry, pushed up government spending at a time when government revenues were stagnant.

The cumulative effect of these developments, which affected both government revenues and spending, was to create budget deficits averaging $184 billion between 1982 and 1987, and ranging between $270 billion and $330 billion in the 1990s.[11]

Faced with deficits of this magnitude, conservatives argue that the government should cut spending, while liberals argue for new taxes. When they debate spending cuts, conservatives argue that Social Security and other entitlement programs should be cut, while liberals prefer to give defense spending the axe. And when they debate tax increases, which is less common, conservatives favor excise or "sin" taxes, while liberals support higher taxes on gasoline or on wealthy individuals. Neither side has argued for a return to previous, more "progressive" tax structures or radically different spending policies. But the choices made in coming years will have an enormous impact on deficits and debt, people and programs.

To appreciate these issues in greater detail, let us turn to the two important developments of the past thirty years: an eroding tax base, and increased government spending.

An Eroding Tax Base

During the past thirty years, two important sources of government revenues—taxes on corporations and on wealthy individuals—declined significantly. As a result, the government relied increasingly on revenue from taxes on middle-income individuals.

In 1952, corporations paid 32.1 percent of the income taxes (as opposed to Social Security and excise taxes) collected by the government, while individuals paid the other 67.9 percent. But by 1980, corporations paid only 12.5 percent of "income" taxes and by 1983 only 6.2 percent.[12] Put another way, in 1955, corporations reported profits of $49.3 billion and paid $20.8 billion in taxes to the federal government. In 1980, corporations made $254.8 billion in profits, a 500 percent increase, but paid only $31.3 billion in taxes, a 50 percent increase. As a result of lower corporate tax rates, and various allowances, credits, deductions, and depreciations,

the effective tax rate on corporate profits had fallen from 42.2 percent in 1955 to 13.1 percent in 1982.[13]

Tax rates for wealthy individuals also declined substantially. During the 1950s, wealthy individuals in the top tax bracket paid 91 percent of their income *over* $200,000 to the government.[14] In the mid-1960s, the Kennedy and Johnson administrations cut the top rate to 77 percent and then 70 percent. (This was similar to rates paid by wealthy individuals during the Great Depression, when President Franklin D. Roosevelt raised tax rates to 63 percent in 1932 and 79 percent in 1936. Rates were then raised to 91 percent during World War II.)[15] After Reagan took office in 1981, the tax rates for wealthy individuals were cut to 50 percent, then to 38 percent, and finally to 28 percent. The Bush and Clinton administrations raised them back to between 32 and 39 percent.[16]

Looking back, we see that taxes on corporations and wealthy individuals were first cut dramatically by President John F. Kennedy and then by President Reagan. And in between Kennedy's big tax cuts in 1964 and Reagan's large tax cuts in 1981–82, both Democratic and Republican presidents and Congresses passed a variety of more modest cuts. (Nixon was something of the exception.) Presidents Lyndon Johnson, Richard Nixon, Gerald Ford, and Jimmy Carter did not change corporate or individual tax *rates*, but instead passed measures allowing various deductions, credits, and exemptions, often called "loopholes," that reduced the "effective" tax rates for corporations and individuals. Although Democratic and Republican legislators generally cut taxes on corporations and wealthy individuals during this period, they sometimes also raised them. After the big tax cuts of 1964 and 1981–82, Congress raised taxes. But these tax increases were modest and did not undo the effect of previous cuts. Johnson passed a small, temporary increase, called a "surtax" to help pay the increasing costs of the war in Vietnam. And the Reagan, Bush, and Clinton administrations all passed modest tax increases because the 1981–82 tax cuts produced huge budget deficits. They hoped modest tax increases would mitigate the impact of earlier cuts. But they did not.

When proposing tax cuts for corporations and wealthy individuals to Congress, Democratic and Republican presidents argued that tax cuts would "stimulate" the economy and that a growing economy would increase government revenues. "Unless we release the tax brake which is holding back our economy," President Kennedy argued, "[the economy] is likely to continue to operate below its potential, federal receipts are likely to remain disappointingly low, and budget deficits are likely to persist."[17]

President Reagan argued much the same thing, saying that a "complete

program of reduction in tax rates" would "provide incentives for the individual, [and] incentives for business to encourage production and hiring of the unemployed and to free up money for investment."[18]

Although Kennedy and Reagan borrowed ideas from different economic theorists—Kennedy from the British economist John Maynard Keynes and Reagan from American economists Arthur Laffer and Robert Mundell—both believed that tax cuts would stimulate the economy and that a growing economy would increase government revenues, even at lower tax rates.

This general economic theory was bolstered, throughout this period, by two other arguments against taxes on corporations and wealthy individuals. Some economists argued that by taxing corporate profits, the government levies two taxes on wealthy individuals. First, it taxes the profits of companies they own as shareholders. And second, it taxes the income that wealthy shareholders receive as income from stock dividends. Other economists agree that the rich are taxed "twice," but they counter that tax rates on both corporations and wealthy individuals have fallen dramatically over the years, so wealthy individuals have little cause for complaint. They also note that poor and working taxpayers are also taxed "twice," first when their paycheck is taxed and again when they pay sales taxes on goods they purchase. (The difference is that states and municipal governments collect this second tax, not the federal government.)[19]

Wealthy individuals have also long complained that high tax rates discourage them from working or investing their money. As Reagan used to argue, "I came into the Big Money making pictures during World War II" (at a time when tax rates on income over $200,000 was 91 percent). "You could only make four pictures, and then you were in the top bracket. So we all quit working after four pictures and went off to the country."[20] If tax rates were lower, Reagan maintained, then he would have made more films, which would have provided employment for other people in the film industry.

Critics of this perspective argue that this is simply a trickle-down approach to economic growth, giving tax cuts to the rich in the hope that they will take their tax savings and invest it productively—in the film industry, for example—rather than "squandering" it on art collections and personal consumption.

Whatever the merits of different arguments for and against tax cuts for corporations and wealthy individuals, the Kennedy tax cuts did not produce large budget deficits, while the Reagan tax cuts did.

The Kennedy tax cuts "worked" because the economy was growing rapidly and incomes were rising in the mid–1960s. President Johnson's

failure to raise taxes to pay for the Vietnam War led to modest budget deficits and to inflation, which became a problem of its own.

The Reagan tax cuts did not "work" in the same way because the economy was not growing in the early 1980s but shrinking. To fight inflation, Federal Reserve Chairman Paul Volcker had forced up interest rates in the early 1980s, sending the economy into a deep recession. In this context, tax cuts did not spur economic growth. And instead of using tax savings to invest in new factories and create new jobs, corporations sought to acquire other companies, a costly process of consolidation, and use profits to pay higher salaries to executives and dividends to stockholders (see chapter 7). According to Harvard economist Benjamin Friedman,

> Despite record internal cash flows . . . business has used an unusually large part of these funds for purposes other than productive new investment. Companies have increasingly distributed their cash flows outside the corporate sector, mostly through payments made to individual and institutional shareholders during the phenomenal wave of corporate reorganizations and recapitalizations that swept over corporate America in the 1980s.[21]

Although wealthy individuals invested heavily in the stock market because corporate mergers bid up stock prices and because corporations paid out greater dividends to shareholders, they also invested heavily in government securities that paid high interest rates, which did little to contribute to economic growth. During the early 1980s, high U.S. interest rates attracted capital from Japan, Europe, and Latin America, but also from U.S. investors, the domestic equivalent of capital flight. In this sense, the fight against inflation created conditions that operated at cross-purposes with the Reagan administration's tax cuts. So instead of encouraging productive investment, tax cuts gave wealthy individuals more money to invest in T-bills, which did little to promote U.S. economic growth. And instead of using their tax savings to purchase domestic goods, which might have helped create jobs for U.S. workers, wealthy and middle-income consumers instead purchased foreign goods, which increased trade deficits instead of reducing the budget deficit.[22]

Because the fight against inflation undermined the economic growth that tax cuts were supposed to produce and because corporations and wealthy individuals did not act as government tax planners expected, the Reagan tax cuts did not stimulate economic growth and led, instead, to reduced government revenue and huge budget deficits.

When the Reagan administration realized that the tax cuts of 1981–82 had greatly reduced government revenues, it passed a series of modest tax

increases. But the combined effect was to leave "in place a net tax reduction approaching $200 billion annually, along with deficits still averaging approximately $150 billion per year," concluded economist Dennis Ippolito.[23] Because its forecasts had relied on substantial economic growth, as well as continued inflation, the Reagan administration's 1981 expectation that tax cuts would yield a $0.5 billion surplus by 1984 turned instead into a $168 billion deficit.[24] David Stockman, the Reagan administration's budget director, later concluded, "Our national savings has been squandered to pay for a tax cut we could not afford."[25]

As a result of tax cuts big and small, cuts approved by both Democratic and Republican administrations during the past thirty years, the government's tax base has eroded. Economists Gregory Mills and John Palmer concluded:

> One consequence of this shift in importance of the different revenue sources is that the projected tax structure is less progressive. . . . The progressive forms of taxation such as individual and corporate income taxes, whose burdens rise at higher income levels, are becoming less significant as sources of income.[26]

By saying that the tax structure is less "progressive," economists mean that it is less "fair," because rich people have a greater capacity to pay taxes, and pay a larger share of their income, at higher tax rates, than do poor people. The aim of a progressive tax structure is to redistribute some wealth from rich to poor. When tax rates are similar for rich and poor, economists describe the tax structure as "regressive." Such a tax structure does little to redistribute wealth. During the middle of this century, the United States had a fairly progressive tax structure. But late-century tax cuts on corporations and wealthy individuals have made it more regressive.

As revenues from corporate and wealthy individual sources have been reduced, the government has increasingly relied on revenue from middle-income taxpayers to balance its budgets. As Ippolito noted, "An important point here is that the middle class [in the 1980s] . . . accounted for almost three-fourths of all returns and nearly 90 percent of all taxes paid."[27] The government's reliance on middle-income taxpayers might not be misplaced if this group were able to make up for revenues lost to tax cuts for corporations and wealthy individuals. If, for example, the income of this group had increased over time, as it did during the 1950s and 1960s, then government revenues would also have increased and "lost revenues" might have been "replaced." But the ability of middle-income

taxpayers to make up revenues lost to various tax cuts was undermined because their income stagnated in the 1970s and '80s (see chapter 7).

As a benchmark, economists use median family income to chart the progress of middle-income households. (The median is the economic "middle": half of all households earn more and half less than this.) In 1973, median family income reached $30,820. It actually declined in the late 1970s and early 1980s during the recession created by high interest rates, then rose back to 1973 levels—$30,853—in 1987.[28] So middle-class incomes have been essentially stagnant for the past twenty years.

But this measure actually understates the problem for middle-income taxpayers. During this period, the average weekly wage for all workers fell from $191.41 a week in 1972 to $171.07 a week in 1986.[29] So how did families keep their annual household incomes steady when their weekly wages fell? Because women in the household entered the workforce in large numbers, and the addition of their earnings kept household income from falling dramatically. Of course, households without two wage earners saw their income decline without relief. "All told, the United States is approaching 20 years of lost income growth," observed Harvard economist Richard Freeman. "That does not make for a very happy society."[30]

If the income of middle-class households had increased during the 1970s and '80s at the same rate as compensation for the executives of U.S. corporations, which grew on average from about $200,000 a year in 1975 to $700,000 in 1988, the median income household would be making more than $95,000 a year instead of $33,742 in 1988, and could easily have paid taxes to cover growing government deficits.[31] Put another way, living standards doubled in the United States between 1947 and 1973. But if middle-income households continued growing at the rate they did between 1973 and 1991, U.S. workers would have to work 268 years to double their incomes.[32]

The reason why incomes have stagnated during the past twenty years, economists say, is that the "productivity" of American workers did not increase substantially. Productivity is a measure of how many goods are produced by each worker. If workers produce more goods or services, they can demand higher pay from the companies that employ them. Between 1947 and 1965, the productivity of U.S. workers increased about 3 percent every year.[33] Workers made more, earned more, and could afford to pay more to the government in taxes. But productivity increased only 2.3 percent between 1965 and 1973, and rose only 0.8 percent a year between 1973 and 1980.[34] If productivity had increased during the past twenty years at just 2 percent annually, the rate it achieved between 1950 and 1973, then workers in 1991 would have earned $45,000 a year instead

of $34,000, and government tax revenues from higher wages would have closed budget deficits and reduced debt.[35]

Neither the productivity nor the pay of U.S. workers increased very much in the 1970s and '80s. Productivity did not greatly increase because savings rates in the United States remained low. U.S. households did not save much money, only about 6.7 percent of their annual income.[36] And many households were heavily indebted, owing substantial sums for home loans and consumer purchases.[37] Europeans save more than twice as much (15.2 percent) and Japanese three times more (18.4 percent) than U.S. families.[38] By saving money, households put money in banks and savings and loans, and companies can borrow this money to invest in increasing worker productivity. Because U.S. workers do not save as much as European or Japanese households, there is less money available to invest, and a scarce supply means that it costs more to borrow money. This and high interest rates made it expensive for U.S. corporations to borrow money in the 1970s and '80s, which meant they did not invest heavily in new factories and machinery that would increase the productivity of U.S. workers. They did borrow money, but they used much of it to buy other companies or build factories overseas. Meanwhile European and Japanese firms invested heavily in building new plants and introducing new machines, such as industrial robots, which enabled the same or small numbers of workers to produce more.[39]

Of course, even when productivity does increase, as it has at low rates in the United States in recent years, there is no guarantee that companies will reward more productive workers with higher wages. It only means that they *can* afford to pay higher wages. The ability of workers to increase wages as productivity increases depends on their bargaining power, their capacity to demand and get higher wages. Although U.S. workers were able to get higher wages as their productivity increased during the 1950s and '60s, their bargaining power slowly diminished in the 1970s and '80s as a result of corporate mergers and downsizing, deunionization, the overseas investment strategies of large corporations, and relatively high levels of unemployment (see chapter 7).

As we saw in chapter 2, the percentage of the U.S. workforce represented by unions in contract negotiations declined from 31 percent in 1970 to 17 percent in 1990. Many corporations have moved factories from the United States to countries with cheaper workers or asked foreign suppliers to produce goods once made in the United States. And unemployment rates have been higher in the past twenty years than they were in the 1950s and '60s. Unemployment rates averaged 7.4 percent in 1993, considerably higher than they did in the mid–1960s, when only 4.2 per-

cent of the workforce was unemployed.[40] And when the economy did expand, U.S. companies were slower and more reluctant to rehire workers than they were previously. When the economy picked up in the early 1990s, U.S. companies created few new jobs. If they had created jobs at the same rate they had during eight previous postwar recoveries, they would have created an additional four million jobs.[41] High levels of unemployment generally make it difficult for workers to demand higher wages. As a result of these developments—slow productivity increases and weakening bargaining power—workers have not been able to increase their incomes substantially in the past twenty years. And the government, which increasingly relies on this group to provide taxes, has not seen its revenues increase substantially either.

Of course, large budget deficits and mounting debt are not only the product of an eroding tax base. They are also the result of increased government spending.

Increased Government Spending

During the 1970s and '80s, the federal government increased spending on social entitlements, principally Social Security, government pensions, and Medicare, and on defense. But because it also increased taxes to pay for increased Social Security benefits, increased defense spending was the main reason why federal deficits grew rapidly in the 1980s.

In the 1950s and '60s, U.S. workers paid more in Social Security taxes than they received in benefits, resulting in large surpluses. In 1972, Congress initiated and President Nixon approved a 20 percent increase in benefits and linked further increases to the rate of inflation through annual cost of living adjustments (COLAs).[42] Rapid inflation during the rest of the decade led to higher benefits and ran down the surpluses accumulated during the 1950s and '60s. By 1981, Social Security was paying out $15 billion more in benefits than it received in taxes (paid for by payroll deductions).[43] (It is important to note, however, that the Social Security deficit did not directly contribute to the government's annual budget deficits because it was kept in separate trust fund accounts.)

Congress and the Reagan administration realized that Social Security would eventually consume its accumulated savings and go bankrupt unless it either reduced benefits or increased taxes to pay for it. Rather than cut benefits, which would have been extremely unpopular, Congress and the Reagan administration decided to increase payroll taxes to keep Social Security solvent. The government also extended tax breaks for Individual

Retirement Accounts (IRAs) as part of its effort to reform Social Security in the early 1980s. As we will see in chapter 7, this contributed to stock price inflation, corporate mergers, and job loss in the 1980s and '90s. The payroll tax increase "covered" the cost of Social Security benefits and created a surplus that could be used to pay benefits when the baby boom generation retired in the next century.[44] With this measure, Budget Director David Stockman observed, "We have imposed payroll taxes sufficient to fund most of Social Security, Medicare, unemployment insurance, and the small social insurance programs . . . for better or ill, then, social insurance is one part of the budget that is in balance."[45]

But the government used Social Security surpluses to cover other debts. As Nixon's Commerce Secretary Peter Peterson observed, "the [surplus] funds are not being saved or invested. Instead, they are being used to help offset each year's overall budget deficit."[46] This means that when people now paying into the system retire, the government will have to find more money to pay their benefits, and it will once again have to decide whether to cut benefits or raise taxes to pay for them, just as it did in 1983.

As a result of these developments, increased government spending on social entitlements led to higher taxes but *not* larger budget deficits, at least not to deficits in the 1980s. Whether it will contribute to deficits at some future date is not yet clear. Some economists estimate that Social Security will start running annual deficits by 2015 and run out of accumulated surpluses by 2036.[47] So while government spending on social entitlements increased in the 1970s and '80s, they were not primarily responsible for burgeoning deficits. Instead, increased defense spending, as well as increased spending for interest payments on the debt and the bailout of the savings and loan industry, made the most significant contributions to government budget deficits in the 1980s.

When he came into office, President Reagan promised to cut taxes, balance the budget, and increase defense spending, which had declined in the 1970s as the war in Vietnam wound down. Reagan kept his promise, increasing the defense department's budget 50 percent, pushing military spending from $201 billion in 1980 to $311 billion in 1987.[48]

As we have seen in chapter 4, two-thirds of the annual U.S. military budget is spent defending U.S. allies in Europe and Japan. (At the same time, the Reagan and Bush administrations cut spending for domestic social programs *other* than Social Security.) Between 1981 and 1987, spending for nondefense programs fell from 28 percent of the budget to 22 percent, while defense spending went up from 23 percent to 28 percent.[49]

As with debates over the merits of cutting taxes on corporations and wealthy individuals, defense spending was the subject of considerable de-

bate in the 1980s and '90s. Some policy makers argued that it contributed to the collapse of the Soviet Union, others argued that it contributed to the economic decline of the United States relative to its allies and competitors in Western Europe and Japan. And policy makers continue to debate what level of defense spending is "appropriate" in the post-Cold War era. But whatever the merits of these arguments, the fact remains that increasing the defense spending in the 1980s, which was accompanied by tax cuts, led to large deficits and growing debt. And many of the benefits of increased military spending flowed to U.S. allies in Western Europe and Japan.

The fight against inflation also contributed to deficits and debt. When Federal Reserve Chairman Volcker raised interest rates to slow inflation, the federal government was forced to spend more money to pay higher interest rates. To raise money to cover its debts, the government sold Treasury bonds. As interest rates rose, it was forced to pay more money to domestic and foreign investors who purchased government securities, which increased overall government spending. And interest rates have remained relatively high, despite a decline in inflation, which also increased government spending and contributed to deficits.[50]

What's more, higher interest rates contributed to the collapse of the savings and loan industry. To bail out S&Ls, the government assumed debts estimated between $200 billion and $500 billion, an amount equal to one or two years of defense spending.[51] The government, in effect, assumed responsibility for private debts, a process very similar to the "socialization" of private debt by Latin American borrowers during their debt crisis. Like them, the U.S. government will ask taxpayers to repay debts incurred by private businesses.

Because the government spent more on defense, interest on the debt, and private industry bailouts, while simultaneously cutting taxes, large budget deficits and mounting debt resulted. Because the national debt increased to nearly $4 trillion by 1992, interest payments on the debt cost the government $303.9 billion a year, slightly more than it spends on defense.[52] "Indebtedness of this kind grows by its own momentum," observed Harvard economist David Calleo.

> Debt can be expected to snowball and interest payments to take an increasing share of federal revenue. . . . Under such circumstances, not only does government crowd out private investment [which can adversely affect the nation's productivity], but debt service crowds out other government spending.[53]

When debt reaches a certain point, higher taxes may do little to reduce debt, as Latin American borrowers discovered in the 1980s, when they increased payments to lenders but nonetheless found themselves deeper in debt.

During the 1980s, an eroding tax base and increased military spending led to burgeoning budget deficits and added trillions to the national debt. As a result, deficits and debt have become the focus of intense political debate in the 1990s, as congressional representatives and the executive wrestle over deficit reduction policies and balanced budget amendments. Tax policy in the 1980s also had important consequences for investors, corporations, and workers. The effort to solve the Social Security crisis in the early 1980s contributed to stock price inflation and job loss in the 1980s and '90s, a development we will examine more closely in the next chapter.

Notes

1. Congressional Quarterly. *Budgeting for America: The Politics and Process of Federal Spending.* Washington, D.C.: Congressional Quarterly, 1982, p. 207.

2. Ibid., p. 199.

3. Ibid., p. 207.

4. Friedman, Benjamin. *Day of Reckoning: The Consequences of American Economic Policy Under Reagan and After.* New York: Random House, 1988, p. 236.

5. Brown, Lester. *State of the World 1985.* New York: Norton, 1984, p. 15.

6. Rosenbaum, David E. "No Painless Way Out for the Next President," *New York Times,* October 4, 1992.

7. Peterson, Peter G. *Facing Up: How to Rescue the Economy from Crushing Debt and Restore the American Dream.* New York: Simon and Schuster, 1993, p. 59.

8. Bradsher, Keith. "Clinton Budget Sees Big Tax Burden for Future Generations," *New York Times,* February 8, 1994.

9. Peterson, 1993, table 4.7.

10. Orr, Bill. *The Global Economy in the 90s: A User's Guide.* New York: New York University, 1992, p. 83.

11. Friedman, 1988, p. 19.

12. Phillips, Kevin. *The Politics of Rich and Poor: Wealth and the American Electorate in the Reagan Aftermath.* New York: Random House, 1990, p. 78.

13. Pechman, Joseph A. *The Rich, the Poor and the Taxes They Pay.* Boulder, Colo.: Westview, 1986, p. 61.

14. Ippolito, Dennis S. *Uncertain Legacies: Federal Budget Policy from Roose-*

velt Through Reagan. Charlottesville, Va.: University Press of Virginia, 1990, pp. 31–37.

15. Phillips, 1990, p. 77.

16. Nasar, Sylvia. "Tapping the Rich May Prove Tricky," *New York Times*, December 12, 1992.

17. Congressional Quarterly, 1982, p. 207. Ippolito, 1990, p. 4.

18. Congressional Quarterly, 1982, p. 207.

19. Kuttner, Robert. *The Economic Illusion: False Choices Between Prosperity and Social Justice.* New York: Houghton Mifflin, 1984, p. 195.

20. Stockman, David. *The Triumph of Politics: How the Reagan Revolution Failed.* New York: Harper and Row, 1986, p. 10.

21. Friedman, 1988, pp. 264–65.

22. Judis, John. "Bush and Kennedy: A Comparison of Economic Policy," *In These Times*, September 30–October 13, 1992, p. 2.

23. Ippolito, 1990, p. 75. Schick, Allen. *The Capacity to Budget.* Washington, D.C.: Urban Institute Press, 1990, p. 136. Friedman, 1988, p. 131.

24. "Budgetary Realities and Promises," *New York Times*, February 11, 1993.

25. Stockman, 1986, p. 379.

26. Mills, Gregory B., and Palmer, John L. *The Deficit Dilemma: Budget Policy in the Reagan Era.* Washington, D.C.: Urban Institute Press, 1983, pp. 24–26. Pechman, 1986, p. 39.

27. Ippolito, 1990, p. 54.

28. Phillips, 1990, p. 15.

29. Ibid., p. 18. Calleo, David P. *The Bankrupting of America: How the Federal Budget Is Impoverishing the Nation.* New York: Morrow, 1992, p. 94.

30. Uchitelle, Louis. "U.S. Wages: Not Getting Ahead? Better Get Used to It," *New York Times*, December 16, 1990.

31. Phillips, 1990, p. 180.

32. Peterson, 1993, table 1.6.

33. Congressional Quarterly, 1982, p. 26.

34. Ibid.

35. Passell, Peter. "What Counts Is Productivity and Productivity," *New York Times*, December 13, 1992. Peterson, 1993, p. 218.

36. Peterson, 1993, table 3.5.

37. Ibid., table 3.12.

38. Ibid., table 3.5.

39. Ibid., table 3.8.

40. Schick, 1990, p. 60. Calleo, 1992, p. 197.

41. "The Economy: Problems . . . and Remedies," *New York Times*, February 14, 1993.

42. Friedman, 1988, p. 78. Peterson, 1993, p. 83.

43. Congressional Quarterly, 1982, p. 79.

44. Friedman, 1988, p. 93.

45. Stockman, 1986, p. 404.

46. Peterson, 1993, p. 108. Calleo, 1992, p. 44.

47. Eckholm, Eric. "Payments to the Retired Loom Ever Larger," *New York Times*, August 30, 1993.

48. Orr, 1992, p. 287.

49. Phillips, 1990, pp. 87–88. Mills and Palmer, 1983, p. 7.

50. Judis, John. "The Red Menace," *New Republic*, October 26, 1992, p. 27.

51. Calleo, 1992, p. 46.

52. "Policies of the 1980s Strain Economy," *San Jose Mercury News*, October 6, 1991.

53. Calleo, 1992, p. 150.

7

Stock Market and Job Loss

Between 1982 and 1996, stock prices soared. The Dow Jones Industrial Average climbed from 777 to over 6,000, the longest bull market in U.S. history. But this was also a period of corporate downsizing, which resulted in massive job losses and stagnant wages for American workers. As we will see, these two developments—rising stock prices and widespread job losses—were closely related.

During the 1980s, new government policies directly or indirectly encouraged investment in the stock market. As new investment flooded into the market, stock prices rose, bid up by growing demand. But while this stock price inflation was good for investors, it put companies under enormous pressure to boost their profits, payouts, and stock prices to meet investors' rising expectations. So corporate managers merged with other firms, sold off parts of their business, introduced new technology, and laid off workers to raise productivity, cut costs, and increase profits. Higher profits could then be used to increase shareholder dividends and boost stock prices. The problem is that as stock prices climbed, job losses have mounted, wages have stagnated, and the gap between rich and poor has widened. The story of these developments begins in 1981, when the Reagan administration first adopted policies that would channel a growing river of money into the stock market.

Social Security and the Stock Market

In 1981, Social Security was in the midst of a serious financial crisis. Recall that a decade earlier, in 1972, the Nixon administration had awarded Social Security recipients a 20 percent increase in benefits and provided an annual cost of living adjustment (COLA) to protect them from inflation,

then running at about 4 percent annually.[1] But as the number of retired people grew and as inflation rose, the cost of the program climbed. By 1981, the government paid out $15 billion more in Social Security benefits than it received in income from payroll taxes, this despite a modest payroll tax increase in 1978.[2]

To deal with this crisis, the Reagan administration proposed cutting Social Security benefits, but a storm of protest prevented it from doing so.[3] Eventually, the administration agreed to retain benefits, though it did so only by increasing payroll taxes substantially, tying COLAs to wages (which climb more slowly than prices), and extending the retirement age.[4] In the short run, these steps solved the immediate crisis. But in the long run, the crisis was simply deferred into the next century, when experts expect Social Security to again run deficits, sometime after 2015.[5]

While debate over the future of Social Security was underway, Reagan administration officials introduced a small change that would have important consequences: they made Individual Retirement Accounts (IRAs) widely available and increased the tax benefits associated with them.

In 1974, the Nixon administration allowed individuals not covered by employer-based pension programs to put up to $1,500 per year into an IRA. In 1981, the government extended the IRA program and its benefits to all working adults, and increased the allowable contribution to $2,000 a year.[6] For individuals who could save $2,000 a year for their retirement (half of those earning more than $50,000 opened IRAs while only 13 percent of those earning under $30,000 did so), IRAs provided three benefits: "First, pre-tax dollars were invested; second, the earnings from those investments grew untaxed; and third, benefits were paid out during years when people generally faced low taxes."[7] Because IRAs provided substantial benefits, and because debate about the crisis in Social Security made people increasingly fearful that the government would not provide adequate benefits when they retired, an increasing number of people opened IRAs.[8] After 1981, annual contributions to IRAs grew rapidly, from $4 billion in 1982 to $29 billion in 1984.[9] And total deposits in IRAs grew from $30.9 billion in 1980 to $370 billion in 1990, then to $1.2 trillion by 1995.[10] The amount of money in 401(k) accounts—the government allows companies to deduct some of the employee's salary and invest it tax-free in a retirement fund—also grew, from $105 billion in 1985 to $675 billion in 1995.[11]

By providing tax breaks to individuals who invested money in retirement funds, the government offered a way for working people to protect themselves in the event that Social Security could not deliver the benefits they expected, and channeled this money into capital markets. This

stream of money would be joined by others in the 1980s, creating a river of cash that would flow into the stock market.

At the same time, in 1981–82, the Reagan administration proposed, and Congress accepted, tax cuts that reduced rates for wealthy individuals from 70 to 50 percent, then to 38 percent, and finally to 28 percent, where they remained for the rest of the decade. In the 1990s, the Bush administration raised them to 32 percent; the Clinton administration to 38 percent.[12] Of course, wealthy individuals could use their tax savings in a variety of ways. They could consume or invest it. And evidently they did both. When they invested money in the early 1980s, wealthy individuals typically invested in bonds rather than stocks. They did so because the high interest rates provided by Treasury bills and other bonds—a product of Fed Chairman Paul Volcker's efforts to fight inflation—compared favorably to returns from the stock market *and* provided greater security. Because not-so-rich investors could also obtain high, safe returns from securities, which were packaged and marketed as certificates of deposit (CDs) by banks and other financial institutions, much of the money deposited in IRAs in the early 1980s was also invested in the bond market. But as inflation slowed, the product of a recession induced by the Federal Reserve's policies for high interest rates and tight money, interest rates gradually fell. And as interest rates fell, investor interest in the stock market grew because stocks typically offered higher returns, though also greater risks. Wealthy investors and individuals with IRAs and 401(k) plans began to invest more heavily in the stock market. They were encouraged to do so both by government tax policies and by its monetary policy, which made the stock market an increasingly attractive destination for domestic investors. Not only did government policy encourage domestic investment in the stock market, it began encouraging foreign investment as well.

Recall that in 1985, the Reagan administration devalued the dollar against the major G-7 currencies in an effort to increase U.S. exports, reduce foreign imports, and shrink U.S. trade deficits. One consequence of this was to reduce the value of U.S. assets—corporations, land, and natural resources—for foreigners. During the early 1980s, they too had invested heavily in U.S. securities because interest rates were higher than they could obtain in other countries. But as interest rates fell, and as the 1985 dollar devaluation made U.S. corporate assets less expensive, foreign investors also began investing in the U.S. stock market.[13] Foreign investment in the United States grew 380 percent between 1978 and 1988, totaling $1.78 trillion.[14] During the first half of this period, most of the money from Western Europe and Japan was invested in U.S. Treasury bonds.[15] But after 1985, a growing share was directed into the stock market. In

1986, foreigners invested $17 billion in the stock market, four times as much as they had in 1985, bringing their total investment in the stock market to $176.4 billion.[16]

Foreign investment in U.S. stocks also grew because it had recently become easier for foreigners to participate in overseas capital markets. The emergence of the Eurocurrency markets (see chapter 4) and the debt crisis in the early 1980s brought creditors and investors in Western Europe and the United States together to manage the crisis.[17] And because new communication technologies made it possible for investors to obtain and share information about distant markets in this period, it became easier for foreign investors to participate in U.S. capital markets, and for U.S. investors to participate in foreign exchanges.[18]

While government tax and monetary policies helped push investors toward the stock market, the stock market exerted its own pull because stock prices had begun to rise in the early 1980s. But here again, two government policies played important roles in this initial rise. First, the Reagan administration cut taxes on corporate profits, which increased the value of corporate stocks and made them more attractive for investors. Second, and perhaps more important, the Reagan administration largely abandoned efforts to enforce U.S. antitrust law, opening the door to a wave of corporate mergers, which stimulated investor interest in the stock market.

The 1890 Sherman Act prohibited the "attempt to monopolize . . . any part of the trade or commerce," while the 1914 Clayton Act prohibited mergers or acquisitions that "substantially lessen competition or . . . tend to create a monopoly."[19] Responsibility for enforcing these antitrust laws was given to the Justice Department and the Federal Trade Commission. But Reagan administration officials did not believe that enforcement of antitrust laws served a useful purpose. Instead, they argued that monopoly was not necessarily bad. William Baxter, head of the Justice Department's antitrust division under Reagan, argued, "There is nothing written in the sky that says the world would not be a perfectly satisfactory place if there were only 100 companies."[20] And Reagan officials wrote that "mergers generally play an important role in a free enterprise economy. They can penalize ineffective management and facilitate the flow of investment capital and the redeployment of existing productive assets."[21]

Because they did not believe that monopoly or mergers were inherently bad, and thought that the government's use of antitrust laws to "intervene" in the market was counterproductive, Reagan administration officials took several steps to curb the government's antitrust litigation. First, they dropped the government's twelve-year-old antitrust suit against IBM

and announced the same day that they had settled its long antitrust suit against AT&T, which provided for the breakup of AT&T but did so on terms favorable to the company.[22] Second, they adopted new guidelines in 1982 (revised in 1984) for assessing whether firms were violating antitrust law. The new Hirschmann-Herfindahl Index made it easier for firms in the same market to merge without triggering a suit by the Justice Department.[23] Justice Department officials also announced that they might withdraw their objections to proposed mergers if the mergers increased the "efficiency" of a business—creating economies of scale or reducing transportation costs.[24] And third, the Reagan administration reduced the budget and cut the staff of the Antitrust Division. In 1980, 474 attorneys worked on antitrust cases, by 1986, only 261 were employed in this division.[25] While these attorneys still filed suits, the number dropped, and they filed far fewer cases than their predecessors in the Nixon, Bush, and Carter administrations: "Restraint-of-trade cases fell from 225 in 1979 to 77 in 1991, monopoly investigations from 20 to 5, and merger investigations from 152 to 82."[26]

The Reagan administration's unwillingness to enforce antitrust law stimulated merger activity throughout U.S. industry. In 1980, 1,565 merger deals were completed, worth $32.9 billion. By 1985, 3,428 mergers were completed, worth $145.3 billion.[27] The number of mergers more than doubled, while the value of deals more than quadrupled.[28]

Corporate managers, investment bankers, and stock market investors supported mergers because they believed that the newly consolidated firm would be more efficient and more profitable. Larger assets and higher profits would increase the value of the firm, making possible higher dividend payouts to shareholders and/or a higher price for the company's stock. The growth in merger activity helped increase stock prices and investor interest in the stock market, or the "market for capital control" as it is sometimes called, in the early 1980s, exerting a substantial pull on investors. Then, as interest rates declined and the dollar was devalued, large and small domestic investors and foreign interests began investing more heavily in the stock market.

One measure of changing investment patterns is provided by the mutual fund industry, which buys multiple stocks and packages them for sale to investors who seek diversified portfolios and who want to leave stock management to others. People who opened IRAs and 401(k) plans typically purchased mutual funds when they invested in the stock market—about 30 percent of the money held in them is invested in mutual funds.[29] In 1984, $5.8 billion of "new" money flowed into mutual funds, according to the Investment Company Institute.[30] This stream of new

money into the stock market grew to $8.4 billion in 1985, then to $21.8 billion in 1986, a dramatic increase that brought the total amount of money invested in mutual funds to $716 billion.[31] During the next ten years, investors would place an additional $514 billion of new money into the stock market.[32]

The flow of new money into the stock market created a strong demand for stocks that helped bid up prices. Between 1982 and 1987, the Dow Jones Industrial Average rose from 777 to 2,722. It has since gone even higher, to above 6,000 in late 1996. This general rise, of course, was not without interruption. On October 19, 1987, the industrial average fell 508 points, a 22.6 percent fall in the value of stocks, a loss of about $1 trillion.[33] The market also posted big declines in 1994 and 1996, though losses were more modest. But after each decline, the market recovered and rose again to new heights.

It is difficult to determine why these "crashes" occurred. Some economists, like Harvard's Claudia Goldin, are skeptical of any assessment: "Explanations for why the stock market went up or down belong on the funny pages."[34] Federal Reserve Chairman Alan Greenspan described the 1987 crisis as an accident waiting to happen.[35] But other economists have plausibly argued that rising stock prices, fueled by investor demand and merger activity, had outstripped company performance, the ability of firms actually to increase efficiency, profits, and payouts.[36]

When investors believe that companies will not meet their expectations, as price-earnings ratios widen, they sell off shares and withdraw money from the market. As demand shrinks, prices fall. In 1987, investors took government proposals to reduce some of the tax benefits associated with some mergers as evidence that it would be more difficult for firms to use mergers to improve their performance.[37] Once investors began selling heavily, they were joined by others who wanted to sell before prices fell very far. But this further weakened demand, and prices cascaded downward.

The 1929 stock market crash had devastating and long-lasting consequences, contributing to a decade-long Great Depression, but the 1987 crash was different. Falling stock prices were followed by fairly rapid recovery and then rapid advance. The difference, in 1987, was that demand for stocks did not completely collapse, as it had in 1929. Because many new investors had their money in IRAs and 401(k) plans, it was difficult for them to withdraw their money quickly or without penalty, so they stayed in the market. In any event, they were investing for their retirement, a long-term proposition. Other foreign and domestic investors might also have withdrawn completely from the market, but the alterna-

tives were not promising. Other stock markets around the world also lost value, and they were generally associated with lower returns (as in Japan) or even higher risk (as in Hong Kong or Singapore). And because interest rates were still low, bond markets were not a terribly attractive option. Demand for stocks was also sustained by corporations themselves, which spent more than $500 billion to buy back their own stocks between 1986 and 1990.[38] They did so because they could purchase stocks at bargain prices and thereby regain more control over their assets and liabilities. This put them in a better position to acquire or repel other companies in the ongoing merger wars.

During the crisis, government tax and monetary policies helped discourage investors from withdrawing from the market. In a sense, they helped sustain demand (much like other Keynesian programs that provide government support during downturns), creating a floor underneath prices, which prevented complete collapse. In a sense too, investors in IRAs and corporate managers helped underwrite the market, upon which their future depended, providing some stability until investor confidence returned.[39] When investors realized that others had not withdrawn their investments and stuck them under their mattresses, when it became evident that demand remained strong despite a major setback, the crisis eased.

By 1990, investment had returned to precrash levels, and then surged. In 1993, for example, the mutual fund industry recorded a $129.5 billion influx of new cash into the market, six times the amount invested in 1986 before the crash.[40] Stock prices have since climbed higher, and higher still.

Business managers, investors, and policy makers have all cheered rising stock prices. But while they celebrate rising stock prices, which provide them with substantial economic or political rewards, they complain if wages or consumer prices rise. They often fail to appreciate the fact that rising stock prices, like rising consumer prices, are an inflationary phenomena. As we have seen, price inflation is a discriminatory economic process. In this context, some firms have a harder time increasing their performance, profits, and payouts—keeping up with the Dow Joneses— than others. This is particularly true for companies that operate in more competitive industries or companies that borrow heavily in capital markets to expand. But even corporations that can more easily improve their performance find it difficult to keep up with investor expectations when stock prices are rising fast. If the price of a company's stock rises (even if this rise is due to strong investor demand rather than increased value), managers come under enormous pressure to increase dividends to investors and keep payouts in line with higher prices. This is not easy to do. It

means that managers increase their company's performance or lose their jobs. "Stockholders are becoming more active, with no tolerance for any kind of mistake or problem," observed Richard Vocacevich, chairman of Norwest Corporation.[41]

In the inflationary stock price environment of the past decade, managers have adopted strategies designed to increase profitability, payouts, and share prices. Mergers and divestitures have been one of the most important strategies, but these have been joined by efforts to increase performance by introducing new technology, restructuring their firms, or moving parts of their business to low-wage factories overseas. The problem is that these strategies have led to widespread job losses, which have contributed to stagnant wages. In this context, stock price inflation is discriminatory because it benefits investors and corporate managers but disadvantages workers.

The Impact on Jobs

In response to stock price inflation, corporate managers have used a variety of strategies to improve performance, profits, payouts, and share prices. Their primary strategy has been to merge with other firms, and sometimes to divest or spin off divisions either to relieve themselves of unmanageable burdens or to raise cash for other parts of the business.[42] Although this strategy is a continuation of practices that began in the early 1980s, it became even more widespread and significant in the 1990s.

In 1995, the value of the nine thousand merger deals reached in the United States totaled $470 billion, while the value of mergers worldwide reached over $600 billion.[43] On just one day—November 7, 1995—mergers worth $19 billion were announced.[44] Compare these figures with the $32.9 billion worth of mergers announced in all of 1980, the year before the current merger-wave began.[45] The value of mergers in 1995 was fourteen times greater than in 1980. All told, mergers worth $2 trillion were consummated between 1981 and 1996.[46]

In the 1980s, Reagan administration officials condoned mergers because they thought that mergers increased business efficiency and because they did not want to use antitrust law to intervene in the economy. In the 1990s, policy makers in the Bush and Clinton administrations also sanctioned accelerating merger activity. But they did so for a rather different reason. They argued that by upsizing U.S. firms, mergers would strengthen U.S. companies and make them more competitive with foreign firms that were largely immune from antitrust law in their own countries.

As Vice President Dan Quayle argued, "To make America more competitive, we are . . . going to have to reexamine our antitrust laws, many of which are anachronistic in this age of global competition."[47] Bush and Clinton did not revise antitrust law, but they did allow merger activity to continue apace.

Corporate managers pursued mergers with enthusiasm. Because stock prices typically increase when mergers are announced, managers can claim that they have increased the value of the firm. And because their compensation is often tied, in part, to stock price performance, they have financial incentives to reap the benefits associated with a rise in the price of the firm's stock. Under these conditions, it is not surprising that corporate managers have sought to acquire other firms or that CEO salaries have soared.[48] In 1995, "CEOs at the largest 500 companies earned $4.06 million on average, or 197 times as much as the average worker, a 15 percent increase from the previous year."[49] This represented a substantial increase from CEO salaries twenty years ago, when "the typical chief executive officer of a large American company earned about 40 times as much as a typical worker did."[50]

Corporate managers no longer direct a company's nuts-and-bolts production of a particular good or service. They manage stock prices, stock-equity ratios, mergers, divestitures, and dividends in an inflationary stock market environment. This new role explains in part why the disparity between CEO compensation and factory-floor wages has grown. It has grown because executive compensation is linked to the stock market, which is willing and able to provide huge rewards to managers for their efforts to increase payouts and stock prices.

Of course, corporate managers must also seek to improve their company's performance. They have done this by introducing new technology and by restructuring the business to increase productivity. New technology is expensive. For industrial firms, the introduction of new technology often requires the construction of whole new factories. For many years, large industrial firms were reluctant to make substantial new investments of this kind. But as they came under increasing pressure from the stock market, from companies that might try to buy them, and from foreign firms that had grown strong in the postwar period, industrial firms began investing in new technology in the 1980s, building new factories, and reorganizing their businesses.[51] Between 1979 and 1995, for example, Caterpillar, a heavy equipment manufacturer, closed nine plants and spent $1.8 billion to modernize its remaining factories. As new technology was introduced, the firm cut its workforce from ninety thousand to fifty-four thousand and increased production. "We've almost doubled our productivity since the mid-1980s," Caterpillar executive James Owens said.[52]

When they reorganized, many firms often moved new manufacturing plants overseas, or contracted with overseas businesses to supply goods, where labor costs were lower. In 1987, for example, "auto makers spent $28 billion on parts manufactured overseas, up from $8 billion ten years before. The Big Three went from importing 500,000 engines in 1983 to 1.92 million in 1987. . . . From 1979 to 1992, thanks to automation, manufacturing output rose 13.1 percent, while the work force declined by 15 percent," writes John Judis.[53] In the 1990s, this process was facilitated by the free trade agreements, which reduced the tariffs or taxes paid by corporations that imported manufactured goods supplied by their own factories or other firms in other countries (see chapter 9).

While the introduction of new technology had periodically transformed heavy industry (in the 1920s and again in the 1980s and '90s), and increased productivity in agriculture (in the 1920s and '50s—see chapter 8), new technology had not been deployed in the service industries.[54] That changed in the 1980s, when firms in the service sector began introducing computer technologies to improve the productivity of white-collar workers in office buildings. Although computer technologies had been available for some years, and they had become cheaper to use, their introduction still required substantial investment.

But despite falling computer prices—"the cost to process 100,000 calculations . . . declined by a factor of 500 from 1952 to 1980, decreasing from $1.26 to one-fourth of one cent"—service-sector firms delayed the introduction of new technology until the 1980s, when they came under pressure to increase productivity and profits and found that the cost of computer-related technologies had fallen far enough to make their use cost-effective.[55] The use of bar codes, scanners, and computers in the retail industry "has contributed to the loss of 400,000 jobs in retailing since 1990."[56] In the banking industry, experts predicted in 1995 that "half of the nation's 59,000 branch banks will close and 450,000 of the 2.8 million jobs in the banking industry will disappear," a product both of mergers and of new technologies like automated tellers (ATMs).[57] As Wall Street economist Stephen Roach observed, "Every time I pass an ATM machine, I see the ghosts of three bank tellers."[58] Or, as another writer explained,

A human teller can handle up to 200 transactions a day, works 30 hours a week, gets a salary anywhere from $8,000 to $20,000 a year plus fringe benefits, gets coffee breaks, a vacation and sick time. . . . In contrast, an automated teller can handle 2,000 transactions a day, works 168 hours a week, costs about $22,000 a year to run, and doesn't take coffee breaks or vacation.[59]

By combining firms, restructuring or relocating business, and introducing new technology, corporate managers in the 1980s and '90s generally increased the productivity of U.S. business, after years of slow or negligible productivity increases.[60] Between 1982 and 1994, "productivity increased about 19.5 percent."[61] And increased productivity enabled firms to raise profits. According to the Commerce Department, for example, "profits for non-financial corporations rose 57 percent between 1992 and 1994."[62]

Higher profits were used to finance mergers, restructure business, introduce new technology, pay higher CEO salaries, increase shareholder dividends, and boost stock prices. But the strategies adopted by corporate managers have also resulted in significant job loss.

Mergers make many workers in combined firms redundant, as occurs when banks with branches across the street from each other merge into a single firm. When corporations move overseas, they eliminate jobs for domestic employees. Internal reorganization programs eliminate workers and assign their jobs to others, often to temporary workers who receive wages that are typically 60 percent of full-time workers' and who receive few if any of the benefits associated with full-time employment.[63] And new technologies make it possible to do the same amount of work, even more, with fewer employees. The net result is massive job loss.

The *New York Times* reported in 1996 that "more than 43 million jobs have been erased in the United States since 1979."[64] Reporters noted that "in one third of all households, a family member has lost a job" and that "one in 10 adults—or about 19 million people, a number matching the adult population of New York and New Jersey combined—acknowledged that a lost job had precipitated a major crisis in their lives."[65] And over time, they said, the pace of layoffs had accelerated, from 1.42 million in 1980 to 3.26 million in 1995.[66] Most laid-off workers find new jobs elsewhere, but "only 33 percent of them earned as much as or more than they had before."[67]

Under these circumstances, it has been hard for workers to demand higher wages, even though productivity gains and higher profits mean that corporate managers *could* increase worker pay. Unionized workers have been increasingly reluctant to strike for higher pay—work stoppages involving more than a thousand workers declined from two hundred fifty a year in 1979 to only twenty-five in 1992—as the risk of job loss has risen.[68]

During most of the postwar period, workers were more willing and also better able to demand and receive higher pay *if* their productivity increased. But massive downsizing has severed this relation.[69] Instead of rising along with productivity, wages have fallen:

Workers in the heavily unionized steel industry . . . saw their wages fall from
$20.37 per hour in 1981 . . . to $16.87 per hour in 1992. . . . The wages of
partially unionized meat-packing workers went from $13.98 per hour in
1981 to . . . $9.15 per hour in 1992. . . . Workers in restaurants and bars—one
of the fastest growing groups in the 1980s—saw their wages fall from $6.14
per hour in 1981 to . . . $5.29 per hour in 1992.[70]

Overall, real wages fell 9.6 percent between 1979 and 1993.[71] Households
were able to maintain their collective income during this period only because an increasing number of women took jobs: 56.6 percent of women
work in paid positions.[72] But while this has helped support family income,
it meant that parents had less time for their children. "Parents are spending 40 percent less time with their children than they did 30 years ago.
More than two million children under the age of 13 have no adult supervi-
sion either before or after school. Paying for day care would use up all or
most of a mother's wages," wrote MIT economist Lester Thurow.[73]

The economic gains made by mergers, restructuring, and new technology have been distributed upward, claimed by corporate managers and
stockholders, not by workers. Between January and June 1995, the value
of stock in 994 public firms (90 percent of the firms on the stock exchange) increased by $673 billion, a sum large enough to give a $5,100
bonus to every American worker, or to feed the entire population for a
year.[74] But most of these gains were distributed to corporate managers
and wealthy shareholders, who own most of the nation's stocks, though
some were distributed to workers who had used IRAs and 401(k) plans
to invest in the stock market. The irony for stockholding workers is that
their participation in the stock market helped fuel the stock price inflation
that pressured companies to adopt strategies that resulted in job losses
and falling wages. Of course, worker-investors have few alternatives and
they have little control over investment decisions made by their mutual
fund managers or over the corporate managers who adopt stock-enhance-
ment, job-loss strategies. This irony was captured by a *New York Times*
article, which ran under the headline "You're Fired! (But Your Stock Is
Way Up)."[75]

These developments have contributed to a growing gap between rich
and poor in the United States. Between 1968 and 1994, the wealthiest 20
percent of the population increased its share of the nation's income from
40.5 percent to 46.9 percent, while "the share of income earned by the
rest of the country's households either declined or remained stagnant,"
the Census Bureau reported.[76] Put another way, the average income for
the top 20 percent of households grew from $73,754 in 1968 to $105,945

in 1994.[77] As a result of growing income inequality, the "gap between rich and poor was wider in the United States . . . than in any other large industrialized country."[78]

As we have seen, these developments were driven during the past fifteen years by stock price inflation, which was fueled by the influx of money into the stock market from diverse sources. Of course, this does not mean that stock price inflation will inevitably continue. Although corporate managers have increased performance, profits, and payouts, which has enhanced stock prices, there are limits to their ability to continue doing so. If stock prices rise too fast or go too high, managers might find it hard to increase dividends at the same pace, a problem that could contribute to a rapid fall in stock prices, as it did in 1987, with potentially serious consequences.[79] In the long run, if job loss continues and wages fall, consumer demand for the goods and services produced by upsized corporations may weaken. This would make it hard for more-efficient firms to produce at full capacity, and to maximize profits and payouts.

Media Mergers and Blockbusters

Corporate mergers resulted in widespread job loss, but also transformed whole industries. Two waves of media mergers, the first in the 1970s and the second in the 1980s and '90s, transformed the communications industry, resulting in the creation of a diminishing number of multimedia firms that practice "product derivation," the repeated sale of the same good in different technological formats.

For most of this century, the communications industry—phone, film, AM radio, TV, print, FM radio, cable, video, and computer—was divided by government antitrust law and by technology. Government antitrust law was repeatedly used to prevent firms from owning multiple communications technologies. Radio and TV were the exception because radio networks were allowed to establish television networks. And antitrust law was used to prevent the monopolization of separate technologies by individual firms. AT&T was for many years the exception because the government allowed it to monopolize phone technology, though as a kind of public utility. In the film industry, for example, the government in 1917 dissolved the Motion Pictures Patent Company monopoly and between 1948 and 1953 forced the major Hollywood studios to divest their movie theater chains.[80]

Because the government generally prevented firms from owning multiple communications technologies, when new technologies were invented

and introduced, they were controlled by a new set of firms. As a result, the communications industry was divided along technological lines into different media.

The problem for different media (with the exception of telephone communications) was that audience demand was relatively stagnant, competition among similar media kept profits low, and the introduction of new media technologies increased industrywide competition for audience share and advertising revenue. These problems first became apparent in the 1970s for Hollywood film studios, which had seen average weekly attendance in movie theaters fall from ninety million in 1946 to forty-five million in 1957 and then to forty million by 1970, largely because moviegoers stayed at home to watch TV.[81] TV networks would experience the same problem later in the decade, when cable TV began siphoning-off viewers in large numbers. The introduction of video players in the 1980s subsequently cut into network and cable TV markets, and the introduction of personal computers later cut into these markets.

To restore profits in media segments where competition was stiff and demand stagnant, corporate managers moved to increase their competitiveness and expand effective demand. This process began first in the film industry, both because Hollywood studios were the first to experience these problems and because other media needed motion pictures and television shows to supply their own markets. Because other media were barred from acquiring Hollywood studios by government antitrust law, nonmedia corporations like Gulf and Western, Transamerica, and Coca-Cola bought studios and moved to restore their profitability.[82]

After they took charge, the new corporate managers increased the productivity of Hollywood studios by reducing the number of films made and increasing their investment in the movies that they did produce. Instead of making both major motion pictures (A-films) and minor B-movies, they eliminated their production of B-movies and shifted resources to A-films. By eliminating B-movies and the double feature, they could reduce the size of their labor force, sell off expensive but unnecessary studio assets, and increase their return from theater admissions (the revenue from one single-feature movie could now cover the cost of making one movie, not two).[83]

As the number of Hollywood films dropped—from three hundred a year in the early 1970s to less than two hundred in the mid-1970s—studios could invest more in each A-film.[84] They spent more on new technology, talent, and advertising to increase the likelihood of success and to distinguish the new Hollywood product from cheaper independent films made in the United States and from films made by film industries in other countries.

To increase the demand for these more expensive films, the studios began making movies designed to attract *repeat* viewers. In practice this meant targeting films at teenage boys, who would watch their favorite movies repeatedly and who usually determined the selection of films on dates. Hollywood focused on young viewers because 70 to 75 percent of the moviegoing audience is under 30 years old.[85] The studios began producing action films to suit this important audience, trying to make action-packed films that could be turned into serials—James Bonds, Star Wars, Godfathers, Halloweens, Aliens, Indiana Joneses—that could persuade viewers to return, again and again. They found that these movies also traveled well and could be shown to young male viewers in countries around the world. In addition to making new films, the studios also began selling old films (those no longer in distribution) to television networks for TV "premiers" and then to cable operators and movie channels.[86] Both strategies helped expand the effective demand for films.

The result was the advent of the Hollywood blockbuster. These enormously profitable films restored the fortunes of the major studios, but they also consolidated the industry. The high cost of making blockbuster films put independent domestic producers and foreign film industries at a disadvantage because they could not easily raise and risk the ever-increasing amount of money required to make a major motion picture. By 1980, "an average studio picture cost $13.7 million. . . . By 1990 total costs had near-tripled to $38.4 million," and by 1994, the average cost had grown to $44 million.[87] And because blockbusters crowded out other films and increased the major studios' share of a relatively fixed market, independent producers and foreign filmmakers had to compete more strenuously for the audience that remained.[88] As a result, the major studios were able to increase their share of domestic and foreign film markets, at the expense of independent and foreign filmmakers. Hollywood studios, for example, increased their share of the Canadian film market from 84.9 percent in 1970 to 95.3 percent in 1978.[89] This development, and the job loss resulting from the decline of film industries in other countries, triggered an intense debate in trade negotiations in the 1980s, as foreign industries tried to protect themselves from the onslaught of Hollywood blockbusters (see chapter 9).[90]

The reorganization of the film industry in the 1970s was followed by a similar reorganization of the network radio and television industry in the mid-1980s. The corporations that bought ABC, CBS, and NBC and founded Fox all invested in new technology to downsize workforces—employment at CBS shrank from forty thousand to less than seven thousand during the 1980s—and increase profitability.[91] And firms in print

media—newspaper, magazines, and trade and textbook publishing—did the same.

While the restructuring of firms within separate media industries became commonplace in the 1980s, so too did mergers between firms in *different* media. Government antitrust law had long prevented media from acquiring businesses in other media. But as the Reagan administration withdrew from antitrust litigation and eased restrictions against consolidation within separate media and permitted cross-media mergers, firms began assembling businesses that could deliver products across the media spectrum. In 1984, the government raised the number of AM, FM, and TV stations that could be owned by a single firm from seven of each (twenty-one total) to twelve of each (thirty-six total), and in 1987 allowed film studios to purchase movie theater chains, permitting studios to reassert control of the retail business that they had lost in the 1950s.[92]

A second, multimedia merger wave quickly followed, with domestic and foreign firms consolidating the communications industry wholesale.[93] As one media industry manager put it, the big media players "are octopuses, all with their hands in each other's pockets. Where one [industry] starts and the other stops will be hard to decide."[94] The number of firms controlling major media declined from fifty to twenty-nine between 1982 and 1987, according to media analyst Ben Bagdikian, and many expect that perhaps only ten firms will control most of the twenty-five thousand media outlets in the United States by the end of the century.[95]

Borrowing from the Hollywood experience, corporate managers who are integrating diverse media into multimedia firms are trying to create goods that can be sold repeatedly in different formats. To do this they seek to control both the software (ideas, stories, images, sounds) and the hardware (the different technologies that deliver software to audiences across the media spectrum) in the United States and around the world. In practice this means obtaining stories from authors or screenwriters to produce books and then films that can be released in different formats.[96] The idea is to sell the same product—a story like *Jurassic Park* or *Twister*—many times. It can be sold first as a book, then produced as a film (or vice versa), which can then be sold to repeat viewers at the multiplex. Theatrical distribution can be assisted by previews of the film on *Entertainment Tonight* and promotion interviews with David Letterman. When its first-run audience has been exhausted, it can be sold to video stores or in supermarkets for viewing on the home VCR. It can then be premiered on network TV, then shown on late-night TV or the movie channels for many years. More recently it became possible for computer owners to access information about the film at its web site, and media

companies expect eventually that viewers will be able to access the film itself (problems with integrating the hardware and ensuring payment has so far delayed this). Not only can the same product—a film—be sold repeatedly in different formats, the ideas, images, and sounds can be repackaged as a Broadway play or Ice Capades show (*Beauty and the Beast*), featured as a ride at a theme park (*Indiana Jones*), or used as decor for bars (*Cheers*), merchandised as the mascot of a hockey team (*Mighty Ducks*) or turned into a video game (or a video game into a movie, as in the case of *Mortal Kombat*).[97] What's more, the sound track can be released on video for MTV, and cuts played on radio stations, then sold on compact disks and cassettes to home listeners. Like the Top 40 song hits of yesteryear, the book, film, and musical goods are designed to be replayed endlessly, using different formats to extend their life span.

To produce goods that can be sold repeatedly in different formats, media firms have invested heavily in new technology and expensive talent. Hollywood, which has become the center of production for communications industry software, has invested heavily in new technology, using computer animation to create new images that could not be produced on sound-stage sets. And they have paid vast sums to domestic and foreign talent in an effort to find bankable stars that can create or maintain audience demand whatever the merits of a particular story.

The introduction of high technology and the intense bidding for bankable talent has dramatically increased the cost of making films, to about $44 million on average in 1994. Because this investment enables studios to produce a high-tech product and attract talent from around the world— directors like Jan de Bont (*Speed*, *Twister*) and actors like Jackie Chan, Claude Van Damme, and Anthony Hopkins—they can distinguish Hollywood films from low-tech foreign films and deprive foreign industries of their creative raw material. "Around the globe, folks just can't get enough of America," *Fortune* magazine reported in 1990. "They may not want our *hardware* any more—our cars or steel. But when they want a jolt of popular culture . . . they increasingly turn to American *software*: our movies, music, TV programming, and home video, which together now account for an annual trade surplus of $8 billion."[98]

Summary

Changed government policies (tax, antitrust, and monetary policies) played a big role in the stock market boom, which contributed to a massive merger wave, downsizing, job loss, and income redistribution. Ironi-

cally, workers have been both helped by the rising value of their IRA investments and hurt by the loss of employment and income associated with this process. In the long run it is unclear whether both developments—the rise of corporate profits and the decline of worker incomes—can be sustained. Corporations, after all, rely on rising levels of consumer demand to maintain growth. If job loss continues and incomes decline, consumer demand may eventually weaken, creating a crisis not only for workers but for corporate managers and investors as well.

Notes

1. Congressional Quarterly. *Budgeting for America: The Politics and Process of Federal Spending*. Washington, D.C.: Congressional Quarterly, 1982, p. 78. Peterson, Peter G. *Facing Up: How to Rescue the Economy from Crushing Debt and Restore the American Dream*. New York: Simon and Schuster, 1993, p. 83. Ball, Robert M. "The Original Understanding on Social Security: Implications for Later Developments," in Theodore R. Marmour and Jerry L. Mashaw, eds., *Social Security: Beyond the Rhetoric of Crisis*. Princeton: Princeton University Press, 1988, p. 34.

2. Kuttner, Robert. *The Economic Illusion*. Boston: Houghton Mifflin, 1984, p. 75. Congressional Quarterly, 1982, p. 79.

3. Marmour and Mashaw, 1988, p. 6.

4. Ball in Theodore R. Marmour and Jerry L. Mashaw, 1988, p. 35.

5. Eckholm, Eric. "Payments to the Retired Loom Ever Larger," *New York Times*, August 30, 1993.

6. Graetz, Michael J. "Retirement Security Policy: Toward a More Unified View," in Theodore R. Marmour and Jerry L. Mashaw, 1988, pp. 109–10.

7. Starr, Paul, "Social Security and the American Public Household," in Theodore R. Marmour and Jerry L. Mashaw, 1988, p. 129.

8. Ibid. More than half of all Americans do not think Social Security will provide money adequate for their retirement. Abelson, Reed. "In Mutual Funds, Sophisticates Prefer a Bit of Naivete," *New York Times*, March 26, 1995.

9. Starr in Theodore R. Marmour and Jerry L. Mashaw, 1988, p. 129.

10. Nolde, Kenneth B. "Bidding War Is Feared for Retirement Savings," *New York Times*, September 30, 1981. Close, Jeff, director of communications, Access Research, personal interview, September 20, 1996.

11. Ibid.

12. Nasar, Sylvia. "Tapping the Rich May Prove Tricky," *New York Times*, December 12, 1992.

13. Norris, Floyd. "From Japan, Wall Street Looks Down Hill," *New York Times*, May 7, 1995.

14. Resnick, Bruce G. "The Globalization of World Financial Markets," *Business Horizons*, November-December 1989, p. 35.

15. Ibid.

16. Bose, Mihir. *The Crash*. London: Bloomsbury, 1988, pp. 17–18, 6.

17. Resnick, 1989, pp. 36–37.

18. Ibid., p. 38.

19. Smiley, Robert H. "Merger Activity and Antitrust Policy in the United States," in Giuliano Mussati, ed., *Mergers, Markets and Public Policy*. Dordrecht: Kluwer Academic, 1995, pp. 64–65.

20. Peritz, Rudolph J. R. *Competition Policy in America, 1988–1992*. New York: Oxford University Press, 1996, p. 278. Eisner, Mark Allen. *Antitrust and the Triumph of Economics*. Charlotte: University of North Carolina Press, 1991, pp. 188–89. Smiley in Giuliano Mussati, 1995, pp. 73–74.

21. Peritz, 1996, p. 281.

22. Eisner, 1991, pp. 187–88.

23. Shughart, William F., III. "Antitrust Policy in the Reagan Administration: Pyrrhic Victories?" in Roger E. Meiners and Bruce Yandle, eds., *Regulation and the Reagan Era*. New York: Holmes and Meier, 1989, pp. 94–95. Mueller, Dennis L., "Mergers: Theory and Evidence," in Giuliano Mussati, 1995, p. 4. Eisner, 1991, p. 197. Smiley in Giuliano Mussati, 1995, p. 74.

24. Ibid., p. 70. Mueller in Giuliano Mussati, 1995, p. 4. Eisner, 1991, pp. 198–99.

25. Ibid., p. 190.

26. Labaton, Stephan. "Rousing Antitrust Law from Its 12-Year Nap," *New York Times*, July 25, 1993.

27. Smiley in Giuliano Mussati, 1995, p. 47.

28. Mueller in Giuliano Mussati, 1995, p. 10. Parzych, Kenneth M. *Public Policy and the Regulatory Environment*. Lanham, Md.: University Press of America, 1993, p. 109. Smiley in Giuliano Mussati, 1995, p. 76.

29. Johnston, David Cay. "In 401(k)s, It's Great to be Young and Bold," *New York Times*, September 3, 1995.

30. "Net New Cash Flow, 1984–1996." Washington, D.C.: Investment Company Institute, 1996.

31. Wyatt, Edward. "For Mutual Funds, New Political Muscle," *New York Times*, September 8, 1996. Close. Access Research, 1996.

32. Wyatt, 1996.

33. Mackay, Robert J. *After the Crash: Linkages Between Stocks and Futures*. Washington, D.C.: American Enterprise Institute for Public Policy, 1988, p. 1.

34. Passell, Peter. "Why Does the Market Keep Going Up . . . When Economic Trends Are Pointing Down," *New York Times*, May 7, 1996.

35. Mackay, 1988, p. 32.

36. Bierman, Harold, Jr. *The Great Myths of 1929 and the Lessons to Be Learned*. New York: Greenwood, 1991, p. 172. Norris, Floyd. "Dividends Are Up, But Not Enough," *New York Times*, May 7, 1996. Bose, 1988, pp. 3–4, 15.

37. Mackay, 1988, pp. 3–4.

38. Smith, Roy C. *Comeback: The Restoration of American Banking Power in the New World Economy*. Cambridge: Harvard University Press, 1993, p. 32.

39. Chernow, Ron. "Lambs Among the Bulls and Bears," *New York Times*, July 26, 1996.

40. Investment Company Institute, 1996.

41. Hansell, Saul. "Wave of Mergers Heads Toward a Record," *New York Times*, October 31, 1995.

42. Smiley in Guiliano Mussati, 1995, p. 49.

43. Norris, Floyd. "The Tao of the Dow, Climbing from One Peak to Another," *New York Times*, November 14, 1995. Gibson, Paul. "The Year of the Do-It-Yourself Megadeal," *New York Times*, December 26, 1995.

44. Norris, Floyd. "Mergers That Try to Keep It Simple," *New York Times*, November 7, 1995.

45. Smiley in Guiliano Mussati, 1995, p. 47.

46. Labaton, 1993. Strom, Stephanie. "This Year's Wave of Mergers Heads Toward a Record," *New York Times*, October 31, 1995.

47. Davidow, Joel. "The Relationship Between Anti-Trust and Trade Laws in the United States," *World Economy*, 14(1), 1991, p. 38.

48. Matier, Philip, and Ross, Andrew. "The Upside of Downsizing," *San Francisco Chronicle*, November 19, 1995.

49. Greenhouse, Steven. "Corporate Greed, Meet the Maximum Wage," *New York Times*, June 16, 1996. Uchitelle, Louis. "1995 Was Good for Companies, and Better for a Lot of C.E.O.s," *New York Times*, March 29, 1996.

50. Cassidy, John. "Who Killed the Middle Class?" *New Yorker*, October 16, 1995, p. 120. In 1960, "the typical CEO of a Fortune 500 company was earning $190,000 a year." (Rifkin, Jeremy. *The End of Work*. New York: Putnam, 1995, p. 173).

51. Rattner, Steven. "If Productivity's Rising, Why Are Jobs Paying Less," *New York Times Magazine*, September 12, 1993.

52. Sterngold, James. "Facing the Next Recession Without Fear," *New York Times*, May 9, 1995.

53. Judis, John. "Why Your Wages Keep Falling," *New Republic*, February 14, 1994, p. 28.

54. Rattner, 1993, p. 96.

55. Rubin, Michael Rogers. *Information Economics and Policy in the United States*. Littleton, Colo.: Libraries Unlimited, 1983, pp. 3–4.

56. Rattner, 1993, p. 97.

57. Hansell, Saul. "Wave of Mergers Is Transforming American Banking," *New York Times*, August 21, 1995.

58. Uchitelle, Louis. "In Refiguring Productivity, U.S. Finds Slower Growth," *New York Times*, February 9, 1996.

59. Rifkin, 1995, p. 144.

60. Rattner, 1993, p. 96.

61. Emspak, Frank. "Where Have All the Jobs Gone?" *Chronicle of Higher Education*, April 5, 1996, p. B2. Uchitelle, February 9, 1996.

62. Emspak, 1996, p. B2.

63. Tilly, Chris. "Short Hours, Short Shrift: The Causes and Consequences of Part-Time Employment," in Virginia L. du Rivage, ed., *New Policies for the Part-Time and Contingent Workforce*. Armonk, N.Y.: Sharpe, 1992, p. 21.

64. Uchitelle, Louis, and Kleinfield, N. R. "On the Battlefields of Business, Millions of Casualties," *New York Times*, March 3, 1996.

65. Ibid.

66. Ibid. See the critique of the report in Cassidy, John. "All Worked Up," *New Yorker*, April 22, 1996, pp. 52–53. Birch, David L. "The Hidden Economy," *Wall Street Journal*, June 10, 1988, p. 23, and the *Times*' response, Uchitelle, Louis, "Despite Drop, Rate of Layoffs Remains High," *New York Times*, August 23, 1996.

67. Ibid. Uchitelle and Kleinfield, 1996.

68. Uchitelle, Louis. "Labor Has a Big Job for Its New Friend Clinton," *New York Times*, June 27, 1993.

69. Emspak, 1996, p. B2.

70. Judis, 1994, p. 28.

71. Ibid., p. 26.

72. Ibid., p. 28.

73. Thurow, Lester. "Companies Merge; Families Break Up," *New York Times*, September 3, 1995.

74. Nasar, Sylvia. "Only a Paper Boom," *New York Times*, June 9, 1995.

75. Norris, Floyd. "You're Fired! (But Your Stock Is Way Up)," *New York Times*, September 3, 1995.

76. Holmes, Steven A. "Income Disparity Between Poorest and Richest Rises," *New York Times*, June 20, 1996.

77. Ibid.

78. Bradsher, Keith. "Widest Gap in Incomes? Research Points to U.S.," *New York Times*, October 27, 1995.

79. Norris, 1996. Norris, Floyd. "Fewer Dividends Getting Trimmed," *New York Times*, January 4, 1995.

80. Garnham, Nicholas. *Capitalism and Communication: Global Culture and the Economics of Information*. London: Sage, 1990, pp. 187, 189.

81. Ibid., pp. 192, 194.

82. Bagdikian, Ben. *The Media Monopoly*. Boston: Beacon, 1987, pp. 24–25.

83. Izod, John. *Hollywood and the Box Office, 1895–1986*. London: Macmillan, 1988, pp. 174–75.

84. Garnham, 1990, p. 181. Izod, 1988, p. 174.

85. Ibid., p. 181. Steinbock, Dan. *Triumph and Erosion in the American Media and Entertainment Industries*. Westport, Conn.: Quorum, 1995, p. 109.

86. Garnham, 1990, p. 197.

87. Steinbock, 1995, p. 99.

88. Izod, 1988, p. 180.

89. Garnham, 1990, p. 171.

90. Ibid., p. 207.

91. Steinbock, 1995, pp. 31, 57.
92. Ibid., pp. 21, 110.
93. Ibid., see chart, p. 19.
94. Ibid., p. 259.
95. Bagdikian, 1987, pp. ix, 4, 21.
96. Ibid., p. 2.
97. Steinbock, 1995, pp. 119–20, 131, 124.
98. Ibid., p. 16.

8

Technology, Food, and Hunger

During this century, successive technological revolutions have increased food supplies in the United States and around the world. But while agricultural technologies have increased world food production, which has grown even faster than world population (see chapter 10), they have also displaced U.S. farmers and contributed to third world hunger.

Agricultural revolutions in the United States raised farm costs and lowered the prices farmers earned for their crops. These developments forced millions of farmers off the land, with important consequences for rural communities, urban consumers, and the environment. In the third world, the introduction of agricultural technologies greatly increased the volume of food produced, but because technology was typically used to grow crops for export and for animal feed, it displaced staple crops and small farmers, contributing to widespread hunger. The irony is that growing food supplies and gnawing hunger go hand in hand in the modern world. In this chapter we will examine the social and environmental problems associated with technological change in agricultural settings, first in the United States, and then in the third world.

Technological Revolutions

There have been three technological revolutions in agriculture during this century, and we may be on the verge of a fourth. The first began in the 1920s, with the introduction of tractors and soybeans. The second got underway in the 1940s, with the introduction of chemical fertilizers and pesticides, hybrid seeds, animal antibiotics, and government-supplied power and water, all elements of what came to be known as the Green Revolution. The introduction of Green Revolution technologies began in

the United States. The introduction and adoption of these technologies by farmers around the world resulted in a third agricultural revolution during the 1960s and '70s. And a fourth revolution, which is associated with the introduction of new biological and genetic technologies, may now be just getting underway.

Each of these technological revolutions transformed agriculture and increased food production. The first revolution began in the 1920s, at a time when seven million family farmers worked the land, using horses for traction. The typical 150-acre farm planted 50 acres of corn or wheat, grew another 50 acres of oats to feed the horses, and kept 50 acres in pasture to rest the land, though they grazed their beef or dairy cattle on this pasture.[1] The arrival in the United States of immigrants from Europe, Latin America, and Asia swelled the population and kept the demand for farm products strong and prices high. Indeed, the prices farmers received were as high as at any time during this century. Because their expenses for land, horses, and housing were low and stable, and prices were high—wheat sold for $100 a ton and corn for $76 a ton—farmers could support their families and nearby rural communities.[2]

Although farm supplies fluctuated annually, depending on the weather, the relation between supply and demand remained fairly close, or balanced from the farmers' perspective. And the existence of millions of small farms supported a vibrant collection of banks, businesses, and small towns across the country. But during the 1920s, the introduction of cheap tractors made by the emerging auto industry transformed U.S. agriculture and led in the 1930s to glut and crisis.

In 1910, only 1,000 farmers used tractors. But by 1920, with earnings from high wartime food prices, farmers had purchased 250,000 tractors from Henry Ford and John Deere, and by 1930, 900,000 farmers owned the new, hard-working machines.[3] The introduction of tractors on the farm was important because it eliminated the need for horses and for the oats they consumed. Farmers could stop growing oats for horses and, instead, plant corn or soybeans. "As powered machinery replaced the horse, more land became available for cash crops," noted Peter Phillips, an agricultural economist.[4] In the 1920s and '30s, many farmers began planting soybeans. Because this legume fixes nitrogen, it can be used in rotation with corn to replenish corn-depleted soil. And because its oils can be used in industry (for paints and varnishes), in food processing (for cooking oil and margarine), and its residue, a protein-rich meal that can be fed to cows, soybeans often took over former oat fields.

These developments enabled farmers to increase the volume of food supplies enormously. In a sense, the widespread adoption of tractors and

soybeans "was equivalent to the discovery and development of a new continent, of a new North America, in the 20th century," argues Jean-Pierre Berlan, an agricultural economist.[5]

The problem was that the new tractor-based agriculture produced huge supplies of food, leading to gluts and lower prices. And the cost of buying and maintaining the new machinery significantly increased costs for farmers. When industry in the United States and around the world laid off millions of workers during the Great Depression that followed the 1929 stock market crash, the demand for food weakened and agricultural prices fell. Wheat prices fell 20 percent, to $79 a ton, in the 1930s.[6] Under these conditions—mounting food supplies and falling demand, at a time when the cost of growing food was rising—many farmers could not earn enough money to survive. As they lost their ability to lease land or repay loans, they were forced to abandon their farms in droves. Perhaps 1.5 million farmers were driven out of farming as a result of the Depression, a process depicted in John Steinbeck's *The Grapes of Wrath*.[7]

Things for farmers might have been even worse if the drought of 1934–36 had not also reduced supplies:

> The calamitous years, which wiped out almost half the corn crop and a large segment of the wheat crop were, in their own peculiar way, an economic blessing since they restored the balance of supply and demand, a prerequisite for economic recovery. No government agricultural policy would have dared to do what the weather did.[8]

The problems associated with this farm crisis were solved, temporarily, by the outbreak of World War II. Because the worldwide war disrupted or destroyed agricultural production in many countries, global food supplies fell. And because war-related industries hired millions of workers and the military drafted millions more into service, the demand for food greatly increased. As a result, prices rose to their highest level in the twentieth century. With wheat prices soaring to $122 a ton and corn to $94 a ton, "net farm income quadrupled, rising from $4.5 billion to $12.3 billion between 1940 and 1945."[9] U.S. farmers, whose production was not disrupted but was instead stimulated by war, again prospered.

After the war, U.S. agriculture was transformed by a second technological revolution. Whereas the introduction of the tractor spurred a substantial increase in food production in the 1920s and '30s, new biological and chemical technologies greatly increased food supplies in the postwar period. The new hybrid seeds, chemical fertilizers, pesticides, and antibiotics, which were developed during the war by government-sponsored

research scientists and then produced and marketed by the emerging seed and agricultural chemical industries, dramatically improved crop yields and increased food supplies.[10] Together with the tractors and farm machinery developed during the earlier period, and the extension of government irrigation projects in the arid West and the provision of electrical power to rural communities, these technological innovations transformed agriculture, resulting in a series of changes known collectively as the "Green Revolution."

The Green Revolution enabled farmers to increase yields 2 percent per acre annually since 1948. They increased corn yields from 38.2 bushels an acre in 1930 to 118 bushels in 1985, soybeans from 21.7 to 34.1 bushels, and wheat from 16.5 to 37.5 bushels in the same period. Milk production per cow increased from 5,314 pounds in 1950 to 13,786 pounds in 1987.[11] The new technologies created food supplies equal to that produced by *another* North American continent.

The extension of U.S. Green Revolution technologies around the world created a third agricultural revolution. Farmers in Europe began adopting the new agrochemical technologies in the 1950s and '60s. They were assisted in this effort by the European Community's Common Agricultural Program (CAP)—a government subsidy program designed to increase food supplies, promote free trade among member countries, and equalize food prices throughout Western Europe. By 1972, European farmers, assisted by new technologies and government subsidies, produced enough food to feed Europe without importing U.S. food, and were on the verge of creating regular surpluses. By 1985, they would export one-third of the food they grew.[12]

The diffusion of Green Revolution technologies in the third world began somewhat later, in the 1960s, and took hold more slowly. But by the 1980s, the new technologies began having an impact on food supplies. Aided by Green Revolution technologies, populous third world countries like India, Pakistan, Indonesia, and China posted major increases in food supplies. India increased grain production by nearly 20 percent, from 131.15 million metric tons (mmt) in 1980 to 190.23 mmt in 1989.[13] China increased its grain harvest from 240 mmt in 1970 to 320 mmt in 1980, then to 407 mmt in 1984[14]; Indonesia from 33.65 mmt in 1980 to 49.11 mmt in 1989; Pakistan from 16.86 to 21.07 mmt in the same period.[15]

The advent of new genetic and electronic agricultural technologies in the 1980s and '90s may result in a fourth revolution. Scientists using genetic engineering are splicing genes from one plant to another, creating "transgenic" products that can increase yields. Computerized mapping of soils and the use of satellites to position farm machinery allow farmers to

work the land with greater precision.[16] Some scientists are also trying to use genetic material from wild and previously neglected local crop varieties to make popular varieties hardier and more productive.[17] Donald Plucknett, a science adviser to the Consultative Group on International Agricultural Research, conducted a 1993 study that found annual yields of grain rising sharply in the late twentieth century. "We all know that there is a biological limit to yield out there somewhere," said Plucknett. "But what surprised me in doing this research is that some of the highest-yielding countries don't seem to be close to it."[18]

Other scientists are dubious about these claims. Elaine Ingham, a plant pathologist at the University of Oregon, responded to the study by saying, "We can keep dumping fertilizer and chemicals on farmland but at what cost to the rest of the ecosystem? Long before we hit the maximum on crop productivity, we are going to have problems with clean water."[19]

Falling Prices, Rising Costs, Failing Farmers

Successive agricultural revolutions greatly increased food supplies. New technologies enabled U.S. farmers to grow three times as much corn in 1985 as they had in the 1950s, probably five times as much as they could in 1920.[20] And because technology enabled farmers to convert land they had once rested in fallow or used to grow feed for horses, they could devote more of their land to corn (the largest crop in the United States) or wheat. In 1989, for example, U.S. farmers produced so much food (278.98 million tons of grain), that they could feed more than half of it to cows, export nearly one-third of it to other countries, and still have enough left over to produce cereal, toast, pasta, and corn chips for U.S. consumers at the lowest prices in the world.[21]

But while new technologies increased food supplies, they created a series of problems for farmers: falling prices, rising costs, and farm failures.

First, rising food supplies resulted in lower prices. In 1920, farmers earned $103 a ton for their wheat.[22] Rising supplies created by tractors and soybeans and falling demand during the Great Depression drove wheat prices down to $79 a ton. High demand during World War II boosted prices up to $122 a ton for wheat and $94 a ton for corn. But after the war, as Green Revolution technologies were introduced, prices fell slowly: to $95 a ton for wheat and $80 a ton for corn in 1954; to $65 a ton for wheat and $53 for corn in 1960; to $62 for wheat and $57 for corn in 1965; and to $54 for wheat and $46 for corn in 1972.

During the 1970s, prices rose again as a result of poor harvests and

grain shortages in the Soviet Union, to $110 for wheat and $79 for corn in 1974.[23] But when Soviet agriculture recovered in the late 1970s, and farmers in the European Community and the third world used Green Revolution technologies to expand their production, prices fell again, to $66 for wheat and $50 for corn in 1980, then to $50 for wheat and $46 for corn in 1984.[24] Expressed in a different way, real prices for wheat, coarse grains, and soybeans declined by one-half between 1945 and 1985.[25]

Falling prices were compounded by a second problem. The new technologies generally raised the cost of growing food, which has increased dramatically in the past fifty years for U.S. farmers. In 1940, it cost farmers about $20 billion to grow their crops. Their costs doubled during the next thirty years, to $40 billion in 1970. Then, during the 1970s, costs rose rapidly, reaching $60 billion in 1980, a 50 percent increase in just ten years.[26] Today it costs farmers three times as much to grow their crops as it did in 1940.

Farm costs doubled between 1940 and 1970 because farmers purchased new machinery and agrochemical technologies to increase production on their farms. Then, in the 1970s, they borrowed substantial sums of money to purchase land or buy new machinery and agrochemical technologies so they could grow and sell more food while prices were high. This sharply increased their costs again.

Whereas farmers, on average, drove 35-horsepower tractors in 1963, they drove 60-horsepower tractors in 1983.[27] Of course, more powerful tractors are more expensive to buy and maintain. The cost of machinery alone increased 40 percent between 1950 and 1980.[28] Farmers also greatly increased their use of agrochemical technologies, particularly chemical fertilizers and pesticides. Farmers used about 2 million tons of nitrogen fertilizer in 1950, but nearly 12 million tons in 1980, a sixfold increase, and their use of pesticides tripled between 1965 and 1985.[29] Because the cost of oil quadrupled between 1973 and 1980, the cost of operating tractors and applying oil-based fertilizers and pesticides increased sharply during the 1970s. And because farmers used about 50 percent more fertilizer to grow food, and paid more for the fertilizer they used, their fertilizer costs rose from $1.6 billion in 1970 to $8.6 billion in 1981.[30]

Of course, technology was not wholly responsible for increasing the cost of growing food in this period. Farmers themselves also borrowed money, not only to buy technology but to purchase land, especially after 1970. Rising debt sharply increased farmers' costs in the 1970s.

Between 1950 and 1970, farm debt—half of it borrowed to purchase technology and half of it to buy land—grew from $12 billion to $53 billion, a fourfold increase.[31] But during the next twelve years, it quadrupled

again, to $216 billion, a sum equal to the debt incurred by all of Latin America in this period.[32] And because the Federal Reserve raised interest rates to curb inflation in 1979, the cost of repaying debt increased sharply, raising the cost of producing food.[33] Whereas farmers collectively devoted only 4 percent of their income to pay the interest on their debts in 1950, and 23 percent in 1970, they spent 75 percent of their income on interest payments in 1980 and 98.9 percent in 1982.[34]

Of course, some farmers borrowed more heavily than others. Generally speaking, young farmers, particularly in the midwestern corn- and soy-belt states, went heavily into debt.[35] Encouraged by high prices during the Soviet grain shortages of the mid-1970s, many farmers borrowed heavily to purchase land so they could expand production. And they were encouraged to do so by bankers, who offered this same advice to both U.S. farmers and third world governments. "The [Farmers Home Administration] almost hauled you in and stuffed money down your shirt," observed Michigan farmer Morie Kranz.[36]

Bankers were eager to lend money both because commodity prices were high and because the value of farm land was increasing. On average the value of agricultural property escalated from $216 billion in 1970 to $754 billion in 1980, and an acre of farmland rose from $600 to nearly $1,200 during the decade.[37] Bankers felt confident lending money so long as the value of farmland—the collateral for their loans—was rising. But when farm prices began to fall, many farmers could not afford to meet rising interest payments and began to go bankrupt. To recoup their loans, bankers foreclosed and sold off farms. Because farmland was sold in large quantities, the price of land began to fall. As farmland prices fell, bankers became less willing to extend loans, and many farmers found it difficult to borrow the money they needed to survive.[38] Like the savings and loans during the same period, many agricultural banks also failed: 79 in 1984, 120 in 1985, and 138 in 1986.[39] But there was not a wholesale collapse of the farm credit industry because government agencies that also loaned money to farmers did not go bankrupt—though they did need a financial bailout to cover their losses during this period—so lending to farmers continued.[40]

Still, "one-fourth of all farm loans—$33.7 billion—from the Farmers Home Administration, federal land banks, production credit associations, commercial banks and life insurance companies were non-performing or delinquent in 1984 and 1985. The farm credit system lost $4.6 billion in 1985 and 1986."[41] As Kenneth Peoples, president of the Farm Credit Assistance Board, noted, "By the mid-1980s, there were from 200,000 to 300,000 farmers [one in five commercial farms] who had exhausted their

options to adjust to adversity and who failed financially. This is perhaps the outstanding statistic of the farm credit crisis."[42]

The falling prices and rising costs associated with the introduction of new technologies created a third problem for farmers: falling farm incomes. Between 1950 and 1990, farm incomes declined by half. Measured in constant 1990 dollars, net farm income declined from $80 billion in 1950 to $60 billion in 1970. Then it rose to $100 billion in 1974, before falling to $35 billion in 1980 and $20 billion in 1982. It then rose to $30 billion in 1985 and $40 billion in 1990, about one-half its 1950 level.[43]

As farm income declined, farmers were forced into bankruptcy and driven off the land. During the past sixty years, declining incomes drove the great majority of U.S. farmers out of business: "From a peak of 7 million farms in 1930, the number of farms declined to 6 million in 1945 and then to 5.6 million in 1950."[44] In 1970, only 2.9 million farms remained. By 1980, there were 2.2 million and by 1994, there were just 1.9 million, the lowest number since 1850.[45] All told, two-thirds of all U.S. farms have disappeared in the past sixty years. And the Office of Technology Assessment estimates that another one million farms will disappear by the end of the century.[46]

The elimination of four or five million farms actually understates the case because the bulk of food produced in the United States is now grown by only 125,000 farmers, only a fraction (6 percent) of the "surviving" farmers.

Although the rate at which farms disappeared would slow over time— 220,000 farms disappeared in 1951, 138,000 in 1961 and only 33,000 in 1983—farms in the 1980s were much bigger (about 400 acres on average) than farms were in the 1950s (about 200 acres on average).[47]

As farmers were driven off the land, surviving farmers purchased their land and expanded. Average farm size grew from 200 acres in 1940 to nearly 500 acres in 1990.[48] And large farmers increased their share of goods grown in the United States. As anthropologist Laura DeLind noted, "[In 1992], a mere 6 percent of all farms (less than 170,000 farms) account for 60 percent of the nation's commodity production and receive 84 percent of the net farm income."[49] And a 1991 USDA study found that 124,000 farmers owned 47 percent of all U.S. farmland.[50]

The displacement of most U.S. farms and the concentration of farming in the hands of a small group of surviving farms had important consequences for agricultural communities that depended on farming as an industry and a way of life. As the Office of Technology Assessment reported in 1991, "The shrinking number of farms and landowners will contribute further to the decline of rural communities and may affect markets for commodities and factors of production."[51]

Rural communities will be adversely affected because when farms disappear, so too do the businesses in agricultural towns. "On average, every time seven farms go under, one business serving a rural community folds," reports Dan Levitas of Rural America.[52] As Iowa farms disappeared in the 1980s, "Farm implement sales in Iowa dropped 42 percent . . . [and between 1980 and 1986] the state lost more than a third of its farm implement dealers."[53]

The decline of farm-related businesses led to declining employment in rural areas, which led to falling incomes for many farm families that had long relied on off-farm income to keep their farms. As David Goodman and Michael Redclift note,

> Rural communities in agriculturally dependent regions have been severely affected by the farm financial situation. . . . Further declines in rural wage rates and increases in unemployment could serve to harm rural places and to reduce the viability of multiple job holding among farm households, which has over the past two decades come to constitute the backbone of farm members in America.[54]

Although many people moved off the farm and into cities, many remained in agricultural areas, where they lived in poverty. "Of the 54 million people living in rural America [in 1990], over 9 million exist below the poverty line, a level of poverty that is nearly as high as in the nation's blighted inner-city neighborhoods," observed Osha Davidson.[55] And of the country's 150 worst " 'Hungry Counties,' 97 percent are in rural areas."[56]

In some regions, whole communities are drying up and blowing away. "The Great Plains is creating a new era of ghost towns," says one scholar.[57] And some counties have fewer residents today than they did in 1890. Declining rural populations—the population decreased in 77 percent of Nebraska's towns between 1980 and 1992—made it hard for those who remain. One reporter noted that "as women become scarce in rural America . . . the men left behind on farms are facing a difficult time finding marriage partners. This epidemic of bachelorhood has led some towns, like Herman, Minnesota, to advertise their surplus of marriageable men in hope of attracting female suitors."[58] Evidently, conditions today are not unlike a century ago, when frontier farmers advertised for mail-order brides.

The environment has also been adversely affected by the intensive use of new agrochemical technologies. They contribute to topsoil erosion, which strips farmland of 3 billion tons of soil every year.[59] Heavy fertil-

izer use releases nitrous oxide, which contributes to global warming (see chapter 10), and contaminates groundwater supplies, while heavy pesticide use contaminates both groundwater and food supplies.

Government officials have not been indifferent to these developments. Beginning in the 1930s, government officials took steps to address the problems associated with rising supplies, falling prices, and the displacement of U.S. farmers. But while the policies developed to deal with these problems were expensive and complex, they did little, in the end, to solve them.

Government Farm Policies

Between 1950 and the 1970s, government officials tried to deal with the problems associated with growing food supplies by introducing two kinds of policies. First, they developed programs designed to increase the demand for U.S. food around the world. Second, they developed programs to curb U.S. food supplies. By increasing demand and reducing supplies, they hoped to keep farm prices from falling too rapidly and avert a rapid displacement of farmers.

In the 1950s, government officials developed two strategies to increase demand for U.S. food around the world: (1) they helped other countries purchase U.S. food at bargain prices or gave it to them free of charge; and (2) they developed new markets for U.S. food.

"Food aid" was the first and most important way that government officials increased the demand for U.S. food in the post-World War II period. In 1954, Congress passed Public Law 480, or the Agricultural Trade Development and Assistance Act. The act was designed to "develop and expand markets for U.S. agricultural commodities, to use the abundant agricultural productivity of the United States to combat hunger . . . and to encourage economic development in the developing countries. . . ."[60]

The new law gave government officials two ways to increase the demand for U.S. food in foreign countries. Under Title I of the act, the U.S. government could sell food to foreign governments on favorable or "concessional" terms, meaning that the U.S. government could sell them food at bargain prices or loan them money at low interest rates to purchase food. The foreign governments would then sell U.S. food in their country and pay for the food (or repay the loan) in their own currency. The U.S. government would then spend the money it earned in the foreign country, using it to build "dams or roads, to buy supplies for [U.S.] military bases or any other projects that involved locally produced goods and

services. It had a multiplier effect on American foreign aid appropriated by Congress and it could be directed to projects independent of Congressional approval."[61]

U.S. officials also provided U.S. food free of charge to select countries under Title II of the act. Since 1955, the government has *given* away about 30 percent of the food exported under the act and *sold* 70 percent on "concessional" terms.[62] But agricultural economist Robert Wood argued that despite giving food away or selling it at low prices, "this program probably cost the U.S. nothing at all because the cost of price support and storage in the absence of the food aid program would have amounted to about as much as 'giving' it away."[63]

U.S. food aid helped increase foreign demand for U.S. food. As Kevin Watkins notes,

> PL 480 paved the way for U.S. world market domination and established an outlet for the farm sector's problematic surplus productive capacity. Between 1954 and 1960, the U.S. share of international grain trade rose from 26 percent to 41 percent, with concessional sales accounting for almost a third of the total. These subsidized exports became a critical source of income support for the U.S. farm sector, which relied increasingly on foreign demand.[64]

By providing cheap or free food to other countries, the U.S. government helped cultivate a taste for first world foods like wheat, which were not previously a staple part of the diet of many people around the world. Massive food aid to Taiwan during the 1950s and '60s created "such a taste for wheat" that "U.S. commercial food exports to Taiwan increased by 531 percent between 1967 and 1974," when U.S. food aid was phased out.[65]

Besides feeding people with cheap surplus food, the U.S. food aid program was also used to promote other economic and political objectives. In her study of seventy-nine countries that received food aid between 1950 and 1990, geographer Janet Kodras found that

> the relative abundance of food resources . . . and the flexibility of food aid as a foreign policy vehicle [made] PL 480 . . . an important mechanism in the pursuit of American global objectives. U.S. food aid has been used in war (the Vietnam conflict) and as a bargaining chip in peace negotiations (the Middle East Accords) . . . as long-term support for an ally (Israel throughout the post-war era) and as an immediate *quid pro quo* for favors gained (establishing military bases in Iceland during the 1950s and Somalia during the 1980s). U.S. food aid has been sent to recalcitrant socialist states (Yugoslavia

and Poland in the 1950s) and to staunchly capitalist regimes (El Salvador, Costa Rica and Honduras during the 1980s). It has been used to build commercial markets for U.S. agriculture (wheat in Taiwan) and to protect U.S. manufacturing concerns (copper in Chile). In these and many other cases . . . food aid was distributed to pivotal states in the dynamic foreign agenda of the U.S. government.[66]

A second way to increase demand was to find new markets for U.S. food in countries where people were able to pay for food. During and after World War II, U.S. farmers found ready markets for their food in Western Europe and Japan. But the recovery of farmers there and the adoption of food self-sufficiency policies, which sometimes excluded U.S. agricultural imports, slowed demand for U.S. food in other first world countries.

In the 1950s and '60s, government officials provided credits and loans to countries that did not need direct or indirect food aid so they could more easily purchase U.S. food.[67] During the 1960s, they sought to stimulate demand in third world countries, and by 1971, countries in Latin America, Asia, and Africa (excluding Argentina and Japan) "accounted for almost half of world imports, on the eve of the first large Soviet purchases."[68] But government officials were reluctant to sell food to communist countries, even though their demand for U.S. food was strong.

As a result of Cold War policies, U.S. government officials did not actively seek new markets in communist countries until the 1970s. But then they did with new enthusiasm. During the 1970s, they also increased sales to East Asian countries such as South Korea and Taiwan, where rapid economic growth increased the demand for food.[69]

While government officials tried to increase the demand for U.S. food, they also tried to curb U.S. food supplies by paying farmers to take land out of production, imposing tariffs on some imported foods to keep domestic supplies low (and prices high), and using subsidy and loan programs to displace farmers slowly.

Government officials tried to reduce food supplies by encouraging or requiring farmers to take land out of production, particularly land that was vulnerable to soil erosion, or by helping farmers store surplus grain in silos. In bad years, when harvests were poor, or in good years, when demand was strong, these two methods of reducing supply were little used. Acreage restrictions were typically lifted in bad years so farmers could produce more to make up possible shortfalls. And they were abandoned in very good years to meet new demand. During the 1960s, between 10 and 20 million acres were idled under various government

programs to reduce supplies, but this land was brought back into production when Soviet grain shortages dramatically increased the demand for U.S. grain in the mid-1970s.[70]

The trouble with acreage-reduction programs was that farmers often took some of their land out of production, then used more fertilizer on the land that remained, thereby actually increasing the volume of food they produced. As Peoples explained,

> Envision the paradox of a mid–1950s farmer receiving a $1,000 subsidy from the U.S. government for setting aside 50 acres of corn ground to reduce the grain surplus, and then using the subsidy check as a down payment on a $5,000 tractor to make . . . the farm more efficient and productive. In effect, the government provided the down payment and then the banker provided the remainder of the financing that enabled the farmer to invest in new machinery to produce higher grain yields on the remaining planted acres.[71]

When too much grain was produced, and falling prices threatened, the government helped farmers store their surplus in the farmer's own silos by offering nonrecourse loans. The government provided low-interest loans so farmers could survive until they sold their grains at a later date for a higher price.[72] "The non-recourse feature meant that a farmer who obtained the loan had a choice of two alternatives: to deliver the farm product (the security for the loan) in lieu of payment or to pay off the loan in cash with accumulated interest and storage costs, if any."[73] Although this program reduced supplies by helping farmers store their surpluses, it was limited by the amount of storage space available to farmers, and this space was insufficient to store supplies that accumulated in the United States during the postwar period.

In a variation on the theme of storing surplus food, the government also bought some commodities like dairy products and either stored them or gave them away through food stamp and school lunch programs in order to reduce the volume of milk and cheese available on the market.[74]

In a second set of farm programs, government officials curbed domestic U.S. supplies by using tariffs (taxes on imported goods) or quotas (limiting the volume of imported produce) to restrict food imports. Restricting foreign imports would cause domestic supplies to be smaller, and prices higher, than they would have been otherwise. Under Section 22 of the Agriculture Adjustment Act of 1951, Congress allowed government officials to impose tariffs or quotas on any farm commodity whose supply the government was trying to manage, and a 1955 amendment allowed officials to place restrictions on any imported foods that interfered with U.S. subsidy programs.[75]

In practice, the government placed stiff tariffs and quotas on dairy products and tobacco during this period, while putting low tariffs on grain. Tariffs on tobacco were very high—50.5 percent in 1988— "reflecting and enhancing the success of the tobacco lobby in acquiring strong support in Congress," while imported dairy products had tariff rates of 12.3 percent and grains of only 2.3 percent.[76]

Although many farmers would have liked the government to reduce the supplies of other food in this way, the government has been unwilling to use tariffs to limit supplies because officials believed that the use of tariffs by other countries would limit overall demand. And the government tried throughout the postwar period to increase overseas demand for burgeoning U.S. food supplies. So it used tariffs to reduce the supply of only a few, politically important crops. Because tobacco and dairy farmers were concentrated in just a few states, they had more political clout than farmers scattered across many different states.

The third important way that government programs limited food supplies was by reducing the number of farms through subsidy and loan programs. These programs were designed to weed out "inefficient" farmers and take their land out of production, thereby reducing food supplies.

During the postwar period, falling farm prices and rising costs would have rapidly ruined many farmers, creating a 1930s-style crisis in the 1950s and '60s. To avoid this, government officials used subsidy and loan programs, developed in the Agricultural Act of 1947, to raise the price that farmers received through "deficiency payments."[77] Each year, U.S. Department of Agriculture (USDA) officials calculated what it would cost the "majority" of farmers (not all farmers) to produce their crop.[78] The government then agreed to pay farmers the difference between the low market price and the higher "target price," a price that was supposed to cover their costs and provide them with enough income to live. But many farmers, a "minority," had higher costs. Perhaps they were more deeply in debt, or their land was more difficult to farm, or they had higher living expenses (medical bills, college tuition for their children). In these cases, government "deficiency payments" did not cover their costs. So every year, a minority of "inefficient" farmers were forced out of farming. Because government officials typically set target prices *below* what many families needed to earn to survive—government officials usually set prices about one-third less than farmers received during the "golden years" of farm prices (1910–14, 1940–52)—about one hundred fifty thousand farmers were driven into bankruptcy and forced off the land every year between 1950 and 1970.

The eviction of millions of farmers occurred *despite* large government

payments, or subsidies, to farmers. "The annual budget of farm programs had risen from an average of $2 billion in the 1950s to over $5 billion by the mid-1960s," writes James Wessel.[79] So despite large subsidies, or rather because of the way government subsidy programs were designed, one-half of all U.S. farmers were forced out of farming between 1950 and 1970, the number of farms falling from six million to three million in just twenty years.[80] So while the government spent billions of dollars on subsidy programs—$6.2 billion in 1968—the program kept half of the farmers in business but helped drive the other half *out* of business. [81]

Many government officials and industry leaders argued that "inefficient" farmers *should* go out of business. They reasoned that the land of bankrupt farmers would be taken out of production, food supplies reduced, and the farmers who survived would eventually be able to earn money without the need for government subsidy. The Committee for Economic Development, a corporate think tank, recommended in 1962 that "excess resources (primarily people) . . . move rapidly out of agriculture" and urged the government to adopt a program that "would involve moving off the farm about two million of the present farm labor force, plus a number equal to a large part of the new entrants who would otherwise join the farm labor force in the next five years."[82]

During the next ten years, nearly two million farmers left farming as a result of falling prices, rising costs, and government subsidy programs designed to smooth and facilitate this process. As agricultural economist Jane Adams has written, government policies "adopted in 1954 allowed commodity prices to decline, with a concomitant sharp drop in farm income."[83] Total farm income fell by half, from $70 billion in 1950 to $35 billion in 1970 (in 1982 dollars).[84] But because the total farm income was divided between a smaller number of farms (three million fewer farms), the income of the remaining farmers increased slightly, from about $10 billion to $12 billion in the same period.[85] As Adams noted, "Only the larger, technologically advanced farmers with large volume and increasing production could survive as farm prices fell."[86]

But while government subsidy programs both displaced "inefficient" farmers and conserved "efficient" ones, the removal of three million farmers did not greatly reduce foods supplies because the "efficient" farmers frequently purchased the land of their bankrupt neighbors and expanded their own operations, producing the same or even greater volume of food on bigger farms.

Government farm policy changed dramatically in the 1970s. Because poor Soviet harvests greatly increased the demand for food, government officials no longer viewed food surplus as the central problem for U.S.

agriculture. Instead they thought the primary problem in subsequent decades would be one of shortage. As a result, they radically changed their approach to agriculture. Rather than trying to reduce U.S. food supplies, they encouraged farmers to expand production. And rather than stimulate demand through food aid programs, they cut back dramatically on the provision of cheap or free food to others and demanded instead that countries now pay for higher priced U.S. food, a development that forced many poor countries to borrow heavily to pay for food imports.

To expand U.S. food supplies, government officials curtailed soil conservation and land set-aside programs, and encouraged farmers to plant the 23.8 million acres of farmland idled in 1972.[87] They offered easy credit and low-interest loans to farmers so they could purchase land, expand production, purchase new machinery and agrochemical inputs, and increase yields.

During this period, there was little need for deficiency payments and nonrecourse loans because, for most crops, the market price regularly exceeded both the government's target price and the cost of producing food for the vast majority of U.S. farmers. The government did not scrap these programs, but they fell into disuse. "With high market prices, loan rates and target prices became irrelevant."[88]

To take advantage of sharply rising world demand, the U.S. government also abandoned its hostility to selling food to communist countries and aggressively pursued new markets in communist countries and rapidly developing countries like South Korea and Taiwan. U.S. agricultural sales were greatly assisted by Nixon's 1971 dollar devaluation, which enabled U.S. grain exporters to undercut other important first world grain producers like Australia, Argentina, and the European Community and to increase the U.S. share of world grain markets. As a result, "exports of agricultural commodities exploded during the 1970s," increasing sixfold, from about $7.3 billion in 1970 to $43.3 billion in 1981.[89] The share of world wheat exports increased from 36 percent in 1970 to 51 percent in 1980, and its share of coarse grain exports rose from 40 percent to 72 percent in the same period.[90]

During the 1970s, the U.S. government virtually abandoned its food aid program, forcing third world countries to purchase food at rising world prices, food that had previously been sold or given to them on concessional terms.

In 1965, the U.S. government had delivered 18 million tons of food to poor countries through the PL 480 program. U.S. officials reduced this to about 10 million tons in the 1970s.[91] But when surging demand pushed up food prices in 1972, the government cut way back so that this food

could enter commercial markets. By 1974, the United States provided only 3 million tons of food through this program, and two-thirds of this went to only two countries: South Vietnam and Cambodia.[92]

As U.S. food aid disappeared, third world countries that had come to rely on first world imports were forced to buy food on global markets at world prices. To do this, many of them borrowed money from the World Bank and commercial banks in first world countries to pay for increasingly costly food imports. Poland, Argentina, Mexico, and Brazil made major grain purchases during this period, using money borrowed from multilateral and commercial banks to finance grain imports.[93] As we have seen, this contributed to rising indebtedness in the 1970s.

But the high prices of the 1970s did not last and food prices fell again at the end of the decade, leading to what the USDA called "the worst economic crisis [for agriculture] since the Great Depression."[94] As a result, the U.S. government reintroduced policies it had abandoned in the 1970s and introduced some new ones.

To reduce supplies, government officials renewed land set-aside measures in 1977 and took further steps in 1983 through the Payment in Kind (PIK) program.[95] "Taking land out of production, reducing supplies and thereby boosting prices are old methods of farm income support," Joseph Belden notes. "The PIK program renewed this approach by offering farmers not cash, but government-owned surplus grain, in exchange for taking acreage out of production. Farmers could then sell the grain or hold it in hopes that prices would rise."[96] In 1983, for example, farmers took 82 million acres out of production, 36 percent of the total, and enrolled in the PIK program.[97]

As prices fell, the government's deficiency program kicked back into gear. But because the government wanted to drive "excess" farmers off the land as a way of reducing food supplies, it set very low target prices that did not cover the costs of many farmers, and it made farm credit difficult to obtain and placed onerous conditions on outstanding debts. U.S. farm debt quadrupled, from $52.8 billion in 1970 to $206.5 billion in 1983.[98] Higher interest rates in the 1980s forced heavily indebted farmers into bankruptcy.

But while U.S. officials renewed or modified long-standing programs to reduce supplies, they also spent considerable effort and money to reduce the supplies of *other* first world farmers, particularly farmers in the European Community.

Like the United States, the European Community had used technological innovation and government subsidies to increase supplies produced by European farmers. And by the early 1980s, they were exporting grain

in large quantities and, for the first time since World War II, competing directly with U.S. farmers for markets in second and third world countries.

Although U.S. farmers could produce food more cheaply, on average, than EC farmers, the EC could deliver food for the same price because it provided more generous subsidies to EC farmers. So the EC could sell at low, world-market prices and still provide a livable income for a majority of EC farmers.[99] In 1980, for example, the EC spent about 83 percent more on its farm program than the U.S. government.[100] This enabled EC farmers to compete for Soviet grain sales, and by 1984, EC and U.S. farmers were "each selling 6.1 mmt of wheat to the USSR."[101]

While subsidies put EC and U.S. farmers on equal footing, the rise in the value of the U.S. dollar after 1980, a strengthening due primarily to high U.S. interest rates, made it more difficult for U.S. farmers to compete in export markets. So to deal with these problems, U.S. officials took two steps in 1985.

First, they adopted the Export Enhancement Program (EEP) in May 1985, subsequently modified by the Food Security Act and Food Security Adjustments Act of 1986. Under the EEP, officials made government-owned food stock available to exporters at no cost so they could more easily compete with the EC. As Katie Snoden, an economist at the Rocky Mountain Institute, explained,

> If Brazil wants to buy 300,000 bushels of wheat . . . but will do so only if it is allowed to pay, say two-thirds of the U.S. market price for it, [U.S.] exporters can petition the [USDA to give them] 100,000 bushels of free wheat. This allows the exporters to buy [other] American commodities at the higher U.S. market rate, and sell them abroad at the lower world price and still make a profit.[102]

Of course, the use of new export subsidies to sell U.S. grain was matched by the European Community, resulting in a subsidy war between the two major first world food suppliers. U.S. officials believed they could use export subsidies to force up EC subsidies to a point where they would become onerous to European taxpayers. U.S. Agriculture Secretary John Block described this strategy as "squeezing the CAP until the pips squeak."[103]

The EEP did raise the cost of farm subsidies to the EC. "In 1986, for example, the EC subsidy for wheat exports was $82.68 per metric ton, while the U.S. subsidy was only $26.56; in January 1987, it rose to $120.25 while the American subsidy rose to $42.89."[104]

The effect of this, and the rising cost of both deficiency payments (a result of rapidly falling prices) and the PIK program (the result of providing commodities to farmers who had removed huge amounts of land from production), was to raise the cost of U.S. agricultural subsidies to $30 billion in 1986, ten times the 1980 level.[105] The cost of EC subsidies meanwhile rose to about $40 billion.[106] Although subsidies hurt the European Community, they probably hurt the United States more because the United States was experiencing massive budget deficits and growing debt in this period while EC countries had much lower deficits.

As a second step, the Reagan administration initiated a second devaluation of the dollar in 1985 through the Plaza accords. U.S. officials hoped that this would improve farmers' ability to sell food on foreign markets. By waging a subsidy war with the EC and devaluing the U.S. dollar, the Reagan administration hoped to reduce the supplies of other first world farmers.

During the mid-1980s, government officials tried to reduce the supplies of U.S. farmers through subsidy and acreage restriction programs, and limit the supplies of EC farmers. But U.S. supplies mounted and EC farmers continued to produce vast quantities of food. In 1991, for example, the EC had stockpiled 23.5 mmt of grain and 290,000 tons of butter, while the U.S. government in 1985 had stockpiled 500 million bushels of wheat and 1.3 million tons of dairy products at a cost of $400 million.[107] The cost of first world food subsidy programs rose, contributing to increasing budget deficits in the United States. The U.S. share of world food markets did not greatly improve despite subsidy programs and a massive dollar devaluation. The USDA reported, "Due to a combination of a weaker dollar and export subsidies, agricultural exports turned up again in quantity in 1987 and made further gains during 1988 in both quantity and value. But rising imports have kept the agricultural balance of trade lower than in the early 1980s."[108]

Between 1980 and 1987, the U.S. share of world agricultural exports had declined from 18 percent to 12 percent, while the EC's share grew from 35 percent to 39 percent. And in the important wheat market, the U.S. share fell from 44.7 percent in 1981 to only 28.6 percent in 1986.[109]

Because these remedies proved ineffective, U.S. officials developed a new approach to the problem of excess supply and insufficient demand. They began negotiating free trade agreements (FTAs) that would reduce supply and increase demand simultaneously (see chapter 9).

In negotiations to revise multilateral trade agreements with more than one hundred countries through the General Agreement on Tariffs and Trade (GATT) and to create new bilateral trade agreements first with

Canada (the U.S.-Canada Free Trade Agreement) and then with Canada and Mexico (the North American Free Trade Agreement, NAFTA), U.S. officials argued that agricultural subsidies would be abolished or greatly reduced and that tariff barriers on food and other commodities eliminated.

U.S. officials reasoned that if first world subsidies were eliminated (a development that would save the U.S. Treasury billions of dollars annually), U.S. farmers and grain producers in Canada, Australia, and Argentina would regain their "natural" competitive advantages over EC farmers, who were more heavily subsidized. As subsidies were reduced and then eliminated, many small farmers in Europe, particularly in France (the major farm producer in Europe), would be forced out of business. And the elimination of other first world suppliers would be greatly reduced. Whereas U.S. officials had long tried to displace inefficient farmers in Iowa and Kansas, in the late 1980s they sought to eliminate inefficient farmers in France and Japan.

U.S. officials also reasoned that if tariffs on food imports could be eliminated around the world, the demand for U.S. food would greatly increase, particularly in Japan, where high tariffs restricted the sale of U.S. food in its lucrative markets. If U.S. farmers could sell more agricultural produce and beef to Japan, U.S. trade deficits might also be reduced.

Lengthy negotiations, which began in 1987, were concluded in 1993 with the adoption of NAFTA and the signing of a revised GATT in 1994. Although measures that would reduce agricultural subsidies and eliminate tariff barriers were bitterly contested by EC negotiators and EC farmers, which delayed negotiations for several years, the agreement reached substantially reduced subsidies and eliminated many trade barriers (see chapter 9).

Farmers and Consumers

The problem with government policies since World War II is that food supplies grew and prices fell despite their efforts to increase demand and curb supplies. One U.S. official described the failure of government efforts to deal with mounting food supplies in the 1950s:

> We sold what we could for cash. What we couldn't sell for cash we would for credit. What we couldn't sell for dollars we sold for foreign currency. What we couldn't get money for we bartered. What we couldn't get anything

for we gave away—what we couldn't export by any means we stored. And still the stocks increased.[110]

In the end, government policies did not help demand keep pace with rising supplies, did not prevent prices from falling, did nothing to reduce farm costs, and did not prevent farmers from being displaced.

Throughout this period, government officials assumed that the displacement of millions of inefficient farmers would take land out of production, reduce the total amount of food grown, and shrink the supply of food. But the ruin of millions of farmers did little to reduce growing food supplies in the United States and around the world. Indeed, the postwar period is quite remarkable in that millions of farmers were eliminated, agricultural communities undermined, and the environment compromised *without* substantially reducing food supplies.

The displacement of millions of farmers was an inefficient way to deal with rising food supplies because it did little to slow the introduction of new agricultural technologies, which were primarily responsible for increasing food supplies and lowering prices. And it was unfair because it eliminated small farmers and helped concentrate food production in the hands of very large farmers—not because they were "better" farmers but simply because they were "bigger." As a 1980 USDA study pointed out, "Growth you now see in farm size has little to do with efficiency. Above about $40,000 to $50,000 in gross sales . . . there are no greater efficiencies of scale. Medium-sized farms are as efficient as the large farms."[111]

While the falling prices associated with successive technological revolutions were bad for a majority of U.S. farmers, they did benefit urban consumers, though not as much as one might expect. Although the prices farmers received fell by more than one-half between 1950 and 1990, the real prices consumers paid at the grocery store did not fall nearly as far.

U.S. consumers spent 20 percent of their disposable income on food in the 1950s and only 14 percent in the mid-1980s.[112] But if the price they paid for food had declined by one-half, as it did for farmers in this period, consumers would have spent only 10 percent of their income on food. So while consumers generally benefited from falling farm prices, they have not benefited as much as they might. They did not because the food-processing industry has not lowered its prices as rapidly as farmers have lowered theirs, and the gap between the price of food at the farm gate and the grocery shelf has grown. In 1950, farmers received about 50 cents on every dollar paid by consumers at the checkout counter.[113] But by 1987, they earned only 25 cents on every dollar spent on food by consumers.[114]

The grain-trade and food-processing industry has been able to increase

the gap between farm prices and sticker prices because it is fairly concentrated, which means that it can bargain down farmers while maintaining consumer demand for its products. Because businesses that purchase and produce food are relatively few in number, while farmers are quite numerous (there are still 1.9 million farmers, despite the fact that four or five million have been put out of business), they are able to drive a hard bargain with farmers and keep prices low. They are in much the same position with food retailers—grocery stores—and consumers. The concentration of industry and the use of massive advertising to maintain consumer demand means businesses are able to keep sticker prices higher than they would if the food-processing industry were less concentrated and more competitive. Between 1950 and 1978, the fifty largest food-processing firms increased their control of industry assets from 36 percent to 64 percent. And grocery chains of more than one hundred stores increased their share of all supermarket sales from 27 percent to 41 percent.[115]

As a result of growing concentration in the industry, food processors were able to increase the gap between farm prices and supermarket prices, despite an overall reduction in the amount that urban consumers paid for food. "Between 1980 and 1987, when farmer's earnings on the wheat in a box of cereal fell by 33 percent, the consumer price of cereal rose 84 percent."[116] As DeLind noted, "In 1990 alone, grain prices declined an average of 11 percent, but commercial cereal prices increased by 6 percent. . . . Stated in a somewhat different manner, a farmer must produce and sell 104 pounds of corn to buy a 25 oz. package of frosted flakes."[117] Put another way, the price that consumers pay for cereal has increased from $2.40 per pound in 1988 to $3.07 per pound in 1992, this at a time of falling grain prices.[118]

In contrast to farmers, who have seen their costs rise and their prices fall, which has led to declining farm incomes, "the 50 food processing firms listed in a *Forbes* magazine industry survey had an average return on equity of 15.1 percent from 1981 to 1986."[119]

Falling farm prices have been good for the grain-trade and food-processing industry, and beneficial to consumers, though less so, and to the industries that employ consumers as workers. Other industries benefit from lower farm and food prices either because it lowers the cost of their raw materials (cornstarch is used as glue in the packaging industry) or because it helps keep wages low. But falling farm prices, coupled with rising costs, have not been good for the majority of U.S. farmers.

Third World Hunger

Technological revolutions have increased world food supplies and allowed third world farmers to make real gains. World food supplies have increased from 631 million tons in 1950 to 1,650 million tons in 1984, a 260 percent increase.[120] As a result, there is more food available *despite* rapid population growth (see chapter 10). The amount of grain available per person has increased from 251 kilograms in 1950 to 380 kilograms in 1985.[121] "History records no increase in food production that was remotely comparable in scale, speed, spread or duration," British economist Michael Lipton has written.[122] Nonetheless, hunger is also widespread. In 1988, the World Bank calculated that one billion people were hungry and malnourished, four times as many people as live in the United States, one of every five people living on the planet.[123]

The number of hungry people is the subject of considerable debate, with estimates of world hunger ranging from 550 million to 1.3 billion. But whatever the exact figure, people in the third world are hungry *not* because population growth has outstripped the available food supply. The problem for people in the third world has been that their effective demand for food has not kept pace with rising supplies, despite rapid population growth. As T. Kelley White, a USDA official, put it in 1989, "Food crises [in the third world] will likely continue to be . . . the consequences of . . . lack of effective demand, rather than a failure of supply."[124]

"On a global basis, it has become an indisputable fact of our times that hunger can no longer be blamed on a shortage of food," writes Joseph Collins, codirector of the Institute for Food and Development Policy. "The telling fact is that in the early 1980s, the number of hungry people was accelerating precisely at a time when global food stocks were building up to record levels."[125] And he notes that it would not take a large amount of food, "only 15 to 20 million tons . . . of the 1,660 million tons [produced in 1987] . . . to raise the diets of . . . the world's undernourished to adequate levels."[126]

According to Collins,

a mere 5.6 percent of the country's food supply, if eaten by the hungry, would make an active life possible for everyone. For Indonesia . . . only 2 percent of the country's food supply would make the difference. . . . A redistribution of only 1.6 percent of . . . Brazil's [supply] would meet all the needs of the 86 million Brazilians estimated in 1984 to be undernourished.[127]

But if world food supplies have increased even faster than the world's population, and if the world's hungry could be fed with a fraction of total supplies, why are so many people hungry?

There are several reasons. First, while new agricultural technologies increased food supplies, their introduction displaced many small farmers. Second, new technologies were typically used to expand the production of export crops and animal feed. This increased the total volume of food but also reduced the domestic supply of staple foods, which poor people eat to survive. And third, the debt crisis reduced incomes and raised prices for poor people, making it more difficult for them to purchase the food that was being produced in ever-greater volume. These developments undermined the poor's "entitlement" to food, which reduced effective demand.

The concept of declining "entitlements" to food was introduced by the economist Amartya Sen in his 1981 book, *Poverty and Famines*. In it he argued that postwar famines were not usually the result of food "shortages" or the product of inadequate food "distribution." He notes that many devastating famines occurred despite the fact that harvests were good and food was widely distributed and readily available:

> Indeed, some of the worst famines have taken place with no significant decline in food availability per head. To say that starvation depends "not merely" on food supply but also on its "distribution" would be correct enough, though not remarkably helpful. The important question then would be: what determines distribution of food between different sections of the community?[128]

According to Sen, people starved because their "entitlement" to land to grow food or income to buy food changed as a result of *economic* developments. He argues that "the entitlement approach views famines as economic disasters, not just as food crises."[129]

The Economics of Famine

During the Great Bengal Famine of 1943, when 1.5 million people died, Sen found that people starved not because harvests were poor—"the [food] supply for 1943 was only about 5 percent lower than the average of the preceding five years"—but because inflation induced by massive government spending on the British war effort in India raised rice prices dramatically, while the wages of agricultural workers who did not own

land to produce food and of fishermen and rural craft workers did not rise to keep pace with increasing food costs.[130] The price of rice, using 1939–40 as an index of 100, increased from 109 in 1941 to 385 in 1942, while the wages of rural agricultural and craft workers rose only from 110 to 125 in the same years. This meant that their ability to purchase enough rice to survive fell precipitously.[131] Poor sharecroppers did not suffer, even though they may have been equally "poor" (in terms of annual income), because their "income" was paid in rice, so its rising price did not affect them.[132] When famine became widespread among rural wage laborers, farmers and merchants also began hoarding rice, further increasing its price. High prices encouraged farmers to grow more rice in 1943 and 1944. The irony of this was that "while the famine killed millions . . . Bengal was producing the largest rice crop in history in 1943."[133] The problem for rural workers was that "institutional arrangements, including wage systems, were slow to adjust to the new reality [of higher prices]."[134] In this case, inflation, not food shortage, led to famine for many.

Thirty years later, in 1974, Bengal, now Bangladesh, was again struck by famine. Although the famine followed a large-scale flood, the harvest was good and food was widely available. The problem this time was that agricultural workers could not work during the summer flood, at the time of their highest annual earnings, and their incomes fell. Farmers and merchants, meanwhile, began hoarding food because they *thought* that the harvest would be poor and that prices would rise. As a result, prices rose at a time when the incomes of many workers had fallen. The fact that farmers had increasingly paid their workers in cash, rather than in kind (in food), made matters worse. As Sen notes, cash wages were "more modern" but they made wage-dependent workers "more vulnerable."[135]

The situation in the 1972–74 Ethiopian famine was the result of somewhat different circumstances.[136] Although a drought reduced food supplies somewhat in one part of the country—the Wollo region—there was plenty of food in the country as a whole, and food prices did *not* rise. The problem was not that food prices rose, but that poor people's entitlement to income to buy food or to land to grow food was reduced.[137] Many tenant farmers were evicted, household servants fired, and cow herders prevented from grazing their cows on land recently brought under cultivation for commercial export crops. "About 50,000 hectares of good land in the Awash Valley were 'developed' in 1970–71 for growing . . . cotton and sugar by a few big companies—mostly foreign owned," Sen records.[138] As a result, these groups lost the means to purchase or grow food. Cattle herders who had been deprived of access to traditional grazing land tried to sell their cows before they died from the drought. But

this glutted the market and caused beef prices to fall, which meant that their ability to purchase grain declined substantially. "The pastoralist, hit by the drought, was decimated by the market mechanism," says Sen.[139] "A remarkable feature of the Wollo famine is that food prices in general rose very little, and people were dying of starvation even when food was selling at prices not very different from pre-drought levels."[140]

Although famines of the kind that Sen describes still occur with alarming frequency around the world—most recently in Somalia—*hunger* is the more common problem for poor people in the third world. Hunger has increased because, borrowing from Sen, the poor's entitlement to food has been eroded by technological developments that displaced farmers and reduced the production of staple foods, and by developments that reduced the income of poor people in different settings.

Reducing Entitlements to Land and Food

The introduction of Green Revolution technologies in the third world helped some farmers to produce more food, earn more money, and expand their landholdings. But the introduction of new mechanical and agrochemical technologies benefited some farmers more than others. Because Green Revolution technologies were designed to increase the production of some first world crops—wheat, corn, and soybeans—farmers who grew these crops realized substantial gains, while farmers growing "traditional" staple foods—beans, cassava, millet—found that the new technologies did not greatly assist them. As Keith Griffin noted,

> Far too much attention has been devoted to the effects of the "Green Revolution" in increasing output of one or two commodities and not enough attention has been given to the performance of the agricultural sector as a whole. For example, in India between 1964 and 1969, wheat production increased 90 percent, but rice production increased by only 4 percent, i.e., less than the population.[141]

Typically, "the development of high-yielding varieties of millet and sorghum has lagged far behind, even though these traditional food crops are considerably more drought-resistant and nutritionally balanced than maize."[142]

Large farmers growing new technology-friendly crops also benefited from better access to government credit and training programs, while their ability to produce on a large scale gave them greater market access

and higher prices.[143] Agricultural economist Andrew Pearse has called these collective benefits:

> the talents-effect after the well-known Biblical parable in which it is re-
> counted that one servant receives ten talents [a form of money] from his
> master and is able to invest and prosper, while the insecurity of his humbler
> fellow restrains him from utilizing the single talent entrusted to him, which
> is wrathfully reappropriated by the master and given to the successful inves-
> tor: "For unto everyone that hath shall be given, and he shall have abun-
> dance; but for him that hath not shall be taken away even that which he
> hath." (Matthew 25, 29)[144]

As a result, "the new technology has hastened the process of [class] differ-
entiation [and] served to consolidate the rich peasantry as a powerful and
dominant class" in many third world countries.[145] The expansion of technology-assisted farmers has concentrated land into fewer hands and displaced millions of farmers from the land. In northwestern Mexico, for
instance, "the birthplace of Green Revolution technologies, the average
farm size over 20 years jumped from 200 to 2,000 acres, with over three-
quarters of those working in agriculture deprived of owning, or even renting, any land at all," notes Collins.[146] "The highly skewed landownership
patterns now found in countries like Brazil, where 2 percent of the farmers own 57 percent of the arable land and more than half of all agricultural
families own none, are but the most obvious legacies of such shifts,"
writes Lester Brown, head of the Worldwatch Institute.[147]

Because small, wealthy elites and prosperous, technology-assisted
farmers have increased their ownership of and control over land in the
postwar period, millions of farmers have been displaced from the land.
"A 1975 . . . UN survey of 83 Third World countries found that typically
only 3 percent of all landowners control a staggering 79 percent of all
farmland, depriving most rural families of owning any land at all," says
Collins.[148]

What happens to third world farmers displaced by the concentration of
landownership? Many of them remain in agricultural areas as landless
workers, seeking employment on large farms and estates. In India, for
example, the number of rural *households* (on average six people per household) who neither own nor lease land nearly doubled between 1961 and
1981, rising from 15 million to 26 million, meaning that an additional 66
million people had become landless in that period.[149] Of course, as Sen
has noted, it is this group of people who are particularly vulnerable to
famine when employment declines or food prices rise sharply.

Because farmers using new machinery and agrochemical technologies typically need less labor and fewer workers than farms using traditional methods, there is not enough work in agricultural areas to support displaced farmers. "In the very areas of northwest Mexico where agricultural production boomed, the average number of days of employment for a farm worker shrank from 190 to 100" between 1973 and 1983 as a result of the introduction of tractors.[150]

When there is little work in agricultural areas, many displaced or landless farmers move in other directions, either to marginal land or to cities.

Many displaced farmers move to more marginal forest, desert, or mountainous lands, where they try to grow subsistence crops. In Brazil, for example, farmers displaced from the fertile São Francisco valley migrate to the Amazon; in Central America they move out of the valleys and up into the hills and mountains; in Sahelian Africa they move into arid grasslands; and in Indonesia they move from the heavily populated island of Java to one of the country's many distant and less populated islands. In some countries, like Brazil and Indonesia, the governments actively encourage "transmigration" programs, providing migrating households with minimal supplies, transportation, and the promise of free land on distant "homesteads."[151] They do this in part because many farmers displaced from agricultural settings would otherwise crowd into the cities, swelling already large urban populations.

Of course farming on marginal land can have serious environmental consequences. The burning of rain forest and the raising of cattle contribute to global climate change (see chapter 11). And farming on marginal land often depletes and erodes the soil, reducing the ability of farmers to grow food. Eventually farmers have to move to new land and start again, usually with the same results.

Throughout the third world, the influx of people displaced from agricultural regions has increased the size of cities. In Africa, for instance, Cairo was the only city with more than one million inhabitants in 1950. But by 1980, there were nineteen cities with one million people and by the end of the century, demographers expect there to be more than sixty such cities, a development that cannot be attributed to population growth alone.[152]

The problem is that few countries have been able to provide employment for displaced agricultural workers in urban areas. And this group, like landless agricultural workers, can be adversely affected by economic developments that reduce employment opportunities (such as recession), or raise food prices (inflation), or increase the cost of imported food (currency devaluations). Displaced poor become vulnerable to hunger and famine.

A second problem is that the new agricultural technologies have primarily been used to expand the production of export crops and animal feed, an expansion that has reduced the availability of "staple" foods or "subsistence" crops.

Most third world farmers grow "staple" crops, foods that comprise the heart of their daily diet. The foods that people eat on a daily basis vary around the world, depending on climate and custom. People in Latin America depend on maize (corn) and beans, in sub-Saharan Africa they rely on sorghum, millet, and maize, in northern Africa on wheat, and in India they rely on rice in wet regions and sorghum and millet in dry parts of the country.[153]

Prior to World War II, when many countries were ruled as colonies by European states, farmers in some parts of what is now the third world were encouraged or forced to grow crops that could be exported to foreign markets: bananas from Central America, cotton from Egypt and Sudan, sugar from the Caribbean, and rubber from Southeast Asia. Generally, the amount of land given to the production of these export crops remained relatively small as a proportion of the total. But as government officials in newly independent countries tried to develop their economies after World War II, they expanded the production of export crops so they could obtain the first world currencies they needed to purchase machinery and import other capital and consumer goods.

By 1975, countries like Costa Rica, Panama, Ghana, and Uganda devoted more land to the production of export crops like coffee, bananas, cocoa, and cotton than to staple cereals that people in those countries typically consume. In extreme cases, like the island country of Mauritius, 90 percent of all arable land was given over to the production of just one crop: sugar.[154] And countries like Brazil, Colombia, Egypt, and Indonesia devote one-third or more of their land to export crops.[155]

In the postwar period, many countries began producing "new" export crops, such as soybeans. Brazil, which grew only 61,000 tons of soybeans in 1950, increased its production to more than 15 million tons by 1980 on its way to becoming one of the world's largest producers.[156] Brazil's soybean crop is either exported or used to feed cows, which are then exported (see chapter 11).

In Brazil and throughout the third world, farmers are increasingly growing crops that feed cows, not people. In a study of twenty-four third world countries in 1990, economist David Barkin found that "at least 5 percent of the total land cultivated in grain showed a shift from human cereal production to commercial grain production for other uses in the past 25 years."[157] He discovered that the "most accelerated rates of con-

version from food to feed [were] occurring in Mexico and Central America, upper South America, eastern and southeastern Asia, northern Africa and western Asia. . . . ."[158]

Large farmers in third world countries grow animal feed rather than food crops because the local demand for food crops is weak, and because cows turn plentiful feed into a higher value food: beef, which can be sold to first world consumers or eaten by domestic elites.

The production of feed rather than food crops has increased dramatically in the past twenty years. In 1970, only 11 percent of the food produced by third world countries was used to feed cows. But by 1990, more than 18 percent was grown for animal feed.[159]

Of course, as farmers grew more feed crops, less of the land was available to produce staple grains. As farmers grew more feed between 1961 and 1986, Barkin found that the production of staple cereals fell: 5 percent in Brazil, 26 percent in Colombia, and 40 percent in Venezuela; 10 percent in South Africa and 16 percent in Tanzania; 10 percent in Thailand and 11 percent in the Philippines.[160]

As feed supplies increased and subsistence supplies declined, the price of staple foods rose.[161] Barkin says of these developments in Colombia, "retail prices for all food grains rose dramatically during the [inflationary 1970s], but prices of [the staple] maize rose faster than did those of rice and wheat."[162]

The increased production of feed crops during the past twenty years, or, in the 1980s, of fresh fruits and vegetables that are shipped from third world countries during their summer season to first world consumers during their winter, or of crops to produce ethanol for car fuel, makes staple food less available and more expensive to the third world poor.[163] As a result of these developments, the poor's entitlement to subsistence food supplies is slowly diminished. "The middle classes and wealthy eat an increasingly rich diet," Barkin concludes, "while undernutrition and malnutrition are common in poor farming communities and urban slums throughout the third world."[164]

The irony is that while Green Revolution technologies increase the volume of world food supplies, they have displaced small farmers and reduced the production of staple foods, upon which poor people depend. Both developments contribute to hunger.

A third problem is that the income of poor people has generally declined in recent years, making it difficult for them to purchase food that is available.

As we have seen, U.S. officials tried to increase the demand for first world foods after World War II by making large quantities of food avail-

able to poor countries, either by giving it away or by selling it cheaply. Although this made food available for many poor people, much of the benefits associated with food aid programs were obtained by a relatively small group of countries. During the 1950s and '60s, cheap food and food aid programs *probably increased* the poor's ability to demand or obtain food, and this helped reduce hunger among the world's poor.

But two developments—the Soviet grain shortages in the 1970s and the debt crisis in the 1980s—weakened the poor's ability to obtain food through the market.

In the early 1970s, government officials reduced the amount of food being provided through U.S. food aid programs and tried to persuade third world recipients to purchase U.S. food instead. The Soviet grain shortages accelerated this process because large Soviet demand led to the sale of U.S. food at high prices, leaving little food left over to be given away through food aid programs.

To obtain the food they had previously received at little or no cost, many third world governments borrowed money from first world lenders—government agencies and commercial banks—to purchase first world foods. They wanted to continue buying first world food because wealthy and middle-class consumers in their countries had come to prefer grains like wheat over traditional domestic varieties. They then used borrowed money to purchase food imports and to subsidize domestic food prices. Many governments provided food subsidies so that urban workers would not demand higher pay, thereby keeping the cost of industrial goods and exports competitive.[165] By borrowing money from first world countries, third world governments could maintain the demand for food even though food provided by U.S. aid programs had disappeared.

But the policy of purchasing food by borrowing money ran into difficulty when U.S. officials raised interest rates and commodity prices began to fall in the early 1980s, events that triggered a debt crisis for many third world countries.

In the 1980s, the World Bank asked third world borrowers to take steps to repay their enormous debts to first world lenders. As part of "structural adjustment" programs designed to assist repayment, third world officials reduced or eliminated government subsidies for food and fuel, and cut the wages of government employees so they could raise more money to repay debt.

These policies helped third world governments repay their debts, but they reduced effective demand and undermined the poor's ability to obtain food. As government food subsidies declined, the cost of food rose, while falling wages meant that the poor found it more difficult to pur-

chase food. These developments eroded the poor's entitlement to food by weakening their ability to demand the food that was available.

At the same time, many governments were also forced to devalue their currencies.[166] This was done to make their exports cheaper, allowing them to sell more of their goods abroad so they could earn foreign currencies that could be used to repay debt, and to make imports more expensive, which would reduce domestic demand for first world goods. This would create trade surpluses that could be used by governments to repay their debts.

But domestic currency devaluations increased the price of imported first world food, grains that people had made part of the daily diet. They also lowered the price that farmers who grew export crops could obtain for food or feed stuffs. Because third world farmers had greatly increased the supply of export crops during the 1970s, prices had already begun to fall in the early 1980s. World coffee production had increased from 1.9 million tons in 1970 to 4.5 million tons in 1979, while world sugar production had increased from 585 million tons to 754 million tons in the same period.[167]

For third world farmers growing export crops, prices fell twice, first as a result of growing third world surpluses and then as a result of domestic currency devaluations. To maintain their income as prices fell, many farmers tried to increase their production of export crops. But this only increased supplies and forced prices downward again. Together these developments reduced the ability of the rural poor, urban workers, and even export farmers to demand food through global and domestic markets.

As a result of these developments, many people go hungry and some starve. Chronic hunger hits children hardest. "Undernutrition affects nearly 40 percent of all children in developing nations and contributes directly to an estimated 60 percent of all childhood deaths," writes Katrina Galway, a U.S. AID official.[168] Typically, children and adults suffering from malnutrition get sick from other diseases.[169] Jeremy Rifkin notes that "chronically malnourished children generally develop smaller body frames and often smaller brains than normal children. If the malnutrition occurs within the first years of their lives, the physical and mental retardation becomes irreversible."[170] The poor survival rates for hungry children is the main reason that the average life expectancy in sub-Saharan Africa is only forty-seven years.[171]

Summary

During the postwar period, food supplies have grown even faster than the population. But growing first world food supplies have displaced millions

of first world farmers and have contributed, along with economic developments that undermine the poor's entitlement to food that is relatively cheap and widely available, to hunger and sometimes famine. In the view of agronomist Dale Johnson, these problems are the result of the fact that "a significant fraction of world farm output is being produced in the wrong place," in the first world, not in the third world where a majority of the world's poor and hungry reside.[172]

"In 1980," one scholar noted, "Third World nations had 75 percent of the world's people, but only 50 percent of the cereal production, 35 percent of the arable land, 35 percent of the meat and eggs, 22 percent of the milk and 15 percent of the tractors."[173] And global climate change may exacerbate this (see chapter 11). In 1994, scientists in the United States and the United Kingdom concluded that global warming, if it occurs, would actually help *increase* food production in temperate first world countries (where food surpluses have been a persistent problem), but *decrease* food production in tropical third world countries (where the availability of subsistence foods has declined). They estimated that "because of global warming, an additional 60 to 350 million people, most of them in the developing [third world], could face critical food shortages by the year 2060."[174]

The irony is that global warming is caused primarily by first world countries, where, for example, in the United States, per capita production of carbon emissions (5 tons annually) is ten times that of China ($\frac{1}{2}$ ton) and one hundred seventy times greater than Zaire.[175]

If global warming followed this pattern, it would simultaneously exacerbate the problem of first world food surpluses and of third world hunger, problems that have persisted and grown sharper during the second half of the twentieth century.

Notes

1. Butler, Nick. *The International Grain Trade*. New York: St. Martin's Press, 1986, p. 12. Friedland, William H., Busch, Lawrence, Buttel, Frederick H., and Rudy, Alan P. *Towards a New Political Economy of Agriculture*. Boulder, Colo.: Westview, 1991, p. 122.

2. Forbes, Malcolm H., and Merrill, Louis J. *Global Hunger: A Look at the Problem and Potential Solutions*. Evansville, Ill.: University of Evansville Press, 1986, p. 117.

3. Friedland et al., 1991, pp. 122–23.

4. Phillips, Peter W. B. *Wheat, Europe and the GATT: A Political Economy Analysis*. New York: St. Martin's Press, 1991, p. 20.

5. Forbes and Merrill, 1986, p. 117.

6. Ibid.

7. Butler, 1986, p. 12.

8. Friedland et al., 1991, p. 117.

9. Goodman, David, and Redclift, Michael. *Refashioning Nature: Food, Ecology and Culture.* London: Routledge, 1991, p. 123.

10. Pearse, Andrew. *Seeds of Plenty, Seeds of Want: Social and Economic Implications of the Green Revolution.* Oxford: Clarendon, 1980, p. 8.

11. Committee on the Role of Alternative Farming Methods in Modern Production Agriculture. *Alternative Agriculture.* Washington, D.C.: National Academy Press, 1989, p. 34.

12. Butler, 1986, p. 32.

13. Orr, Bill. *The Global Economy in the 90s: A User's Guide.* New York: New York University Press, 1992, pp. 65–66.

14. Butler, 1986, p. 133.

15. Orr, 1992, p. 65.

16. Feder, Barnaby J. "Out of the Lab, A Revolution on the Farm," *New York Times,* March 3, 1996.

17. Wheeler, David L. "The Search for More-Productive Rice," *Chronicle of Higher Education,* December 1, 1995, p. A12.

18. Wheeler, David L. "Expansion of Agricultural Research Said to Have Fueled Dramatic Increases in Yields of Corn, Rice and Wheat," *Chronicle of Higher Education,* September 22, 1993, p. 10.

19. Ibid.

20. Summers, Mary, and Tufte, Edward. "The Crisis of American Agriculture: Minding the Public's Business," unpublished paper, January 10, 1988, p. 16. Committee, 1989, p. 32.

21. Mansholt, Sicco. "The GATT Agricultural Negotiations: A Time to Ponder the Consequences," unpublished paper, no date, see table.

22. Forbes and Merrill, 1986, p. 117.

23. Ibid. Long, Robert E. *The Farm Crisis: The Reference Shelf,* vol. 59, no. 6. New York: Winston, 1987, p. 14. Hopkins, Raymond F., and Puchala, Donald J. "The Global Political Economy of Food," *International Organization,* Summer 1978, 32, 3, p. 584. Summers and Tufte, 1988, p. 7.

24. Forbes and Merrill, 1986, p. 117.

25. Ibid. Rifkin, Jeremy. *Beyond Beef: The Rise and Fall of the Cattle Culture.* New York: Dutton, 1992, pp. 160–61. Hudson, William J. "Population, Food and the Economy of Nations," in David Pimentel and Carl W. Hall, eds., *Food and Natural Resources.* San Diego: Academic Press, 1989, p. 284.

26. Summers and Tufte, 1988, p. 15. Committee, 1989, p. 32.

27. Ibid., p. 37.

28. Peoples, Kenneth L., Freshwater, David, Hanson, Gregory D., Prentice, Paul T., and Thor, Eric P. *Anatomy of An American Agricultural Credit Crisis: Farm Debt in the 1980s.* Washington, D.C.: A Farm Credit Assistance Board Publication, 1992, p. 23.

29. Ibid. Davidson, Osha Grey. *Broken Heartland: The Rise of America's Rural Ghetto.* New York: Free Press, 1990, p. 42. Flaherty, Diane. "The Farm Crisis," in Robert Cherry et al. *The Imperiled Economy. Book II, Through the Safety Net.* New York: Union for Radical Political Economics, 1988, p. 41.

30. Ibid., pp. 40–41. Wessel, James. *Trading the Future: Farm Exports and the Concentration of Economic Power in Our Food Economy.* San Francisco: Institute for Food and Development Policy, 1983, p. 84.

31. Belden, Joseph N. *Dirt Rich, Dirt Poor: America's Food and Farm Crisis.* New York: Routledge and Kegan Paul, 1986, p. 32.

32. Ibid. Friedland et al., 1991, p. 115.

33. Peoples, 1992, p. 14.

34. Belden, 1986, p. 34.

35. Peoples, 1992, pp. 49–58.

36. Wessel, 1983, pp. 41–42.

37. Long, 1987, p. 19. Peoples, 1992, p. 25.

38. Ibid., p. 40.

39. Davidson, 1990, p. 56.

40. Peoples, 1992, p. 43.

41. Committee, 1989, p. 92.

42. Peoples, 1992, p. 92.

43. Peoples, 1992, p. 18.

44. Ibid., pp. 4, 12. Murdock, Steve H., and Leistritz, F. Larry. *The Farm Financial Crisis: Socioecononomic Dimensions and Implications for Producers and Rural Areas.* Boulder, Colo.: Westview, 1988, pp. 30–31. Vogeler, Ingolf. *The Myth of the Family Farm: Agribusiness Dominance of U.S. Agriculture.* Boulder, Colo.: Westview, 1981, p. 4.

45. Holmes, Steven A. "Farm Count at Lowest Point Since 1850: Just 1.9 Million," *New York Times,* November 10, 1994. Vogeler, 1981, p. 4.

46. Long, 1987, p. 78.

47. Ibid., p. 10. Committee, 1989, p. 54.

48. Peoples, 1992, p. 12.

49. DeLind, Laura. "Cheap Food: A Case of Mind Over Matter," paper prepared for conference on "Diversity in Food, Agriculture, Nutrition and Environment," organized jointly by the Agriculture, Food and Human Values Society and the Association for the Study of Food and Society, June 4–7, 1992, East Lansing, Michigan, p. 8. Brooks, Nora L., Stucker, Thomas A., and Bailey, Jennifer A. "Income and Well-Being of Farmers and the Farm Financial Crisis," *Rural Sociology,* 51, 4, 1986, p. 396. Murdock and Leistritz, 1988, p. 33.

50. "U.S. Says Number of Farm Owners Is at Lowest Level in the Century," *New York Times,* December 29, 1991.

51. Ibid.

52. Wessel, 1983, p. 71.

53. Davidson, 1990, p. 55.

54. Raikes, Philip. *Modernizing Hunger: Famine, Food Surplus and Farm Policy in the EEC and Africa.* Portsmouth, N.H.: Heinemann, 1988, p. 80.

55. Davidson, 1990, pp. 73–74.

56. Ibid., p. 77.

57. Heath, Thomas. "Once-Thriving Small Towns on Plains Face Extinction," *San Francisco Chronicle*, November 11, 1995. Margolis, John. "The Reopening of the Frontier," *New York Times Magazine*, October 15, 1995, p. 52.

58. Johnson, Dirk. "Home on the Range (And Lonely, Too)," *New York Times*, December 12, 1995.

59. Brown, 1989, p. 48.

60. Butler, 1986, p. 26.

61. Bernstein, Henry, Crow, Ben, Mackintosh, Maureen, and Martin, Charlotte. *The Food Question: Profits Versus People*. New York: Monthly Review Press, 1990, p. 18. Garst, Rachel, and Barry, Tom. *Feeding the Crisis: U.S. Food Aid and Farm Policy in Central America*. Lincoln: University of Nebraska Press, 1987, p. 21. Wallerstein, Mitchell. *Food for War—Food for Peace: United States Food Aid in a Global Context*. Cambridge: MIT, 1980, p. 36.

62. Taylor, 1993, p. 234.

63. Wood, Robert E. *From Marshall Plan to Debt Crisis: Foreign Aid and Development Choices in the World Economy*. Berkeley: University of California, 1986, p. 36.

64. Watkins, Kevin. "Agriculture and Farm Trade in the GATT," *CAP Briefing*, 20. London: Catholic Institute for International Relations, March 1989, p. 3.

65. Taylor, 1993, p. 239.

66. Ibid., pp. 243–44. Paarlberg, Robert L. *Food Trade and Foreign Policy: India, the Soviet Union and the United States*. Ithaca: Cornell University Press, 1985, p. 116.

67. Soden, Katie. *U.S. Farm Subsidies*. Snowmass, Colo.: Rocky Mountain Institute's Agricultural Program, 1988, p. 16.

68. Goodman and Redclift, 1991, p. 154.

69. Friedland et al., 1991, pp. 84–85. Paarlberg, 1985, p. 131. Butler, 1986, p. 55.

70. Brown, Lester. *State of the World 1989*. New York: Norton, 1989, p. 57. Wallerstein, 1980, table 1.1. Goodman and Redclift, 1991, p. 124.

71. Peoples, 1992, p. 2.

72. Soden, 1988, p. 10.

73. Johnson, 1973, p. 35.

74. Soden, 1988, p. 7.

75. Watkins, 1989, p. 3.

76. Taylor, Peter J. "The Globalization of Agriculture," *Political Geography*, 12, 3, May 1993, pp. 254–55.

77. Johnson, 1973, p. 36.

78. Committee, 1989, p. 74.

79. Wessel, 1983, p. 29.

80. Vogeler, 1981, p. 4.

81. Johnson, 1973, p. 50.

82. *An Adoptive Program for Agriculture.* New York: Committee for Economic Development, 1962, pp. 25, 59.

83. Adams, Jane H. "The Decoupling of Farm and Household: Differential Consequences of Capitalist Development on Southern Illinois and Third World Family Farms," in *Comparative Studies in Society and History*, 30, 3, July 1988, p. 465.

84. "Good Times are Back on the Farm, For a Bit," *The Economist*, March 10, 1990, p. 25. Belden, 1986, p. 42.

85. *The Economist*, 1990, p. 25.

86. Adams, 1988, p. 465.

87. Brown, 1989, p. 57.

88. Peoples, 1992, p. 31.

89. Lehman, 1993, p. 26. Libby, Ronald T. *Protecting Markets: U.S. Policy and the World Grain Trade.* Ithaca: Cornell University Press, 1992, p. 50.

90. Butler, 1986, p. 16.

91. Wallerstein, 1980, p. 54.

92. Ibid. Taylor, 1993, p. 241. Hopkins and Puchala, 1978, p. 633. Wallerstein, 1980, p. 15.

93. Long, 1987, p. 68. Wood, 1986, p. 21.

94. Danaher, Kevin. "U.S. Food Power in the 1990s," *Race and Class*, 30, 3, 1989, p. 31.

95. Wallerstein, 1980, p. 17.

96. Belden, 1986, p. 44.

97. Ibid.

98. Committee, 1989, p. 91.

99. Libby, 1992, p. 37.

100. Ibid., p. 83.

101. Ibid., p. 62.

102. Soden, 1988, p. 15.

103. Watkins, Kevin. "Changing the Rules: The GATT Farm Trade Reform and World Food Security." *GATT Briefing*, 4. London: European Network on Agriculture and Development, 1990, p. 2.

104. Libby, 1992, p. 73.

105. Watkins, Kevin. "Agriculture and Food Security in the GATT Uruguay Round." *Review of African Political Economy*, 50, 1991, p. 40.

106. Tarditi, Secondo, Thomson, Kenneth J., Pierani, Pierpalo, and Croci-Angelini, Elisabetta. *Agricultural Trade Liberalization and the European Community.* Oxford: Clarendon, 1989, p. 2.

107. Cohen, Roger. "Life Can Be Sweet on Europe's Subsidized Farms," *New York Times*, April 12, 1992.

108. Porter, Jane M., and Bowers, Douglas E. *A Short History of U.S. Agricultural Trade Negotiations.* Washington, D.C.: U.S. Department of Agriculture, 1989, p. 19.

109. Libby, 1992, p. 13.

110. Paarlberg, 1985, p. 108.

111. Adams, 1988, p. 465.

112. Brown, 1992, p. 68. Friedland et al., 1991, pp. 126–27.

113. Friedland et al., 1991, p. 126. See Butler, 1986, p. 18.

114. Rifkin, 1992, p. 163.

115. Belden, 1986, p. 5.

116. Friedland et al., 1991, p. 128.

117. Wessel, 1983, p. 158.

118. "Does Cereal Cost Too Much?" *Weekly Reader*, 77, 2, September 15, 1995, pp. 1–2.

119. Brown, 1992, p. 77.

120. Brown, Lester. "Natural Limits," *New York Times*, July 24, 1993. Brown, 1987, p. 59. Sen, Amartya. *Poverty and Famines: An Essay on Entitlement and Deprivation*. Oxford: Clarendon Press, 1981, p. 158. Stevens, William K. "Feeding a Booming Population Without Destroying the Planet," *New York Times*, April 5, 1994.

121. Pimentel, Marcia. "Food as a Resource," in David Pimentel and Carl W. Hall, 1989, p. 426.

122. Lewis, Paul. "Food Production and the Birth Rate in a New Race," *New York Times*, May 10, 1992.

123. Collins, Joseph. "World Hunger: A Scarcity of Food or a Scarcity of Democracy," in Michael T. Klare and Daniel C. Thomas, eds., *World Security: Trends and Challenges at Century's End*. New York: St. Martin's, 1991, p. 345. Hopkins and Puchala, 1978, p. 812. Griffin, Keith. *World Hunger and the World Economy: And Other Essays in Development Economics*. London: Macmillan, 1987, p. 4. Grigg, David. *The World Food Problem 1950–1980*. London: Basil Blackwell, 1985.

124. Stokes, Bruce. "Crowds, Food and Gloom," *National Journal*, September 16, 1989, p. 2263.

125. Collins, 1991, p. 346.

126. Ibid.

127. Ibid., pp. 346–47.

128. Sen, 1981, p. 7.

129. Ibid., p. 162.

130. Ibid., pp. 52, 75.

131. Ibid., pp. 54, 63, 64, 66.

132. Ibid., pp. 69–70.

133. Ibid., pp. 77–78.

134. Ibid., p. 78.

135. Ibid, p. 50.

136. Ibid., p. 86.

137. Ibid., p. 96.

138. Ibid., p. 104.

139. Ibid., pp. 105, 107.

140. Ibid., p. 112.

141. Griffin, Keith. *The Political Economy of Agrarian Change: An Essay on the Green Revolution.* London: Macmillan, 1974, pp. 62–63.

142. Brown, 1993, p. 72.

143. Danaher, 1989, p. 39.

144. Pearse, 1980, p. 5.

145. Friedland et al., 1991, p. 194. Pearse, 1980, p. 165.

146. Collins, 1991, p. 350.

147. Brown, 1993, p. 71.

148. Collins, 1991, p. 350.

149. Brown, 1987, pp. 29–30.

150. Collins, 1991, pp. 350, 360.

151. Shenon, Philip. "Rearranging the Population: Indonesia Weighs the Pluses and Minuses," *New York Times*, October 8, 1992.

152. Timberlake, 1985, p. 42.

153. Barkin, David, Batt, Rosemary L., and DeWalt, Billie R. *Food Crops vs. Feed Crops: Global Substitution of Grains in Production.* Boulder, Colo.: Rienner, 1990, p. 17.

154. Dinham and Hines, 1983, p. 187.

155. Hopkins and Puchala, 1978, p. 260.

156. Tullis, F. LaMond, and Hollist, W. Ladd. *Food, the State and International Political Economy: Dilemmas of Developing Countries.* Lincoln: University of Nebraska Press, 1986, p. 133. Goodman, David, and Redclift, Michael. *The International Farm Crisis.* New York: St. Martin's Press, 1989, pp. 275, 277.

157. Barkin, 1990, p. 18. Brown, 1992, p. 76.

158. Barkin, 1990, p. 20.

159. Hopkins and Puchala, 1978, p. 599.

160. Barkin, 1990, p. 120.

161. Ibid., p. 27.

162. Ibid., p. 34.

163. Tullis and Hollist, 1986, p. 147. Forbes and Merrill, 1986, p. 154. Yotopoulous, Pan A. "Middle-Income Classes and Food Crises: The 'New' Food-Feed Competition," *Economic Development and Cultural Change*, 33, 3, April 1985, p. 480.

164. Barkin, 1990, p. 1.

165. Goodman and Redclift, 1989, p. 209.

166. Ibid., p. 52.

167. Dinham and Hines, 1983, pp. 189, 193.

168. Rifkin, 1992, p. 177. Barry, 1987, p. 17.

169. Timberlake, 1985, p. 48.

170. Rifkin, 1992, p. 178.

171. Timberlake, 1985, p. 48.

172. Johnson, 1973, p. 23.

173. Franke, Richard W. "The Effects of Colonialism and Neocolonialism on

the Gastronomic Patterns of the Third World," in Marvin Harris and Eric B. Ross, eds., *Food and Evolution*. Philadelphia: Temple University Press, 1987, p. 463.

174. Pitt, David E. "Computer Vision of Global Warming: Hardest on the Have Nots," *New York Times*, January 18, 1994.

175. Jackson, Robert M. *Global Issues 94–95*. Guilford, Conn.: Dushkin, 1994, p. 81.

9

Free Trade Agreements

In 1986, U.S. officials asked other countries to negotiate new trade agreements that would open doors to U.S. goods around the world. U.S. officials were determined to conclude new agreements with their trading partners to solve a series of economic problems.

U.S. officials wanted to reduce the massive U.S. trade deficit, which had grown from $25.3 billion in 1980 to $122 billion in 1985. The 1985 dollar devaluation was designed to make U.S. goods cheaper to foreign buyers. If foreign consumers purchased more U.S. goods, the trade deficit would shrink. But in the year after the Plaza accords, the U.S. trade deficit continued to rise, increasing from $122 billion to $155 billion. This development convinced U.S. officials that a currency devaluation would not alone increase the sale of U.S. goods abroad. They believed that restrictive trade policies and government practices in other countries made it difficult to sell even inexpensive U.S. goods in foreign markets. So U.S. officials asked governments in first and third world countries to adopt new trade rules that would open their doors to U.S. goods. As Carla Hills, the chief U.S. negotiator in trade talks from 1986 to 1992, put it, "I would like you to think of me as the U.S. Trade Representative with a crowbar, where we are prying open [foreign] markets, keeping them open so that our private sector can take advantage of them."[1]

U.S. officials were particularly keen on opening up markets for U.S. agricultural goods. They regarded this as a problem for two reasons. First, U.S. farmers were losing markets to European competitors—the U.S. share of the world wheat market declined from 55 percent in 1980 to 31.5 percent in 1986—which resulted in falling farm prices and declining incomes. Second, U.S. government spending on agricultural subsidies, which were used to help farmers compete with European farmers, had increased to $30 billion in 1986, a tenfold increase from 1980. Large ag-

ricultural subsidies contributed to large and growing government budget deficits. To increase agricultural sales, which would simultaneously reduce the U.S. *trade* deficit and the U.S. *budget* deficit, government officials proposed for the first time to open global agricultural markets.

In addition to agricultural trade, U.S. officials were determined to conclude trade agreements that would end foreign restrictions on food and raw material exports, eliminate their "tariffs" or taxes on U.S. goods that they imported, reduce regulations and restrictions that made it difficult to sell U.S. goods in foreign markets, make uniform government regulations that were necessary for the safe conduct of trade around the world, and prevent U.S. technology from being copied and used by competitors. "There is no question about it," Carla Hills said of far-ranging U.S. trade proposals. "This round of [trade] talks is a bold and ambitious undertaking."[2]

To reach agreement on trade issues with other countries, U.S. officials pursued negotiations in three settings. First, they initiated a new round of talks through the General Agreement on Tariffs and Trade (GATT), a set of trade rules adopted by first and third world countries in 1947. Members of GATT periodically revise the rules of the agreement in negotiations called "rounds." Until 1986, negotiations in most of GATT's successive rounds were concerned with the gradual reduction of tariffs or taxes on imported goods. In 1947, for example, governments around the world collected tariffs amounting to about 40 percent of the price of imported goods. By 1986, after seven rounds of negotiation, members had agreed to reduce tariffs to about 5 percent on average.[3] Because GATT sets trade rules for most, though not all countries (most communist countries did not participate in GATT during this period), U.S. leaders used GATT negotiations as a way to open doors for U.S. goods around the world. Called the "Uruguay Round," because the first meeting was held at a seaside resort in Uruguay, the global trade negotiations that began in 1986 would continue for seven years, ending in December 1993. The U.S. Congress would approve them one year later, on December 1, 1994.

While a new GATT agreement was being negotiated by more than one hundred countries, U.S. officials also opened and concluded regional trade agreements with neighboring countries. The U.S.-Canada Free Trade Agreement, which was signed in 1988, and the North American Free Trade Agreement (NAFTA), which was ratified by the United States, Canada, and Mexico in 1993, were both designed to accomplish similar trade goals. U.S. officials used regional free trade agreements (FTAs) both as a model for GATT negotiations—they contained many provisions that U.S. officials wanted GATT members to adopt—and as a fall-back posi-

tion should GATT members fail to adopt U.S. proposals. Because GATT negotiations deadlocked on several occasions, largely as a result of disputes over U.S. agricultural proposals, U.S. officials worried that the Uruguay Round might not revise trade rules sufficiently. So they decided to rewrite trade rules outside of GATT, beginning first with their closest neighbors and largest trading partners: Canada and then Mexico. (The United States conducts more trade with Canada than it does with Japan.)[4]

In addition to these global and regional trade initiatives, U.S. officials also used Section 301 of the Trade Acts of 1984 and 1988 to conduct one-on-one trade negotiations with other countries. If U.S. trade officials found that other countries denied U.S. corporations "reasonable" access to domestic markets, dumped their goods in the United States at below-market prices, or failed to protect the patents and copyrights of U.S. firms, Section 301 allowed them to impose retaliatory sanctions and tariffs on goods from these countries. The threat of "Super 301" sanctions frequently forced countries—most of them third world countries—to begin bilateral negotiations with the United States to settle trade disputes. As one observer noted, "By 1990, more than half of the 32 cases under Section 301 investigation involved developing countries. . . ."[5] And in these negotiations, U.S. trade officials asked that trade policies be revised to open doors to U.S. goods. In effect, Super 301 law was used to persuade other countries to comply with U.S. trade demands then being made in regional and global trade negotiations.[6]

By negotiating new trade relations through GATT and regional free trade agreements like NAFTA, and applying U.S. trade laws, U.S. officials hoped to open doors to U.S. goods in foreign markets. During the trade negotiations that followed, U.S. government economists predicted that a revised GATT agreement could increase world trade by $200 billion a year.[7] Other economists were less optimistic. Some critics argued that trade would increase by only about $20 billion a year. And others, such as Jadgish Bhagwati, economic adviser to the director general of GATT, argued that "it's almost astrological to try and forecast specific numbers. What economists are really better at is rules and devising principles."[8] Although economists disagreed about the precise economic benefits of free trade agreements, U.S. officials expected new trade rules to expand trading opportunities and solve a variety of economic problems for government and business.

U.S. Proposals to Solve Problems

Generally speaking, U.S. officials used negotiations on global, regional, and bilateral free trade agreements to solve four problems related to agri-

culture, exports, taxes and regulation, and technology. Let us first examine agricultural issues.

Agricultural Subsidies

First, U.S. officials wanted to open doors to U.S. agricultural produce in foreign markets by eliminating subsidies for farmers in the United States and around the world. They wanted to eliminate agricultural subsidies because the large and growing cost of subsidies ($30 billion in 1986) contributed to massive U.S. budget deficits. Of course, a reduction of government subsidies would force many U.S. farmers out of business. But government officials had long viewed this as a good thing because they thought the elimination of "inefficient" farmers would reduce supplies and increase prices for farmers who remained in business. The problem was that officials thought it would be difficult and unwise to reduce U.S. subsidies unilaterally because heavily subsidized European farmers would then undersell nonsubsidized U.S. farmers. As U.S. trade negotiator Daniel Amstutz explained, "The bottom line is that we must reject the 'go it alone' approach and move toward a global solution. The new round of trade negotiations is a major opportunity for making that move. . . . The international bargaining table is where the solution lies."[9] And President Reagan argued, "No nation can unilaterally abandon current [subsidy] policies without being devastated by the policies of other countries. The only hope is for a major international agreement that commits everyone to the same actions and timetable."[10]

So U.S. officials proposed eliminating agricultural subsidies everywhere because they believed that U.S. farmers, and grain producers in Canada, Australia, and Argentina, could then undersell European farmers, who were competitive in global markets only because they received even larger subsidies than those provided U.S. farmers. Without subsidies, many European farmers would go out of business. Because "the 12 countries of the European Community [have] more than 10 million farmers, compared with only two million in the United States," a smaller European farm population would reduce burgeoning food supplies, which would lead to higher prices for farmers who remained in business.[11]

In trade negotiations with Canada and Mexico, U.S. officials went further, proposing that subsidies for other industries also be eliminated, reasoning that businesses in other countries could not compete effectively without subsidies. And they persuaded Canadian and Mexican government officials that this would benefit taxpayers and reduce government expenses at a time when all were experiencing large budget deficits.

Export Restrictions and Import Quotas

Second, U.S. officials wanted to open foreign markets where governments restricted the sale or export of food, raw materials, and energy supplies. And they proposed banning export restrictions in new free trade agreements.

During the 1970s and '80s, many third world countries began restricting the sale or export of their commodities, either to raise prices for their goods or to protect domestic industries. For example, oil-producing countries that joined OPEC used the organization to restrict the supply of oil and drive up its price. Coffee-producing countries used the International Coffee Agreement, which was organized in 1958, to establish export quotas for coffee-growing countries, restrict supplies and keep prices high. Although OPEC was better able to raise prices than the coffee cartel, the ability of countries to restrict exports by collaborating with other countries led to higher prices and sometimes to inflation in the first world countries that imported these goods. Third world countries also restricted the export of some raw materials to protect domestic industry. Indonesia and countries throughout Southeast Asia restricted the export of tropical timber because they wanted to build up their domestic plywood industries—Indonesia became the world's largest plywood maker—rather than export raw timber to plywood manufacturers in Japan.

U.S. officials wanted to reduce the ability of third world commodity cartels to limit supplies, which raised prices and contributed to inflation, so they proposed that export restrictions be prohibited in new trade agreements. Although this proved difficult to do with respect to OPEC in GATT negotiations, U.S. officials persuaded Canada and Mexico not to restrict the sale of food, energy, or raw materials to the United States. In NAFTA, for example, Canada agreed to provide natural gas and Mexico agreed to furnish oil to the United States at current levels, even if they faced energy shortages in their own countries.

Taxes and Regulations

Third, U.S. officials wanted to eliminate taxes and regulations that made U.S. goods more expensive or difficult to sell in foreign markets.

When GATT was founded in 1947, its members were determined to reduce "tariffs" or taxes on imported goods, and its name—General Agreement on *Tariffs* and Trade—reflected this goal. Then and now, U.S. officials believed that tariffs were bad because they made U.S. goods more expensive and therefore harder to sell in foreign markets. But despite this

ideology, countries around the world, the United States among them, imposed tariffs on imported goods both to raise money for the government (tariffs were the chief source of revenue for the U.S. government in the nineteenth century) and to protect domestic industry. If tariffs on imported goods made them cost more than products made by domestic industry, consumers would purchase domestic goods, even though foreign goods were more cheaply made. But high tariffs in the postwar period made it difficult for countries like the United States to export goods. This hurt employment in export-oriented industries and made consumers pay high prices for the goods they purchased. So the United States and other GATT members agreed to reduce their tariffs on many, though not all, imported goods. Seven rounds of GATT negotiations reduced average tariffs from about 40 percent in 1947 to about 5 percent in 1985.[12] But many countries retained high tariffs on some imported goods like textiles and agricultural produce to protect their textile industry and domestic farmers. In the case of agriculture, they were able to do so because the United States insisted in the 1950s that agricultural tariffs be excluded from tariff-reduction negotiations in GATT.

In negotiations over new global and regional free trade agreements, U.S. officials sought to lower tariffs on manufactured goods, which were already quite low, and reduce them on goods that were not previously covered, like agricultural produce. U.S. officials were particularly keen on reducing tariffs that made it difficult to sell U.S. beef and food to Japan.

U.S. officials also wanted to do more than reduce tariffs. They wanted to eliminate government regulations that made it difficult to sell U.S. goods in foreign markets even though they were not explicitly tariffs. Although GATT had slowly reduced tariffs, many countries used government regulations or nontariff trade barriers to restrict imports. "As tariff barriers within the GATT have fallen, nontariff barriers in most countries have risen," one trade economist explained.[13]

U.S. officials wanted to reduce nontariff trade barriers because they *acted like tariffs* even though they were not taxes. As United Technologies executive Harry Gray argued,

> Such barriers as quotas, package and labeling requirements, local content laws, inspections procedures and discriminatory government procurement policies all inhibit world trade. We need conditions that are conducive to expanded trade. This means a world-wide business environment that's unfettered by government interference.[14]

To a large extent, U.S. proposals to reduce government regulations in other countries mirrored the Reagan administration's efforts to reduce

costly and burdensome government regulations in the United States. But they represented a significant departure from GATT because GATT members had restricted previous negotiations to tariff reductions. Historically, GATT members paid little attention to nontariff barriers because they were harder to measure and because many countries argued that they did not have the same detrimental impact on economic activity that tariffs did.

Of course, some government regulations are designed to ensure the safety and integrity of trade. Governments do not want to import contaminated foods or dangerous products that put consumers at risk, so they adopt health and safety restrictions that apply to imported goods. U.S. officials objected to some of these regulations arguing, for example, that European restrictions on U.S. beef raised with hormones were unfair. "More and more governments are looking for and finding alleged problems about [food] composition or how it was grown," Hills argued in 1990. "As quotas and tariffs on farm products are reduced or eliminated as a result of the Uruguay Round, politicians will look for other ways to curb imports. If new and unjustified health and safety food standards are adopted, the U.S. will retaliate."[15]

While U.S. officials objected to some health and safety regulations, they recognized that others were necessary for trade. But the problem with necessary regulations was that *different* regulations applied to the same goods in different jurisdictions. Producers of everything from tomatoes to cars to aircraft found it costly and burdensome to comply with regulations that varied from one country to the next or, in the United States, from one state to another. To deal with problems caused by different kinds of regulation, U.S. officials argued that necessary regulations should be made uniform or "harmonized," as they put it, around the world. And they argued that international scientific organizations should be given authority to determine what regulations should be uniformly applied by all. In the case of agriculture, U.S. officials proposed that responsibility for setting food safety standards be assigned to *Codex Alimentarius*, a scientific U.N. agency based in Rome. *Codex* sets regulatory standards for food, but compliance with its regulations has been voluntary. U.S. officials proposed that countries around the world adopt *Codex* standards as their own.

Reagan administration officials not only wanted to harmonize international regulations, they also wanted to make regulations in different U.S. states uniform. They argued, for instance, that strict California laws that were more stringent than federal laws should be preempted and uniform federal regulations put in their place. "The food industry will find it very

difficult to maintain its efficient distribution system if the states are free
to impose food safety and labeling requirements different from those of
the federal government," warned John Cady, president of the National
Food Processors Association. "I would rather deal with one federal go-
rilla than 50 state monkeys," another industry representative added.[16]

Reagan administration officials also wanted to make government regulations more easily understood, more "transparent" to outsiders. Many
countries established Byzantine regulations that only domestic firms
could master, or they relied on "informal" or "arbitrary" rules and regulations that put importers at a disadvantage. U.S. officials argued that
these rules should be codified and clarified so that importers could compete on a level economic playing field.

Patents and Piracy

The fourth problem that U.S. officials wanted to address in new free
trade agreements was the unauthorized use of U.S. inventions by overseas
competitors.

Although U.S. industries have higher labor costs than many foreign
industries, they also possess more advanced and sophisticated technologies, which allow them to produce goods more cheaply than low-wage
competitors. But during the 1970s and '80s, U.S. firms found that benefits
of advanced technology could be captured by others. They found that
while a new technology—such as a new pharmaceutical drug, hybrid seed,
computer chip, or Hollywood movie—could be extremely costly to in-
vent, test, and manufacture, it could be cheaply copied by others. Because
many countries did not recognize U.S. patent, copyright, and trademark
laws, which assign a monopoly to the inventor of a new technology for
seventeen years and allows them to sue others if they "infringe" on the
patent by using their invention without permission or payment, businesses in other countries copied and used technologies invented elsewhere. So, for example, manufacturers in Southeast Asia made imitation
Levi's jeans and reproduced copies of *The Terminator*, thereby profiting
from the sale of goods invented elsewhere.

U.S. officials were determined to safeguard the technological superior-
ity of U.S. firms and prevent unauthorized use or "piracy" as it is called
by foreign competitors. Gerald Mossinghoff, president of the Pharmaceutical Manufacturers Association, said that "patent piracy in just four
countries—Argentina, Brazil, India and Turkey—cost U.S. research-based
pharmaceutical firms almost $1 billion annually."[17] Altogether, U.S. com-
panies would receive $61 billion a year if piracy of U.S. technological

inventions or "intellectual property rights" as they are called were ended, according to the U.S. International Trade Commission.[18]

To protect inventions originating in the United States and other first world countries, U.S. officials argued that the protection given to inventors by U.S. patents, copyrights, and trademarks should be recognized by countries and their duration extended from seventeen to twenty years. In NAFTA negotiations, U.S. officials went further, proposing that copyrights, which protect songs like Madonna's "Material Girl" and movies like Disney's *Aladdin*, be extended to fifty years.

The Negotiations

Although U.S. officials made these ambitious and complicated proposals to solve U.S. economic problems, both foreign *and* domestic, they received crucial political support from other countries. A number of food-exporting countries outside Europe, which became known as the "Cairns Group" (Australia, Canada, New Zealand, Fiji, Brazil, Uruguay, Argentina, Malaysia, Indonesia, the Philippines, Thailand, Colombia, and Chile), supported U.S. agricultural proposals in heated disputes with members of the European Community. While the EC members opposed U.S. proposals on agricultural matters, they welcomed U.S. initiatives to end export restrictions, reduce tariff and nontariff barriers, and protect technological inventions from unauthorized use. EC members also wanted to reduce the economic power of third world commodity cartels, open doors to their goods in foreign markets, and protect their own technological advantages. And many governments in first and third world countries believed that they too would benefit from open doors and expanded trade. Many of the civilian democrats that came to power in Southern Europe, Latin America, East Asia, and Eastern Europe during the 1970s and '80s agreed with U.S. officials that these proposals would expand trade and increase their own economic opportunities (see chapter 12). And in the early 1990s, many former communist countries, which had previously not participated in GATT, became members, frequently supporting many of the proposals initiated by the United States.

Of course, some countries objected to some or all of these proposals. But they were too small or isolated to have much impact on negotiations. "The big markets dictate the trading rules," one senior U.S. negotiator said. "The U.S. can't do it independently, and the EC can't do it independently, but when the two lock arms, they can determine the fate of the round."[19]

While GATT negotiations continued, the United States concluded free trade agreements with Canada in 1988 and then with Canada and Mexico in 1993. The first was relatively uncontroversial. But the second, NAFTA, was the subject of a brief, intense debate in Congress before it was ratified. Debate was brief in part because Congress allowed U.S. trade officials to negotiate regional and global free trade agreements under special fast-track authority. This meant that the president could conduct negotiations and then submit the finished agreement to Congress for approval within sixty days. Because they were "agreements," not "treaties," they needed approval by a simple majority in both houses, with the important stipulation that they could not be amended. Congressional representatives agreed to vote for or against the entire set of complex trade rules contained in the agreement. Presidents Reagan, Bush, and Clinton asked for, and Congress granted, special fast-track authority because they did not want individual representatives to complicate negotiations or obstruct agreements reached between multiple governments.

The Uruguay Round negotiations were nearly completed in 1990, but reached an impasse when U.S. and EC officials could not reach an agreement on reducing agricultural subsidies. After fits and starts, talks resumed and negotiations were eventually completed on December 14, 1993. The final document, which was 22,000 pages long and weighed 385 pounds, was signed by 109 countries on April 15, 1994.[20] "This [is] the single largest trade agreement ever," said President Clinton in April 1994. "It writes new rules of the road for world trade well into the next century."[21] The U.S. Congress approved GATT on December 1, 1994.

When GATT members signed the new agreement, they adopted many but not all of the proposals made earlier by U.S. officials. Export restrictions were banned, tariffs and quotas reduced, nontariff trade barriers restricted, some regulatory standards were made uniform, and patent protection was extended. But some important U.S. proposals were not adopted in full measure.

In agriculture, U.S. officials had proposed eliminating subsidies completely. But EC governments opposed this, largely because farmers in France mounted large and vehement protests against U.S. proposals. The dispute over agricultural subsidies very nearly led to the collapse of Uruguay Round negotiations. The EC agreed to reduce its sales of subsidized grain by 21 percent, far lower than the 100 percent reduction favored by the United States. "In the end, none of [the U.S.] negotiating objectives was achieved," said a disappointed Heinz Hutter, chief executive of Cargill, one of the world's largest grain-trading firms. "But it was unrealistic to think so much could be done so quickly against entrenched [European] interests."[22]

U.S. officials had greater success in negotiations with Canada and Mexico. Generally speaking, regional free trade agreements incorporated more of the U.S. proposals, and used stronger language and stricter provisions, than those reached in GATT.

Still, the free trade agreements adopted in 1993–94 were generally a "success" for U.S. policy makers because they will likely open doors to U.S. goods in foreign markets, lower prices and enhance access to third world raw materials, and protect the technological advantages of first world firms. It may be too early to measure success, but there is some indication that free trade agreements already have expanded trade.

Problems Associated With Free Trade Agreements

The new free trade agreements (FTAs) create a series of problems for people in different settings. After reviewing some of the problems related to specific provisions in the new agreements, we will discuss some of the general problems associated with them.

Reducing Subsidies

The first problem is related to the reduction of agricultural subsidies in GATT and the reduction of industrial subsidies in regional free trade agreements (the U.S.-Canada FTA and NAFTA). Although the EC agreed only to a partial reduction of its agricultural subsidies, the 21 percent reduction it conceded in GATT negotiations will no doubt drive some of the EC's ten million farmers out of business. To some extent, European farmers will experience a winnowing process like that experienced by U.S. farmers since World War II. If the farm population in the EC were reduced in proportion to the 20 percent cut in subsidies, some two million farmers would be displaced—as many farmers as now exist in the United States. It would be difficult to predict which farmers would be most affected by reduced subsidies, but it is likely that the EC would target relatively "inefficient" farmers who receive large subsidies, many of them in the United Kingdom, Portugal, Spain, Greece, Ireland, and Germany rather than the more efficient Dutch and politically active French farmers. France is the largest agricultural producer in the EC and its farmers are better organized and more efficient than most. They have organized massive protests on a national scale and effectively challenged the government to hang tough in negotiations with the United States.

Provisions in regional FTAs did not eliminate agricultural subsidies,

but they contained language that allows member countries to sue one another if they think that agricultural or industrial subsidies give producers an unfair advantage or "distort trade." Under the U.S.-Canada FTA, for example, U.S. timber producers complained that Canadian timber manufacturers received an unfair, trade-distorting subsidy because the government of British Columbia paid the cost of replanting trees cut down by Canadian firms in the province's forests. (U.S. timber companies must themselves pay the cost of replanting clear-cut forest on privately owned land in the United States.) This tree-replanting "subsidy" enabled Canadian firms to export and sell lumber in the United States at prices lower than U.S. firms.

Under regional FTAs and GATT, firms may not themselves sue other countries to force them to comply with provisions in the agreement. Only governments can. So U.S. timber producers asked U.S. trade officials to review their case and sue the Canadian government on their behalf. After "finding" that U.S. firms were "injured" by Canadian "subsidies," U.S. trade officials sued the Canadian government, asking it to remove the subsidies through the arbitration process established by the FTA. Arbitration panels, with trade experts nominated by both parties to a dispute, determine whether a provision of the agreements has been violated. They then issue a ruling if they believe it has. In this case, they ruled that the tree-replanting program was a subsidy that violated the agreement.

At this point in the process, different things can happen. The Canadian government can comply with the ruling and ask provincial authorities to stop funding the tree-replanting program. (Its ability to insist may depend on the constitutional relation between federal and provincial government in Canada. In the United States, the Constitution assigns considerable authority to the federal government, but also reserves important rights for state and local government.) But the Canadian government can also refuse to comply with the arbitration panel ruling. Because arbitration panels have no power to enforce their rulings, and because most FTAs do not have any organizational authority for insisting that governments change their trade policies, enforcement of arbitration panel rulings is usually left up to the "injured" party.

Free trade agreements allow governments injured by countries that violate the agreements to "retaliate" against the violator by imposing punitive taxes on goods imported from that country. (It is illegal to impose retaliatory tariffs without a favorable ruling.) So, in this case, the U.S. government could levy heavy tariffs on Canadian timber products, making it difficult for them to compete in U.S. markets. If the United States did so, the Canadian government could still refuse to comply. But high

retaliatory tariffs would no doubt harm some Canadian manufacturers, who would then ask their own government to comply with the ruling so they could get on with business as usual. This process is designed to put economic pressure on governments to comply with trade agreements by enlisting both foreign governments and domestic manufacturers in the process. In this particular case, mounting economic pressure on the provincial government forced it to change its forest policy and end tree-replanting subsidies. Private companies in British Columbia must now bear this cost themselves.[23]

Environmentalists in Canada and the United States criticized the application of the free trade agreement in this case because it undermined what they regarded as a sensible way to ensure that clear-cut forests were replanted and the woods used on a more sustainable basis, something that might not occur if private firms have to pay for this themselves. Environmentalists and other consumer and labor groups also worried that this kind of ruling would set a precedent for attacks on other "subsidies" that they regarded as useful or necessary, and they warned that it could undermine the authority of state and local governments. They noted, for instance, that U.S. businesses have argued that Canadian health care and unemployment programs violate free trade agreements. Because Canadian employers do not have to pay for health care benefits, as many do in the United States, U.S. businesses argue that national health care in Canada unfairly aids Canadian firms. And because self-employed lobster fishermen in Canada can receive unemployment benefits in the off-season, while their U.S. counterparts cannot (self-employed businesspeople cannot collect unemployment benefits in the United States), U.S. lobster men argue that unemployment benefits underwrite Canadian lobster exports. These disputes have not yet been resolved, but critics argue that language in free trade agreements permits a broad assault on important environmental and social programs. If, for example, U.S. proposals to eliminate agricultural subsidies completely had been adopted, programs that promote soil and water conservation, education and scientific research, farm credit and loans, and food aid to foreign countries could have been contested as unfair subsidies to trade.

Critics of new free trade agreements also argue that rulings like that in the Canadian tree-replanting case and language in the new GATT could substantially undermine the authority of state and local governments. New language in GATT, for example, requires contracting parties to "take such reasonable measures as may be available to it to ensure observance of the provisions of this agreement by regional and local governments and authorities within its territory."[24] And NAFTA requires members to

"take all necessary steps, where changes to domestic laws will be required to implement their provisions . . . to ensure conformity of their law with these agreements."[25]

Former California Governor Edmund G. Brown Jr. opposes the preemption of state government by free trade agreements. "Our constitutional system rests on democratic accountability with significant legal and regulatory differences recognized among states and localities," he argued. "NAFTA . . . in the name of taking down trade barriers would curtail local preferences and thereby undermine the ability of diverse communities to control their own destiny."[26]

Ending Export Restrictions and Import Quotas

A second set of problems is related to provisions in free trade agreements that reduce export restrictions on food, energy supplies, and natural resources and restrict import quotas on different commodities.

Many countries now limit the export of oil or coffee in order to reduce global supplies and thereby raise the price they receive for these goods. Although consumers around the world welcome lower-priced gas and coffee, lower prices would make it much more difficult for exporting countries to buy things from abroad, repay debts, invest their earnings in domestic development projects, raise standards of living, or close the growing economic gap between first and third world countries. Prices for oil, food, and natural resources fell dramatically during the 1980s, and free trade agreements that prevent countries from reducing or managing the supply of these goods will likely contribute to the downward pressure on prices. NAFTA, for example, prohibits Mexico and Canada from reducing their energy exports to the United States to a level below the average of the previous three years. This provision was designed to guarantee delivery of Mexican oil and Canadian natural gas and electricity to the United States.[27] By agreeing to maintain energy exports, Mexican and Canadian officials will find it difficult to increase prices.

In the case of food, a prohibition of export restrictions could be particularly devastating. If a poor country experienced a bad harvest, and its government could not prevent other countries from buying and exporting its food, domestic food supplies could fall and prices rise. If food prices rise without a commensurate rise in income, many poor people might starve.

Without export restrictions, government officials in many countries will have a harder time managing their natural resources. Pacific Rim countries belonging to the International Tropical Timber Organization

have banned the export of raw logs to Japan and restricted timber exports. They did so either to promote domestic industry, as Indonesia did to build up its plywood industry, or to manage its forest resources, as Thailand did to reduce the soil erosion and flooding associated with rapid deforestation.

The GATT ban on export restrictions would not only affect third world countries, it could also affect people and the environment in first world countries.

Japanese officials claim that U.S. government restrictions on raw log exports from *federal* forests, which are designed to protect jobs at U.S. mills, and new federal restrictions on logging in old-growth forests, which are designed to protect endangered spotted owls, would violate the GATT ban on export restrictions. Some U.S. forest industries support the Japanese position, urging an end to federal export restrictions and regulations because they can get high prices from Japanese buyers as a result of dollar devaluations, which make it more profitable to cut and ship raw logs than to mill the wood first, and because they want greater access to public forest supplies.[28] The ratification of GATT means that it could be very hard for U.S. officials to defend Forest Service restrictions and regulations that help manage public forests.

Just as free trade agreements attempt to reduce export restrictions, they also seek to do away with import quotas, which restrict supplies and force up prices. At present, U.S. beef, sugar, peanut, and tobacco farmers all benefit from U.S. restrictions on the import of these goods from other countries. Many of them would be forced out of business if large supplies of foreign produce entered the United States and lowered prices. Consumers would benefit, but ranchers and farmers would lose. The point is that free trade agreements have very different consequences for different groups of people.

In Japan, for example, the end of restrictions on rice imports will help consumers, who now pay more for staple foods than consumers in most of the world. But it will likely devastate the farm population and contribute to the migration of young people from rural areas to the cities. As journalist Roger Cohen observed,

> In opening its market to imported rice for the first time, Japan was taking more than a small trade step. Rice cultivation is central to Japan's religion, culture and folklore and the bar on imports symbolized its sacredness. Each spring, the Emperor plants the first seedling on the grounds of the Imperial Palace. But in the end, the Japanese government decided that access to markets outweighed these considerations.[29]

But while they managed to reduce or eliminate restrictions on food, raw materials, textiles, and even cars in new free trade agreements, U.S. officials were unable to persuade other countries to lift import restrictions on Hollywood films and TV programs. "I am disturbed by the refusal of the EC to negotiate seriously," said Jack Valenti, president of the Motion Picture Association of America, the main lobbying group for the Hollywood-based entertainment industry. "I feel . . . disappointment that we were unable to reach a fair conclusion."[30]

European officials disagreed with this assessment. Jack Lang, France's minister of culture, said the decision *not* to eliminate restrictions on U.S. film, TV, and music imports was "a victory for art and artists over the commercialization of culture."[31]

Import restrictions on cultural goods were extremely contentious issues because Hollywood, the center of the U.S. communications industry, is capturing global markets with film, TV, and music products. In France, for example, 60 percent of the films shown in theaters and 50 percent of the programs aired on French TV are made in Hollywood.[32] And U.S. cultural industry supremacy is even more pronounced in other countries around the world. In Brazil, eight of the ten top-grossing films in 1990 were made in Hollywood; in Hungary, Hollywood films captured nine of the top ten spots.[33] Hollywood earns more than $8 billion a year for its film and video exports, and growing income from foreign sales added jobs in Hollywood, where the film and TV industry employs 414,700 workers. Hollywood has been able to capture foreign markets because it has developed advanced technology and has the ability to raise and risk $44 million on the average film. Technology and capital enable it to attract skilled directors and actors from around the world (Louis Malle and Peter Weir, Arnold Schwarzenegger and Mel Gibson) and produce technologically sophisticated movies like *Jurassic Park.* Hollywood also frequently owns or controls distribution networks and theater outlets in other countries. In Indonesia, for example, the company that monopolizes film distribution pushes Hollywood films. "As a result," writes journalist Philip Shenon, "the Indonesian film industry is dying, with fewer than 30 films expected to be produced [in 1992], half of [1991's] output."[34] And since World War II, the industry has been able to expand Hollywood's dominance at the expense of foreign film industries. Valenti once boasted, "The motion picture industry is the only U.S. enterprise that negotiates on its own with foreign governments."[35]

In Europe and elsewhere, government officials established import quotas on Hollywood products to protect domestic industries, preserve indigenous cultures, and restrict television violence.[36] In recent years,

France and Spain restricted the amount of time that could be devoted to Hollywood films and TV and radio programming in media outlets. And they levied taxes on film tickets to raise money to support their domestic film industries. Hollywood director Steven Spielberg criticized these moves, saying that "filmmakers can find no comfort when their film is barred or restricted or otherwise frustrated when they try to take out work to the global public."[37]

But a group of European directors led by Wim Wenders and Bernardo Bertolucci responded by saying,

> We are only desperately defending the tiny margin of freedom left us. We are trying to protect European cinema against its complete annihilation [by Hollywood films like Spielberg's *Jurassic Park*, which swallowed up a huge share of European ticket sales in 1993]. The dinosaurs of 1993, that's us. We are facing extinction and we are merely fighting for our survival. Do you seriously think that our European films are really so bad that they deserve to reach 1 percent of American audiences, while American films fill more than 80 percent of European screens?[38]

Reducing Tariffs

The reduction of taxes and regulations on imported goods, and the creation of uniform laws that are necessary to protect the health and integrity of trade, were a centerpiece of negotiations over new free trade agreements. Although the reduction and elimination of taxes and regulations that hinder trade were designed to benefit consumers, they contribute to three kinds of problems.

First, the reduction of tariffs on imported goods will reduce government revenues. By reducing tariffs to zero, NAFTA will cut U.S. revenues by about $4 billion a year, and cut about $3 billion in tax revenues for Canada and for Mexico. The elimination of income from this source comes at a time when each country is facing large budget deficits and where they must actually *increase* government spending to facilitate implementation of the agreement. U.S. Commerce Secretary Ron Brown estimated that the government would spend $2 billion a year for ten years to build roads, bridges, and sewers along the border. It would also spend an undetermined amount for maintaining and expanding U.S. customs and border patrols to prevent people from crossing borders.

The United States also agreed to provide $1 billion to assist trade through a new North American Development Bank, and authorized the U.S. Treasury to spend billions of dollars to defend the current value of

the Mexican peso if the new agreement led to speculation or trade deficits that devalued the peso. This is just what happened in December 1994, when the value of the peso fell by nearly 40 percent as a result of a $30 billion trade deficit that Mexico ran up in NAFTA's first year. To forestall a further depreciation of the peso, the U.S. government provided the Mexican government with a $9 billion line of credit to stabilize exchange rates.[39]

As it turned out, tariff reduction also provides tax relief for U.S. corporations. U.S. firms control about 40 percent of the Mexican and 40 percent of the Canadian export economy.[40] As economist Sidney Weintraub notes, "An important feature of the U.S.-Mexico industrial relationship is that more than one-half of their trade in manufactured goods takes place between affiliated companies. This is also true of U.S.-Canada industrial trade."[41]

Because U.S. corporations operating in Mexico and Canada export much of the goods they produce to the United States, or import goods from the United States to sell in Mexico and Canada, tariff reduction amounts to a large tax cut for U.S. firms operating in foreign countries. And this tax relief is not available to U.S. firms that operate only in the United States.

While U.S. firms operating in Canada and Mexico will receive tax cuts, it is not clear that they will pass along their savings to consumers in the form of lower prices. As Rene Osario, a Hewlett-Packard representative, said, "Tariff reduction will free investment for *other* things.[42]

Tariff reductions in GATT will cost the U.S. government another $3 billion a year in lost revenues, a problem for U.S. policy makers because Congress must either cut spending or increase taxes to replace lost revenue under current deficit-reduction rules.[43]

The new GATT does not entirely eliminate tariffs, allowing governments to retain some tariffs, though at lower levels. One issue that the new tariff-reduction agreements in GATT did not address was the differential tariffs used by first world countries to discriminate against third world countries. First world countries typically place low tariffs on raw materials imported from third world countries, but very high tariffs on their manufactured goods. So, for example, first world countries placed a tiny 0.1 percent tariff on raw rubber imports from third world producers, but levied a 16.5 percent tariff on rubber footwear.[44] The effect was to discourage third world countries from making goods that might compete with first world producers. Across-the-board tariff reduction might benefit consumers, but it would leave discriminatory tariff structures in place, structures that often disadvantage poor countries.

Second, the elimination of nontariff trade barriers, or government regulations that act *like* tariffs because they make it more difficult to sell goods in foreign markets, may adversely affect consumers and the environment.

In 1992, for example, the Canadian government passed new regulations designed to protect the health of imported puppies. They did so because U.S. firms that sold puppies to Canadian pet stores shipped puppies under conditions that exposed them to disease and kept them in transit for more than thirty-six hours, which the government regarded as cruel. "[The new regulations] will reduce the number of [Canadian] families that are traumatized by purchasing imported dogs that die or suffer from disease," officials of Agriculture Canada explained.[45]

But U.S. pet industry officials objected, arguing that the regulations would increase the cost and reduce pet ownership in Canada, and asked the U.S. government to sue Canada because, they said, the regulations were a nontariff trade barrier that violated the U.S.-Canada Free Trade Agreement.

Although the dispute over the puppy trade is a minor affair, it illustrates how regulations designed to protect consumers, and in this case, animals, can be attacked under new free trade agreements as obstacles to trade. Environmental and consumer advocates argue that provisions in new free trade agreements could be used to challenge or modify regulations imposed by the Convention on the International Trade in Endangered Species, the Montreal Protocol, which limits the production of ozone-depleting chemicals, recycling laws, and the U.S. Marine Mammal Protection Act (MMPA). On June 25, 1991, Mexico sued the United States in GATT after U.S. officials blocked the import of Mexican tuna because Mexican fishermen caught tuna using methods that resulted in the death of dolphins, marine mammals protected under provisions of the MMPA.[46] The GATT arbitration panel assigned to hear the dispute ruled for Mexico, arguing that member countries could not discriminate against goods produced in ways they viewed as "unacceptable." This means that Canada could not restrict the import of puppies raised in a manner Canadians regarded as "inhumane," that the United States could not restrict the import of goods manufactured by prisoners (as many goods are in China), by children (as they are in many parts of the world), or by workers denied the right to organize unions (as they are in many countries). Critics of FTAs argue that rulings like that in the Mexican tuna case open the door to other challenges that obstruct trade, even if these regulations are designed to protect consumers, the environment, or workers.[47]

Of course, free trade agreements would not eliminate all regulations that affect trade, in part because government regulations that affect trade

are considered under free trade agreements on a case-by-case basis. This takes time, and arbitration panels, which are made up of trade experts, do not always agree on the interpretation and application of provisions in free trade agreements.

Where regulations are seen as necessary to protect the safety and integrity of trade, FTAs assign authority to regulate trade to international agencies like Codex Alimentarius, which sets standards and regulates trade in food. These scientific agencies would then be responsible for creating uniform regulations that would apply around the world. But the effort to create uniform global standards leads to a third problem: uniform standards may result in regulations with lower standards than now apply in many countries.

Codex, for example, now sets standards for the amount of pesticide residues allowed in imported fruits and vegetables. But these levels are often lower than standards set by the U.S. Environmental Protection Agency (EPA). Codex regulations, for example, allow banana producers to export fruit containing fifty times as much residual DDT, a pesticide banned in the United States since 1970, as the U.S. EPA now permits.[48] The EPA accepts only about 20 percent of Codex standards for residual pesticides, rejecting the majority because they are too low.[49] If Codex assumes authority for setting global food regulations, existing standards of food safety could be lowered significantly in many countries. This would not mean, of course, that consumers would be forced to consume bananas from countries that applied large amounts of DDT on their crops. But they would have to learn more about the fruit they purchase and exercise greater caution because they could not rely on government agencies to intervene on their behalf at the border. Nor does it mean that Codex would always set lower standards. Indeed, for many countries observance of Codex standards might be higher than the ones they now use. And sometimes Codex agrees to higher standards. In 1991, for example, U.S. officials asked Codex to approve the use of hormones to raise beef, a position opposed by European representatives to Codex because the EC bans the import of hormone-raised beef. A Codex scientific committee rejected the U.S. proposal on a 27 to 13 vote.[50]

But whether it sets high or low standards, environmental and consumer groups argue that Codex should not be given authority to set uniform standards for the world because it preempts the ability of local, state, and national governments, which are composed of elected representatives, to set standards acceptable to the communities they represent. Voters in California, for example, regularly pass referendums that set health and safety standards that are more stringent than those adopted by the federal gov-

ernment. Using free trade agreements to assign this authority to international agencies that are not accountable to consumers or voters is unfair, critics argue.

Extending Patent Protection

Although Hollywood was unable to eliminate restrictions on its film exports in GATT, it was able to obtain expanded patent protection for its films, songs, and merchandise, everything from *Dumb and Dumber* to Mickey Mouse slippers. GATT and other free trade agreements extended patent, trademark, and copyright protection around the world and granted protection for longer periods of time. These measures were of great concern not only to Hollywood, but also to pharmaceutical, chemical, and agricultural companies who argued that their inventions or "intellectual property rights" were being pirated or used without their authorization by competitors in other countries. But the extension of protection for inventions may promote monopoly and raise the cost of food and drugs in other countries.

In the United States, patents, trademarks, and copyrights are used to give inventors of technologies, drugs, brand names, songs, and books a monopoly over the use of that invention for a given period of time, seventeen years for a patent approved by the U.S. government. Because they are government-granted monopolies, patent law does not promote competition or trade in goods or ideas, it *restricts* them. Trade economist Alan Deardorff writes:

> As its name suggests, intellectual property "protection" is a surprising issue for the GATT [because] . . . the GATT's mission has always been to prevent, or at least circumscribe, countries' efforts to "protect" their domestic industries. Now, [in the case of patents] the GATT is being called upon to *extend* protection, not restrict it . . . the goal of Uruguay Round negotiations in restricting this free flow may be viewed as perverse.[51]

The first problem with the restriction of patent protection and monopoly is that it strengthens the technological advantages of first world countries, which have the educational systems and research infrastructures—skilled engineers and scientists, government-funded research universities, and programs such as NASA and the National Academy of Sciences—necessary for invention in the modern world. As a result, inventors in first world countries own the bulk of the world's patented inventions. According to one study,

Only one percent of the patents are owned by third world nationals. Of the 3.5 million patents in existence worldwide in the 1970s, only about 200,000 were granted to developing countries. Most of these third world patents, some 84 percent, were owned by transnational corporations from the richest five countries. . . . [52]

A second problem is that patent protection may lead to higher prices for consumers. (Generally free trade agreements seek to lower consumer prices.) Many countries that provide patent protection do so for short periods of time. Canada, for example, protects drug patents for only seven to ten years, about half the duration of U.S. patents. According to the U.S. General Accounting Office, Canada's shorter-term patent laws kept drug prices there 32 percent lower than drug prices in the United States.[53] And many countries prevent patents from being awarded for some technologies or require patent holders to license their products at a low cost. In India, for example, "patents cannot be given for a method of agriculture or horticulture" or for medical processes that "render [humans, plants, or animals] free of disease. . . ."[54] Both Canada and India require foreign drug companies to license their products at a low cost so that medicine can be made more cheaply available to consumers. Oxfam's Kevin Watkins argues, "Compulsory licensing is widely used in India and other developing countries in order to limit the abuse of monopoly power conferred by patents."[55]

By making patent laws in countries around the world conform with U.S. patent laws, consumers may see prices for drugs and other essential goods rise.

A third problem is that first world inventors are patenting goods or ideas drawn initially from others. On March 3, 1993, two hundred thousand Indian farmers rallied in Delhi to protest GATT proposals to extend patent protection to seed and agricultural chemical companies.[56] They regarded this as a problem because it means seed companies can demand a royalty for the use of patented seeds or chemicals in third world countries, demanding further that farmers pay royalties on seeds saved from the previous harvest. Under the new rules, "a farmer purchasing [patented] seed would have the right to grow the seed but not the right to make seed," argued Indian economist Vandana Shiva.[57]

Seed companies maintain that they need patent protection to protect costly invention. "Even though it has been a tradition in most countries that a farmer can save from his own crop, it is under [current] circumstances not equitable that farmers can use this [patented] seed and grow a commercial crop out of it without payment of royalty [to its inventors],"

argued Hans Leenders, secretary general of the International Association of Plant Breeders for the Protection of Plant Varieties.[58]

The irony of this position is that much of the raw material for new drugs, seeds, and chemicals comes from rain forests and the farms and gardens of poor people in the third world (see chapter 11). Some of this material—wild and cultivated varieties of plants, grains, and vegetables—has been gathered by first world scientists who do not pay for cuttings and specimens. Shiva notes that a variety of Turkish barley was donated to U.S. farmers to combat a yellow dwarf virus, saving U.S. farmers $150 million a year in crop losses, and "a wild tomato variety taken from Peru in 1962 has contributed $8 million a year to the American tomato processing industry by increasing the content of soluble solids."[59] And the "baseball" tomatoes, which can be harvested by machine, that are sold in U.S. supermarkets are the result of cross-breeding tomato varieties taken from Latin American countries during the 1950s and '60s. "Yet none of these benefits have been shared with Peru, the original source of the genetic material," notes Shiva.[60] According to some estimates, "wild varieties contributed $340 million per year between 1976 and 1980 to the U.S. farm economy," and the "total contribution of wild germplasm to the U.S. economy has been $66 billion."[61]

So, having taken genetic material from third world sources, processed it, and patented this process or invention, first world scientists are not in the position of selling it back to people who initially supplied the material.

Much the same is true of ideas. Most of Disney's major cartoon productions are based on fables and folklore originally told by people in other countries. *The Little Mermaid* had Danish origins, *Beauty and the Beast* and *Cinderella* were told in France and Italy, and *Aladdin* was a story that originated in the Middle East. But by copyrighting its own particular version (in words, music, and images), Disney can then sell these stories to people around the world and deny others the right to use them.

General Problems

New free trade agreements contain provisions that affect subsidies, export restrictions and import quotas, taxes and regulations on imported goods, and patents on inventions. While they may provide benefits, they also contribute to a variety of problems. But in addition to the problems associated with specific provisions, the new free trade agreements contribute to three *general* problems.

In the abstract, free trade agreements are designed to open doors so that businesses can participate and compete with each other in markets around the world. Consumers will benefit from this because increased competition, and the decline of burdensome government taxes and regulations, will permit businesses to specialize and deliver their goods at the lowest possible price. Free trade agreements will no doubt open doors, but they may open markets not to competition between businesses but to large-scale transnational corporations. According to the World Bank, "transnational corporations (TNCs) control 70 percent of world trade. In 1990, the world's largest 350 TNCs accounted for almost 40 percent of world merchandise trade, which then totalled $3.485 trillion. The top 500 TNCs control two-thirds of world trade."[62]

As a result, large TNCs may capture most of the economic benefits provided by free trade agreements. When NAFTA cut tariffs, U.S. corporations operating in Canada and Mexico received tax cuts that were unavailable to firms based only in the United States. Because three to six TNCs control 85 to 90 percent of world wheat, corn, coffee, cotton, and tobacco exports, 90 percent of forest product exports, and 90 to 95 percent of iron ore exports, the reduction of import and export restrictions will provide immediate benefits to a small number of large firms.[63]

The problem is that when a small number of large firms control world trade in a given industry, free trade agreements may not lead to greater competition and lower prices, which is what economists expect them to do. If free trade agreements included antitrust or antimonopoly provisions of the kind embodied in U.S. antitrust law, they might stimulate competition and lower prices. The Sherman Antitrust Act of 1890, for example, prohibits companies from engaging in practices that unfairly restrain trade, reduce competition, or raise prices.[64] In that sense, U.S. antitrust law has long been used as an important way to promote "free trade," at least *within* the United States. But the new free trade agreements do not include antitrust provisions. When U.S. officials initiated new free trade agreements in the mid-1980s, they did not propose that antitrust provisions be included in negotiations. Instead they insisted that patent monopoly law be extended.

Indeed, many government officials have argued that U.S. antitrust laws should be eliminated. In 1989, Vice President Dan Quayle argued, "To make America more competitive, we are . . . going to have to reexamine our anti-trust laws, many of which are anachronistic in the age of global competition."[65] More recently, Lester Thurow, an adviser to President Clinton, said that antitrust laws were "out of date. Big companies do sometimes crush small companies, but better that small American compa-

nies be crushed by big American companies than that they be crushed by big foreign companies."[66]

As a consequence, the new free trade agreements contain no antitrust provisions, measures that might be used to prevent "big foreign companies" from crushing small companies in the United States or elsewhere, or from using their economic power unfairly to restrain international trade. The new free trade agreements sometimes prohibit governments from restraining trade, but they do nothing to prevent private companies from acting in ways that unfairly reduce competition and raise prices. Under these circumstances, where large TNCs control much of the world's trade, and much of this trade is within firms located in different countries, free trade agreements may not be able to deliver the goods—greater competition and lower consumer prices—that their proponents expect.

A second general problem is that the creation of *regional* free trade agreements may discriminate against countries that do not belong to regional trade blocs, a development that runs counter to the idea that free trade agreements should end trade discrimination.

One of the central provisions in GATT is that its trade rules should *apply equally to all* of a country's trading partners. So if the United States imposes a tariff on goods from one country, it must equally tax the same goods from other countries. Article XXIV allows regional trade arrangements that remove barriers so long as they do not raise trade barriers with countries that do not belong. But this rule has not been closely observed, and a number of regional trade groups have emerged over the years that created "free trade" among a particular group of countries but discriminate against countries outside this group. The European Union (EU) is the most prominent such group or "trade bloc," as they are sometimes called, but there are other smaller ones in Asia, Africa, and Latin America.[67] The creation of a U.S.-Canada FTA and then a NAFTA has created another large and powerful trade bloc. And countries that belong to GATT, but not to the EU or NAFTA, had complained that these regional FTAs discriminate against them.

Newly democratic countries in Eastern Europe complain that the EU is raising new trade barriers to them even as it negotiates a reduction of trade barriers in GATT. "The process of liberalization and the opening of [EU] markets to us is going slowly," complained Andrzej Arendarski, Poland's minister for trade and foreign economic relations. "It is our intention to press our partners [in the EU] to change their attitudes."[68] But the EU has been reluctant to do so, putting import restrictions and tariffs on as much as one-half of the goods imported from Eastern European

countries.[69] And these restrictions make it difficult to export goods and use export earnings to pay back loans from EU countries.

Countries in Latin America also worry that NAFTA will exclude them from the U.S. market. When they negotiated the NAFTA, U.S. officials promised to extend it to other Latin American countries, first Chile and then eventually all of Latin America. But a recent U.S. government report found that "Mexico is reportedly *not* interested in allowing other countries in the region into an arrangement that offers considerable benefits, which were achieved because of its relationship to the United States."[70] Governments in Latin America, but also in Asia, fear that NAFTA will discriminate against them because the United States cannot grant preferential trading status to members of GATT and even greater trade preferences to members of NAFTA, without adversely affecting the former. As one economist warned, new trade blocs may "set a dangerous precedent for further special deals, fragmentation of the trading system, and damage to the interests of non-participants."[71]

A third problem is that while free trade agreements will no doubt increase the volume of trade, the economic benefits associated with expanding trade opportunities will not be equally shared.

Indeed, economists and government officials *expect* this to happen. As Robert Gilpin explains,

> It is important to stress what liberal [free trade] theory does *not* assert. Liberals do not argue that everyone will necessarily gain from trade. . . . Rather [they] assert that there are potential gains. . . . Furthermore, liberal theory does not argue that everyone will gain equally. . . . Instead, it maintains that everyone will gain in absolute terms, although some will gain relatively more. . . . The argument for free trade is based not on grounds of equity and equal distribution but on increased efficiency and the maximization of world wealth.[72]

"Our trade policy is guided by a simple credo," Mickey Kantor, the U.S. Trade Representative in the Clinton administration, observed at the conclusion of the GATT negotiations. "We want to expand *opportunities* for the global economy."[73] But it is important to note that the goal of U.S. officials was expanded opportunities. They did not argue that the benefits of expanded opportunities would be widely shared.

In this regard, it is noteworthy that the volume of world trade has increased ten times since GATT was formed in 1947. But the economic benefits associated with this dramatic increase in trade—an increase made

possible in part by a general reduction of tariffs—has not been widely shared. As we have seen, the gap between first and third world countries has grown in this period, despite the expansion of trade. And according to Tim Lang and Colin Hines, "Developing nations' share of global wealth fell from 22 percent between 1980 and 1988."[74] Although trade may not alone have caused the gap between rich and poor countries to grow—falling commodity prices, indebtedness, and inflation probably played bigger roles in this period—expanded trade has not provided substantial benefits either. During the postwar period, most of the world's trade has been conducted among first world countries. There is little evidence to suggest that new free trade agreements will substantially change this.

Winners and Losers

Because free trade agreements are a complex set of rules, it is difficult to determine how they will affect the countries that adopt them, how they will impact different industries and the people who work in them. But it is clear that they will produce both winners and losers. A quick examination of the U.S. glass industry, French agriculture, and riziculture in Japan and the United States shows how free trade agreements can have very different consequences for different groups of people.

For glass manufacturers in the United States, NAFTA will have very different economic consequences. As journalist Keith Bradsher reports, Corning Glass, the largest and most technologically advanced glassmaker in the world, will benefit from the FTA because it will be able to sell more high-tech glass in Mexico, in part because Corning merged with Mexico's largest glass producer—Vitro SA—so that it could increase its access to Mexican markets. As a result, "the 660 workers of the automated Corning factory [in Martinsburg, West Virginia] can expect greater job security than they have now and new jobs may be added."[75] And workers in Vitro's plants will also benefit from the companies' ability to sell more low-tech glassware in the United States. "But about 2,000 workers in small handmade glass factories [in West Virginia] face possible financial ruin," Bradsher reports.

> Even with tariffs that currently add up to 38 cents to the cost of each dollar's worth of imported glass, half of the local industry has already gone bankrupt in the last decade, partly because of Mexican competition. "If that duty is released, it's just going to kill us," said Michael Hall, president and part

owner of a small company . . . which makes high-quality glass flower vases and drinking glasses in two kilns set up in a warehouse in rural Ellenboro.[76]

Because it saw NAFTA as beneficial, Corning broke ranks with other glassmakers that had long opposed tariff reduction and "aggressively advocated the free trade agreement." By contrast, small glassmakers opposed the agreement but were unable to mount an effective lobbying campaign against the agreement in Washington. "When you're salesman, president and janitor, it's hard to have time to lobby," said Kenneth B. Dalzell, head of the sixty-employee Dalzell Corporation, explaining why he did not respond to West Virginia Senator John D. Rockefeller IV's request for his views on the agreement.[77]

In France, the conclusion of GATT negotiations created very different reactions among farmers. French winemakers like Louis Lator, who exports 90 percent of his wine, mostly to the United States and the United Kingdom, welcomed the agreement because it provided greater access to U.S. markets. He and other vintners campaigned vigorously for passage of the agreement, arguing that wine was more important to the French economy ($6 billion a year in export sales) than wheat ($4.5 billion in exports) and that the complaints of wheat farmers should be ignored. "The average Frenchman doesn't . . . realize that a living history museum [French wheat farmers] is not the same thing as international trade."[78]

But wheat farmers like Regis D'Hondt, who operates a 300-acre wheat farm, disagreed, arguing that the reduction of agricultural subsidies in GATT will ruin many farmers. And most economists agree that GATT will reduce France's farmers (half of them wheat farmers) by more than half, from eight hundred thousand to three hundred thousand by the year 2000.[79] To prevent this, French farmers, though not vintners, staged large and often violent protests during GATT negotiations, once even using tractors to blockade Euro-Disney.[80]

The decision by Japanese and South Korean officials to end their decades-long bans on imported rice had different consequences for rice growers in Japan, South Korea, and the United States. The end of the ban on rice imports will lower prices and ruin many small-scale rice farmers in Japan and South Korea, and spur the exodus of young rural farmers to the cities. "Frankly, rice farming is not that profitable," said Kanichi Sugawara, a sixth-generation rice farmer in Furukawa. "But we keep on going because we want to preserve that faith. Religious faith is not a matter of cheap or expensive."[81] Some domestic rice farmers will survive because they can produce varieties that some consumers prefer, even at high prices. Despite large and determined protests by farmers, Japanese offi-

cials agreed to end the ban for a variety of reasons. Recent rice shortages had pushed up prices, which led consumers to support an end to the ban. Whereas only 41 percent of Japanese consumers supported an end to the ban in 1988, 62 percent did so in 1993.[82] They also responded to lobbying by Japanese industry. According to Andrew Pollack, "The big push [for an end to the ban] has come from Japan's powerful export-oriented industries, which would benefit from a new global trading system under the GATT."[83]

While GATT will adversely affect Japanese and South Korean rice farmers, it will benefit some but not all rice farmers in the United States. "California rice growers who specialize in the short-grain rice favored in Japan, would clearly benefit from an opening in the Japanese rice market," reported journalist David Sanger.

> [But] Gulf coast rice growers, who raise long-grain rice, America's dominant rice crop, would be unlikely to win a big stake of the Japanese market [though they] would benefit if the move raises world rice prices. "This is an extremely significant, very positive development for the California rice industry . . ." said John W. Kenward of the Rice Grower's Association in California.[84]

As these examples illustrate, FTAs can produce complex outcomes, with very different consequences for people within a particular industry or country. But the problems associated with these changes for small U.S. glassmakers, French wheat growers, and Japanese and South Korean rice farmers are not addressed in free trade agreements. Indeed, efforts to mitigate the impact of change for these groups might result in measures—taxes, regulations, subsidies, import or export restrictions—that FTAs are trying to eliminate. Not only are free trade agreements expected to produce economic losers, they are supposed to prevent governments from taking steps that might "protect" the losers from the impact of the agreements.

Although government officials who negotiated and adopted FTAs usually concede there may be some losers, they argue that there will be more winners in the long run. But in countries where the losers outnumber the winners, or where the losers organize to resist their loss, government officials have suffered political losses of their own.

After Canadian officials negotiated the U.S.-Canada FTA, the economy went into a tailspin. As a result of the agreement, which allowed U.S. corporations based in Canada to move their operations south to lower-wage regions in the United States, and a steep recession, the Canadian

economy lost 510,000 jobs in just three years.[85] Prime Minister Brian Mulroney, who had negotiated the agreement, saw his popularity plummet to record lows because voters opposed his economic policies and his handling of Quebecois separatism (see chapter 13). And in the October 1993 elections, his Progressive Conservative Party, which had controlled Parliament with 153 seats, lost every seat but two, a collapse even more dramatic than losses experienced by communist parties after the demise of communist regimes in the Soviet Union and Eastern Europe after 1989 (see chapter 12).[86]

And in Mexico, Zapatista insurgents in the southern state of Chiapas launched an armed rebellion on January 1, 1994, a move designed to protest NAFTA, which took effect on that day. "The free trade agreement is the death certificate for the Indian peoples of Mexico, which are expendable for the Government of Carlos Salinas de Gortari," said rebel leader Subcommandante Marcos.[87] With 20 percent of the population reporting "no income" and 40 percent reporting income of less than $3.32 a day, with falling prices for coffee, the major agricultural product of the region, and a central government that provided few of the services it offered elsewhere in the country (half of the residents in Chiapas lack potable water), NAFTA was not the only problem in Chiapas, but it symbolized to Zapatistas the government's indifference to economic losers.[88]

These political problems were not anticipated by the governments that negotiated and adopted FTAs in Canada and Mexico. Of course, FTAs will probably not create these same problems in many or even most countries. But it is likely that political problems will emerge in some countries where the expected economic benefits associated with free trade agreements do not materialize or where they produce numerous losers of the kind described here.

Notes

1. Lang, Tim, and Hines, Colin. *The New Protectionism*. New York: New Press, 1993, p. 26.

2. Environmental News Network. *GATT: The Environment and the Third World, A Resource Guide*. A Project of the Tides Foundation. Berkeley: Environmental News Network, 1992, sec. 3, p. 3.

3. Avery, William P., ed. *World Agriculture and the GATT*. Boulder, Colo.: Rienner, 1993, p. 1.

4. Passell, Peter. "Regional Trade Makes Global Deals Go Round," *New York Times*, December 19, 1993.

5. Watkins, Kevin. "GATT and the Third World," *Race and Class*, 34, 1, 1992, p. 36.

6. Davidow, Joel. "The Relationship between Anti-Trust and Trade Laws in the United States," *The World Economy*, 14, 1, 1991, p. 47. Raghavan, Chakravarthi. *Recolonization: GATT, the Uruguay Round and the Third World*. Penang, Malaysia: Third World Network, 1990, p. 73.

7. Einstein, David. "GATT Prospects are Brightening," *San Francisco Chronicle*, December 3, 1993.

8. Lang and Hines, 1993, p. 56.

9. Paarlberg, Robert L. "Why Agriculture Blocked the Uruguay Round: Evolving Strategies in a Two-Level Game," in William P. Avery, 1993, p. 42.

10. Paarlberg, 1993, p. 32.

11. Cohn, Theodore H. "The Changing Role of the United States in the Global Agricultural Trade Regime," in William P. Avery, 1993, p. 31.

12. Avery, 1993, p. 1.

13. Gilpin, Robert. *The Political Economy of International Relations*. Princeton: Princeton University Press, 1987, p. 195.

14. Environmental News Network, 1992, Sec. 1, p. 2.

15. "New Trends to Agriculture Exports Seen Under Guise of Food Safety," *Inside U.S. Trade*, Special Report, March 16, 1990, p. S-8.

16. Moore, W. John. "Stopping the States," *National Journal*, July 21, 1990, p. 1758.

17. Advertisement. "The New Age of Trade," *New York Times*, April 15, 1994.

18. Chomsky, Noam. "Notes on NAFTA: The Master of Mankind," *The Nation*, March 29, 1993, p. 412.

19. Bradsher, Keith. "Asians and Latins Object to GATT Deals," *New York Times*, December 8, 1993. Lang and Hines, 1993, p. 50.

20. Riding, Alan. "Seven Years of Struggle Ends as 109 Nations Sign Trade Accord," *New York Times*, April 16, 1991.

21. Bradsher, Keith. "US and Europe Clear the Way for a World Accord on Trade, Setting Aside Major Disputes," *New York Times*, December 15, 1993.

22. Advertisement. *New York Times*, April 15, 1994.

23. Tester, Frank James. "Free Trading the Environment," in Duncan Cameron, ed., *The Free Trade Deal*. Toronto: Lorimer, 1988, p. 207.

24. Grimmet, Jeanne J. *Environmental Regulation and the GATT*. Washington, D.C.: Congressional Research Service, 1991, p. 38.

25. Ferriss, Susan. "NAFTA Coming Into Focus," *San Francisco Examiner*, June 19, 1994.

26. Brown, Edmund G. "Race to the Bottom," *San Jose Mercury News*, September 15, 1992.

27. Tester, 1988, pp. 204–13. Shrybman, Steven. "The Environmental Costs of Free Trade," *Multinational Monitor*, March 1990, p. 20.

28. Arden-Clarke, Charles. "Conservation and Sustainable Management of Tropical Forests: The Role of ITTO and GATT." Gland, Switzerland: World Conservation Center, 1990, pp. 6, 9.

29. Cohen, Roger. "A Realignment Made Reluctantly," *New York Times*, December 15, 1993.

30. Bradsher, December 15, 1993. Weintraub, Bernard. "Clinton Spared Blame by Hollywood Officials," *New York Times*, December 16, 1993.

31. Cohen, December 15, 1993.

32. Weintraub, Bernard. "Directors Fight for GATT's Final Cut and Print," *New York Times*, December 12, 1993.

33. Mitra, Meera. "A Question of Indianness Amid Western Influence," *World Paper*, March 1992, p. 11.

34. Shenon, Philip. "Giant U.S. Film Studios Overwhelm Indonesia's," *New York Times*, October 29, 1992.

35. Cockburn, Alexander. "In Bed With America," *American Film*, November-December 1991, p. 42.

36. Kolbert, Elizabeth. "Canadians Act to Restrict Violence on TV," *New York Times*, January 11, 1994. Cohen, Roger. "France and Spain Are Adopting Quotas on U.S. Arts Imports," *New York Times*, December 22, 1993.

37. Weintraub, December 12, 1993.

38. Ibid.

39. Anthony DePalma. "US Helps Teetering Mexico Peso," *San Francisco Chronicle*, January 3, 1995.

40. Morici, Peter. "Grasping the Benefits of NAFTA," *Current History*, 92, 1993, p. 51. Wilkerson, Bruce W. "Trade Liberalization, the Market Ideology, and Morality: Have We a Sustainable System?" in Ricardo Grinspun and Maxwell A. Cameron, eds., *The Political Economy of North American Free Trade*. New York: St. Martin's Press, 1993, p. 35.

41. Weintraub, Sidney. "Free Trade in North America: Has Its Time Come?" *The World Economy*, 14, 1, 1991, p. 59.

42. Personal interview, March 5, 1993.

43. Friedman, Thomas L. "Congress Loath to Finance GATT Treaty's Tariff Losses," *New York Times*, April 13, 1994.

44. Perry, G. *Trade Liberalization and Export Promotion*. Washington, D.C.: World Bank, 1982, p. 136.

45. Farnsworth, Clyde H. "Next Trade War Target May Be Dogs," *New York Times*, December 2, 1992.

46. Phillips, David. "Dolphins and GATT," in *The Case Against Free Trade: GATT, NAFTA and the Globalization of Corporate Power*. San Francisco: Earth Island Press, 1993, p. 135.

47. Lang and Hines, 1993, pp. 65–66, 68.

48. Ritchie, Mark. "GATT, Agriculture and the Environment," *The Ecologist*, 20, 6, 1990, p. 216.

49. Bredahl, Maury E., and Forsythe, Kenneth W. "Harmonizing Phyto-Sanitary and Sanitary Regulations," *The World Economy*, 12, 2, 1989, pp. 196–97.

50. Lang and Hines, 1993, p. 103.

51. Deardorff, Alan V. "Should Patent Protection Be Extended to All Developing Countries?" *The World Economy*, 13, 4, 1990, p. 498.

52. "Of Minds and Markets: Intellectual Property Rights and the Poor," *GATT Briefing*, 2, July: European Network on Agriculture and Development, 1990, p. 2.

53. Freudenheim, Milt. "For Canada, Free Trade Accord Includes Higher Prices for Drugs," *New York Times*, November 16, 1992.

54. Shiva, Vandana. "Biodiversity and Intellectual Property Rights," in *The Case Against Free Trade*, 1993, p. 112.

55. Watkins, Kevin. "GATT and the Third World: Fixing the Rules," *Race and Class*, 34, 1, 1992, p. 38.

56. Shiva, 1993, p. 55.

57. Shiva, Vandana. "The Crisis of Diversity," *Third World Resurgence*, 13, 1991, p. 11.

58. Shiva, Vandana. "The Seed and the Earth: Biotechnology and the Colonisation of Regeneration," in Vandana Shiva, *Close to Home: Women Reconnect Ecology, Health and Development Worldwide*. Philadelphia: New Society, 1994, p. 135.

59. Shiva, 1993, p. 119.

60. Watkins, 1992, pp. 37–38.

61. Shiva, 1993, p. 119.

62. Lang and Hines, 1993, p. 34.

63. Brown, Michael Barrat. *Fair Trade: Reform and Realities in the International Trading System*. London: Zed Books, 1993, p. 51.

64. Davidow, 1991, p. 39.

65. Ibid., 38.

66. Morris, David. "Free Trade: The Great Destroyer," in *Case Against Free Trade*, 1993, p. 140.

67. Lang and Hines, 1993, pp. 43–44.

68. Stevenson, Richard W. "Europe Says Barriers to Trade Hurt Its Economies," *New York Times*, March 1, 1994.

69. Ibid.

70. Bradsher, Keith. "U.S. Memo Says Mexico May Bar NAFTA Growth," *New York Times*, March 1, 1994.

71. Schott, Jeffrey J. "Trading Blocs and the World Trading System," *The World Economy*, 14, 1, 1991, p. 3.

72. Gilpin, 1987, p. 179.

73. Advertisement. *New York Times*, April 15, 1994.

74. Lang and Hines, 1993, pp. 8, 113, 161.

75. Bradsher, Keith. "An Industry's Winners and Losers Once a Free-Trade Pact Is Signed," *New York Times*, July 21, 1992.

76. Ibid.

77. Ibid.

78. Christie, Alix. "Trade Talks Are Tearing France," *San Francisco Chronicle*, November 28, 1993.

79. Ibid.

80. Riding, Alan. "In Paris Protest, Farmers Sing Blues," *New York Times*, September 30, 1991.

81. Ibid.

82. Pollack, Andrew. "For Rice Lobby, the Bowl Dries Up," *New York Times*, December 13, 1993.

83. Ibid.

84. Sanger, David E. "Ending Sacred Trust, Japan Will Open Rice Market," *New York Times*, December 8, 1993.

85. Campbell, Bruce. "Restructuring the Economy: Canada Into the Free Trade Era," in Ricardo Grinspun and Maxwell A. Cameron, 1993, p. 100. Uchitelle, Louis. "NAFTA and Jobs: In a Numbers War, No One Can Count," *New York Times*, November 14, 1993.

86. Bradsher, Keith. "U.S. Says Chrétien Will Not Undo NAFTA," *New York Times*, October 27, 1993.

87. Golden, Tim. "Left Behind, Mexico's Indians Fight the Future," *New York Times*, January 9, 1994.

88. Ibid.

10

Population Growth

During this century, the world's population has grown rapidly, doubling from 2 to 4 billion between 1925 and 1976, and reaching 5.3 billion by 1990.[1] Much of this growth occurred after World War II. While the world's population increased annually by 20 million people during the 1940s, it increased by more than 50 million every year in the 1950s, 65 million a year in the 1960s.[2] In 1966, the United Nations estimated that world population would reach 7.5 billion by the end of the century.[3] These projections persuaded government officials around the world that rapid population growth was a serious problem and that steps should be taken to slow it. In 1969, President Nixon announced that the U.S. government would "give population [control] and family planning a high priority," and called on other governments to take "prompt action" to slow population growth.[4] And in 1974, the United Nations convened its first world population conference in Bucharest, Romania.

At the time, government officials expected that population growth would lead to a series of problems: food shortages and hunger, conflict and war, environmental destruction, and the depletion of natural resources. Events in the mid-1970s initially seemed to confirm their worst fears. But since then, a series of social and technological developments changed the expected course of events and led to a different understanding of the problems associated with rapid population growth. By 1994, when the United Nations convened its third conference on population and development in Cairo, the problems and politics associated with population growth had changed dramatically.

To understand how population issues have changed in the past twenty-five years, it is important first to describe what government officials and demographers in the late 1960s and early 1970s expected to happen as a

217

result of rapid population growth and examine the steps they took to address these problems.

The Population Bombs

Widespread public recognition of population growth as a global social problem emerged slowly in the 1950s and '60s. It was assisted by the publication of two books with the same title: *The Population Bomb*. In 1954, T. O. Greissimer published a pamphlet with this title that was widely distributed by the Hugh Moore Fund, a private foundation started by the Dixie Cup Corporation. In it, Greissimer argued that "the population bomb threatens to create an explosion as disruptive and dangerous as an explosion of the atom bomb, and with as much influence on prospects for progress or disaster, war or peace."[5]

Then in 1968, Paul Ehrlich published a book with the same title that borrowed some of Greissimer's ideas and extended them to explore the environmental consequences of population growth. These two books, and the work of private philanthropical groups like the Hugh Moore Fund, and the Population Council, a group organized in 1952 by John D. Rockefeller III, helped bring rapid population growth to the attention of policy makers and the public.[6]

In the 1950s and '60s, authors and policy makers who worried about rapid population growth noted that improved sanitation and health care in the postwar period helped more children survive infancy and enabled adults to live longer. It was common in nineteenth-century Europe for one-quarter of all infants to die before the age of 2.5 years, and one-half of adults by age 37.5. But a century later, one-fourth had not died until age 62.5, and one-half had not died until age 72.5.[7]

While these developments lowered death rates in countries around the world, people continued to have children at pre–1950 rates. Because people adjusted their behavior slowly to changed circumstances—healthier babies and longer lives—world population grew rapidly. Policy makers concerned about population growth worried that it would result in a series of social, political, and environmental problems.

First, they thought that the growing population had or would soon outstrip the amount of food available to eat, resulting in a Malthusian crisis: too many people, too little food. "The battle to feed all of humanity is over," Ehrlich argued. "Sometime around 1958, the stork passed the plow."[8] He expected this to lead to widespread hunger and starvation.

"In the 1970s," Ehrlich predicted in 1968, "the world will undergo famines—hundreds of millions of people are going to starve to death. . . ."[9]

Ehrlich and others who supported this view were often called "Malthusians" because this argument relies on Robert Malthus's 1798 *Essay on Population*, which proposed that "the power of population is indefinitely greater than the power in the earth to produce subsistence [food] for man."[10]

Ehrlich explained that he came to understand Malthus and the meaning of the population bomb,

> one stinking hot night in Delhi. . . . My wife and daughter and I were returning to our hotel in an ancient taxi. The seats were hopping with fleas. The only functional gear was third. As we crawled through the city, we entered a crowded slum area. The temperature was well over 100, and the air was a haze of dust and smoke. The streets seemed alive with people. People eating, people washing, people sleeping. People visiting, arguing, and screaming. People thrusting their hands through the taxi window, begging. People defecating and urinating. People clinging to buses. People herding animals. People, people, people, people. As we moved slowly through the mob, hand horn squawking, the dust, noise, heat, and cooking fires gave the scene a hellish aspect. Would we ever get to our hotel? All three of us were, frankly, frightened. It seemed that anything could happen—but, of course, nothing did. Old India hands will laugh at our reaction. We were just some overprivileged tourists, unaccustomed to the sights and sounds of India. Perhaps, but since that night I've known the *feel* of overpopulation.[11]

The growing gap between population and food supply would lead first to starvation, population control advocates expected. And the onset of starvation would lead to a second problem: war. As one population control group explained in a 1967 newspaper ad, "There can be no doubt that unless population is brought under control at an early date, the resulting human misery and social tensions will inevitably lead to chaos and strife—to revolutions and wars, the dimensions of which it would be hard to predict."[12] During the 1960s, many U.S. government officials viewed social unrest, communist insurgency, and guerrilla warfare in poor countries as the likely political product of "overpopulation."[13]

Third, the new Malthusians argued that a growing population would increase levels of pollution and waste, which would result in environmental degradation. As Ehrlich wrote, "The causal chain of [environmental] deterioration is easily followed to its source. Too many cars, too many factories, too much detergent, too much pesticide . . . inadequate sewage

treatment plants, too little water, too much carbon dioxide—all can be easily traced to *too many people*."[14]

Ehrlich and others subsequently modified this somewhat, arguing that environmental degradation was a product not only of population size but also of the level of affluence and the kind of technology used to produce goods, an argument summed up by this formula: Impact = Population × Affluence × Technology, or I = PAT.[15] But in 1990 he still maintained that "Global warming, acid rain, depletion of the ozone layer, and exhaustion of soils and ground water are all related to population size."[16]

And fourth, the new Malthusians believed that the growing population would consume finite natural resources such as minerals and oil at an accelerated rate, resulting in raw material shortages and rising prices for the goods produced by industrial societies.[17] As the Club of Earth argued in 1988, "Overpopulation and rapid population growth are intimately connected with . . . [the] rapid depletion of non-renewable resources. . . ."[18]

Because they expected rapid population growth to lead to starvation, war, environmental degradation, and the depletion of natural resources, private groups and government officials began advocating population control in the late 1960s and early 1970s. And they urged governments to adopt programs that would slow population growth. These included the creation of educational family planning programs, the distribution of contraceptives, and sometimes the provision of clinics that performed abortions and sterilizations, usually on a voluntary but sometimes on an involuntary basis. Population control advocates in government and the private sector believed that rapid population growth was such an urgent problem that drastic steps needed to be taken quickly. Some even advanced the concept of triage as a way to address the problem.

During World War I, doctors at military field hospitals in France developed a policy to deal with incoming casualties who could not all be cared for by limited medical staffs. They divided casualties into three groups, hence the name "triage," from the French for "three parts." The first group was composed of soldiers who would die even if they were treated. The second, those who would survive without immediate treatment. The third, those who could be saved only if they were treated immediately. Under this policy, doctors treated the third group and left the other two to live or die.[19]

Population control advocates borrowed this idea and applied it to population control programs. For some, "triage [means] directing [food] aid to those countries with the greatest chance of survival while abandoning others to famine."[20] Ehrlich and others argued that U.S. food aid should

be given to countries like Pakistan, which might eventually become "self-sufficient" and able to feed its own population, but withheld from countries like India, which would not be able to feed its population even with substantial food aid.[21] In a food-short world, feeding people who could not eventually feed themselves would be a waste of scarce resources, population controllers argued.[22] Some even argued that some health care programs should be withdrawn from countries where population growth was rapid.[23]

The concept of triage was important because it was adopted by some governments as a component of population control policy. In the United States, for example, government officials in the Johnson and then Nixon administrations increased spending for the U.S. Agency for International Development's (AID) population control program from $35 million in 1968 to $123 million in 1972, a nearly fourfold increase.[24] But at the same time, they cut AID's funding for overseas health care programs by nearly one-third, from $164 million to $60 million, in the same period.[25] In 1966, U.S. officials first insisted that countries receiving U.S. food aid institute birth control programs so that they could, in President Johnson's words, "prevent the shadow of hunger from becoming the nightmare of famine."[26] In the 1970s, when food shortages developed as a result of poor Soviet grain harvests, the Nixon administration curtailed its food aid program and insisted that poor countries pay for food imports (many of them borrowed heavily to do so), a policy that used the concept of triage as a rationale.

Events in the 1970s initially seemed to confirm the expectations of population control advocates. A 1972 famine in Bangladesh and the war that followed it in 1973–74, and the world grain shortages that resulted from poor Soviet harvests, raised the prospect of widespread hunger and acute famine. The OPEC oil embargo, which sharply raised prices, signaled to many the depletion of this important but finite natural resource. But in the years that followed, a number of social and technological developments occurred that challenged the predictions of population controllers and led to a different understanding of the relation between population growth and hunger, population and war, population and environmental degradation, and population and natural resource depletion.

Crisis Deferred

During the 1970s and '80s, the world's population grew more slowly and food production increased more rapidly than population control advo-

cates expected. And because global per capita food production actually increased despite continued population growth, the Malthusian crisis that Ehrlich and others expected to emerge in the 1970s was averted or, at least, deferred.

The population bomb did not "explode" in the 1970s or '80s largely because two social-technological revolutions altered the relation between population growth and food supply. The "Sexual Revolution" that transformed gender relations around the world slowed population growth in first and many third world countries, while a "Green Revolution" greatly increased food production in many countries, even in countries with little land and large populations like India and China. Population control advocates like Ehrlich did not anticipate or fully appreciate these developments because they wrote, in the late 1960s, on the eve of both revolutions, which had then only just begun. To understand why the Malthusian crisis was averted, let us first examine why population growth slowed, and then examine why food supplies grew in the 1970s and '80s.

Slowed Population Growth

Although the world's population continued to grow during the 1970s and '80s, it did not grow nearly as fast as expected. In the late 1960s, population control advocates and the United Nations predicted that world population—then 3.5 billion—would more than double to 7.5 billion by the end of the century. But it grew more slowly, to 5.3 billion in 1990 and an expected 6.1 billion by the year 2000.[27] This means that there will be about 1.4 billion fewer people than demographers expected, a substantial difference.[28] This was due primarily to declining birth rates. As Harvard economist Amartya Sen noted, "Indeed, the growth rate of world population is already firmly declining—it came down from 2.2 percent in the 1970s to 1.7 percent between 1980 and 1992."[29]

Rates of population growth slowed most dramatically in first world countries. "In France, the United Kingdom and the United States, the [fertility] rate is 1.8 births per women," a rate well below the level (2.1) that would lead eventually to a "stable population size."[30] As Ehrlich admitted in his 1990 book, *The Population Explosion*, "Average birth rates in . . . the United States are already below replacement reproduction."[31]

Growth rates slowed dramatically in first world countries like the United States as a result of a series of technological and social developments that can collectively be described as the Sexual Revolution. The development of new contraceptive technologies—the pill, intrauterine devices, diaphragms, and spermicides—which became widely available only

in the mid-to-late 1960s, the abolition in 1973 of federal government restrictions on abortions, changed social attitudes about sexuality and gender roles that emerged as a result of the counterculture and women's movements in the 1960s and 1970s, and the widespread entry of women into the labor force, led to lower birth rates in the United States. By 1976, the birth rate had fallen to 1.7, well below "replacement reproduction."[32]

The rapid decline in U.S. birth rates occurred largely as a result of technological change and voluntary social developments, not as a result of government-directed population control programs. The government did abolish most restrictions on the use of contraceptive technologies in the 1960s and on the use of abortion to terminate pregnancy in 1973, but it did little to reduce the size of the domestic population or develop population control programs in the United States.[33] Most family planning programs were developed by private for-profit businesses and nonprofit corporations like Planned Parenthood. The U.S. government, however, did fund population control programs in other countries. For example, U.S. AID spent "$3.9 billion on population and family planning assistance throughout the third world" between 1968 and 1988.[34]

Similar developments contributed to lower birth rates in most first world countries, even in France, Italy, and Spain, where the Catholic Church opposed the use of most contraceptive technologies and abortion and where the governments did little to promote domestic population control. Between the late 1960s and early 1990, fertility rates dropped from 2.5 to 1.5 in Italy, from 2.9 to 1.7 in Spain, and to a low 1.8 rate in France.[35]

Population growth also slowed dramatically in many, though not all, third world countries. Although the introduction of new technologies and changed social attitudes may have contributed to declining birth rates there, government population control programs, often developed with the assistance of first world population control advocates and institutions, played a significant role.

In the mid-1960s, "only 12 governments had national population programs, which were funded primarily by the United States and other foreign aid donors."[36] But by 1994, "130 national governments . . . subsidized family planning services, including 65 developing country governments which specifically seek to slow population growth."[37]

Some populous third world countries have greatly slowed population growth in a very short time. In China, fertility rates fell from 2.8 in 1979 to 2.0 by 1991; in the Indian state of Kerala, they fell from 3.0 to 1.8 in the same period; and in Brazil, they fell from 5.75 in 1970 to 4.35 in 1980 and to 3.2 in 1990.[38] While fertility rates fell rapidly and dramatically in all these regions, they did so for very different social reasons.

In China, fertility rates fell as a result of coercive and noncoercive government programs. Long-standing government programs designed to raise literacy rates and provide education, health care, and employment helped lower fertility rates, as noncoercive programs like these have done in many parts of the third world. The government's adoption in 1979 of a coercive one-child policy, which rewards families with only one child and punishes families who have more than one child, also reduced fertility rates and slowed population growth. "While China may get too much credit for its authoritarian measures, it gets far too little credit for the other, more collaboratory and participatory policies it has followed, which have themselves helped to cut down the birth rate," argues Sen.[39]

By contrast, in the Indian state of Kerala, a region much like China in social and economic terms, fertility rates fell even more dramatically than they did in China, and did so in the absence of coercive government measures. Instead, fertility rates fell in response to improved health care and education for women, what Sen describes as "collaborative" and "participatory" government programs.[40]

In Brazil, fertility rates fell in the absence of either coercive *or* collaborative *government* programs. "What distinguishes Brazil is the absence of any government birth control program. Brazil has experienced the largest self-induced drop in human history . . . compressing 100 years of fertility decline into 20 years," said Canadian demographer George Martine.[41] Despite the lack of government birth control programs and the opposition of the Catholic Church, Brazilians began using contraceptives in large numbers. Contraceptive use increased from only 5 percent of married women in 1965 to two-thirds of married women in 1989, and 27 percent of them have been sterilized (compared to 17 percent in the United States).[42]

Social scientists argue that Brazilians have reduced family size because their incomes have declined (largely as a result of the debt crisis) while their expectations have risen (largely as a result of TV). To get more with less, men and women have, in effect, downsized their families and had fewer children.[43]

In China, Kerala, and Brazil, fertility rates fell for very different reasons, in unexpected ways. In the 1960s, population control advocates recommended that governments adopt coercive measures to slow population growth, particularly in populous third world countries. In some countries, population growth slowed, not as a result of coercive government programs, but as a result of collaborative government programs or voluntary individual decisions. So, for a variety of reasons, population growth slowed and world population did not increase as rapidly as population

control advocates expected. Not only did the population grow more slowly, but food supplies increased more rapidly than Malthusians anticipated.

Growing Food Supplies

World population grew from 2.5 billion to 5.3 billion between 1950 and 1990, the largest, fastest increase in human history.[44] But world food production grew even faster. In 1950, farmers produced 631 million metric tons of grain, but 1,688 million metric tons in 1990, a 260 percent increase, "outstripping population growth by a wide margin and raising the grain harvested per person by 40 percent."[45] And the production of meat rose at the same rate, from 24 million to 62 million tons, while the fish catch increased from 22 million to 100 million tons.[46] "History records no increase in food production that was remotely comparable in scale, speed, spread or duration," British economist Michael Lipton has written.[47] And global environmental analyst Lester Brown concurs, "Much of the world *is* better fed than it was in 1950."[48]

What's more, food production has increased dramatically in the world's most populous countries in recent decades. India increased its food production per capita by 23 percent in the past decade and China by 39 percent, according to the U.N. Food and Agriculture Organization.[49] "The *largest* increases in the production of food—not just in the aggregate but also per person—are actually taking place in the third world, particularly in the region that is having the largest absolute increases in the world population, that is, in Asia," writes Sen.[50]

As a measure of this progress, food prices have generally fallen. In 1992, the United Nations reported that the price of "basic foods" had fallen 38 percent during the 1980s.[51] Contrary to what population controllers expected, food production has grown more rapidly than population, and it has grown most rapidly in areas they least expected it. Recall that Ehrlich advised cutting food aid to India because, he believed, it would never achieve food self-sufficiency. As it turned out, India eventually became a grain *exporter*.

The rapid growth in food production, even in the third world, was largely a product of the Green Revolution, the combination of new technologies and farming practices that emerged first in the United States after World War II, and then spread to Europe, Japan, and eventually the third world. The Green Revolution advanced rapidly during the 1970s, as farmers in Western Europe, North America, and the third world responded to Soviet grain shortages and high world food prices by adopting new

technologies and expanding production. Population controllers, who expected famines to develop in the mid-1970s, did not anticipate these developments because they wrote on the eve of the Green Revolution.

Of course, while world food supplies grew more rapidly than population in recent decades, this does not mean they will continue to do so, and food production slowed somewhat during the late 1980s. Nor does it mean that increasing food supplies will eliminate or even reduce hunger. As we have seen, a substantial proportion of world food supplies is fed to cattle and other animals, a large percentage of agricultural land is devoted to inedible export crops, and populations in rich countries consume much more per person than inhabitants in poor countries. In the United States, for example, residents consume 860 kilograms of grain per person, nearly three times the world average (323 kilograms per person) and nearly nine times as much as the average Haitian (100 kilograms per person).[52] And because many people have found that their entitlement to food has been adversely affected by economic developments—declining incomes, debt crisis, currency devaluations, unemployment, budget cuts—they may experience hunger even though food prices have generally fallen. The result is that a large percentage of the world's growing population—about one billion in 1990—are hungry *despite* growing food supplies. And unless these economic and social patterns of food production and consumption change, people will continue to hunger, even starve.

Because population has grown more slowly and food supplies more rapidly than population controllers expected, a Malthusian crisis characterized by widespread famine did not materialize in the 1970s or '80s. The crisis was averted or deferred by the Sexual Revolution and the Green Revolution and, to some extent, by governments and individuals who heeded the advice of population control advocates and developed programs or change behaviors that slowed population growth.

The Malthusian crisis was not the only problem that population-control advocates expected to result from rapid population growth. They also expected it to lead to war, environmental degradation, and the depletion of natural resources. But events in the 1970s and '80s would change expected relations, just as they changed the relation between population growth and food supply.

War, Environmental Degradation, and Resource Depletion

In the 1950s and '60s, population control advocates argued that rapid population growth would lead to war, as countries struggled for control of food and other scarce resources. But the evidence that population

growth leads to war is quite weak. Most of the wars fought since 1970, or indeed throughout the post-World War II period, were triggered not by population pressures, but by the political and social problems associated with partition, superpower rivalry, or ethnic conflict. It would be difficult to argue, for instance, that Arab-Israeli wars, the Soviet invasion of Afghanistan, or U.S. interventions in Vietnam, Grenada, Panama, or the Persian Gulf were the outgrowth of population pressures. On a few occasions, famine and war have been related, but the relationship has been different from what population controllers expected.

Since 1970, famine and war have occurred in Bangladesh (1971–74), Cambodia (1975–80), Ethiopia (1980s), Somalia (1990–91), and Rwanda (1994). With the exception of Bangladesh, war has *preceded* famine in each case. Most political analysts have argued that war in these countries was triggered by social and ethnic conflict and that war, by displacing people and disrupting food production, contributed to hunger and famine. If this is true, then the relation between population growth and hunger and war needs to be reexamined. In these cases, war probably contributed to famine, not famine to war.

In their initial assessment during the 1960s, population control advocates expected that population growth was responsible for pollution and would lead to severe environmental degradation. A growing awareness of environmental problems after Earth Day in 1970 made this seem a plausible assumption. But during the 1970s and '80s, scientists began to argue that worrisome environmental problems such as ozone depletion and global warming were more a product of affluence and technology than a consequence of overpopulation (see chapter 11).

In 1974, scientists discovered that man-made gases called chlorofluorocarbons (CFCs) that were used in aerosol sprays, solvents, and styrofoam destroyed the ozone layer, which protects people and plants from the sun's damaging rays. They also observed that small populations using advanced technology were responsible for most of the atmospheric pollution resulting from CFC use. Populations in the Northern Hemisphere, most of them affluent in global terms, emitted 88 percent of all CFCs, while poor populations in the Southern Hemisphere released only 12 percent of the total.[53]

Much the same is true of global warming. During the mid-1980s, scientists discovered that the burning of fossil fuels and forests had increased the level of carbon dioxide in the atmosphere. They predicted that high carbon dioxide levels would trap heat in the atmosphere and make the planet warmer. They also calculated that "with only 25 percent of the world's people, the industrialized nations of the North generated nearly

three-quarters of all carbon dioxide emissions, accounting for about half of the manmade greenhouse gases in the atmosphere."[54] According to environmental scientist Kirk Smith, the average American annually produces 5.2 tons of carbon dioxide while the average Indian produces only 0.22 tons, about 4 percent as much.[55]

In this case, small affluent populations, which use advanced technologies like cars to consume energy resources at a rapid rate, make a bigger contribution to pollution and environmental degradation than large but poor populations. For example, "75 percent of the 2,500 billion tons of waste generated in 1985 worldwide" is produced by developed countries.[56] And according to Sen, "it remains true that one . . . American has a larger negative impact on the ozone layer, global warmth and other elements of the earth's environment than dozens of Indians and Zimbabweans put together."[57]

Findings like these altered the perception that growing populations, particularly in the third world, were primarily responsible for global environmental degradation. Instead, pollution and environmental degradation are now seen more as products of technology and consumption patterns by small but affluent populations. Again, these developments were not well understood by population controllers in the 1960s, who wrote before ozone depletion and global warming were even recognized as serious environmental problems.

During the 1960s, population control advocates warned that a growing population would consume natural resources at a more rapid rate, leading to the depletion of key, finite natural resources like oil and minerals. And during the 1970s, events initially confirmed this last set of expectations. Successive oil embargoes drove oil prices to record levels and the price of many other minerals increased sharply. Economists predicted that oil prices would continue to rise as supplies dwindled, feeding inflation and crippling energy-dependent industrial economies.

But events took a different turn in the 1980s. High oil prices stimulated the search for new supplies, and substantial amounts were found in the North Sea. Automobile manufacturers began producing more fuel-efficient cars, and "gasoline consumption per mile fell by 29 percent between 1973 and 1988."[58] Consumers lowered their thermostats and installed weather stripping and insulation in their attics to conserve heat, and utility companies provided rebates on energy-efficient appliances. As a result of new oil discoveries, the development of new technologies, and changed social behavior, oil supplies increased, the demand for oil leveled off, and prices fell. By the end of the 1980s, the price of oil had fallen to pre-embargo levels.

Similar developments occurred with regard to other natural resources. The invention of new fiber-optic cable made from glass, which is produced from sand or silica, a very common material, reduced the demand for and price of copper cable, which is made from a relatively scarce mineral. In the 1960s, military planners worried that declining supplies of tungsten, a rare metal used to make high-performance jet airplane parts, could compromise their ability to build sophisticated military aircraft. But that fear has abated because the most advanced jet aircraft now use composite-material technology that replaces much of the need for tungsten.

In 1980, the economist Julian Simon bet population control advocate Paul Ehrlich that the price of finite natural resources would fall during the next decade, as people found new supplies, used them more efficiently, and developed substitutes. Ehrlich accepted the wager, arguing that a growing population would deplete natural resources and increase their price by the end of the decade. Simon allowed Ehrlich to choose five commodities and bet $1,000 on the outcome. Ten years later, the *New York Times Magazine* reported the outcome. In 1980, Ehrlich had purchased $200 worth of five metals: copper, chrome, nickel, tin, and tungsten. By 1990, the price of all five metals had *declined*, copper to $163, chrome to $120, nickel to $193, tin to $56, and tungsten to $86.[59] Simon won the bet because technological and social changes increased supplies and/or reduced demand, causing the price of these metals to fall. As the *New York Times Magazine* explained,

> Prices fell for the same . . . reasons they had fallen in previous decades—entrepreneurship and continuing technological improvements. Prospectors found new lodes, such as the nickel mines around the world that ended a Canadian company's near monopoly of the market. Thanks to computers, new machines and new chemical processes, there were more efficient ways to extract and refine the ores for chrome and other metals. For many uses, the metals were replaced by cheaper materials, notably plastics, which became less expensive as the price of oil declined (even during this year's crisis in the Persian Gulf, the real cost of oil remained lower than in 1980). Telephone calls went through satellites and fiber-optic lines instead of copper wires. Ceramics replaced tungsten in cutting tools. Cars were made of aluminum instead of tin and the [international tin] cartel collapsed.[60]

As a result of these developments, the problems that population-control advocates expected to occur did not materialize or, if they did, not in ways that were expected. As we have seen in previous chapters, government policies have often failed to produce expected results or, if they did,

had unanticipated social consequences. Dollar devaluations, high interest rate policies, third world development lending, tax-cut programs, new agricultural technologies, superpower partition, and economic crises in dictatorships had unexpected social, political, and economic consequences, which government officials and social scientists did not anticipate or appreciate. Much the same is true of problems associated with population growth.

The inability of population control advocates to anticipate the course of subsequent events should not be too surprising, particularly because they were writing on the eve of dramatic and far-reaching social and technological revolutions. And the developments that changed the expected course of events did not mean that rapid population growth was not a problem. Indeed it is. Population growth remains a serious global problem, just as hunger remains a difficult issue. But while population growth is a serious global problem, the character of the problem has changed and people think differently about it.

Changing Programs and Policies

Population growth is still a problem. World population may still double or triple in size before it stabilizes sometime in the next century. And while food production expanded more rapidly than population during the postwar period, there is no guarantee that it will continue to do so, particularly if soil erosion continues at high levels. Nearly one billion go hungry in any case. Unless they can obtain the means to grow or purchase food they will remain hungry, and population growth will likely increase the number of hungry people in the world. But the social and technological developments of the past twenty-five years have shifted the focus of government officials and social scientists concerned about population growth.

In the 1960s, officials were worried primarily about *world* population growth. But as population growth slowed dramatically in most first world and some third world countries, they worried less about global population increases and more about high fertilities rates and rapid growth in some regions, in particular countries. In most African countries, fertility rates remain very high. And economic decline during the 1980s—due largely to indebtedness and falling commodity prices for the goods they produce—has made it difficult for governments to provide effective programs that could slow population growth. They have been unable to increase their food production substantially, largely because governments

lack the means to build infrastructures that can assist or stimulate food production. Population growth remains high in India, which "adds more people to the world's population each year than all the countries of sub-Saharan Africa combined."[61]

To slow population growth in Africa, India, and elsewhere, government officials in many countries now believe that coercive government policies—like the Indian government's forced sterilization campaigns of the early 1970s—were counterproductive. Objections to this campaign led to the ouster of the government that sponsored it and discredited other, non-coercive family planning programs. "If we had concentrated more on the . . . human resources element—female literacy, education—in the 1950s and '60s, [India] would have a population of about 600 million now [instead of 800 million]," said government science adviser Sam Pitroda.[62] Many social scientists believe that China's one-child policy may have done less to slow population growth than its proponents claim and led to other problems, such as a decline in the number of female children, the result of widespread abortion of females by couples who want male heirs.[63]

As a result, the focus of most population control efforts has shifted from coercive "emergency" measures to noncoercive government programs and voluntary private efforts. "There is no imminent emergency that calls for a breathless response," argues Sen. "What is called for is systematic support for people's own decisions to reduce family size through expanding education and health care, and through economic and social development."[64]

Generally speaking, government officials and social scientists agree that fertility rates can be reduced by making inexpensive contraceptive technologies more widely available—"40 to 50 percent of women of reproductive age in 18 developing countries [100 million altogether] desire no more children but have no access to family planning," notes the World-watch Institute's Jodi Jacobson—by providing better maternal and infant health care, educating women, and teaching them to read, by promoting gender equality, particularly in the workplace, and by increasing the age at which women may legally marry.[65] But while there is general agreement that these steps can work, their effectiveness depends on the particular design of the program and its applicability to very specific social and cultural settings. How to do this is the subject of considerable experimentation and debate.

Government officials in many countries have also shifted their attention to the problems associated with population *movement*, not just growth. "By the year 2005 . . . more than half of the world's people will live in urban areas," write officials of the U.N.'s Population Division.[66]

While cities have increased in size as a result of population growth (about 60 percent), they have also done so because people have moved to cities from rural areas (40 percent).[67] In 1950, for instance, no city in Africa had more than one million inhabitants. But by 1970 there were 19 cities with more than one million inhabitants, by 1990 there were 59, and there may be as many as 109 by the year 2000.[68] Mexico City grew from 3.5 million in 1950 to about 18 million in 1990, a fivefold increase.[69]

Because most cities lack the infrastructure to accommodate swelling populations, sanitation, crowding, traffic, and the provision of basic services—water, electricity—all become serious health and social problems. And because few cities can provide employment for growing populations, poverty and hunger become common. "Already," Paul Kennedy writes, "the sheer concentration of people—143,000 per square miles in Lagos, Nigeria and 130,000 per square mile in Djakarta, Indonesia, compared with New York's mere 11,400 per square mile . . . [results in cities that] have become increasingly centers of poverty and social collapse."[70]

While poor countries worry about internal migrations that result in rapid urbanization, government officials in rich countries, where fertility rates have plummeted, express concern about migration across national borders. But most migration takes place within national borders, and most cross-border migrants stay within the less developed world. Of the one hundred million international migrants in 1992, the World Bank estimated that only one-third moved to Western Europe, North America, and Australia, and about 1.5 percent of the total migrated to the United States.[71]

Some population control advocates in first world countries have shifted their attention from population growth to immigration. As Ehrlich argued in 1990, "Migration from poor to rich nations represents a very different kind of threat. . . . To the degree that immigrants adopt the lifestyles of their adopted countries, they will begin consuming more resources per person, and to do disproportionate environmental damage."[72] John Tanton, founder of an anti-immigrant group, Federation for American Immigration Reform, argues,

> More and more countries, most of them poor and less developed, are reaching the point of excess population, resource depletion and economic stagnation. Their "huddled masses" cast longing eyes on the apparent riches of the industrial west. The developed countries lie directly in the path of a great storm from the third world.[73]

This perspective is ironic because it was European populations that grew rapidly in the nineteenth century—increasing their share of world

population from 22 percent in 1800 to 35 percent in 1930—and migrated across the globe, settling in North America and Australia—"over 50 million Europeans moved overseas between 1846 and 1930."[74]

Although substantial numbers of migrants move to the industrialized countries, economists are divided about the consequences of immigration. Some argue that it contributes to the economy, while others maintain that it is a drain on government expenditures and harms the economy. The historical evidence suggests that earlier migrations were generally beneficial, though not without social and economic costs. And there is considerable evidence that migrants who sent earnings home to families played a significant role in the economic development of poorer countries. The money sent back to the Philippines by migrants in 1989, for example, contributed more to the islands' economy than all foreign direct investment that year.[75] If this is generally true, the admission of some immigrants to wealthy countries may assist economic development in poor countries, and economic development there may help provide jobs, thereby reducing migration, and lower fertility rates, which could slow population growth (economic development and higher incomes have contributed to declining fertility in many settings).

Just as the focus on population control efforts has shifted, the earlier emphasis on food production has changed over the years. In the 1960s, most government officials and international aid organizations focused their efforts simply on increasing overall food production. But as it became clear that food production and hunger could both grow together, and that hunger was caused not simply by population growth but by a decline in the poor's "entitlement" to food (their ability to grow or purchase food), government officials and agricultural experts shifted their attention to these issues. While scientists keep trying to increase yields, they now emphasize the importance of conserving topsoil and developing sustainable land-use systems. Many social scientists now argue that less food should be produced for animals and more for human consumption and that efforts should be made to provide land and subsistence foods for the poor.

There is less emphasis on the effect of growing poor populations on environmental degradation or resource depletion, though there is some because poor populations can contribute to resource depletion and pollution by cutting trees and burning fuel wood, which can also lead to soil erosion. Instead, the attention of government officials has turned to the role that the use of advanced technologies—such as automobiles—and the demand for resources in affluent industrialized societies play in global pollution and resource consumption.

Changing Politics

During the past twenty-five years, social developments have changed people's understanding of population growth and the problems associated with it. As this occurred, the programmatic emphasis of governments around the world has shifted. Not surprisingly, the politics surrounding global population issues has been transformed in unexpected ways, creating different political alignments at each of the three U.N. conferences on population, which were held in Bucharest in 1974, Mexico City in 1984, and Cairo in 1994.

The first U.N. population conference was organized at the initiative of the United States and other first world countries. At the meeting, the U.S. delegation, appointed by Republican President Nixon, "put forward a forceful policy agenda favoring urgent global action to reduce high fertility, including demographic targets" for every country.[76] These proposals were opposed by most third world countries, whether capitalist or communist, Muslim or Catholic.[77] They argued that "development was the best contraceptive," and maintained that "population will take care of itself" so long as the industrialized countries agreed to provide economic aid and improve the terms of trade.[78] Third world countries were joined by the communist countries, notably the Soviet Union and China. Following Karl Marx, who had criticized Malthus, government officials in the Soviet Union and China regarded population size and growth as a nonissue or, in the case of China, as a "very good thing."[79]

During the next ten years, population growth slowed dramatically in first world countries, population control programs were adopted by many third world countries, and in 1979, China reversed its position and adopted forceful population control measures. But while many countries joined the U.S. "side" of the population debate, the United States abandoned it. After he was elected president in 1980, Ronald Reagan, who ran on an anti-abortion, pro-life platform, reversed U.S. population control policy and cut off U.S. aid for foreign family programs that included abortion. And at the 1984 U.N. population conference, the U.S. delegation argued that rapid population growth was "a neutral phenomenon . . . not necessarily good or ill." And U.S. delegates argued that the population boom "was a challenge, it need not have been a crisis."[80] Ironically, this was a position previously held, but recently abandoned, by communist countries.

As a result, most industrialized capitalist countries, most communist countries, and many third world countries supported global population control efforts, while the United States joined Catholic and some Islamic

third world countries that regarded population growth as unimportant and viewed many population control programs as pernicious.

One consequence of the U.S. position at the 1984 conference was that global funding for family planning and population control programs declined, primarily because the United States, which had previously been the primary donor, cut its funding. The withdrawal of U.S. funding had a significant impact on population growth. "During the 1970s, world contraceptive use grew by 53 percent and average family size declined by 22 percent. . . . [But] during the 1980s, . . . contraceptive use grew by less than 20 percent and family size declined less than 8 percent," observed Sharon Camp, a representative of Population Action International.[81]

When Democrat Bill Clinton was elected president in 1992, the U.S. position changed again, moving back to support for population control programs, the position held by Nixon in the early 1970s. At the 1994 U.N. conference in Cairo, a new political alignment had emerged. For the first time, the United States was allied with communist China in support of global population control programs, a position supported by industrialized countries in Europe and Japan, and by many third world countries. On the other side, many Catholic third world countries, which had opposed population control programs at the previous two meetings, were joined by a large number of Muslim countries. This new alliance was unusual because the two religions have historically been at odds. These countries objected to language in the conference report that they believed approved of abortion "as an international right or as a means of family planning."[82] Some Islamic countries—Iraq, Saudi Arabia, Sudan, and Lebanon—boycotted the conference altogether.[83] While language on abortion became an extremely contentious issue at the meeting, most countries around the world—173 of 189—nonetheless permit it.[84] To some extent, the new global political alignment on population issues pitted countries with "secular" identities (capitalist and communist) against countries with "religious" identities (Catholic, Muslim).

Although population growth is an issue today, as it was in the 1960s, the problems, programs, and politics associated with it have changed substantially. And these changes have occurred largely as a result of technological, social, and political developments that were not very well understood when rapid population growth first became a global issue.

Notes

1. Kennedy, Paul. *Preparing for the 21st Century*. New York: Random House, 1993, p. 22.

2. Vu, My T. *World Population Projections, 1985*. Baltimore: Johns Hopkins University Press, 1985.

3. Hauser, Philip M. "World Population: Retrospect and Prospect," in National Academy of Sciences, *Rapid Population Growth: Consequences and Policy Implications*. Baltimore: Johns Hopkins University Press, 1971, p. 110.

4. Mass, Bonnie. *Population Target: The Political Economy of Population Control in Latin America*. Toronto: Women's Press, 1976, p. 63.

5. Ibid., p. 40.

6. Ibid., p. 37. Teitelbawm, Michael S. "The Population Threat," *Foreign Affairs*, Winter 1992–93, p. 66.

7. Hauser, 1971, p. 107.

8. Ehrlich, Paul R. *The Population Bomb*. New York: Ballentine Books, 1968, p. 37.

9. Ibid., prologue.

10. Malthus, Thomas Robert. "An Essay on the Principle of Population," in Garrett Hardin, ed., *Population Evolution and Birth Control*. San Francisco: Freeman, 1969, p. 7.

11. Ehrlich, 1968, pp. 15–16.

12. Mass, 1976, p. 60.

13. Ibid., pp. 46–47, 137.

14. Ehrlich, 1968, pp. 66–67.

15. Ehrlich, Paul R., and Ehrlich, Anne H. *The Population Explosion*. New York: Simon and Schuster, 1990, p. 58.

16. Ehrlich, Paul R., and Ehrlich, Anne H. "The Population Explosion," *Amicus Journal*, Winter 1990, p. 25.

17. Ehrlich, 1968, p. 133.

18. Ehrlich and Ehrlich, *Amicus*, 1990, p. 26.

19. Ehrlich, 1968, p. 159.

20. Mass, 1976, p. 138.

21. Ehrlich, 1968, pp. 160–61.

22. Ibid., p. 166.

23. Bandarage, Asoka. "A New Malthusianism?" *Peace Review*, 6, 3, Fall 1994, p. 294.

24. Mass, 1976, pp. 48, 58.

25. Ibid.

26. Ibid., p. 50.

27. Berreby, David. "The Numbers Game," *Discover*, April 1990, pp. 48–49.

28. Lewis, Paul. "World Population Will Top 6 Billion," *New York Times*, May 15, 1990. Stevens, William K. "Feeding a Booming Population Without Destroying the Planet," *New York Times*, May 10, 1992.

29. Sen, Amartya. "Population: Delusion and Reality," *New York Review of Books*, September 22, 1994, p. 69.

30. Jacobson, Jodi. "Planning the Global Family," in Lester Brown, *State of the World 1988*. New York: Norton, 1988, p. 152.

31. Ehrlich and Ehrlich, 1990, p. 193.

32. Haub, Carl, and Riche, March F. "Population by the Numbers," in Laurie Ann Mazur, ed., *Beyond the Numbers: A Reader on Population, Consumption and the Environment*. Washington, D.C.: Island Press, 1994, p. 103.

33. Teitelbawm, 1992–93, p. 68.

34. Donaldson, Peter, and Tsui, Amy Ong. "The International Family Planning Movement," in Laurie Ann Mazur, 1994, p. 115.

35. Kennedy, 1993, p. 36. Jacobson, 1988, p. 152.

36. Camp, Sharon L. "The Politics of U.S. Population Assistance," in Laurie Ann Mazur, 1994, p. 123.

37. Ibid.

38. Sen, 1994, p. 70. Brooke, James. "Births in Brazil Are on Decline, Easing Worries," *New York Times*, August 8, 1989.

39. Sen, 1994, p. 70.

40. Ibid.

41. Brooke, 1989.

42. Ibid.

43. Ibid.

44. Brown, Lester. "Feeding Six Billion," *Worldwatch*, September-October 1989. Reprinted in John Allen, ed., *Environment 91/92*, Guilford, Conn.: Dushkin, 1991, p. 62.

45. Ibid., p. 66. Brown, Lester. "Facing Food Insecurity," in Lester Brown, *State of the World 1994*, New York: Norton, 1994, p. 177.

46. Ibid., p. 181.

47. Timberlake, Lloyd. *Africa in Crisis: The Causes, the Cures of Environmental Bankruptcy*. London: International Institute for Environment and Development, 1985, p. 18.

48. Mann, Charles C. "How Many Is Too Many?" *The Atlantic*, February 1993. Reprinted in John L. Allen, ed., *Environment 94/95*, Guilford, Conn.: Dushkin, 1994, p. 39.

49. Sen, 1994, p. 66.

50. Ibid.

51. Ibid., p. 67.

52. Postel, Sandra. "Carrying Capacity: The Earth's Bottom Line," in Laurie Ann Mazur, 1994, p. 52.

53. Bidwai, Praful. "North vs South On Pollution," *The Nation*, June 22, 1992, pp. 856, 854.

54. Mazur, 1994, p. 3.

55. Bidwai, 1992, p. 853.

56. Sagoff, Mark. "Population, Nature and the Environment," in Laurie Ann Mazur, 1994, p. 35.

57. Sen, 1994, p. 68.

58. Mazur, 1994, p. 5.

59. Tierney, John. "Betting the Planet," *New York Times Magazine*, December 2, 1990, p. 81.

60. Ibid.

61. Camp in Laurie Ann Mazur, 1994, p. 127.

62. Crossette, Barbara. "Why India Is Still Failing to Stop Its Population Surge," *New York Times*, July 8, 1989.

63. Sen, 1994, p. 69.

64. Ibid.

65. Jacobson in Lester Brown, 1988, pp. 155, 165. Mazur, 1994, p. 7.

66. Chen, Nancy Yu-Ping, and Zlotnick, Hania. "Urbanization Prospects for the 21st Century," in Laurie Ann Mazur, 1994, p. 343.

67. Ibid., p. 344.

68. Ibid., p. 352. "Squeezing in the Next Five Billion," *The Economist*, January 20, 1990, p. 22.

69. Chen and Zlotnick in Laurie Ann Mazur, 1994, p. 356.

70. Kennedy, 1993, pp. 26, 27.

71. Sharry, Frank. "Immigration and Population Policy in the United States: Collision or Consensus?" in Laurie Ann Mazur, 1994, p. 384.

72. Ehrlich and Ehrlich, 1990, p. 62. Sharry in Laurie Ann Mazur, 1994, p. 380.

73. Ibid., p. 381.

74. Kennedy, 1993, p. 42.

75. Zlotnick, Hania. "International Migration: Causes and Effects," in Laurie Ann Mazur 1994, p. 372.

76. Teitelbawm, 1992–93, p. 67.

77. Ibid.

78. Ibid., p. 68.

79. Ibid., p. 71.

80. Ibid., p. 72.

81. Camp in Laurie Ann Mazur, 1994, p. 129.

82. Cowell, Alan. "U.S. Negotiators Push for a Truce Over Population," *New York Times*, September 5, 1994.

83. Crossette, Barbara. "Population Meeting Opens with Challenge to the Right," *New York Times*, September 6, 1994.

84. Butturini, Paula. "Pope on a Crusade," *San Francisco Examiner*, September 4, 1994.

11

Global Climate Change

On June 23, 1988, NASA scientist James Hansen told Congress he was "99 percent certain" that global warming had begun. "It is time to stop waffling so much and say that the evidence is pretty strong that the greenhouse effect is here," he argued.[1]

Scientists first warned of global warming a century ago. Nobel laureate scientist Svante Arrhenius argued in 1896 that increasing levels of carbon dioxide in the atmosphere would raise its temperature.[2] Since then, the amount of carbon dioxide in the atmosphere has increased about 27 percent, from 280 parts per million to 356 parts per million, as have other important heat-trapping gases such as methane, chlorofluorocarbons (CFCs), and nitrous oxide.[3] Hansen and others have argued that these gases, which were largely a by-product of human activity, retained heat from the sun, creating a "greenhouse effect" that has warmed the planet. The Earth's temperature is about one degree Fahrenheit hotter today than it was a century ago.[4] And the U.N.'s Intergovernmental Panel on Climate Change (IPCC), a scientific task force first assembled in 1988 to assess the problem, predicts that global temperatures will increase between 1.4 and 6.3 degrees during the next century unless drastic steps are taken to curb greenhouse gas emissions.[5] If this occurs, the IPCC reported, "the rate of change is likely to be greater than that which has occurred on Earth any time since the end of the last ice age."[6]

Rapidly rising temperatures could create serious problems for people in different settings, scientists argue. Rising temperatures could melt polar ice and raise sea levels, inundating islands and low-lying coastal plains where millions live. A one-meter rise would flood deltas on the Nile, Po, Ganges, Mekong, and Mississippi Rivers, displacing millions of people and swamping the croplands now used to feed them.[7] Higher sea levels could drown coral reefs, destroying the fish and ruining the livelihood of

239

people who depend on reefs in the Caribbean and the Pacific.[8] And warmer water could increase the strength of hurricanes and typhoons, causing greater damage for people living along their path in the Western Atlantic and Western Pacific.[9] The insurance industry is particularly concerned about this prospect because windstorms caused $46 billion in losses between 1987 and 1993.[10]

Higher temperatures could also disrupt agriculture. While farmers in northern latitudes—North America and northern Europe and Asia—could benefit from higher temperatures, longer growing seasons, and higher levels of carbon dioxide (which plants use to grow), even modest increases could devastate farmers in tropical zones in Asia, Africa, and Latin America. Rice yields decline significantly if daytime temperatures exceed 95 degrees, and in many Asian countries, temperatures are already near this limit.[11] One group of scientists predicted that cereal prices could increase between 25 and 150 percent by the year 2060, a development that would cause hunger and starvation for between 60 million and 350 million poor people, most of them in the tropics.[12]

The prospect that global warming could have its most serious impact on people in relatively poor and populous tropic countries is ironic given the fact that most of the gases believed to contribute to global warming are generated by small populations in relatively rich northern countries, particularly the United States. In 1960, the United States produced one-third of all global carbon dioxide emissions and about 20 percent in 1987; its per capita annual production of 5.03 tons was nearly five times the world per capita average of 1.08 tons, but 13 times that of Brazil and 167 times that of Zaire.[13] This irony is not lost on poor countries, who are now being asked to reduce or defer fossil fuel consumption as a way to mitigate the effects of global warming. Brazil, for example, has rejected calls to reduce burning of tropical woods in the Amazon basin. President José Sarney argued that the industrial nations were conducting "an insidious, cruel and untruthful campaign" against Brazil to distract attention from their own large-scale pollution, acid rain, and "fantastic nuclear arsenal" that threaten life.[14] Chinese officials maintain that they need to consume vast quantities of coal to provide electricity for China's growing economy. At present, "the average Chinese consumes less than 650 kilowatt hours [annually], barely enough to burn a 75-watt bulb year round . . . and 120 million rural Chinese . . . live without electricity in their homes or villages."[15] But if it does expand coal-fired electricity production to light villages, run refrigerators, and power industry, as the government plans, China would overtake the United States as the world's largest producer of carbon dioxide by the year 2020.[16]

Because the environmental and social consequences of rising temperatures are not uniform, but unevenly distributed, it might be best to describe these developments as products of "global climate change" rather
than "global warming," which suggests that temperature change will be
experienced by people in much the same way everywhere.[17] What's more,
it might be better to use the phrase "global climate change," given the
scientific uncertainties about the process and the debate surrounding
claims that the world is warming significantly and that human activity is
largely to blame.

Although Senator Al Gore, later vice president, asserted that "there is
no longer any significant disagreement in the scientific community that
the greenhouse effect is real and already occurring," global climate change
remains the subject of scientific debate. While a majority of scientists
share Gore's view that the greenhouse effect is demonstrable, a minority
disagree, making two kinds of objections to the conclusions reached by
the IPCC.[18]

First, some scientists argue that the Earth may not be warming much,
if at all. S. Fred Singer, former director of the U.S. weather satellite program, notes that satellite data collected between 1979 and 1994 showed
"no appreciable recent warming."[19] Other scientists agree that modest
warming, about one degree, has occurred in the past one hundred years,
but argue that this is well within the range of natural temperature change.
They note that global temperatures in the 1980s, when some of the hottest
years of the past century were recorded, were slightly lower than those
recorded during the Middle Ages, some five hundred years ago, "when
Scandinavians grew grain near the Arctic Circle," and more than two degrees cooler than global temperatures six thousand years ago.[20]

Second, some scientists argue that there is little proof that higher temperatures are the product of human activity and increased atmospheric
concentrations of greenhouse gases. They note that global temperatures
actually *declined* between 1940 and 1970, data that greenhouse proponents do not dispute, at a time when industry expanded and world carbon
dioxide emissions tripled.[21] If human activity and atmospheric concentrations of carbon dioxide and other waste gases were closely related to temperature change, then global temperatures should have increased during
this period, they maintain. The fact that they did not suggests that temperature change may be a result of "natural fluctuation" rather than a
product of human activity.[22]

Because some scientists believe that the relation between human activity
and temperature change is weak, they express little confidence in the computer models that use rising carbon dioxide levels to predict higher tem-

peratures in the next century.[23] "I do not accept the model results [used by the IPCC and others] as evidence," Richard Lindzen of MIT argues. Trusting them, he says, "is like trusting a ouija board."[24] Lindzen and others argue that computer models of climate change do not adequately account for natural variation or environmental processes—increased cloud cover, water vapor—that may mitigate warming tendencies. "I don't think we've made the case yet" that serious climate change is now occurring, he argues.[25]

This kind of skepticism finds some support in the IPCC report, which conceded in 1992 that "it is not possible at this time to attribute all, or even a large part, of the observed global-mean warming to the enhanced greenhouse effect [the extra warming attributable to human-produced gases] on the basis of the observable data currently available."[26] More recently, in 1995, the IPCC expressed greater confidence in the relation, writing that the warming of the past century "is unlikely to be entirely due to natural causes and that a pattern of climatic response to human activity is identifiable in the climatological record."[27] But criticism still persists. Lindzen argues that because computer models do not estimate natural variability accurately, there is "no basis yet for saying that a human influence on the climate has been detected."[28]

At issue, of course, is whether drastic steps should be taken to reduce the emission of greenhouse gases. If human activity does in fact contribute to global warming, as a majority of scientists believe, then their call for a 50 to 60 percent cut in greenhouse gas emissions, effectively returning emissions to 1950 levels, should be heeded. But if climate change is not a product of human activity, then efforts to reduce greenhouse emissions would be both ineffective and socially disruptive, particularly for poor countries that are trying to use carbon sources to promote economic growth. "Poverty is already a worse killer than any foreseeable environmental distress [associated with global warming]," Lawrence Summers, former chief economist of the World Bank, has argued. "Nobody should kid themselves that they are doing Bangladesh a favor when they worry about global warming."[29]

Although scientific uncertainty makes global climate change a difficult issue, it is nonetheless possible to develop a constructive approach. If steps were taken to solve environmental problems that are serious in their own right, problems that may also contribute to global climate change, then people could address real as well as potential problems, a strategy that would minimize both social and environmental risks. There are, for example, sound environmental and social reasons to reduce energy consumption and car use and slow deforestation. Because these activities also

release vast quantities of carbon dioxide, efforts to curb the consumption of fossil fuels and wood might also reduce global warming. (The carbon dioxide released by these activities accounts for about half of all greenhouse gases.) The same is true for other activities that produce other greenhouse gases. A reduction of world cow herds would reduce hunger and deforestation, and also curb emissions of methane, which makes up about 18 percent of all greenhouse gases.[30] The ban on CFCs, scheduled to take effect at the turn of the century, will slow destruction of the ozone layer, about which there is no serious scientific dispute, and reduce its contribution (about 14 percent) to global climate change. And if nitrogen fertilizer use was curbed, the problems associated with groundwater pollution could be addressed and nitrous oxide levels in the atmosphere (about 6 percent of the total) could be reduced. However, in the case of nitrous oxide, fertilizer reductions could adversely affect global food supplies and contribute to hunger, which suggests that efforts to curb fertilizer use should be approached with great caution.

In this context, it is important not just to curb human activities that adversely affect the environment and may contribute to global climate change, but to do so in ways that are equitable and sensible. Any effort to address environmental problems should take into account the social impact of proposed solutions. With these issues in mind, let us look at pressing environmental problems that might be addressed, both because they contribute to known environmental and social problems, and because they may contribute to global warming. We will look first at human activities that produce carbon dioxide, the main greenhouse gas, and then at activities that produce methane, CFCs, and nitrous oxide.

Power, Forests, and Cars (Carbon Dioxide)

In the early 1970s, long before global warming became a concern, environmentalists urged energy conservation. They argued that the profligate use of coal and oil to generate electricity for home and industry contributed to serious environmental and economic problems.[31] (Coal and oil are used to generate more than one-half of the electricity around the world.) Because coal often contains sulfur, combustion in power plants contributes acid rain, which ruins forests near and far.[32] While oil burns cleaner than coal, the production of oil creates toxic waste that is hard to discard safely and the transport of oil across oceans frequently results in spills that harm marine life.

The use of oil to produce electricity or to fuel cars also contributes

to serious economic problems, environmentalists argue. Countries that import oil spend vast sums to purchase it, contributing to trade deficits and sometimes debt. For the United States, "oil imports alone have accounted for three-fourths of [its] trade deficit since 1970," and the United States has paid $1 trillion since 1970 for imported oil.[33] For countries without substantial domestic supplies, the economic costs can be higher. During the 1970s, many Latin American countries borrowed heavily and fell deeply into debt to pay for oil imports. What's more, competition for control of oil supplies has recently led to two wars in the Persian Gulf—the 1980–90 Iraq-Iran War and the 1990–91 Gulf War—which forced consumer countries to increase defense spending and intervene militarily to protect supplies from the region. "Even before Iraq invaded Kuwait, U.S. forces earmarked for gulf deployment were costing taxpayers around $50 billion a year—nearly $100 a barrel for oil imported from the Persian Gulf."[34] And Allied intervention to dislodge Iraqi troops cost tens of billions more.

Energy conservation can solve many of these environmental and economic problems. During the 1970s, when oil prices rose, it became cost-effective to curb energy use by persuading consumers to conserve and by introducing new technologies to produce and use electricity and fossil fuels more efficiently. Between 1973 and 1986, these steps—lowering thermostats, insulating homes, driving less, and improving gas mileage in cars—enabled the U.S. economy to grow without expanding energy use, a development that helped the environment and resulted in $150 billion in annual energy savings.[35] But as oil prices fell in the mid–1980s, many conservation measures were abandoned and technological improvements were deferred, resulting in growing levels of energy consumption. Energy consumption could again be curbed through consumer conservation programs and the introduction of new technologies—fuel cells, photovoltaic cells, computerized electricity distribution systems, gas-turbine engines, and solar-hydro-geothermal technologies—to create what engineers call a "nega-watt revolution": producing more energy with less.[36] Some economists have urged U.S. officials to pursue energy-efficient policies in part because they would make U.S. industry more competitive with businesses in Europe and Japan, where ongoing conservation practices have lowered the real cost of energy for domestic industry.[37] If the rich countries developed and introduced energy-saving technologies, their cost would decline and they would become more affordable for poor countries. And because the power sector accounts for one-third of global carbon dioxide emissions, energy conservation would also help avert potential warming.

Deforestation

During the early 1980s, environmentalists recognized that tropical deforestation had become a problem. Attention was first drawn to Brazil, where 33 percent of the world's tropical forests are located (58 percent are in Latin America, 23 percent in Southeast Asia and the Pacific, and 19 percent in Africa), and where deforestation was rapidly accelerating.[38]

In 1981, the United Nations estimated that 7.3 million hectares of tropical forest were burned or cut every year, and some environmental groups argued that as much as 11.3 million hectares were lost annually.[39] These figures were revised downward in the early 1990s, to about 1.5 million hectares.[40] But more recent studies indicate that deforestation has accelerated again, particularly in the Amazon.[41] But whatever the precise rate, deforestation remains a serious and growing problem, especially if the vast temperate Siberian forest (the size of the continental United States) is opened to intensive cutting, which experts expect to occur as a result of the breakup of the Soviet Union and the entry of foreign companies into the Russian economy (see chapter 12).[42]

Environmentalists have identified four problems with tropical deforestation. First, deforestation in the tropics, where rainfall is heavy—a one-hour downpour in Ghana can dump more rain than showers in London deliver in a month—leads to rapid runoff, triggering floods and eroding soils.[43] Runaway forest soils fill streams with sediments, kill fish, and clog reservoirs behind dams, shortening their life span and reducing their ability to irrigate fields and generate electricity.[44]

Second, tropical woods do not easily recover from deforestation. Some scientists estimate that it takes tropical forests between one hundred fifty and a thousand years to recover fully from a clear-cut, in contrast to temperate woods, which can be cut more often on a sustainable basis.[45] Because tropical forests do not easily recover, deforestation is typically associated with the loss of plant and animal species. Again, scientists debate the rate of extinction, or argue that tropical rain forests are not the only or most important reservoirs of plant and animal species (one scientist argues that savannas may be more important for *mammal* species), but the fact is not disputed that deforestation leads to extinction in species-rich, tropical forest environments.[46] If Latin American forests are reduced to 50 percent of their original size, scientists estimate that 15 percent of forest plant species and 12 percent of bird species would be lost.[47] The problem with species loss is that it undermines the genetic base for cultivated plants and domestic species that are used by people throughout the world, and for pharmacology, which relies on biological

resources for human drugs.[48] For example, scientists recently discovered a primitive corn species in a tiny corner of a Mexican rain forest that was threatened with destruction. Because the surviving corn is a perennial, resistant to a variety of plant viruses, and hardy in cold and elevated climates, the plant holds great promise for plant geneticists who hope to infuse modern corn with some of the rain forest corn's genetic properties.[49] The irony is that species loss is reducing genetic resources just when genetic engineering technologies are being deployed to make effective use of them.[50]

Third, deforestation adversely affects indigenous Indian populations, particularly in Latin American and Pacific island forests. The destruction of rain forests and exposure to outside populations have reduced their number. In 1994, one entire village of Jaguapure Indians threatened to commit suicide unless seized lands were returned, and suicide rates among remnant tribes is high.[51] The opening of forests and the introduction of long-isolated cultures have resulted in the import and export of disease. River blindness and malaria have been taken into the forests, while scientists think that dengue fever, the Ebola virus, and perhaps AIDS have been brought out of disrupted rain forest environments.[52]

Deforestation also adversely affects other populations. In India and Africa, where there are few residual forest tribes, deforestation has increased fuel wood costs and forced poor people to forage further and longer for fuel to cook meals.[53]

Fourth, deforestation accelerates carbon dioxide emissions. Although undisturbed tropical forests emit carbon dioxide on balance, forest clearing and burning have greatly increase net carbon dioxide emissions, adding "perhaps 1 to 2.6 billion tons of carbon dioxide to the atmosphere annually, or between 20 and 50 percent as much as the burning of fossil fuels.[54] It matters, of course, how forests are cut. Selective cutting for valuable hardwoods produces less destruction and fewer emissions than conversion to tropical plantations. And these uses do less to destroy forest cover or release carbon dioxide than clear-cutting or burning, as occurred on a grand scale in 1976, when Volkswagen set 25,000 hectares of Amazonian forest afire to clear land for a cattle ranch.[55]

Although there are good reasons to curb deforestation in the tropics, and to prevent deforestation in temperate Siberian woods, different social solutions are needed because the economic causes of deforestation vary regionally.

In Latin America, the primary cause of deforestation is cattle ranching, from which beef is exported to the fast-food hamburger industry in the United States.[56] Central American ranchers, for example, export 85 to 95

percent of their beef to the United States.[57] The migration of poor farmers into the forests, where they engage in subsistence agriculture, also contributes to deforestation in Latin America. Governments in the region typically provide subsidies to cattle ranchers and assist the settlement of migrant farmers. They do so to promote beef exports that can be used to repay debt—deforestation accelerated after the onset of the debt crisis—and to provide land for small farmers displaced by the introduction of large-scale Green Revolution agriculture in the fertile valleys, as in Brazil, or for poor landless farmers in countries where fertile land is monopolized by elites, as in Central America.[58]

In this context, deforestation might be slowed if the United States curbed consumption or imports of Latin American beef and if governments in the region introduced land reform to provide land to poor farmers and ease pressure on marginal agricultural environments. They might also encourage "sustainable" forestry—rubber tapping, nut harvesting—for indigenous and some settler groups already living in the woods. Of course, first world countries would probably have to extend substantial debt relief and economic aid to persuade governments in the region to conserve forests rather than use them as a source of export earnings or a way to absorb displaced rural populations.

The causes of deforestation in Southeast Asia are rather different. In Thailand, Malaysia, Indonesia, Papua New Guinea, and the Philippines, most tropical hardwoods are cut and exported to Japan, which imports 53 percent of the world's tropical hardwoods for use in construction and paper manufacture.[59] Taiwan and South Korea are also big tropical timber importers. While timber exports are the main cause of deforestation in this region, conversion to tropical plantations—rubber, palm, and coffee—and the migration of subsistence farmers into the woods, which in Indonesia is directed by a government "transmigration" program designed to reduce population density on Java, also contribute to deforestation.[60]

In this context, deforestation might be slowed if Japan and the other tropical timber importers curbed hardwood consumption—much of the imported plywood is used once for concrete-building forms and then simply discarded—and if the Indonesian government emphasized birth control policies rather than "transmigration" programs. Thailand has banned the export of tropical timber, and other countries have banned the export of raw logs, in an effort to protect and manage their forests more effectively, though new free trade agreements may undermine their ability to use export controls to protect their resources. And while conversion of forests to plantations contributes to species loss, it is less damaging than conversion to pasture or agriculture, and may represent a kind of compromise for countries needing export earnings.

In India and tropical Africa, the use of forests for fuel wood and subsistence agriculture is the main cause of deforestation, though countries in West Africa export some timber to European consumers.[61] The destruction of forests for fuel woods is particularly acute where population densities are high. In this context, birth control programs to reduce population density, the introduction of agro-forestry programs—where villages are given resources to plant fast-growing trees for fuel—the provision of more efficient stoves to use fuel more effectively and, in some cases, the provision of cheap fuel alternatives, like kerosene, can help reduce pressure on the forests. These steps can improve conditions for poor households, which may spend hours searching for fuel woods or may switch to faster-cooking but less nutritious foods where fuel is scarce or too expensive.[62] While these programs have proven effective, they are also costly for governments with few resources, which means that rich countries would have to provide economic aid if they were to be adopted widely.

Automobiles

At the first Earth Day rallies in 1970, students sometimes bashed or buried cars, which they saw as symbols of environmental pollution and waste. Although smog and oil spills were then recognized as problems associated with cars, the explosive growth of the world car fleet and the widespread use of automobiles have since brought a host of other car-related environmental and social problems into sharp relief.

In 1950, there were 50 million cars worldwide, 75 percent of them in the United States. This number doubled by 1960, doubled again by 1970, and doubled again by 1990, an eightfold increase to more than 400 million cars.[63] And experts expect the world car fleet to reach 530 million by the end of the century, with much of the growth occurring in the former communist countries.[64]

Of course, the exploding car population intensifies and widens the impact of cars on the environment. But perhaps more important is the extensive *use* of cars. By 1990, U.S. owners drove their cars 2 trillion miles every year, the equivalent of a roundtrip from Earth to Pluto every day of the year.[65]

The practice of driving interplanetary distances results in the consumption of vast quantities of oil, about 6 billion barrels a year. As has already been noted, the production, transportation, and use of oil are associated with a whole set of environmental, economic, and political problems. And when burned to power a car, the oil is converted into a complex set of

waste gases, carbon dioxide among them.[66] The average car produces its weight in carbon dioxide every year; the world car fleet generates about 14 percent of all carbon dioxide emissions.[67] But carbon dioxide emissions were long neglected because it is not a toxic gas, like most of the other one thousand assorted pollutants created by internal combustion engines.[68] Early efforts to reduce auto pollution focused on lead in gasoline, benzene, carbon monoxide, nitrogen oxides, unburned hydrocarbons, aldehydes, particulates, and trace metals because they contributed to smog and were known to have adverse effects on human health. More recent efforts have identified the release of CFCs from auto air conditioners (the number one source of CFC emissions in the United States) and carbon dioxide as problematic, even though they are not toxic to humans. And more attention is now being paid to tiny particles of soot, which may be responsible for as many as 50,000 to 60,000 deaths annually in the United States, affecting primarily young children with respiratory problems.[69]

While cars release toxic pollutants, nontoxic gases, and particulates that adversely affect human health or the environment, they are also responsible for considerable death and injury. Worldwide, 265,000 are killed every year in auto accidents, and ten million more are injured.[70] Death rates are highest in poor countries, where cars share roads with pedestrians, bikes, and animals, and lower in rich countries where governments spend heavily to segregate traffic, police roads, improve auto safety, and increasingly, prosecute drunk drivers.[71] But even in the rich countries, cars are prodigious killers. In the United States, cars kill about fifty thousand annually, and have killed three million during the century since the car was invented. Nearly twice as many Americans have died on the highway than on the battlefield in all of this country's wars since 1776.[72]

In social and economic terms, the growth of car fleets has persuaded governments to build highways and transform cities to accommodate them, developments that have contributed to the deterioration of urban neighborhoods and downtown businesses, fueled urban sprawl, and consumed rural farms near cities. Because mass transit systems become more expensive and less efficient as cities sprawl—mass transit carries only as many people in the United States today as it did in 1900—people rely more heavily on the automobile for transport, at considerable personal expense.[73] A study by the Hertz Corporation reported that Americans devote 15 percent of their income on automobile transportation, and the average male spends sixteen hundred hours a year in his car.[74] The government too spends vast sums supporting private transportation, particularly on road construction, maintainence, and police services. The California Department of Transportation reported that the state spent $2,500 more

for each vehicle on the road than it received from car owners in taxes and fees.[75] The cost to taxpayers of government automobile subsidies is now only becoming apparent, largely because the interstate highways and bridges are due for repair, at staggering cost.

During the 1970s, some of the problems associated with car use were addressed by government policy and market forces. Clean air legislation required cars to get better mileage and emit fewer pollutants. The elimination of lead from gasoline was particularly important, though U.S. manufacturers began exporting tetraethyl lead to other countries after the U.S. ban took effect. The introduction of safety belts, crash standards, and speed limits reduced fatalities 6 percent, even though the car population grew 50 percent.[76] At the same time, rapidly rising oil prices spurred technological innovation, resulting in smaller, more fuel-efficient cars, many of them from Japan, and reduced consumer use.

But many of the gains made during the 1970s eroded during the 1980s. The growing car population undermined technological improvements. "All of the progress we are making through technology is being eaten up by growth," one official of the California Air Resources Board reported.[77] The Reagan, Bush, and Clinton administrations cut mass transit systems, reduced fuel-efficiency standards, and increased speed limits. These relaxed government policies undercut previous environmental and safety gains. And falling oil prices after 1985 encouraged consumers to increase car use. In the past ten years, consumers have purchased trucks, jeeps, and minivans in increasing numbers, which is a problem because these vehicles get poor gas mileage, lowering the average fuel efficiency of the U.S. fleet. According to the Environmental Protection Agency, some forty million Americans live in cities that do not meet federal clean air standards, despite two decades of pollution-reduction efforts.[78]

Many environmentalists and government officials have proposed higher taxes, tickets, and tolls as a way to curb auto use in the United States. They note that a 50-cent-a-gallon increase in the gas tax would produce $55 billion in annual revenue, providing income to reduce budget deficits and discouraging car use.[79] Although the Clinton administration raised the gas tax by only 4 cents, state officials around the country have increased registration fees, tickets, and tolls to raise money for strapped state budgets. In California, state officials raised registration fees and slapped a 40 percent penalty on drivers who paid one day late, while cities hiked parking tickets and tolls to finance budgets and reduce congestion. San Francisco, for example, increased its parking ticket revenues from $5.5 million in 1990 to $42 million in 1993, a sevenfold increase.[80]

The problem with this approach is that it is an inefficient and unfair

way to reduce car use. The rising cost of fuel, fees, taxes, and tolls is felt first by low-income drivers, discouraging them from hitting the road. But this is not an efficient way to curb use because poor people own few cars and drive them sparingly. Families with annual incomes over $35,000 own three times as many cars, driving them three times as often and three times as far as families earning under $10,000.[81] And the increasing popularity of gas-guzzling cars, vans, and trucks among well-to-do drivers means they consume more than three times as much gas. Higher costs are inefficient because they do little to curb use by people who have the greatest impact. And they are unfair because, in a country where mass transit systems are inadequate, poor people need cars to get to work just as much as wealthy families do. There are also regional inequalities. In Wyoming, the average commuter pays $243 a year in gas taxes, the average New Yorker only $91.[82] An across-the-board tax increase would have a greater impact on drivers in western states, where commutes are long, than on drivers in the East. There is a more efficient and equitable way to curb car use: gas rationing. But it is such an anathema to consumers and politicians—this despite demonstrable success during World War II—that it does not yet figure in any political discussion of car use.

Increasing car ownership and use in the United States and around the world is the source of serious environmental and social problems, global climate change among them. There are good reasons to reduce car use. But the automobile is so deeply embedded in the economic, social, and psychological life of the wealthy countries, particularly the United States, that it will be difficult to curb car ownership or use.

Swamps, Rice, and Cows (Methane)

After carbon dioxide, methane is the most important greenhouse gas, representing about 18 percent of all the gases with climate-changing potential.[83] Most of the methane in the atmosphere, about 65 percent, is emitted from "natural" processes, from anaerobic fermentation in wetlands, peat bogs, and swamps.[84] Human activity is responsible for about 35 percent of all methane emissions. Rice cultivation accounts for about 20 percent of this and animal husbandry contributes about 15 percent.[85]

Although the use of synthetic fertilizer could lower methane emissions from rice cultivation, it would be difficult to reduce methane from this source without jeopardizing rice production, which feeds so much of the world.[86] But while it would be difficult to reduce rice production, there are sound human and environmental reasons to reduce animal herds, par-

ticularly of cows. Cows release about 80 million metric tons of methane into the atmosphere, considerably more than other domestic animals: ten times more than sheep, fifty times more than pigs.[87] What's more, the expansion of the world cow herd, which increased from 500 million to 1.2 billion between 1950 and 1990, has contributed to two important human and environmental problems.[88]

First, cows consume vast quantities of grain that might otherwise feed a hungry and growing world population. As we have seen, cows consume about one-third of the world's grain, nearly 70 percent of the grain grown in the United States.[89] And in recent years, feed grain for cows has increasingly replaced grain grown for human consumption in the third world, which has reduced the supply and increased the price of staple foods for poor people.[90] Many countries, particularly in Latin America, have increased cattle production to supply beef for the U.S. market and earn money that can be used to repay debt. But the expansion of cattle ranching, with its resulting "protein flight," has reduced the amount of land devoted to agriculture and has led to rural job loss because ranching employs very few workers (one worker for every 47.6 hectares, compared with one worker for every 2.9 hectares in agriculture).[91] Cattle ranching has thereby contributed to rising prices and falling incomes for rural families in many countries, one reason why "one-third of rural families [in Mexico] never eat meat or eggs and 59 percent never drink milk."[92]

While the expansion of the world cattle herd contributes to hunger in poor countries, it contributes to obesity and disease in wealthy countries where consumers eat vast quantities of beef.

Between 1945 and 1976, per capita beef consumption in the United States grew from 71 pounds to 129 pounds annually.[93] Nearly 40 percent of this was consumed as hamburgers, a postwar phenomenon associated first with the spread of backyard barbecue grills (unlike pork, which was preferred by Americans before the war, hamburger patties do not fall through the grate onto the charcoal) and later with the spread of fast-food hamburger franchises.[94]

The growing consumption of beef protein created a diet heavy in fat: 37 percent of calories in U.S. diets comes from fat.[95] As a result, obesity has become a serious problem. More than thirty-four million Americans are overweight according to the Centers for Disease Control, and the number of women considered obese rose from 13.3 percent to 17.7 percent between 1960 and 1980.[96] More important, fat-heavy diets and obesity contribute to disease and death. The U.S. Surgeon General estimated that 1.5 million deaths in 1987 were related to dietary factors and said that diets high in saturated fat and cholesterol contributed to the high incidence of heart attack, colon and breast cancer, and stroke in America.[97]

Second, the world's cow herd contributes to a series of environmental problems. The expansion of cattle herds in tropical regions has led to extensive deforestation, particularly in Latin America, and increased carbon dioxide emissions. Outside rain forest settings, cattle grazing on desert fringe areas or on marginal lands can lead to desertification, as it has in the Sahel of Africa, or to the degradation of grasslands.[98] Cows also consume large quantities of water, far more than other domesticated animals, which can drain water resources in arid regions.[99] On pasture land, cattle waste can foul streams—"an ungrazed part of a stream in Montana produced 268 more trout than did a grazed part of the same stream"— while waste from feed lots can contaminate groundwater supplies—"the organic waste generated by a 10,000-head feed lot is equivalent to the human waste generated in a city of 110,000 people."[100]

But after increasing for many years, beef consumption in the wealthy countries began to fall in the past two decades. From a high of 129 pounds per capita in 1976, U.S. beef consumption fell to 78.2 pounds by 1983, back to World War II levels.[101] This rapid decline was a product of two developments: rising grain prices during the 1970s and changing diets.[102] As Americans became more concerned about diet and health in the 1970s and '80s, consumers reduced their purchase of beef, which was growing more expensive because feed prices had soared, and increasingly turned to chicken, fish, and pasta. As a result of falling consumer demand, the growth of the world cow herd slowed and then stabilized at about 1.25 billion head by 1990.[103]

While this was a welcome development in human and environmental terms, further cattle herd reductions would be possible and beneficial. A reduction in dietary fat in the United States, say from 37 to 30 percent, a level most dietary scientists believe is necessary, would reduce beef consumption by 20 percent.[104] And if fat made up only 14 percent of American diets, a level that some scientists believe is optimal because it would greatly reduce health risks, beef consumption would fall and the world cow herd could shrink dramatically, releasing large amounts of grain for human consumption. "If the 130 million metric tons of grain that are fed yearly to U.S. livestock were consumed directly as human food, about 400 million people--1.7 times larger than the U.S. population—could be sustained for one year," Cornell scientist David Pimentel estimated.[105] Of course, even scientists who argue that "we are basically a vegetarian species and should be eating a wide variety of plant food and minimizing our intake of animal food," do not argue for a completely vegetarian diet or an agriculture without animal husbandry.[106] Rather, they argue that consumption of animal protein should be reduced in wealthy countries,

that consumers should rely on other animals that produce protein more efficiently (chickens and pigs), and that cow herds should be reduced but not eliminated so they can continue to provide milk, cheese, traction, and manure in many agricultural systems.

Coolants and Spray Cans (CFCs)

In 1985 British scientists discovered that a set of gases called chlorofluorocarbons (CFCs) were responsible for depleting ozone in the atmosphere.[107] CFCs were first invented by Du Pont scientist Thomas Midgley in 1930.[108] Because CFCs were nontoxic, nonflammable, noncorrosive, and inert, they soon found widespread application as coolants in refrigerators and air conditioners, propellants in spray cans, and blowing agents in plastic and styrofoam. Later, related gases called halons found use in fire extinguishers: "Used in Army tanks, in which engine and munition fires can spread like lightning, [automatic] halon fire extinguishers . . . can snuff out a raging gasoline fire in thousandths of a second."[109]

In 1974, scientists warned that while CFCs were beneficial in many respects, when they were released into the atmosphere, sunlight would detach chlorine from the rest of the molecule, and that chlorine would then attack and deplete ozone.[110] If this occurred, researchers warned, CFCs could weaken the ozone layer, the planet's protection against harmful ultraviolet radiation from the sun. They predicted that higher radiation levels would increase the incidence of skin cancer, particularly among Caucasians, make cataracts more common, and suppress the human immune system, which fights off viruses, tumors, and other infectious diseases.[111] Increased radiation would also harm plants, particularly crops like soybeans, and affect marine organisms in waters up to 100 feet deep.[112] Scientists noted, however, that the effects would be hard to predict because radiation levels around the globe would increase unevenly, and because places with heavy cloud cover would block much of the radiation, whereas areas with direct sunlight would receive heavier doses.[113]

Scientists found evidence in 1985 that CFC levels and ozone depletion were closely related and discovered serious ozone depletion over Antarctica. This discovery of an "ozone hole . . . larger than the United States and taller than Mount Everest" spurred efforts to reduce and eventually ban CFCs and other ozone-depleting gases, halons, and later methyl bromide.[114]

In 1987, twenty-four countries adopted the Montreal Protocol on Substances That Deplete the Ozone Layer, agreeing to freeze CFC produc-

tion at 1986 levels, followed by a 20 percent reduction by 1993 and another 30 percent reduction in 1998.[115] During the next few years, as evidence mounted that ozone depletion was accelerating and becoming more serious, signatories to the Montreal Protocol took additional steps. In 1989 they agreed to eliminate all CFC production by the end of the century, and in 1992 moved the deadline up to 1996.[116] The rich countries also agreed to provide $500 million to poor countries to help them reduce their reliance on CFCs.[117] The Bush administration used provisions of the Clean Air Act to ban some substances not covered by the Montreal Protocol.[118] And in 1995, one hundred governments agreed to phase out methyl bromide, a powerful ozone-depleting pesticide used in agriculture.[119]

Governments acted with rare unanimity and considerable speed because the scientific evidence was not disputed (as it has been with global warming), because CFC contributed to ozone depletion but also to global warming (accounting for about 14 percent of greenhouse gases), because ozone depletion was accelerating rapidly—ozone was being depleted twice as fast in 1992 as it had been in 1985—and because the particular properties of CFCs made delay damaging. CFCs have long atmospheric life spans: CFC 11 lasts 76 years in the upper atmosphere, CFC 12 for 139 years.[120] And because they are now stored in foams, refrigerators, and spray cans, they will be slowly released as these containers erode, pumping ozone-depleting gases into the atmosphere even after their manufacture has stopped. As a consequence, a CFC ban in the year 2000 would only reduce CFCs to current levels in 2073. By moving up the deadline to 1996, governments thought CFC levels would fall back to current levels much sooner, by 2053. These realities made for rare agreement. As U.S. delegate Richard Benedick explained, "We're seeing something completely unprecedented in the history of diplomacy. Politicians from every block and region of the world are setting aside politics to reach agreement on protecting the global environment."[121]

These developments produced real and immediate benefits and created fewer economic problems than many first expected. Scientists found that production and use of CFCs slowed even before the Montreal Protocol took effect and, as a result, that ozone depletion slowed dramatically. "Here is a beautiful case study of science and public policy working well," said NASA scientist James Elkins.[122] And the cost to industry and consumers of replacing CFCs with other technologies proved less expensive than industry officials first predicted. The switch to other technologies even resulted in energy-saving designs, which could result in savings of up to $100 billion during the next eighty-five years.[123] While efforts to

reduce CFCs have been successful, it is important to note that they occurred not so much because they contributed to global warming, but because they contributed to other serious social and environmental
problems.

Synthetic Fertilizer (Nitrous Oxide)

Synthetic nitrogen fertilizers emit nitrous oxide, a gas associated with
global climate change. There are also natural sources of nitrous oxide
emissions in oceans and soils, but as with methane emissions, little can
be done about them. About one-third of all nitrous oxide emissions are
associated with human activity. Of these, synthetic fertilizer use is the
most important.[124] The increasing use of nitrogen fertilizers—global fertilizer use grew from 14 million tons in 1950 to 121 million tons in 1984—
contributes not only to global warming (about 6 percent of the total), but
also to groundwater pollution and algae blooms, which deprive rivers,
estuaries, and oceans of oxygen, killing fish and other marine life.[125]

But while there are problems associated with nitrogen fertilizers, global
climate change among them, the use of fertilizer greatly increases world
food production, which is essential for a growing population. As the
Worldwatch Institute estimated, "Eliminating [synthetic fertilizer] use
today would probably cut world food production by at least a third," an
extremely serious problem for the "billion and a half people now fed with
the additional food produced with chemical fertilizer."[126]

Under these circumstances it is difficult to imagine or suggest that synthetic fertilizer use should be dramatically reduced or eliminated as part
of an effort to reduce global warming. There are, however, some steps
that could be taken to reduce fertilizer use and nitrous oxide emissions
on the margins.

Because natural gas is used to produce synthetic fertilizers like anhy-
drous ammonia, fertilizer prices rise and fall with energy prices. When
energy prices rose in the 1970s, fertilizer use slowed somewhat, curbing
pollution and nitrous oxide emissions.[127] Most agronomists also think that
changed farm practices could reduce some fertilizer-related problems.
They argue that farmers could apply fertilizers more carefully, an important consideration because their effectiveness is relatively ephemeral.[128]
They urge farmers to use more natural manures for fertilizer, much of it
now wasted in cattle, pig, and chicken feed lot systems, which do not
apply waste to farmlands, because natural manures release less nitrous
oxide and require less energy (and carbon dioxide emissions) to pro-

duce.[129] And they urge farmers to plant nitrogen-fixing crops like alfalfa along with nitrogen-depleting crops like corn to reduce synthetic-fertilizer inputs and also reduce farmer costs, an important consideration if small-scale farmers are to survive.[130]

Because these practices would likely produce only modest reductions in synthetic fertilizer use, people concerned about global climate change will probably have to devote their attention to curbing *other* greenhouse gases, which in any event play a more significant overall role.

Notes

1. Shabecoff, Philip. "Global Warming Has Begun, Expert Tells Senate," *New York Times*, June 24, 1988.

2. Switzer, Jacqueline Vaughn. *Environmental Politics: Domestic and Global Dimensions*. New York: St. Martin's Press, 1994, p. 269.

3. Rensberger, Boyce. "As Earth Summit Nears, Consensus Still Lacking on Global Warming's Cause," *Washington Post*, May 31, 1992.

4. Stevens, William K. "Experts Confirm Human Role in Global Warming," *New York Times*, September 10, 1995.

5. Flavin, Christopher. "Slowing Global Warming," in Lester Brown, *State of the World 1990*. New York: Norton, 1990, p. 17.

6. Kennedy, Paul. *Preparing for the 21st Century*. New York: Random House, 1993, p. 108. Stevens, William K. "Earlier Global Warming Harm Seen," *New York Times*, October 17, 1990. Leggett, Jeremy. "The Nature of the Greenhouse Threat," in Jeremy Leggett, ed., *Global Warming: The Greenpeace Report*. Oxford: Oxford University Press, 1990, p. 2.

7. Kennedy, 1993, p. 110.

8. Stevens, William K. "Violent World of Corals Is Facing New Dangers," *New York Times*, February 16, 1993.

9. McKibben, Bill. *The End of Nature*. New York: Random House, 1989, pp. 95–96.

10. Leggett, Jeremy. "Gone with the Winds," *World Paper*, April 1993, p. 13.

11. Kennedy, 1993, pp. 111–12.

12. Pitt, David E. "Computer Vision of Global Warming: Hardest on Have-Nots," *New York Times*, January 18, 1994. Pedrick, Claire. "A Moveable Feast: Climate, Bread and Butter," *World Paper*, April 1993, p. 11.

13. Flavin, 1990, p. 19. Kennedy, 1993, p. 117.

14. Simons, Marlise. "Brazil, Smarting from the Outcry Over the Amazon, Charges Foreign Plot," *New York Times*, March 23, 1989.

15. Tyler, Patrick E. "China's Power Needs Exceed Investor Tolerance," *New York Times*, November 7, 1994.

16. Tyler, Patrick E. "China's Inevitable Dilemma: Coal Equals Growth," *New York Times*, September 29, 1995.

17. Stevens, William K. "In a Warming World, Who Comes Out Ahead?" *New York Times*, February 5, 1991.

18. Michaels, Patrick J. *Sound and Fury: The Science and Politics of Global Warming*. Washington, D.C.: Cato Institute, 1992, p. 3.

19. Singer, S. Fred. "Global Climate Change: Fact and Fiction," in John L. Allen, ed., *Environment 93/94*. Guilford, Conn.: Dushkin, 1993, p. 186. Kerr, Richard A. "Is the World Warming or Not?" *Science*, 267, February 3, 1995, p. 612. Michaels, 1992, p. 53.

20. Rensberger, 1992. Stevens, William K. "In New Data on Climate Changes, Decades, Not Centuries Count," *New York Times*, December 7, 1993. Stevens, William K. "Climate Roller Coaster in Swedish Tree Rings," *New York Times*, August 7, 1990.

21. Stevens, William K. "With Climate Treaty Signed, All Say They'll Do Even More," *New York Times*, June 13, 1992. Singer, 1993, p. 17. Brown, Lester. "A False Sense of Security," in Lester Brown, *State of the World 1985*. New York: Norton, 1985, p. 15.

22. Singer, 1993, p. 186.

23. Flavin, 1990, p. 17.

24. Stevens, William K. "A Skeptic Asks, Is It Getting Hotter, Or Is It Just the Computer Model?" *New York Times*, June 18, 1996.

25. Ibid.

26. Rensberger, 1992.

27. Stevens, William K. "Experts Confirm Human Role in Global Warming," *New York Times*, September 10, 1995.

28. Ibid.

29. Nasar, Sylvia. "Cooling the Globe Would Be Nice, But Saving Lives Now May Cost Less," *New York Times*, May 31, 1992.

30. Kelly, Mick. "Halting Global Warming," in Jeremy Leggett, 1990, p. 86. Leggett in Jeremy Leggett, 1990, p. 17.

31. Renner, Michael. "Reinventing Transportation," in Lester Brown, *State of the World 1994*. New York: Norton, 1994, p. 64.

32. Postel, Sandra. "Protecting Forests," in Lester Brown, *State of the World 1984*. New York: Norton, 1984, p. 82.

33. Romm, Joseph J., and Lovins, Amory B. "Fueling a Competitive Economy," *Foreign Affairs*, Winter 1992–93, p. 47.

34. Ibid, p. 49.

35. Ibid., p. 48.

36. Renner, 1994, p. 69.

37. Romm and Lovins, 1992–93, p. 50.

38. Caufield, Catherine. *Tropical Moist Forests*. London: Earthscan, 1982, p. 7. Meyers, Norman. "Tropical Forests," in Jeremy Leggett, 1990, p. 377.

39. Caufield, 1982, p. 1. Postel, Sandra, and Heise, Lori. "Reforesting the Earth," in Lester Brown, *State of the World 1988*. New York: Norton, 1988, p. 85.

40. Budiansky, Stephen. "The Doomsday Myths," in John L. Allen, ed., *Envi-

ronment 95/96. Guilford, Conn.: Dushkin, 1995, p. 35. "Instant Trees," *The Economist,* April 28, 1990, p. 93.

41. Schemo, Diane Jean. "Burning of Amazon Picks Up Pace, with Vast Areas Lost," *New York Times,* September 12, 1996.

42. Stevens, William K. "Experts Say Logging of Vast Siberian Forest Could Foster Warming," *New York Times,* January 28, 1992.

43. Caufield, 1982, p. 10.

44. Pearce, Fred. "Hit and Run in Sarawak," *New Scientist,* May 12, 1990, p. 47. MacDougall, A. Kent. "Worldwide Costs Mount as Trees Fall," *Los Angeles Times,* June 14, 1987. Postel in Lester Brown, 1984, p. 84.

45. Wolf, Edward C. "Avoiding a Mass Extinction of Species," in Lester Brown, 1988, p. 110. Anderson, Patrick. "The Myth of Sustainable Logging: The Case for a Ban on Tropical Timber Imports," *The Ecologist,* 19, September–October 1989, p. 166. Recent studies have shown that even temperate woods do not recover as easily or as fast as foresters have long assumed. Dold, Catherine. "Study Casts Doubt on Belief in Self-Revival of Cleared Forests," *New York Times,* September 1, 1992.

46. Caufield, 1982, p. 10. Budiansky, 1995, p. 34. Petit, Charles. "Scientist Argues Against Focus on Rain Forests," *San Francisco Chronicle,* February 21, 1992.

47. Wolf in Lester Brown, 1988, p. 103.

48. Pimentel, David, Armstrong, Laura E., Flass, Christine A., Hopf, Frederic W., Landy, Ronald B., and Pimentel, Marcia H. "Interdependence of Food and Natural Resources," in David Pimental and Carl W. Hall, eds., *Food and Natural Resources.* San Diego: Academic Press, 1989, p. 42.

49. Meyers, Norman. "Loss of Biological Diversity and Its Potential Impact on Agriculture and Food Productivity," in David Pimental and Carl W. Hall, 1989, pp. 52–53.

50. Ibid., p. 53.

51. Caufield, 1982, p. 19. *San Francisco Chronicle,* March 11, 1996.

52. Caufield, 1982, p. 33. Preston, Richard. "Crisis in the Hot Zone," *The New Yorker,* October 26, 1992, p. 62.

53. Postel in Lester Brown, 1984, p. 83. MacDougall, 1987.

54. Postel and Heise in Lester Brown, 1988, p. 94.

55. Caufield, 1982, p. 37.

56. Postel in Lester Brown, 1984, p. 77. Singer, in Robert Allen, 1992, p. 86. Harrison, Paul. *The Third Revolution: Population, Environment and a Sustainable World.* London: Penguin, 1993, pp. 95–96.

57. Caufield, 1982, p. 34.

58. "How Brazil Subsidizes the Destruction of the Amazon," *The Economist,* March 18, 1989, p. 69. Harrison, 1993, p. 96; Caufield, 1982, pp. 24–25.

59. Schwarz, Adam. "Timer Troubles," *Far Eastern Economic Review,* April 6, 1989, p. 86. Caufield, 1982, p. 29.

60. Ibid., p. 28. Postel in Lester Brown, 1984, p. 77.

61. Postel and Heise in Lester Brown, 1988, pp. 88–89.

62. Ibid., p. 88.

63. Motor Vehicle Manufacturers Association. *World Motor Vehicle Data, 1988 Edition*. Detroit: 1988. Attshuler, Alan. *The Future of the Automobile: The Report of MIT's International Automobile Program*. Cambridge: MIT Press, 1984, pp. 2–3, 13. Brown, Lester, Flavin, Christopher, and Norman, Colin. *Running on Empty: The Future of the Automobile in an Oil Short World*. New York: Norton, 1979, p. 86.

64. Attshuler, 1984, p. 113.

65. Allen, Alexandra. "The Auto's Assault on the Atmosphere," *Multinational Monitor*, January-February 1990, p. 23.

66. Attshuler, 1984, p. 4.

67. Flavin, Christopher, "Slowing Global Warming," in Lester Brown, *State of the World 1990*. New York: Norton, 1990, p. 23. Attshuler, 1984, p. 58. Greenpeace, *The Environmental Impact of the Car: A Greenpeace Report*. Seattle: Greenpeace, 1992, p. 15.

68. Ibid., p. 19.

69. Hilts, Philip J. "Studies Say Soot Kills Up to 60,000 in U.S. Each Year," *New York Times*, July 19, 1993.

70. Greenpeace, 1992, p. 48. Attshuler, 1984, p. 5.

71. Zuckerman, Wolfgang. *End of the Road: From World Car Crisis to Sustainable Transportation*. Post Mills, Ver.: Chelsea Green, 1993, p. 134.

72. Schaeffer, Robert. "Car Sick: Autos Ad Nauseum," *Greenpeace Magazine*, May–June 1990, p. 15.

73. Ibid.

74. Brown, Flavin, and Norman, 1979, p. 17. Zuckerman, 1993, pp. 85–86. Romm and Lovins, 1992–93, p. 86.

75. Zuckerman, 1993, p. 215.

76. Attshuler, 1984, pp. 66–67, 70.

77. Brownstein, Ronald. "Testing the Limits," *National Journal*, July 29, 1989, p. 1918.

78. Reinhold, Robert. "Hard Times Dilute Enthusiasm for Clean Air Laws," *New York Times*, November 25, 1993. Sterngold, James. "A Back-and-Forth Smog War," *New York Times*, September 12, 1996.

79. Wald, Matthew L. "50–Cents-a-Gallon Tax Could Buy a Whole Lot," *New York Times*, October 18, 1992.

80. Matier, Phillip, and Ross, Andrew. "State Drives Up Car Costs," *San Francisco Chronicle*, June 21, 1993.

81. Motor Vehicles Manufacturer Association, 1988.

82. Wald, 1992.

83. Ehrlich, Anne. "Agricultural Contributions to Global Warming," in Jeremy Leggett, 1990, p. 401.

84. Ibid., pp. 402–3.

85. Ibid., p. 403.

86. Ibid., p. 407.

87. Ibid., p. 404. McKibben, 1989, p. 15. Durning, Alan Thein, and Brough, Holly B. "Reforming the Livestock Economy," in Lester Brown, *State of the World 1992*. New York: Norton, 1992, p. 74.

88. Ibid., p. 68.

89. Ibid., pp. 69–70.

90. Ibid., p. 76; Sanderson, Steven E. "The Emergence of the 'World Steer': International and Foreign Domination in Latin American Cattle Production," in F. LaMond Tullis and W. Ladd Hollist, eds., *Food, the State and International Political Economy: Dilemmas of Developing Countries*. Lincoln: University of Nebraska Press, 1986, pp. 133–34, 139–40.

91. Edelman, Mark. "From Costa Rican Pasture to North American Hamburger," in Marvin Harris and Eric B. Ross, eds., *Food and Evolution*. Philadelphia: Temple University Press, 1987, pp. 553, 554–55. Sanderson in F. La Mond Tullis and W. Ladd Hollist, 1986, p. 146.

92. Ibid., p. 129.

93. Skaggs, Jimmy M. *Prime Cut: Livestock Raising and Meatpacking in the United States, 1607–1983*. College Station: Texas A&M University Press, 1986, p. 166.

94. Rifkin, Jeremy. *Beyond Beef: The Rise and Fall of the Cattle Culture*. New York: Dutton, 1992, pp. 260, 264.

95. Durning and Brough in Lester Brown, 1992, p. 74.

96. Rifkin, 1992, p. 166.

97. Ibid., p. 171.

98. Durning and Brough in Lester Brown, 1992, pp. 72–73. Kennedy, 1993, pp. 98–99.

99. Cervinka, Vashek. "Water Use in Agriculture," in F. La Mond Tullis and W. Ladd Hollist, 1986, pp. 148–49. Durning and Brough in Lester Brown, 1992, pp. 70–71.

100. Rifkin, 1992, pp. 206, 221.

101. Ibid., pp. 206, 221.

102. Skaggs, 1986, pp. 181–82.

103. Ehrlich in Jeremy Leggett, 1990, p. 405.

104. Durning and Brough in Lester Brown, 1992, pp. 81–82.

105. Pimental et al. in David Pimentel and Carl W. Hall, 1989, p. 36. Rifkin, 1992, p. 161.

106. Ibid., pp. 73–74.

107. Shea, Cynthia. "Protecting the Ozone Layer," in Lester Brown, *State of the World 1989*. New York: Norton, 1989, pp. 77–78.

108. Shea in Lester Brown, 1989, p. 85.

109. Browne, Malcome W. "As Halon Ban Nears, Researchers Seek a New Miracle Firefighter," *New York Times*, December 15, 1992.

110. Shea in Lester Brown, 1989, pp. 78–79.

111. Ibid., pp. 82–83. Wicker, Tom. "Bad News From Above," *New York Times*, April 10, 1991.

112. Shea in Lester Brown, 1989, p. 83. Browne, Malcome W. "Broad Effort Underway to Track Ozone Hole's Effects," *New York Times*, January 6, 1992.

113. Stevens, William K. "Clouds May Retard Ozone Depletion," *New York Times*, November 21, 1995.

114. Shea in Lester Brown, 1989, p. 78.

115. Ibid., p. 93.

116. Whitney, Craig R. "Banning Chemicals That May Harm Ozone," *New York Times*, March 3, 1989. Perlman, David. "Scientists Discover Huge Increase in Threat to Ozone," *San Francisco Chronicle*, February 4, 1992. Whitney, Craig R. "80 Nations Favor Ban to Help Ozone," *New York Times*, May 3, 1989. Stevens, William K. "Threat to Ozone Hastens the Ban on Some Chemicals," *New York Times*, November 26, 1992.

117. Ibid. Whitney, Craig R. "Industrial Countries to Aid Poorer Nations on Ozone," *New York Times*, May 6, 1989.

118. Schneider, Keith. "Bush Orders End to Making of Ozone-Depleting Agents," *New York Times*, February 13, 1992.

119. Stevens, William K. "100 Nations Move to Save Ozone Shield," *New York Times*, December 10, 1995.

120. Shea in Lester Brown, 1989, p. 88.

121. Browne, Malcome W. "Ozone Fading Fast, Thatcher Tells Experts," *New York Times*, June 28, 1990.

122. Stevens, William K. "Scientists Report an Easing in Ozone-Killing Chemicals," *New York Times*, August 26, 1993.

123. Doniger, David, and Miller, Alan. "Fighting Global Warming Is Good for Business," Center for Global Change, College Park, University of Maryland, circa 1990.

124. Ehrlich in Jeremy Leggett, 1990, pp. 410–13.

125. Hudson, William J. "Population, Food and the Economy of Nations," in David Pimental and Carl W. Hall, 1989, pp. 201–3. French, Hilary F. "Clearing the Air," in Lester Brown, *State of the World 1990*. New York: Norton, 1990, p. 106. Brown, Lester. "Reducing Hunger," in Lester Brown, 1994, p. 29.

126. Ibid. Ehrlich in Jeremy Leggett, 1990, p. 419.

127. Brown in Lester Brown, 1994, p. 31.

128. Andow, David A., and Davis, David P. "Agricultural Chemicals: Food and Environment," in David Pimentel and Carl W. Hall, 1989, p. 195.

129. Ibid. Ehrlich in Jeremy Leggett, 1990, pp. 414, 416.

130. Meyers, Norman. "Loss of Biological Diversity and Its Potential Impact on Agriculture and Food Productivity," in David Pimentel and Carl W. Hall, 1989, p. 59. Ehrlich in Jeremy Leggett, 1990, p. 416.

12

Dictatorship and Democracy

In late 1989, communist dictatorships in seven Eastern European countries suddenly fell, most of them peacefully, and civilian democrats assumed power for the first time in more than forty years. The simultaneous collapse of seven communist dictatorships, capped by the dramatic opening and then destruction of the Berlin Wall, the most visible symbol of dictatorship in one-party states, was the high-water mark of contemporary democratization. But democratization in Poland, East Germany, Czechoslovakia, Hungary, Bulgaria, Romania, and Albania was not the first nor the last episode of democratization in recent years. Events in Eastern Europe were only one act in a global drama spanning the past twenty years, a process that first toppled "capitalist" dictatorships in southern Europe, Latin America, and East Asia, then destroyed communist regimes in Eastern Europe and the Soviet Union, and more recently, brought an end to whites-only rule in South Africa.[1]

The rise of democracy in at least thirty countries around the world since 1974 was not only welcome but remarkable for two reasons.[2] First, democratization or the transfer of political power from dictators or one-party regimes to civilian democrats occurred *peacefully*. With the exception of some violence in the Philippines, Romania, and the Soviet Union, and considerable violence in South Africa, the transfer of power was achieved without bloodshed. Second, dictators themselves often initiated the process, taking steps that made possible open elections and a return to civilian authority. Few analysts or dissident movements opposed to dictatorship expected dictators to propose dramatic reforms or to surrender power without a fight. But many of them did just that, opening negotiations with their opponents, quitting their offices, and retiring from public life. Of course, dissident movements and popular protests played an important role in some countries, particularly in South Korea, Poland,

and South Africa. But in most cases, mass movements organized protests only after dictators initiated reform. Democratization might therefore be described as a "devolutionary" process because the transfer of political power was peacefully achieved and because it did not result in the kind of violent "revolutionary" change associated with the American, French, or Russian Revolutions.

Contemporary democratization occurred in great regional waves, moving westward around the world. It began in southern Europe in the mid-1970s, then moved west across the Atlantic to Latin America. The dictatorships in major Latin American countries began folding in the mid-1980s, and most of the remaining dictatorships disappeared by the end of the decade. In the late 1980s, several countries in East Asia democratized, followed in 1989 by the collapse of communist regimes in Eastern Europe. A few years later, the Soviet Union democratized and dissolved into separate republics (as did Yugoslavia and Czechoslovakia—see chapter 13). And then South Africa abandoned apartheid, adopted majority rule, and finally inaugurated a black president in 1994.

In each of these geographic regions, democratization had rather different *causes*. For example, the debt crisis contributed to democratization in most Latin American countries, while in East Asia it was rapid economic growth that helped trigger democratization. Economic stagnation was a primary cause of democratization in the Soviet Union and Eastern Europe, while trade sanctions, embargo, and divestment played a major role in South Africa. In these different regions, economic crises of one sort or another, compounded by problems associated with military defeat, the illness or death of an aging dictator, popular uprising, or changed superpower policy forced dictators to surrender power.

Although democratization had very different causes in each region, its political and economic *consequences* were much the same everywhere. In political terms, democratizing countries drafted new constitutions, held elections, and allowed numerous and diverse political parties to participate. In economic terms, most democratizing countries opened their economies to foreign investment and trade, sold state-owned assets and industries to private investors and entrepreneurs, and reduced military spending and downsized armies.

Of course, people in many countries expected democratic politics and economic policies to solve the problems that first confronted dictators and helped force them from power. Unfortunately, civilian democrats in many countries have been unable to solve their problems. And where democratic politics have been corrupted or new economic policies have failed, new dictators once again threaten to assume power.

To understand the prospects of democratizing states, we will look first at the problems that led to the collapse of capitalist dictatorships and communist regimes in different regions during the past twenty years. Then we will examine the common political and economic strategies adopted by most civilian democrats after they assumed power. In this context we will discuss the problems and prospects of democratizing states around the world.

Southern Europe: Falling Behind

Although fascist dictatorships in Italy and Germany were crushed by Allied forces during World War II, dictatorships in Portugal and Spain survived the war, largely because they stayed neutral in the conflict. In Portugal, António de Oliveira Salazar, a former economics professor, had assumed power in 1930; in Spain General Francisco Franco defeated republican forces during a bitter civil war and became dictator in 1939. The Iberian dictatorships, which would survive until the early 1970s, were joined by Greece in 1967, when a military coup established a dictatorship on the Ionian peninsula.

By Western European standards, Portugal, Spain, and Greece were poor countries. After World War II, dictatorship in Portugal and Spain, and civilian and later military government in Greece, made some economic gains, but their improvements in per capita incomes and literacy were based on relatively weak economies. Because none of them had substantial industries that could compete in overseas markets, they all imported more than they exported and posted trade deficits for every year between 1946 and 1974. As the Turkish economist Caglar Keyder noted, "None of the southern European countries (except Spain in 1951 and [again] in 1960) ran a commodity surplus in all the years between 1946 and 1974. This is to say that none of [them] ever reached a point when their economies generated sufficient exports to pay for their imports. . . . ."[3]

Most economies and the dictators who run them cannot long survive persistent trade deficits of this sort. But Iberian and Ionian dictatorships were able to make up for their industrial deficiencies and grow somewhat during this period (Spain more than Portugal or Greece) because they exported *workers*, not industrial goods, imported free-spending Western European tourists, and received significant infusions of cash from external sources.[4] As Raymond Carr and Juan Aizpurua note

> The economy was refueled from abroad: by tourist earnings, by the remittances of emigres working abroad, and by foreign loans. Only these invisible

earnings and loans made it possible to realize . . . plans for rapid growth without running up against the balance of payments problems that bring growth to a grinding halt in most poor economies.[5]

After World War II, Western European countries, with the assistance of the U.S. Marshall Plan, recovered and began to grow. They soon experienced labor shortages, in part because the war had killed or crippled many potential workers. So they began hiring workers from Europe's periphery, particularly from Spain, Portugal, southern Italy, Greece, and Turkey. Workers in those countries, particularly in rural areas, were eager to seek work abroad because they faced poverty and unemployment at home. During the 1960s, nearly one million Portuguese workers left the country to work in France and West Germany, and in the early 1970s, one hundred thousand were emigrating annually.[6] In Spain, half a million workers had left the province of Andalusia during the 1950s. This emigration emptied rural villages. The Castilian novelist Miguel Dlibes wrote of one village: "Cartiguera is a dying village, in agony. Its winding streets, invaded by weeds and nettles, without a dog's bark or a child's laugh to break the silence, enclosed pathetic gravity, the lugubrious air of the cemetery."[7]

But while this was a difficult and sometimes painful process, it greatly reduced domestic unemployment, providing a safety valve for dictatorships, and helped boost their economies because emigrants sent "remittances" or money they earned abroad back to families who stayed behind. In Spain, for example, emigrants' remittances made up about one-half of the annual trade deficit in the 1960s.[8]

While they exported workers, governments in Spain, Portugal, and Greece also imported tourists and spent much of their budgets to build the hotels, resorts, and infrastructure needed to develop this industry. For example, the number of tourists visiting Spain exceeded the number of people living in Spain by 1973.[9] These tourists spent money and created jobs, and this too helped what the economist Paul Samuelson called "market fascism" in Spain to survive.[10]

All three countries also received large infusions of economic aid from external sources. Although the United States had fought to destroy dictatorships in Europe during World War II, it provided financial support to Iberian dictatorships after the war in return for the establishment of U.S. military bases there in the 1950s, and provided economic and military assistance to Greece, a country bordering communist dictatorships in Eastern Europe.[11] Portugal also relied on another source of external wealth during the postwar period: its colonies in Africa. Portugal derived

considerable income from its exploitation of Mozambique, Angola, and Guinea-Bissau, and the Salazar dictatorship refused to relinquish its colonies, despite armed rebellion by independence movements and the withdrawal of other European states from Africa during the period of decolonization in the 1950s and '60s.

Buoyed by income from emigrant workers, tourists, and superpower aid, the dictatorships in Portugal, Spain, and later Greece managed to keep their economies afloat during the 1950s and '60s. Of the three, Spain was the most successful, recording rapid rates of growth, which some economists then described as a "miracle." But much of Spain's postwar growth simply recovered economic ground lost during the Depression, Civil War, and World War II.[12] By the end of the 1960s, it was clear that despite some modest gains, the rest of Western Europe was leaving these countries behind economically. In the 1970s, conditions that had made possible modest economic growth changed, confronting dictatorships with serious economic crises.

The crisis began when the United States devalued the dollar in 1971, making the value of Portuguese, Spanish, and Greek currencies rise. This made it more difficult for them to export goods, and it increased their already large trade deficits. This problem was compounded by rising oil prices. When OPEC countries cut oil supplies and raised prices following the 1973 Yom Kippur War, the economic crisis deepened. Portugal was particularly hard hit because OPEC countries refused to sell oil to the dictatorship, now headed by Marcello Caetano, because it had allowed U.S. forces to use Portuguese bases to assist the Israeli war effort.[13]

The oil crisis of 1973–74 not only raised the cost of oil for countries with little oil of their own, which increased their trade deficits, it also triggered a global recession. In response, Western European countries laid off immigrant workers and sent them home. This led to rising domestic unemployment and discontent and greatly reduced the money received from emigrant workers' earnings, which further increased trade deficits. And during the recession, fewer European families vacationed abroad, reducing tourist receipts.[14]

Of the three, the Portuguese dictatorship found itself in the most difficult straits. This was because its decade-long wars to prevent the independence of its Africa colonies had drained its treasury. "By 1974, a population of less than 9 million was sustaining a 200,000-man army in Africa and spending over 45 percent of its annual budget on the military," notes Kenneth Maxwell.[15] "The burdens of the African campaigns on a small, poor nation with limited resources and retarded economic and social infrastructures proved unsustainable."[16] With tongue-in-cheek, *The Economist* then described Portugal as "Africa's only colony in Europe."[17]

The economic crisis triggered by new conditions in the 1970s was compounded in Portugal, Spain, and Greece by military and political problems. For Portugal, massive military spending on wars in Africa did not help the military defeat armed independence movements. In 1973, Antonio de Spínola, a leading Portuguese general, published a book arguing for a political solution. His book, *Portugal and the Future*, convinced many, particularly in the military, that Portuguese defeat was imminent.[18] Military officers who were radicalized by their experience in Africa then organized the Armed Forces Movement (AFM), which sought to overthrow the Caetano dictatorship, democratize the political system, and end Portugal's anticolonial wars in Africa. On April 25, 1974, AFM units in Portugal overthrew the Caetano regime.

Military defeat also played an important role a few months later in Greece. To deflect growing discontent at home, the "Colonels," as the Greek military dictatorship was known, supported a coup in Cyprus during the summer of 1974. The coup was led by Greek-speaking Cypriots who wanted to overthrow the government of Archbishop Makarios III so that the Mediterranean island could then be "united" with Greece.[19] But the coup prompted fighting between the island's Greek- and Turkish-speaking residents, a development that triggered an invasion of the island by Turkish forces and brought Greece and Turkey to the brink of war. Faced with humiliation in Cyprus and a potentially disastrous war with its more powerful neighbor, military leaders in Greece refused to wage war and demanded that the junta surrender power to a civilian government on July 24, 1974.[20]

In both Portugal and Greece, military defeat in wars abroad either turned elements of the military against the dictatorship (Portugal) or discredited it completely (Greece). Neither dictatorship could survive the loss of legitimacy associated with military defeat.

In Spain, the economic crisis triggered by dollar devaluation and OPEC embargo was compounded not by military defeat but by a crisis of succession. Born in 1892, Franco was 83 in 1974. Increasing age and bouts of illness had forced him to designate King Juan Carlos as his successor in 1969. In the years before his death Franco tried to create political institutions that would survive him. (This was also a problem in Portugal, where Salazar appointed Caetano as his successor in 1968, shortly before he died.) But dictators find it difficult to transfer power to successors without interruption, largely because dictatorship requires aggregating, not delegating power. So when Franco died in November 1975, Juan Carlos appointed a prime minister who began to dismantle the political institutions of the dictatorship and move the country toward civilian,

democratic government, a protracted process that took three more years. Elites in Spain moved toward democracy because they wanted to join the Spanish economy with the rest of Western Europe. But the European Community would not let Spain share the substantial economic benefits of EC membership so long as it remained a dictatorship. So by abandoning dictatorship, elites hoped to join the EC, which would help Spain overcome both the immediate economic crisis and chronic economic backwardness and promote new economic development. Franco's death gave them the political opportunity to pursue a democratization policy that many regarded as an economic necessity.[21]

Spanish elites who pressed for democratization (called *aperturistas*) and those arguing for continued dictatorship (*immobilistas*) were also mindful of the social and political turmoil prompted by the coup and collapse of the Caetano regime in neighboring Portugal, a revolution that brought to power communists and then socialists. They were also aware of the trials and convictions of military leaders and torturers in Greece following democratization there. For Spanish elites, a carefully managed devolution of power from Francoist dictatorship to civilian democracy seemed a good alternative to events in either Portugal or Greece.

In all three countries, political intermediaries played important roles in the devolution of power. In Portugal, a movement of Marxist military officers served as intermediaries; in Greece, the military president and a former prime minister living in exile in Paris managed the government before full-scale elections were held; in Spain, a king and his technocratic allies in government oversaw the devolutionary process.[22] All of them made democratization and entry into the European Community their primary political and economic objective.[23] When elections were held, socialist governments assumed power in all three countries, a development that would have been unimaginable in the early 1970s, since socialist and communist parties were banned or severely restricted by dictatorships in all three countries.[24] All three soon joined the European Community: Greece in 1981, Spain and Portugal in 1986. And this development proved to be a great boon to their economic fortunes in the 1980s.

The transition to democracy on the Iberian peninsula did not go unnoticed in Latin American dictatorships, where most countries were once colonies of Portugal and Spain. In 1978, just as democracy arrived in Spain, seventeen of the twenty Latin American countries were governed by military or "authoritarian" governments, according to political scientist Robert Pastor.[25] Unlike dictators in Portugal and Spain, most Latin American dictators would survive the 1970s. But the debt crisis that

emerged in the early 1980s would create problems that would sweep most of them from power and establish democratic civilian governments by the end of the decade. By 1990, "17 of the 20 countries and over 90 percent of its population [could be] said to live under democratic governments," writes Pastor. "More of Latin America is now democratic . . . than at any time in the previous 160-year period of the continent [since] the struggle for separation from Spain and . . . Portugal."[26]

Latin America: Debt and Devolution

Most Latin American dictatorships had come to power in the 1950s and '60s, though a few, like Chile's General Augusto Pinochet Ugarte, seized power in the 1970s. Modest economic growth throughout the 1960s provided economic credibility to dictators and the bureaucracies associated with them. The alliance between military rulers and bureaucratic elites formed the social basis of what political scientists called "bureaucratic authoritarian regimes" in the region.

The 1973 oil crisis and the recession associated with it created many of the same economic problems for Latin American dictatorships that it did for regimes in southern Europe. It increased the cost of imported oil and food, which raised prices and contributed to inflation, and created trade deficits, which weakened their currencies. But while it created immediate problems for some Latin American countries, the oil crisis also presented dictatorships with an opportunity. Rising oil prices were good for oil-producing countries (which in Latin America included Mexico and Venezuela) and new revenues from higher oil prices found their way into financial pools that were then made available to third world borrowers by first world lenders. Because Latin American dictators had access to low-cost credit through private U.S. banks and international lending agencies, they could borrow money to cover trade deficits and invest in their economies. By borrowing money, dictators were able to create jobs, build dams and roads, increase exports, raise military spending, cover budget deficits, and create the kind of economic growth that enhanced their legitimacy. Dictators across the continent borrowed about $350 billion between 1970 and 1983, funds that helped them achieve rapid rates of economic growth. The Brazilian dictatorship, which borrowed the largest amount, also recorded the highest rates of growth, a development that many economists described as a "miracle." Dictators then pointed to this miraculous economic development, in much the same way that Benito

Mussolini boasted of having made Italy's trains run on time, as proof of their competence.

Massive borrowing enabled Latin American countries to avert the problems that undermined southern European dictatorships in the early 1970s. The Iberian and Ionian dictatorships found it more difficult to borrow, either because first world lenders were more reluctant to advance loans to them or because their own conservative economic policies, which stressed self-sufficiency (a residue of fascist ideology), prevented them from asking for loans. But having used borrowed money to address their economic problems in the 1970s, Latin American dictatorships created economies that were vulnerable to changed conditions in the 1980s. This vulnerability increased when first world lenders insisted in the late 1970s that loans be tied to floating, not fixed interest rates, rates that subsequently rose dramatically.

Economic conditions changed when the U.S. Federal Reserve raised interest rates to fight inflation in 1979 and 1980. Because most of their loans were tied to U.S. interest rates, dictators had to make higher interest payments on money they had borrowed in the 1970s. What's more, high U.S. interest rates attracted Latin American investors, who withdrew their money from domestic bank accounts and invested in U.S. government securities. This capital flight from Latin America made it more difficult for countries to purchase imports and repay debt. It also eroded the tax base, depriving Latin American dictatorships of money at a time when they needed it most.

While higher interest rates increased costs, falling commodity prices reduced the income of Latin American countries. The prices Latin American countries could get for their beef, food, timber, minerals, or oil began to fall after 1980 for two reasons. First, borrowed money had been used by dictatorships and private industry to increase their production of exports, and increased production glutted markets. Second, high U.S. interest rates triggered a recession in the United States and around the world, which reduced the demand for goods produced in Latin America and other third world countries. Rising supplies and falling demand led to falling prices. This meant that Latin American dictatorships were earning less while being asked by first world lenders to pay more.

By 1982, when Mexico announced that it could no longer make payments on its $90 billion foreign debt, most of the Latin American dictatorships faced a serious economic crisis. One World Bank official described Argentina's economy, then saddled with $40 billion in foreign debts, as a "financial Hiroshima."[27]

Although the debt crisis undermined the economic legitimacy of dicta-

tors throughout Latin America, the crisis did not alone lead to the collapse of dictatorship. But economic crisis was compounded by political disaster in Argentina, and events there soon led to the collapse of the regime, a development that helped trigger democratization elsewhere.

On April 2, 1982, Argentine troops crossed 300 miles of South Atlantic Ocean and landed in Port Stanley, the capital of an island group the British call the Falklands and the Argentines call the Malvinas.[28] General Leopoldo Galtieri and the rest of Argentina's military junta apparently believed that the British would surrender the islands without a fight and that capture of the islands would bolster domestic support for the regime. Instead, the invasion triggered a ruinous war with the United Kingdom, which destroyed the regime's credibility at home.

Within days of the invasion, a British fleet had shipped south, to land troops on the islands on May 21. They quickly defeated Argentina's ill-equipped army, cut off from Argentina by the British navy, and forced its surrender on June 14.

As it turned out, the war in the Falklands/Malvinas was for Argentina's dictatorship what war in Cyprus was for the Greek junta: a humiliating defeat that forced them both from power. In Argentina, power was first assumed by another military government. But deteriorating economic and political conditions soon forced this government to call elections and it transferred power to a civilian government the following year.

The collapse of dictatorship in Argentina, a large and relatively wealthy country in Latin American terms, reverberated across the continent. Dictators in other countries recognized that they shared many of the same economic problems. They also noted that U.S. policy toward dictatorship had undergone an important shift.

For many years, U.S. officials permitted, condoned, or even encouraged dictatorship throughout much of Latin America. And the United States had provided food aid and military loans to dictators during the 1960s and '70s. But during the Falklands war, U.S. officials did not support or defend the Argentine dictatorship. In fact, in a phone call with Galtieri just one day before the Argentines seized the islands, President Reagan told him, "I do not want to fail to emphasize pointedly that the relationship between our two countries will suffer seriously."[29] Galtieri evidently expected the United States to ignore the conflict, and the junta even suggested to the United States and other Latin American governments that they were obligated to come to Argentina's "defense" under the mutual-security provisions of the 1947 Rio Treaty. They were greatly disappointed when they received no diplomatic assistance from the United States or other dictatorships, and they felt betrayed after they learned that

the U.S. government had provided important military assistance to the United Kingdom during the war. Dictators across the continent regarded these developments as an indication that U.S. policy had shifted and that they could no longer count on U.S. support in the event of a crisis.

In Brazil, the debt had grown from $12.6 billion to $90 billion between 1973 and 1982, inflation had soared into quadruple digits, and the economy had become, from the government's perspective, unmanageable. For more than a decade, the dictatorship had said it was moving toward eventual democratization, but it moved at a glacial pace. Economic crisis and changed political conditions sped up the process after the collapse of the dictatorship in neighboring Argentina in 1983 and in Uruguay in 1984. Brazil's dictators returned power to civilian authority in 1985.

Events then shifted to the Philippines, a country that more closely resembles Latin American countries in political and economic terms than its Asian neighbors. Like many Latin American countries, the Philippines were colonized and catholicized by Spain, then brought into the U.S. sphere of influence during the Spanish-American War. In 1972, President Ferdinand Marcos declared martial law and assumed dictatorial powers. Like the Latin American dictatorships, the Marcos regime borrowed heavily in the 1970s, the country's foreign debt growing to $26 billion by 1985, an amount equal to the country's annual GNP.[30] For the Marcos regime, profound economic crisis was joined by political turmoil when opposition leader Benigno Aquino was assassinated by government soldiers in 1983. His murder triggered social protest and massive capital flight, leading to a moratorium on debt payments and a real decline in the economy.[31] During 1984 and 1985, the economy registered "negative growth," shrinking by nearly 9 percent in those two years.[32] Faced with deteriorating economic and political conditions, Marcos called a snap presidential election for early 1986, an election he expected to win over the disorganized opposition.[33] But opposition candidate Cory Aquino, widow of the slain Benigno Aquino, won despite massive election fraud. When Marcos refused to surrender power, civilians and some army units took to the streets, while U.S. officials invited Marcos to find exile in Hawaii. Foreign push and domestic shove soon forced Marcos from office and into exile in 1986.

In Argentina, Brazil, and the Philippines, and throughout Latin America, dictatorships confronted debt-related economic crisis. Because first world lenders insisted that dictators institute "austerity" programs to ensure repayment of debt, dictators found themselves in the difficult position of introducing extremely unpopular economic policies. To make these policies succeed, dictators needed the acquiescence or cooperation

of other social groups, particularly wealthy elites and middle classes. But these groups demanded that they obtain political power and a return to democracy if they were to assume responsibility for managing the economic crisis. Under the circumstances, the dictatorships could not easily refuse. What's more, they recognized that U.S. support for dictatorship had eroded and they worried about the alternatives to a managed or controlled democratization process. They feared popular revolts of the kind that had emerged in Portugal and later threatened in the Philippines. And they worried about events in Greece, where dictators and torturers were tried and jailed for their criminal conduct in office. Many dictators had reason to fear the Greek example. In Argentina, the military had waged a "dirty war" against civilian dissidents during the 1970s and '80s, kidnapping, torturing, jailing, and murdering its opponents. As one army general explained, "We are going to kill 50,000 people: 25,000 subversives, 20,000 sympathizers, and we will make 5,000 mistakes."[34]

Many officials in dictatorial regimes had also illegally profited from their offices, siphoning off borrowed public money into private bank accounts. When civilian government returned in Argentina, many people demanded that officials in the dictatorship be tried and punished for economic and political crimes. Military officials lobbied desperately to prevent this, while army units staged mutinies and attempted coups to discourage the civilian government from prosecuting those responsible for the dirty war.

Throughout Latin America, the generals concluded that a "managed" devolution of power would be preferable to the alternatives. So they devised constitutions that would transfer power while retaining some prerogatives and protections from legal proceedings after they surrendered power. As a result, dictators in Argentina, Uruguay, Brazil, Peru, Ecuador, El Salvador, Panama, Honduras, Bolivia, and Paraguay transferred power, returned to the barracks, or retired from public life.[35] In 1990, even General Pinochet returned power to civilian government in Chile.

East Asia: Growing Pains

In 1950, South Korea was the economic equal of Kenya or Nigeria, while Taiwan was comparable to Egypt. But during the next thirty years, the economies of South Korea and Taiwan grew by leaps and bounds. Between 1962 and 1980, South Korea's GNP increased 452 percent, growing from $12.7 billion to $57.4 billion, a development that distanced it from its former companions in the third world. And by 1983, *The Economist*

noted, the 18 million people in Taiwan exported more goods than 130 million Brazilians or 75 million Mexicans.[36]

Economic growth in South Korea and Taiwan, which was the envy of third world countries everywhere, was made possible by three important developments. First, both South Korea and Taiwan had been colonized by Japan at the beginning of the century. Japanese colonial administrators developed important economic infrastructures and tied the colonial economies to Japan. Close economic relations survived the war, and when Japan began its remarkable economic ascent, it pulled them along. It is important to note, however, that Japanese economic growth always exceeded that of its former colonies, which meant that their rise, while significant, was not as spectacular as that of Japan.[37]

Second, after the Korean War began in 1950, South Korea and Taiwan began receiving substantial economic and military benefits from the United States, largely because U.S. policy makers regarded them as frontline states in the battle against communism. To shore up Chiang Kai-shek's one-party dictatorship in Taiwan and the military governments that ruled South Korea after 1962, the U.S. government provided $5.6 billion in economic and military aid to Taiwan and $13 billion to South Korea between 1945 and 1978. U.S. aid to Korea was greater than aid to all of Africa ($6.89 billion) and India ($9.6 billion), and nearly as much as to all of Latin America ($14.8 billion) in the same period.[38] The United States also opened its markets to importers from Korea and Taiwan, giving them preferential trading privileges enjoyed by few other countries, while allowing them to erect formidable trade barriers against U.S. imports so they could protect and nurture domestic industry.

Third, the dictatorships in South Korea and Taiwan instituted land reform, thereby creating an urban workforce that could work in their growing export industries. They banned labor unions and strikes to keep wages low, a policy designed to give their export industries a competitive advantage in U.S. and world markets. And they used high tariff barriers to protect domestic industry from foreign competition and fostered the growth of large, export-oriented monopoly firms, what the Koreans call *chaebols* and the Taiwanese call *caifa*, to create businesses that could compete with large transnational firms in first world countries.[39]

These three developments—Japanese colonialism before 1945, U.S. assistance after 1945, and domestic economic policy that capitalized on economic opportunities—enabled the South Korean and Taiwanese economies to grow rapidly, providing considerable economic legitimacy for the dictators that directed them. But changing economic and political conditions in the 1970s and '80s caught South Korea and Taiwan in an

economic squeeze that made it increasingly difficult for the dictatorships to maintain rapid rates of growth.

For Taiwan, problems began in 1972, when President Nixon suddenly recognized communist China and cut off much of U.S. economic, military, and diplomatic aid to the nationalist government. Although these developments shocked the dictatorship, which viewed changed U.S. policy as a betrayal (much as dictators in Greece, Argentina, and the Philippines viewed other U.S. policies), the U.S. government did not curtail Taiwan's trading privileges, so it could still export goods to the United States.

Then, in the early 1980s, both South Korea and Taiwan began to experience growing competition from other Asian countries—China, Thailand, and Indonesia—that adopted their "model" of economic growth and developed export industries that relied on workers who were paid even lower wages. Workers received $643 a month in Taiwan and $610 in South Korea in 1988; workers received $209 in Indonesia, $132 in Thailand, and $129 in Malaysia.[40] Lower wages enabled businesses in other Asian countries to manufacture goods at prices that undercut firms in South Korea and Taiwan.

While new Asian competitors pushed from below, the United States began to push from above. Because East Asian countries were so successful at selling their goods in U.S. markets, while blocking the sale of U.S. goods in their countries, the United States began running large trade deficits with South Korea, Taiwan, and most importantly, Japan. Persistent trade deficits strained U.S. support for East Asian dictatorships. To reduce its trade deficits with Asian countries and improve its competitiveness in overseas markets, the U.S. government in 1985 devalued the dollar. This forced up the value of the South Korean currency by 30 percent. "We can absorb wage increases," a South Korean executive explained, "but we can't take any more [currency] appreciation."[41]

In 1987, U.S. officials also began restricting its preferential trading relations with East Asian countries, making it more difficult and more expensive for them to sell goods in U.S. markets.[42] And they demanded that East Asian countries lower their trade barriers so that U.S. firms could sell more goods there, using bilateral and multilateral trade talks to press their case.[43]

At the same time, domestic social groups began pressing for change. Rapid urbanization had moved many people off the land and into the cities, but housing shortages and real estate speculation had pushed up housing costs for workers and the middle class. In Taipei, land is more expensive than in Manhattan, but workers earn only half as much as their

counterparts in New York City.[44] Workers grew weary of working long hours with little pay—South Koreans worked 54.3 hours a week on average.[45] Although the economy grew and per capita income increased, this did not mean that wages also increased. The dictatorships restrained wage increases and kept them from growing as fast as the economy. Workers who labored hard for their country became increasingly unhappy about their inability to share in its rewards. As a result, legal and illegal labor disputes rose sharply in the mid-1980s. In South Korea, for example, the number of disputes rose from 276 in 1986 to 3,749 in 1987, a thirteenfold increase.[46] Legal and illegal strike activity forced up wages, despite the dictatorships' determined efforts to arrest labor leaders and curb wage increases, and this made South Korean goods more expensive and less competitive on world markets. What's more, industrial workers, and increasingly, middle-class workers, joined student demonstrators demanding an end to dictatorship and a return to democracy. Although the dictatorship had been able to contain and isolate student radicals for some years, it became more difficult to do so when economic demands echoed political demands and workers and white-collar employees joined student protests.

For South Korea and Taiwan, economic success invited lower-wage Asian countries to emulate them, first world countries to retaliate against them, and domestic workers to protest against them.

In Taiwan, these economic problems were compounded by a succession crisis. The Republic of China was created in 1948 when nationalist armies under General Chiang Kai-shek fled from the Chinese mainland after being defeated by communist armies and took refuge on Taiwan, creating a dictatorship that ran the country under martial law for the next thirty-nine years. When Chiang Kai-shek died in 1975, power invested in the one-party regime passed to his son, Chiang Ching-kuo. By the time he inherited his father's power, Chiang Ching-kuo was sixty-five, already an old man. Near the end of his life, in 1986, he began casting around for a successor and began to consider reform that could eventually transform Taiwan into a multiparty democracy, finally lifting martial law in 1987. When he died in 1988, power passed to Lee Teng-hui, who, like Juan Carlos in Spain, initiated a leisurely reform process that eventually led to open elections in 1992.[47]

And in both South Korea and Taiwan, dictatorships closely observed the hapless demise of the Marcos dictatorship in 1986. Although the Philippines was more like Latin American countries in economic and political terms, it was an Asian society in geographic terms. And its proximity to South Korea and Taiwan made dictators fear the spread of Corazon Aquino's "People Power" to restive populations in their own countries.

By 1986–87, as economic growth slowed from double-digit to single-digit rates, the dictatorships in South Korea and Taiwan had become extremely anxious about economic and political developments. Cho Soon, South Korea's minister of economic planning, warned that without economic reform, "Our country will collapse like some of the Latin American countries," such as Argentina.[48] And military leaders like Roh Tae Woo concluded that greater democratic participation was necessary if the country was to move ahead economically. During the late 1980s, military regimes in South Korea and Taiwan saw democratization as a way to share power with the middle class and to create a multiparty system dominated by a center-right party as a way to restore the government's legitimacy, deflect popular protest, and get the economy moving again.

In South Korea it was Roh Tae Woo who initiated reform in 1987, arguing that "this country should develop a more mature democracy," transforming himself from military leader to presidential candidate.[49] After he won election in 1987 as president when dissident leaders split the opposition vote, he took steps that resulted in the 1992 election of dissident civilian Kim Young-sam. "Now we have finally created a truly civilian-led government in our country," Kim said after the vote.[50]

In 1992, Thailand joined South Korea and Taiwan when the military government stepped down and transferred power to civilians. Like them, Thailand experienced many of the problems associated with rapid growth. When government troops massacred student and middle-class demonstrators demanding political reform in May 1992, the military regime was discredited. Acting as an intermediary, King Bhumibol Adulyadei then assumed the role that Juan Carlos had played in Spain and managed a transfer of power to civilian government by September.[51]

During the late 1980s, communist dictatorships in China and Vietnam also initiated some economic and political reforms to address the economic problems that confronted them. The aging political leadership of communist parties in China and Vietnam faced the problem of choosing more youthful political successors, a problem shared by rulers in Taiwan. In 1989, students and workers in Beijing occupied Tiananmen Square and demanded political reform, much as demonstrators in Seoul had been doing for some years. It appeared, during the spring of 1989, that these developments in China might lead to democratization there, just as it was then doing in South Korea and Taiwan. But the massacre of protesters camped in Tiananmen Square and the arrest of dissidents throughout the country aborted reforms that seemed in the offing. Events in China did not lead to the collapse of dictatorship. Nor did the Vietnamese regime devolve power, though it too was experiencing a deep economic crisis.

Communist regimes in East Asia did not democratize like capitalist dictatorships in southern Europe, Latin America, and East Asia, or like communist dictatorships that would subsequently democratize in Eastern Europe and the Soviet Union. They did, however, reform their economies and adopt many of the same economic policies that civilian democrats deployed in many democratizing states, an approach that in China has been called "market Leninism."[52] Communist regimes in Asia survived, at least for the present, because they possessed considerable political legitimacy derived from having fought and won wars against colonial powers and domestic rivals. The Chinese communists fought the Japanese in China, U.S. and U.N. forces in Korea, and nationalist rivals during a long civil war. The Vietnamese communists had fought for independence against France, Japan, and the United States, and in 1975 defeated the South Vietnamese regime after U.S. troops withdrew. Their ability to defeat formidable opponents, and their programs designed to improve conditions for the rural population, gave them a reservoir of support they could draw on during the economic and political crises of the 1980s. (Fidel Castro's communist regime in Cuba survives for many of the same reasons.) By contrast, communist dictatorships in Eastern Europe (with the exception of Yugoslavia—see chapter 13) assumed power not as a result of their own efforts but because they were installed by the Soviet Union and backed by the Red Army. And dictators in Eastern Europe and the Soviet Union had long since exhausted the patience of the domestic population, so when crisis struck in the 1980s, they found themselves isolated and vulnerable.

The Soviet Union and Eastern Europe: Decline and Democratization

Democratization in the Soviet Union and Eastern Europe was a product of economic crisis originating in the Soviet Union. This crisis was rooted in the stagnation of collectivized agriculture and the heavy burden of military spending in the postwar period. "By the beginning of the 1980s," Soviet leader Mikhail Gorbachev observed, "the [Soviet Union] found itself in a state of severe crisis which has embraced all spheres of life."[53]

During the 1920s and '30s, the Soviet dictatorship under Joseph Stalin forced small and medium-sized farmers to join large-scale, state-owned collectives. By increasing farm size and mechanizing agriculture under state authority, the government hoped to increase agricultural output and use much of the wealth it produced to finance industrial development.

But collectivization was an extremely disruptive process, as the regime killed farmers who opposed these measures or sent them to Siberia, and agricultural output faltered, contributing to famine in some regions.

After World War II, agriculture revived and the large-scale collective farms increased production, for a time. Because the communist regime continued siphoning off agricultural resources to finance industrial growth and, during the Cold War, the military, there was little investment in agriculture and few incentives for farmers to increase yields or produce more food. Crop yields in the Soviet Union were only about half those obtained in the United States.[54] These problems reached crisis proportions in the mid-1970s, when Soviet grain harvests failed, a development that sent world grain prices soaring. Because farm production failed to keep pace with the growing Soviet demand for food, the Soviet Union had to import more food. The cost of food imports doubled from $5.1 billion to $10.2 billion between 1974 and 1978, a development that increased the Soviet trade deficit.[55] And because farmers in the 1970s and '80s began selling a growing share of their crops through unofficial or black markets that offered higher prices, there was less food available in state stores. Consumers found it difficult to obtain food using ration coupons, though they could purchase higher-priced food on black markets.[56] The result was long lines, frayed tempers, and considerable resentment.

The Soviet regime might have invested more heavily in agriculture if it had not been preoccupied with military spending. But during the Cold War, the Soviets spent heavily to develop and maintain its status as a military and political superpower. According to military analyst Ruth Sivard, the Soviets spent $4.6 trillion between 1960 and 1987, or between 12 and 15 percent of its annual GNP, on the military.[57] Other economists argued that the Soviets spent even more, as much as 20 to 28 percent of GNP.[58] (By comparison, the United States spent only 6 to 8 percent of its GNP on the military during the Cold War.)

Massive military spending enabled the Soviet regime to expand its political influence, maintain an occupying army in Eastern Europe, assist socialist movements and communist governments abroad, and obtain substantial income from arms sales to other countries—$64 billion worth of arms between 1973 and 1981.[59] But it did not provide substantial economic benefits in the Soviet Union or secure military advantages abroad.

Domestically, heavy military spending absorbed scarce supplies of capital, skilled labor, and natural resources, diverting resources from other sectors of the economy, particularly from agriculture and consumer industries. As a result, it retarded economic growth and contributed to stagnation and decline.[60] The Soviet invasion of Afghanistan in 1979 greatly

increased military spending and stimulated an arms race with the United States in the early 1980s, a development that further increased military spending. Gorbachev later said that increased military spending during the Afghan war and the arms race of the 1980s had "exhausted our economy."[61]

It also became apparent in the 1980s that massive military spending had not enabled the Soviets to produce weapons that could compete with U.S. and Western European arms on battlefields in Afghanistan and the Middle East. In 1982, for example, during an air battle over Lebanon, Israeli pilots flying U.S. and French jets "shot down 80 Soviet-made planes [flown by Syrians] while losing none of their own."[62] This kind of lopsided battlefield performance was dramatically underscored during the 1991 Persian Gulf War, when the U.S.-led coalition crushed Iraqi forces, which were supplied with Soviet arms, destroying four thousand Soviet-built tanks in the process. The failure of Soviet weaponry in battlefield competition led Soviet military planners to conclude that the entire Soviet military model was "obsolete."[63] Soviet Marshal Dmitry Yazov admitted, "What happened in Kuwait necessitates a review of our attitude toward the [Soviet Union's] entire defense system."[64]

Soviet economic problems worsened after 1985. Falling world oil prices reduced income from oil exports, one of its major sources of foreign currency, and increased its trade deficit. To cover the trade deficit so that it could import the food and technology it needed from the West, the Soviet Union began borrowing heavily. The Soviet debt to Western European governments and banks nearly quadrupled between 1984 and 1989, growing "from $10.2 billion at the end of 1984 to $37.3 billion at the end of 1989."[65] And the regime's attempts to stimulate the stagnating economy led to growing budget deficits (see chapter 6 on U.S. budget deficits in the same period). "In 1981–85, the budget deficit only averaged 18 billion rubles per year, [but] in 1986–89, it averaged 67 billion rubles," a more than threefold increase.[66]

The Soviet economic crisis was compounded by two political crises. First, the communist regime faced not one but three crises of succession between 1982 and 1985. When Leonid Brezhnev died suddenly after reviewing the annual parade celebrating the anniversary of the Bolshevik Revolution on November 10, 1982, a political battle to choose his successor ensued. Brezhnev's chosen successor, Konstantin Chernenko, was passed over and Yuri Andropov selected as the new Soviet leader. But Andropov died after a long illness on February 9, 1984. A second succession crisis then ensued. Andropov's choice, Mikhail Gorbachev, who represented the young, reform-minded wing of the Communist Party, was passed over and Brezhnev's old protégé, Chernenko, was chosen instead.

But he died a year later, on March 10, 1985, and Mikhail Gorbachev, then fifty-four, assumed power.[67]

Second, by the time the protracted succession crisis had been sorted out, it had become evident that the Soviet Union faced military defeat in Afghanistan. The looming defeat by anticommunist mujahadeen rebels supplied with U.S. arms undermined the legitimacy of a regime that relied on its military standing as a political cornerstone, much as military defeats undermined the legitimacy of dictatorships in Portugal, Greece, and Argentina.

After he assumed power in 1985, Gorbachev took steps to address the economic crisis. By reducing military spending, transferring these resources to other sectors of the economy, and allowing some privatization of state-owned farms and industry to give farmers and workers incentives to increase the quantity and quality of food and consumer goods, Gorbachev hoped to jump-start the languishing economy. But dramatic economic restructuring, called "perestroika," antagonized the military and the Communist Party bureaucracy that directed agriculture and industry. To overcome opposition within the Communist Party and push ahead with economic reform, Gorbachev needed to develop a wider social constituency that could provide political support for reform outside the party. So Gorbachev promoted political reform and limited democratization, what he called "glasnost" (openness), as a way to rally wider popular support for perestroika, demilitarization, and reform. As Gorbachev explained, democratization was "a guarantee against the repetition of past errors, and consequently a guarantee that the restructuring process is irreversible." There was no choice, he said; it was "either democracy or social inertia and conservatism."[68]

Because reduced military spending was a central part of perestroika, Gorbachev devoted considerable attention to Soviet military and foreign policy. He withdrew the Soviet army from Afghanistan, stopped aid to the communist regime in Ethiopia (see chapter 13), and initiated arms control agreements with the United States and its NATO allies in Western Europe. The 1987 Intermediate-Range Nuclear Forces Treaty, which removed intermediate-range nuclear missiles from Europe, was the first arms control agreement to reduce the size of superpower arsenals, and Gorbachev also initiated talks that led to a reduction of conventional troops in Europe. Gorbachev pursued détente with China and sought an end to the long Cold War with the United States. And he renounced longstanding Soviet claims that it had a right to use military force in Eastern Europe to support communist dictatorships there, a "right" that the Soviets exercised in East Germany in 1953, in Hungary in 1956, and in

Czechoslovakia in 1968. The Soviets had also threatened to intervene in Poland in 1981, when the independent labor union Solidarity threatened to topple the communist government, but had refrained when Polish General Wojciech Jaruzelski assumed power and crushed the incipient revolt without Soviet military assistance.

By renouncing the right to intervene in Eastern Europe, Gorbachev undercut client dictatorship that had first been installed by the Soviets in the late 1940s. At a press conference on October 25, 1989, Soviet Foreign Minister Gennady Gerasimov was asked whether the Soviet Union still adhered to the Brezhnev Doctrine, which was used to justify Soviet intervention in Eastern Europe. He said it did not. Instead, he said, new Soviet policy would be called the "Sinatra Doctrine," because the American singer Frank Sinatra "had a song, 'I did it my way.' So every country decides in its own way which [economic and political] road to take."[69] The Soviet adoption of a new foreign policy toward Eastern Europe fatally weakened communist dictatorships and fueled the rise of dissident opposition movements in Poland, East Germany, Hungary, Czechoslovakia, Romania, Bulgaria, and Albania. By the end of 1989, just two months after Gerasimov's press conference, communist dictatorships in all these countries had been swept from power. Some tried to initiate and manage a devolution of power to dissident democrats so that they could retain some power. But an economic crisis rooted in stagnation and debt—recall that Eastern European countries were the first casualties of the debt crisis in the early 1980s—left them without any economic credibility, while the new Soviet policy deprived them of any remaining political legitimacy or military power.

Because they possessed a very narrow social base, with little economic credibility or political legitimacy, communist dictatorships in Eastern Europe collapsed like a house of cards at the first appearance of organized dissent or concerted civic action. In East Germany, it was the flood of migrants from East Germany to Hungary and then to West Germany that brought down the dictatorship, while in Poland it was an organized labor movement. In Hungary and Czechoslovakia newly organized dissident movements negotiated an end to dictatorship. In Romania, street demonstrations and mob action brought a bloody end to the brutal regime of Nicholae Ceausescu.

The dramatic events of 1989 had important consequences for the Soviet Union. The collapse of communism in Eastern Europe, the emergence of protest movements in some Soviet republics, and the extension of reforms in response to a deepening economic crisis led in August 1992 to a coup by hard-liners in the military and Communist Party who were deter-

mined to restore one-party dictatorship. But whereas Chinese hard-liners had been able to crush dissent and maintain dictatorship, Soviet hard-liners found few allies. Instead, people in Moscow and important elements of the army rallied to Russian President Boris Yeltsin, forcing the coup to collapse. These developments led, by the end of 1992, to democratization but also to the division of the Soviet Union into fifteen independent countries (see chapter 13).

South Africa: Embargo, Defeat, and Democratization

On February 2, 1990, South Africa's President Frederik W. de Klerk told the country's whites-only parliament that he was legalizing the outlawed African National Congress (ANC) and other black political organizations and would soon release ANC leader Nelson Mandela, who had been imprisoned for twenty-seven years. Although he told one Western diplomat, "Don't expect me to negotiate myself out of power," de Klerk did just that.[70] One year later, he introduced changes that removed "the remnants of racially discriminatory legislation which have become known as the cornerstones of apartheid," and began a process of negotiation and constitutional reform that would lead in April 1993 to elections that swept Mandela to power as the country's first black president. When Mandela was inaugurated on May 10, 1994, joyous black crowds chanted in Xhosa, "Amandla! Ngawethu!" (Power! It is ours!).[71]

De Klerk initiated the devolution of power in response to a worsening economic and political crisis in South Africa. During the 1950s and '60s, "the apartheid system probably aided economic growth in South Africa" because it locked in low wages for black South African workers.[72] But by the late 1960s, "this position began to change" because low wages discouraged businesses from spending money to introduce new technology that would increase productivity and make South African goods more competitive on world markets, so economic growth began to slow.[73]

In 1976, South African police killed several black demonstrators protesting apartheid in Soweto, an action that triggered a wave of protests and strikes that continued during the 1970s and '80s. During the second half of the 1980s, "5,000 people died and more than 30,000 were jailed without charge."[74] Black protests called international attention to and condemnation of apartheid. Spurred by protests in South Africa and in Western countries, companies and countries began to withdraw investment from South Africa, levy economy sanctions, and eventually reduce much of their trade with South Africa. By the end of the 1980s, sanctions

and disinvestment had brought the South African economy to a standstill. Economists estimated in 1989 that average income had fallen 15 percent from 1980 and that economic sanctions were costing the economy $2 billion a year.[75]

While the economy stagnated, military spending grew, both because the government was waging an internal war against domestic black protesters and because it deployed troops to fight a communist guerrilla movement in Namibia and intervened in neighboring Angola to overthrow the communist government there. These costly external wars led in 1988 to the South African army's defeat by Angolan and Cuban troops at the battle of Cuito Cuanavale in 1988. As Kevin Danaher and Medea Benjamin noted, "The defeat forced the South Africans to sign a peace treaty [with Angola] on December 22, 1988, requiring them to withdraw from Angola [after a thirteen-year occupation] and a phase-out of their decades-long control of Namibia."[76]

When de Klerk became president on August 15, 1989, after the illness and resignation of hard-line President P. W. Botha, known by associates as the "Old Crocodile," he confronted a worsening economic, military, and political crisis. During the next six months, he came to view an end to apartheid as the key to ending the crisis. By ending apartheid, de Klerk hoped that domestic turmoil would wane, military expenditures could be reduced, and foreign investors and Western governments could be persuaded to end economic sanctions and reinvest in the economy. (As in southern Europe, improved economic relations depended on ending dictatorship.) The collapse of communism during the six months between his appointment as president and his dramatic February 2 speech made de Klerk's decision easier, he said, "because it created a scenario where the communist threat . . . lost its sting."[77]

By initiating a devolution of power, de Klerk sought to manage events so that the white minority could reserve their economic power and retain some political power in a post-apartheid state. And democratization in South Africa has encouraged democratization in other African countries. About half of the continent's forty-eight countries have since held or have promised to hold multiparty elections, though this process is only now getting underway, with as yet limited results.[78]

Democracy and Development

Contemporary democratization is largely a product of economic crisis. The problems associated with different kinds of economic crises were

compounded by political problems related to the death or illness of dictators, defeat in war, and public protest by dissident groups. Faced with difficult economic and political problems, dictators and one-party regimes realized they needed to take drastic steps to resolve their problems. But to be successful, radical economic and political reform needed broad public support. And other social groups refused to accept responsibility for solving economic problems they did not create unless they could obtain real political power. As Walden Bello and Stephanie Rosenfeld have written, "Economic policies that are not supported by a rough consensus forced by democratic means are likely to founder over the long run. Democracy, one might say, has become a factor of production."[79]

Under these circumstances, dictators devolved power to civilian democrats, trying to manage the process so that they could retain some residual political power and possibly protect themselves from prosecution for economic crimes (corruption) or violations of human rights (illegal arrests, torture, murder of dissidents). As we have seen, the devolution of power was abrupt in some places and protracted in others, and dictators had only limited success in managing the democratization process.

Once they assumed political power, civilian democrats had to address difficult economic problems. Although the origin and character of economic crises differed from one region to the next, and from one country to the next within these regions, civilian democrats everywhere adopted a common economic approach that they hoped would solve their separate problems. In nearly all democratizing states, civilian democrats have (1) opened their economies to foreign investment and trade, (2) sold off or privatized state-owned public assets and industries, and (3) cut military spending. But while this common set of economic policies has produced economic benefits in some democratizing states, they have also created economic, social, and political problems of their own.

Opening the Economy

Around the world, civilian democrats have reduced tariff barriers, opened their economy to foreign investors, and lifted currency exchange restrictions. Lower tariff barriers are designed to make imported goods more readily available to domestic consumers who have long craved many goods from other countries and to force domestic industries to lower their prices and improve the quality of their goods, or go out of business. Foreign competition and the threat of bankruptcy are supposed to shake up domestic industries that have grown inefficient and wasteful as a result of government protection under dictatorship. By opening the economy to

foreign investment, governments hoped that foreign companies would in-ject new money, management skills, and technology into the economy, thereby providing jobs in industries that can compete on world markets. And by lifting currency restrictions, government economists expected world currency markets to appraise their currency and set exchange rates at realistic levels. As a result, the currencies of most democratizing states were devalued, which made their goods cheaper and easier to sell abroad, a development that helped them increase their exports and reduce their trade deficits. These three measures were designed to achieve what the Brazilians called a "competitive integration" with the world economy.[80]

The problem for many countries, however, is that when tariff barriers were lowered, domestic consumers bought expensive imported goods: Nike shoes, Levi's jeans, foreign cars. This orgy of consumer spending on imports created trade deficits, which forced down the value of their currency. And while a devalued currency should have made their goods easier to sell on overseas markets (which should have improved their trade balance), their goods were often regarded as shoddy by consumers else-where. The result was that they found it difficult to sell their goods at any price. Foreign investors did open some new factories and purchased some government-owned industries at bargain-basement prices (currency de-valuations made businesses cheaper for foreign buyers). But the large-scale investment that many governments expected did not materialize, largely because global economic activity has been slow and there is excess capacity in many industries, and partly because investors are waiting to see whether governments can control inflation and create a favorable busi-ness climate and strong consumer market before risking substantial sums of money. And the widespread sale of public assets and industries has glutted investment markets, which has slowed sales and lowered prices.

Selling Off State Assets

Civilian democrats around the world have sold public assets that had previously been controlled by dictators, bureaucrats, and their friends and families, an economic system that Peruvian economist Hernando de Soto has described as "buddy-buddy" or "crony capitalism."[81] Civilian demo-crats hoped that the sale of public assets would raise money that could be used to repay debts or reduce government budget deficits and cut the cost of subsidizing inefficient industries. The sale of public assets was also supposed to provide new economic opportunities for domestic investors, who were expected to emerge as a new class of energetic entrepreneurs.

As a result, the sale of national banks, airlines, telephone companies,

shipping lines, cement factories, port facilities, and land has been widespread. In Eastern Europe, assets worth more than $100 billion have been offered for sale.[82] In Brazil, the sale of ninety-two "parastatal" firms and a port authority by the end of 1992 had been valued at $62 billion.[83]

Privatization has been less extensive in East Asia, though South Korea sold off seven firms in 1990, because both South Korea and Taiwan have few public assets compared with countries in southern Europe, Latin America, or Eastern Europe, and because the state supports large *private* monopolies, *chaebols*, which they are unwilling to break up.

The problem with this strategy is first that few domestic investors can afford to purchase large companies, while currency devaluations make them cheaper, in real terms, for foreign investors. Foreign firms have snapped up the best offerings at bargain prices, but they are not interested in purchasing poor-quality companies, and the worldwide sale of so many properties has glutted investment markets. With first world airline companies battling each other for scarce travelers, the last thing they need to do is buy up the Argentine airline fleet. In Eastern Europe, Poland has managed to sell only a fraction of the firms it offered for sale, and Germany has sold only a fraction of the eight thousand or so former East German state firms.[84] In Czechoslovakia, and in many former Soviet republics, the governments abandoned plans to sell most of their assets on the open market and instead gave or sold vouchers to residents who used them to buy shares in privatized firms. The idea was to sell the firms to domestic buyers and then use the money raised to introduce technology, improve productivity, and increase competitiveness.[85] But it is not clear that this experiment will provide sufficient capital, that the money collected from small investors will flow to the right firms, that these firms will use the money wisely, or that newly privatized firms will be able to compete effectively against well-established, large-scale firms from Western Europe, North America, or East Asia. So far, the attrition rate of recently privatized firms has been high, and business failures have contributed to rising unemployment in many democratizing states.

Demilitarizing the Economy

Demilitarization has been most dramatic in Eastern Europe and the Soviet Union. Under Gorbachev, the Soviet Union began withdrawing troops from Afghanistan and Eastern Europe and cut military spending and troop levels. This made possible the devolution of power to democrats in Eastern Europe, who promptly slashed military spending, cut

troop levels, disbanded party militias, and withdrew from the Warsaw Pact, causing its demise in 1991.[86]

After the 1992 coup failed and the Soviet Union democratized and divided, military spending fell in most of the former republics. The decline was dramatic. In 1987, the Soviet Union had 3.9 million troops under arms and spent $356 billion on defense. In 1994, the Russian government (the largest of the former Soviet republics) had 2.1 million troops under arms and spent only $29 billion on defense.[87]

In Latin America, successive Argentine presidents have cut military spending in half, scaled back the draft, and cut the army to one-half its Falklands/Malvinas size.[88] And armies across the continent have been scaled back. Julio María Sanguinetti, who became Uruguay's president in 1985, described the changed political atmosphere: "If you get a group of Latin American politicians together in a room and ask, 'Who wants to be foreign minister?' everyone will wave his or her hand in the air. But if you ask, 'Who wants to be defense minister?' everyone stares at the floor."[89]

East Asian states are the exception to this general rule. After Tiananmen Square, the Chinese increased military spending and their democratizing neighbors did the same. South Korea increased its military spending both because its disagreements with North Korea remain unresolved and because the United States cut back its military spending on the peninsula, which forced the South Korean government to assume a greater share of defense costs.

Although military spending in East Asia has increased somewhat, the general trend is to demilitarize, and world military expenditures are down 14 percent from 1987 levels.[90]

Governments have demilitarized for a variety of economic reasons. Most governments believe that heavy military spending did little to contribute to economic growth and may even have put their economies at a disadvantage in global competition with states that devoted a smaller percentage of their GNP to military expenditures, like Germany and Japan. In a study on the relation between military spending and economic growth, A. F. Mullins found that "in general, those states that did best in GNP growth . . . paid less attention to military capability than others. This relation . . . holds right across the range from poor states to rich states and from weak states to powerful. Those that did poorly in GNP growth . . . paid more attention to military capability."[91]

Continuing Economic Crises and Democracy

During the 1970s and '80s, economic crises of different sorts created problems that contributed to the collapse of dictatorships around the

world. The civilian democrats who assumed power then attempted to solve their separate crises by opening their economies, selling off state assets, and reducing military spending. Some have had more success than others, but difficult economic problems remain for most countries.

In Spain, for example, the economy boomed during much of the 1980s, largely because membership in the European Community (now the European Union) provided real benefits. But growth slowed dramatically in the 1990s and unemployment grew to a staggering 21.5 percent in 1993, the highest in the EU and twice the average of other EU countries.[92] The problem was that despite improved economic performance, Spanish industry was still not competitive with other European heavyweights. "We were seduced into believing we were in the major league," explained Spanish business consultant Jaime Mariategui. "But when you are racing a Spanish SEAT [a car made in Spain] against a Mercedes, eventually you [must] face reality."[93] And pointing to the anemic 1 percent growth in 1992 and 1993, and the collapse of Spain's stock market, journalist Roger Cohn observed, "The danger seems real that Spain, having made a great leap, could slip back."[94] A spokesman for a large Spanish firm complained, "Europe means progress, but right here progress means unemployment, and I don't know if that is acceptable."[95]

In Latin America, many new democracies have also recorded impressive economic growth in recent years, but the number of people in poverty has nonetheless increased. "The resumption of economic growth has been bought at a very high social price, which includes poverty, increased unemployment and income inequality, and this is leading to social problems," observed Louis Emerij, an economist at the Inter-American Development Bank in 1994.[96] By the end of the decade, 192 million people or 37 percent of the population will live in poverty. "Growth has really been on only one end of the spectrum, the wealthy. The rich are getting richer and the poor are getting poorer. And this will generate social conflict," argued U.N. official Peter Jensen.[97]

In 1992 a Harvard University study found that "the vast majority of people in Eastern Europe live in economic conditions demonstrably worse than those under the inefficiencies of central planning."[98] And in the former Soviet Union, a deepening economic crisis has actually lowered the life expectancy of adult men and led to a decrease in the population, a development that British demographer David Coleman described as

an incredibly clear picture of a society in crisis. A decline in life expectancy this dramatic has never happened in the postwar period. . . . It shows the

malaise of society, the lack of public health awareness and the fatigue associated with people who have to fight a pitched battle their whole lives just to survive.[99]

Under these circumstances, it should not be surprising that in a 1994 opinion poll, two-thirds of Russians believed that things were "better" under communism than they are "now."[100] In Eastern Europe, substantial minorities, and sometimes majorities, agreed.[101]

Of course, economists and policy makers who defend the economic policies of democratizing states argue that contemporary problems are the product of *previous* economic policy—the residual effects of discredited dictators—or that they are *temporary* problems associated with a difficult "transition" process. That may be. But many people in these countries nonetheless associate these problems with the democrats who recently assumed power. And unless democratic governments speedily solve some economic problems, public disenchantment may grow.

In some countries, continuing economic crisis, which differs in important ways from the crises that preceded the fall of dictatorship, has created political problems for democratic governments, and dictatorship again threatens. In Peru, a democratically elected president, Alberto Fujimori, closed parliament and the courts and assumed dictatorial powers. And in some Eastern European and former Soviet states, former communists have returned to power in recent elections, ousting the democrats who took power after communism collapsed. Just as the current economic crisis differs from the one that preceded the collapse of dictatorship, the advocates of a new kind of authoritarianism differ from their dictatorial predecessors. In Brazil, for example, Congressman Jai Bolsonaro argues that "Real democracy is food on the table, the ability to plan your life, the ability to walk on the street without getting mugged." He believes that "Fujimorization is the way out for Brazil" and says, "I am in favor of dictatorship" because "we will never resolve serious national problems with this irresponsible democracy."[102]

Economic crisis, it seems, can create serious problems for dictators and democrats alike. Although dictatorship has collapsed in countries around the world during the past twenty years, many economic and political problems remain. Unless democratic governments can solve some of these problems and make some demonstrable economic progress, the threat of dictatorship, in some form, will remain.

Notes

1. Schaeffer, Robert. "Democratic Devolutions: East Asian Democratization in Comparative Perspective," in Ravi Palat, ed., *Pacific-Asia and the Future of the*

World-System. Westport, Conn.: Greenwood, 1993. Schaeffer, Robert. *Power to the People: Democratization Around the World.* Boulder, Colo.: Westview, 1997.

2. Huntington, Samuel P. "Democracy's Third Wave," in Larry Diamond and Marc F. Plattner, eds., *The Global Resurgence of Democracy.* Baltimore: Johns Hopkins University Press, 1993, p. 3.

3. Keydar, Caglar. "The American Recovery of Southern Europe: Aid and Hegemony," in Giovanni Arrighi, ed., *Semiperipheral Development: The Politics of Southern Europe in the Twentieth Century.* Beverly Hills, Calif.: Sage, 1985, pp. 141–42.

4. Arrighi, Giovanni. "Fascism to Democratic Socialism: Logic and Limits of a Transition," in Giovanni Arrighi, 1985, p. 265. Arrighi, Giovanni. "World Income Inequalities and the Future of Socialism," *New Left Review,* 189, September–October 1991, p. 47. Keydar in Giovanni Arrighi, 1985, p. 145.

5. Carr, Raymond, and Aizpurua, Juan Pablo Fusi. *Spain: Dictatorship to Democracy.* London: George Allen and Unwin, 1979, p. 57.

6. Maxwell, Kenneth. "The Emergence of Portuguese Democracy," in John H. Herz, ed., *From Dictatorship to Democracy: Coping with the Legacies of Authoritarianism and Totalitarianism.* Westport, Conn.: Greenwood, 1982, p. 233.

7. Carr and Aizpurua, 1979, pp. 68, 67.

8. Baklanoff, Eric N. "Spain's Emergence as a Middle Industrial Power: The Basis and Structure of Spanish-Latin American Economic Relations," in Howard J. Wiarda, *The Iberian-Latin American Connection: Implications for U.S. Foreign Policy.* Boulder, Colo.: Westview, 1986, p. 139. Logan, John. "Democracy from Above: Limits to Change in Southern Europe," in Giovanni Arrighi, 1985, p. 164.

9. Malefakis, Edward. "Spain and its Francoist Heritage," in John H. Herz, 1982, p. 218.

10. Arrighi in Giovanni Arrighi, 1985, p. 265.

11. Logan in Giovanni Arrighi, 1985, p. 163.

12. Arrighi, 1991, p. 47.

13. Maxwell in John H. Herz, 1982, p. 235.

14. Baklanoff in Howard J. Wiarda, 1986, p. 140.

15. Maxwell in John H. Herz, 1982, p. 235.

16. Ibid.

17. Ibid.

18. Morrison, Rodney J. *Portugal: Revolutionary Change in an Open Economy.* Boston: Auburn House, 1981, p. 2. Logan in Giovanni Arrighi, 1985, p. 158.

19. Ibid., p. 270.

20. Psomiades, Harry J. "Greece: From the Colonels' Rule to Democracy," in John H. Herz, 1982, p. 253.

21. Malefakis in John H. Herz, 1982, p. 220.

22. Psomiades in John H. Herz, 1982, p. 258.

23. Harsgor, Michael. *Portugal in Revolution* (Washington, D.C.: Center for Strategic and International Studies). Beverly Hills, Calif.: Sage, 1976, p. 28. Logan in Giovanni Arrighi, 1985, pp. 166, 168.

24. Maxwell in John H. Herz, 1982, p. 238.

25. Pastor, Robert A. *Democracy in the Americas: Stopping the Pendulum.* New York: Holmes and Meier, 1989, p. xi.

26. Ibid., p. ix.

27. Smith, William C. *Authoritarianism and the Crisis of the Argentine Political Economy.* Stanford: Stanford University Press, 1989, p. 249.

28. Wynia, Gary W. *Argentina: Illusions and Realities.* New York: Holmes and Meier, 1986, p. 3.

29. Ibid., p. 15.

30. Aquino, Belinda A. "The Philippines: End of an Era," *Current History*, April 1986, p. 158.

31. Bresnan, John. *Crisis in the Philippines: The Marcos Era and Beyond.* Princeton: Princeton University Press, 1986, p. 145.

32. Aquino, 1986, p. 158.

33. Bresnan, 1986, p. 142.

34. Smith, 1989, p. 232.

35. Hartlyn, Jonathan, and Morley, Samuel A. *Latin American Political Economy: Financial Crisis and Political Change.* Boulder, Colo.: Westview, 1986, p. 1.

36. Johnson, Chalmers. "Political Institutions and Economic Performance: The Government-Business Relation in Japan, South Korea and Taiwan," in Frederic C. Deyo, ed., *The Political Economy of the New Asian Industrialism.* Ithaca: Cornell University Press, 1987, p. 136.

37. Cumings, Bruce. "The Origins and Development of the Northeast Asian Political Economy: Industrial Sectors, Product Cycles and Political Consequences," in Frederic Deyo, 1987.

38. Cumings in Frederic Deyo, 1987, p. 67. Koo, Hagen. "The Interplay of State, Social Class, and World System in East Asian Development: The Cases of South Korea and Taiwan," in Frederic Deyo, 1987, p. 167. Bello, Walden, and Rosenfeld, Stephanie. *Dragons in Distress: Asia's Miracle Economies in Crisis.* San Francisco: Food First Books, 1990, p. 4.

39. Johnson in Frederic Deyo, 1987, p. 147.

40. Bello and Rosenfeld, 1990, p. 15.

41. Ibid., p. 9.

42. Ibid.

43. Cooper, John F. "Taiwan: A Nation in Transition," *Current History*, April 1989, p. 174.

44. Ibid.

45. Gibney, Frank. *Korea's Quiet Revolution: From Garrison State to Democracy.* New York: Walker, 1992, p. 83.

46. Bello and Rosenfeld, 1990, p. 43.

47. Cooper, 1989, p. 176.

48. Bello and Rosenfeld, 1990, p. 21.

49. Haberman, Clyde. "Korean Declares 'Sweeping' Change Is the 'Only' Way," *New York Times*, July 5, 1987.

50. Sanger, David E. "Korea's Pick: A Pragmatist," *New York Times*, December 20, 1992.

51. Wright, Joseph J., Jr. "Thailand's Return to Democracy," *Current History*, December 1992, pp. 421–23.

52. Kristof, Nicholas D. "China Sees 'Market-Leninism' as Way to Future," *New York Times*, September 6, 1993.

53. Goldman, Marshall I. "The Future of Soviet Economic Reform," *Current History*, October 1989, p. 329.

54. Cook, Edward C. "Agriculture's Role in the Soviet Economic Crisis," in Michael Ellman and Vladimir Kontorovich, eds., *The Disintegration of the Soviet Economic System*. London: Routledge, 1992, pp. 199, 200.

55. Ellman, Michael. "Money in the 1980s: From Disequilibrium to Collapse," in Michael Ellman and Vladimir Kontorovich, 1992, p. 196.

56. Ellman and Kontorovich, 1992, p. 1. Cook in Michael Ellman and Vladimir Kontorovich, 1992, p. 210.

57. Sivard, Ruth. *World Military Expenditures, 1987–88*. Washington, D.C.: World Priorities, 1987, pp. 5, 54–55. Sen, Bomnath. "The Economics of Conversion: Transforming Swords to Plowshares," in Graham Bird, *Economic Reform in Eastern Europe*. Brookfield, Ver.: Elgar, 1992, p. 21.

58. Epstein, David F. "The Economic Cost of Soviet Security and Empire," in Henry S. Rowen and Charles Wolf, Jr., eds., *The Impoverished Superpower*. San Francisco: Institute for Contemporary Studies, 1990, p. 153.

59. Smith, Alan. *Russia and the World Economy: Problems of Integration*. London: Routledge, 1993, pp. 74, 88–89. Klare, Michael T. *American Arms Supermarket*. Austin: University of Texas Press, 1984, p. 312.

60. Gold, David. "Conversion and Industrial Policy," in Suzanne Gordon and Dave McFadden, eds., *Economic Conversion*. Cambridge: Ballinger, 1984, p. 195.

61. Schememann, Serge. "The Sun Has Trouble Setting on the Soviet Empire," *New York Times*, March 10, 1991.

62. Kramer, Mark. "Soviet Military Policy," *Current History*, October 1989, p. 351.

63. Blitz, James. "Gloom for the Russians in Gulf Weapons Toll," *Sunday Times* (London), March 3, 1991.

64. Ibid.

65. Smith, 1993, p. 158.

66. Ellman and Kontorovich, 1992, pp. 25, 114.

67. White, Stephen. *After Gorbachev*. Cambridge: Cambridge University Press, 1993, pp. 1–8.

68. Khanin, Grigorii. "Economic Growth in the 1980s," in Michael Ellman and Vladimir Kontorovich, 1992, p. 29.

69. Dahrendorf, Ralf. *Reflections on the Revolution in Europe*. New York: Times Books, 1990, p. 16.

70. Sparks, Allister. "Letter from South Africa: The Secret Revolution," *The New Yorker*, April 11, 1994, p. 59.

71. Wren, Christopher S. "Mandela, Freed, Urges Step-Up in Pressure to End White Rule," *New York Times*, February 12, 1991.

72. Moll, T. C. " 'Probably the Best Laager in the World': The Record and Prospects of the South African Economy," in John D. Brewer, *Can South Africa Survive? Five Minutes to Midnight*. New York: St. Martin's Press, 1989, p. 153.

73. Ibid., pp. 153, 144.

74. Baker, Pauline H. "South Africa on the Move," *Current History*, May 1990, p. 197.

75. "How Do South Africa Sanctions Work?" *The Economist*, October 14, 1989, p. 45. Baker, 1990, p. 200.

76. Danaher, Kevin, and Benjamin, Medea. "Great White Hope de Klerk Brings *Glasnost* to Pretoria," *In These Times*, February 7–13, 1990, p. 10.

77. Baker, 1990, p. 197.

78. Darnton, John. "Africa Tries Democracy, Finding Hope and Peril," *New York Times*, June 21, 1994.

79. Bello, Walden, and Rosenfeld, Stephanie. "Dragons in Distress," *World Policy Journal*, 7, 3, 1990, p. 460.

80. Roett, Riordan. "Brazil's Transition to Democracy," *Current History*, March 1989, p. 149.

81. Brooke, James. "Peru Rises Up Against Red Tape's 400-year Rule," *New York Times*, August 8, 1989.

82. Greenhouse, Steven. "East Europe's Sale of the Century," *New York Times*, May 22, 1990.

83. Pang, Eul-Soo, and Jarnagin, Laura. "Brazil's Catatonic Lambada," *Current History*, February 1991, p. 75.

84. Engleberg, Stephen. "First Sale of State Holdings a Disappointment in Poland," *New York Times*, January 13, 1991. Protzman, Ferdinand. "Privatization Is Floundering in East Germany," *New York Times*, March 12, 1991.

85. Passell, Peter. "A Capitalist Free-For-All in Czechoslovakia," *New York Times*, April 12, 1992.

86. Nelson, Daniel N. "What End of Warsaw Pact Means," *San Francisco Chronicle*, April 24, 1991.

87. "The World's Shrinking Armies," *New York Times*, May 30, 1994.

88. Ibid. Wynia, Gary W. "Argentina's Economic Reform," *Current History*, February 1991, pp. 59–60.

89. Brooke, James. "Latin Armies Are Looking for Work," *New York Times*, March 24, 1991.

90. "The World's Shrinking Armies," May 30, 1994.

91. Mullins, A. F., Jr. *Born Arming: Development and Military Power in New States*. Stanford: Stanford University Press, 1987, p. 103.

92. Whitney, Craig R. "Western Europe's Dreams Turning Into Nightmares," *New York Times*, August 8, 1993.

93. Cohen, Roger. "Spain's Progress Turns to Pain," *New York Times*, November 17, 1992.

94. Ibid.

95. Ibid.

96. Nash, Nathaniel C. "Latin American Speedup Leaves Poor in the Dust," *New York Times*, September 7, 1994.

97. Ibid.

98. Brucan, Silvia. "Shock Therapy Mauls Those Who Unleashed It in Eastern Europe," *World Paper*, June 1994, p. 3.

99. Specter, Michael. "Climb in Russia's Death Rate Sets Off Population Implosion," *New York Times*, March 6, 1994.

100. Burawoy, Michael. "Reply," *Contemporary Sociology*, 23, January 1994, p. 166.

101. Ibid.

102. Brooke, James. "A Soldier Turned Politician Wants to Give Brazil Back to Army Rule," *New York Times*, July 25, 1993.

13

The Spread of Separatism

In the summer of 1991, an ethnic movement in Eritrea declared its independence from Ethiopia, movements in Slovenia and Croatia declared their independence from Yugoslavia, and movements in Latvia, Lithuania, and Estonia declared their independence from the Soviet Union. One year later, Slovaks announced they would separate from Czechoslovakia. These announcements effectively divided these countries into two or more parts. The success of these "separatist" movements was significant globally for four reasons.

First, they were the first ethnic *minorities* to create independent states of their own in the post-World War II period. Although many ethnic movements had tried to create separate states in the postwar period, most notably by Biafrans in Nigeria and Katangans in the Congo, the only one to secede successfully was in what was to become Bangladesh. But the movement to separate Bengal from Pakistan was supported by a *majority* of people in both parts of Pakistan. Until 1991, no *minority* groups had been able to depart from a country recognized as legitimate by members of the interstate system.

Second, these ethnic independence movements were able to separate from the countries they had inhabited as a result of their own initiative, not as a consequence of superpower partition. Significantly, each of these countries was divided by internal forces, not foreign hands. Third, their success resulted in the emergence of new states in the interstate system: two in Ethiopia, two in Czechoslovakia, five in Yugoslavia, and fifteen or more in the Soviet Union. Fourth, these dramatic developments encouraged the proliferation of separatist movements around the world, reviving the fortunes of old separatist movements and stimulating the formation of new ones on virtually every continent.

It is difficult to determine just how widespread separatist movements

have become because scholars use different criteria to count them. Some scholars estimate that there may be as many as five thousand "nations" in the world, while others argue that there are fewer ethnic nations, perhaps two hundred thirty-three "politically active communal groups," that might form the basis of new states.[1]

Of course, not all these groups want to obtain independence in separate states of their own, but many do. This is a problem because the interstate system, which consisted of one hundred sixty-eight sovereign states in 1981, does not easily accommodate changes that would permit each "nation" to receive a "state" of its own.[2] While the number of states in the system has more than tripled in this century, from about fifty in 1900 to nearly one hundred ninety today, there are very few states anywhere in the world that are composed of only one "nation"—"fewer than 20 are ethnically homogeneous, in the sense that minorities account for less than 5 percent of the population"—and the number of states would have to increase significantly to accommodate all of them.[3]

During this century, the creation of new states has been a difficult and often violent process. In recent years, ethnic separatism has led to conflict and war in some but not all places. The partition by Eritreans of Ethiopia was the culmination of a thirty-year war that resulted in the death of five hundred thousand people from fighting and millions more from starvation in the region. The breakup of Yugoslavia led to bitter fighting between some of the successor states (Serbia, Croatia, and Bosnia-Herzegovina) but not all of them (Slovenia and Macedonia). The Baltic states (Latvia, Lithuania, and Estonia) departed peacefully from the Soviet Union, but ethnic war has raged in some regions of the former Soviet Union, both before and after they became independent republics. In December 1994, for example, Soviet troops moved into Chechnya to prevent it from seceding, a development that led to bitter fighting. In Czechoslovakia, as in the Baltics, the departure of Slovakia has been described by participants as a "velvet divorce," referring to the peaceful "velvet revolution" that brought an end to communist rule in 1989.

Although separatist movements in some countries have managed to depart without triggering conflict, for every velvet divorce there has been a "charred Yugoslavia." In February 1993, the *New York Times* listed forty-eight "ethnic wars" then occurring in countries around the world and one year later listed "more than 100 . . . battles taking place within countries" between different ethnic groups.[4]

To understand separatism as a significant global development, we need first to examine why separatist independence movements emerged, explain why they succeeded in 1991–92, and explore the problems associated with the proliferation of movements like them in other countries.

Contemporary separatism emerged as a product of two related but historically sequential developments. Separatist movements first emerged after World War II. They were largely a product of decolonization, which denied some people states of their own and assigned them to states that they did not meaningfully choose. Then in the 1980s and '90s, separatism in Eastern Europe and the Soviet Union emerged in response to democratization, which enabled some groups to seek power on their own terms. Movements that emerged in response to decolonization (Eritrean and Baltic movements) and groups that emerged in response to democratization (in Yugoslavia, Czechoslovakia, and republics in the Soviet Union) both achieved success in 1991–92. After examining the emergence of separatism during these two eras, we will discuss the problems associated with these developments and examine their impact on the interstate system, individual states, and the political relations within them.

Decolonization and Separatism

Separatist movements first emerged in response to both the problems and the promises of the new "republican" interstate system that took shape after World War II.[5] The new system was republican because it was based on nation-state republics, like the United States, rather than on colonial empires. Although the new republican interstate system replaced a system dominated by European colonial empires before the war, one of the problems associated with building a new system was that many people were arbitrarily assigned to states they did not themselves make or choose. At the same time, the new interstate system promised that all "nations" would enjoy the right to "self-determination," the right to choose their own form of government.

Problems

At summit meetings during and after the war, the great powers agreed in principle that the interstate system should consist of independent, republican nation-states. But because much of the world was still controlled by European empires or occupied by victorious Allied armies, it was difficult to create immediately a system of self-governing states made up of ethnically homogeneous "nations." What's more, the superpowers were intent on doing this in a way that promoted or protected their own global political interests. So, for example, they agreed that Europe should be divided into U.S. and Soviet spheres of influence, based largely on the

areas controlled by their armies at the end of the war. This meant that the United States agreed not to interfere in Soviet-controlled Eastern European countries, much to the consternation of people there, while the Soviet Union agreed to withdraw its support for communists engaged in a civil war for control of Greece, which was assigned to the U.S. sphere.

The United States and Soviet Union also agreed to partition some states (Korea, China, Vietnam, and Germany) and allowed the British to partition others (India and Palestine) in the decolonization process. These partitions angered many residents, who thought partition was either unnecessary or unfair.[6] In other cases, European empires transferred power to independence movements in their former colonies, but they adjusted the territorial borders of these states, though these boundaries often made little social or political sense. And they sometimes allowed the new republics to invade, annex, or incorporate adjacent territories not originally assigned to them, often over the objections of their inhabitants, so long as they did not infringe on the claims of powerful states. So, for example, the superpowers did not strenuously object when the new Indian government forcibly incorporated some of the princely states, such as Hyderabad and Kashmir, when communist China invaded and annexed Tibet in 1950, and when Indonesia invaded and annexed Irian Jaya in 1963 and later invaded and annexed East Timor in 1973, an island that had just won its independence from Portugal.

Of course, many people objected to the treaties, partitions, invasions, annexations, and incorporations that assigned them to states they did not make, to governments they did not choose.

Eritrea, for example, had been an Italian colony that was occupied by the British during World War II and then administered after the war as a U.N. Trust Territory. The United Nations decided in 1952 to transfer British authority to a government that was "independent" but also "federated" with Ethiopia, which had long claimed that Eritrea belonged to Ethiopia. Under Ethiopian pressure—the Ethiopians had banned Eritrean independence parties and labor unions in the region—the Eritrean assembly voted to end its relative autonomy in 1962 and become part of Ethiopia.[7] Eritreans who opposed these successive assignments—to Italy, then to Britain, the United Nations, semiautonomous government, and finally Ethiopia—organized a movement demanding unqualified independence and, in 1961, began conducting a guerrilla war against Ethiopia, starting a civil war that raged for thirty more years.

The Baltic countries—Lithuania, Latvia, and Estonia—also passed through a succession of assignments, punctuated by a brief period of self-government. Although they had been autonomous countries in the mid-

to-late eighteenth century, they were incorporated by the Russian empire during the nineteenth and early twentieth centuries. When the Russian empire collapsed in 1917, movements in the Baltic demanded and fought for independent states, which they achieved in a treaty with the Soviets in 1920. Authoritarian governments or dictators then ruled during most of the next twenty years in the three independent states. In the Hitler-Stalin Pact of 1939, all three states were assigned to and then occupied by the Soviet Union, which deported and massacred tens of thousands of people. When war between Germany and the Soviet Union erupted in 1941, movements in all three countries launched insurrections against Soviet rule, and after German forces occupied the three states, many people joined the German war effort.[8] The Soviet army reoccupied the Baltic states in 1944, deporting or killing people they regarded as German collaborators, though anti-Soviet guerrilla activity continued until 1952, when the Lithuanian Freedom Army laid down its arms.[9] Although the United States did not recognize the wartime Soviet annexation of the Baltic states as legal, it did not actively contest it.

Not only did many people object to the way they were assigned states in the new interstate system, they also objected to the way that governments in the new republics treated minority populations. When independence movements assumed power in postcolonial states, they often adopted policies designed to create a singular national identity, trying to persuade the diverse peoples living in these states to think of themselves as "Indonesians" or "Nigerians." In many respects, they strived to emulate the experience of many Europeans, who first organized modern "states" and then tried to create "nations" within them. As the Italian nationalist Massimo d'Azeglio observed after the unification of Italy in 1860, "We have made Italy, now we must make Italians."[10] He said this because on the eve of unification, "only 2 and one-half percent of the population [on the peninsula] used the [Italian] language for everyday purposes."[11]

This has proved to be a more difficult task than nationalists and state officials imagined. For example, in Italy today, the League of the North has demanded independence for people living in northern Italy, a region they call Padania.[12]

After independence it became common for governments in the new republics to adopt a single administrative language, which they insisted be taught in school, and made command of this language a prerequisite for employment in the civil service or advancement in the army. Of course, this kind of policy assisted native speakers of the chosen language while disadvantaging people who spoke other languages. Although dis-

criminatory language, religious, and economic policies were designed to promote singular national identities, they often antagonized ethnic minorities that resided in or had been incorporated into the new states. And these ethnic minorities frequently organized separatist movements to reject assimilationist identities and reassert identities of their own.

One such group was the Karen in Burma. Because Baptist and Seventh-Day Adventist missionaries converted many Karen to Christianity, British colonial officials "favored [the Karen], educating and recruiting them for the military and police force," in the years before World War II.[13] During the war, when Japanese forces invaded and occupied Burma, the Karen fought for the British while other, Buddhist groups supported the Japanese.[14] Although the Karen and other minorities were guaranteed important rights when the British gave independence to Burma in 1948, anti-Christian policies and attacks on Karen villages triggered a Karen revolt, which was joined for a time by communists and other ethnic groups.[15] After some initial success, the rebels were driven back to Burma's border with Thailand. Karen guerrilla forces demanding an independent state they call "Kawthoolei" or "The Land of the Lilies" have battled government forces since then.[16]

Promises

When the United States and Soviet Union began building the new interstate system during World War II, they made "self-determination" one of its intellectual cornerstones. By self-determination, U.S. and Soviet leaders meant that colonies should be able to secede from empires and that people in independent states would then choose their own form of self-government. To promote self-determination, U.S. and Soviet officials pressed for the decolonization of European empires and the creation of independent nation-states. In this context, the attempt by ethnic minorities to seek power in independent states of their own was a modern, legitimate, and rational goal.

Separatism is a modern political objective because the idea that state power would be a useful way to protect or promote a social group is relatively new, a product of late nineteenth century thought. It was only in the 1880s, for example, that socialist movements in Europe decided that control of state power might advance and protect the interests of working-class people. They began to see state power as important because the authority of European governments to levy taxes, raise armies, regulate the economy, and provide social services had greatly expanded during the nineteenth century. During this century, many social movements con-

cluded that state power could greatly assist them if they could somehow obtain it.[17]

The attempt by separatist and other groups to obtain state power was given considerable legitimacy because the new interstate system recognized self-determination as a basic principle. But while the superpowers promoted self-determination to people around the world, they gave it a fairly narrow meaning, which was not widely appreciated. By "self-determination," U.S. and Soviet leaders meant that colonies should be able to secede from empires and create independent states. They did not mean to suggest that people within independent states should be allowed to secede from newly created *republics*. After all, the U.S. government had fought a long Civil War in the 1860s to prevent the secession of the latter kind (though they had previously fought to obtain their independence from imperial Britain). But many groups did not appreciate this distinction, arguing that self-determination should be permissible for people living in colonies *and* for minorities residing in the new republics. They sometimes argued that the state they inhabited was an "empire" and that they had a right to secede from it, just as colonies could secede from empires. Throughout the postwar period, for example, Baltic movements argued that the Soviet Union was not a republic but an empire and that they were not republics but colonies. Whatever the historical merits of this argument, separatist movements could plausibly argue that the demand for independent states was legitimate, given the fact the interstate system recognized self-determination as a basic principle.

And the separatist demand for state power was a rational goal because the new interstate system provided substantial political and economic rewards to groups that managed to obtain states of their own. With state power, groups could become members of the United Nations, which would recognize their governments as sovereign and protect them from external aggression. Government officials of states could borrow money from the World Bank, receive trading privileges through GATT, and field teams in Olympic competitions. Movements that did not possess states of their own—Kurds, Palestinians, Karens—could not claim the benefits associated with state power in the new interstate system.

Because ethnic minorities in many countries realized that state power could provide real benefits, they organized separatist movements to redeem the system's promise of self-determination. They expressed their determination to redeem this promise in different ways. A Maori political party in New Zealand calls itself Mana Motuhake (self-determination), and argues that it will provide them with *turangawaewae*, which means having a place upon which the feet can stand.[18]

Other separatists describe state power as having a "house" of their own. A San Juan cab driver who supports independence for Puerto Rico told me, "You don't come into my house and tell me what to do."[19] And when Slovak separatists jostled Czechoslovakia's President Václav Havel during a visit to Bratislava in 1990, they shouted, "This is our house! We want a free Slovakia!"[20]

During the postwar period, separatist movements emerged in response to the problems and promises of the new interstate system in countries around the world. They commonly appeared in third world countries where colonies were becoming independent, but also in European states, which were themselves undergoing a transition from imperial to republican states. University of California sociologist Donald Horowitz noted,

> The independence of Asia and Africa was being felt in Europe and America. The grant of independence to the former Belgian territories in Africa (Zaire, Rwanda and Burundi) helped stimulate the ethnic movement of Flemings in Belgium itself. If, they said, tiny Burundi can have an autonomous political life, why should we be deprived of the same privilege? . . . In Canada, some French-speaking Quebeckers also cited African independence as a precedent for their own.[21]

Because these movements emerged in response to the problems and promises of the new interstate system, one might have expected some of them to have won independent states of their own. But they did not. Despite real grievances and determined efforts, they almost all failed, at least until 1991.

Separatist movements failed to achieve their independence between 1945 and 1991 for two reasons. First, with the exception of the movement in Bengal (which did manage to create a separate state), separatist movements were comprised of ethnic *minorities*, which meant that they faced unequal struggles against majority populations and governments that were determined to consolidate their power in postcolonial republics. These governments waged bloody civil wars against separatist guerrillas and minority populations without much restraint because the superpowers did not object to the use of power against minority populations. The superpowers did not object because they regarded these wars as "internal" affairs.

The second reason separatist movements failed is that they could not secure superpower support for their efforts throughout this period, even if their claims for a separate state had considerable legal and historical merit. The 1920 Treaty of Sevres promised the creation of an independent

state for the Kurds, a group that lives in territory that straddles borders in Iraq, Iran, Turkey, and Syria, which makes it an ethnic minority in each of the post-Ottoman states. Although the U.S. government recognized the merits of Kurdish claims and even supported Kurdish guerrillas fighting in Iraq, a secret 1975 congressional intelligence report

> made it abundantly clear that an independent Kurdistan was not on the [U.S.] agenda. Instead the U.S. government "preferred . . . that the insurgents simply continue a level of hostilities sufficient to sap the resources of our [Iranian] allies" neighboring country [Iraq, then a U.S. foe]. This policy was *not* imparted to our clients [the Kurds] who were encouraged to continue fighting.[22]

Some years later, after the 1991 Gulf War against Iraq, the United States again supported the Kurds' right to self-determination in principle, but denied it in practice, stopping short of helping create an independent Kurdistan, largely because such a policy would antagonize Turkey, an important U.S. ally in NATO.[23]

Although the superpowers supported decolonization, they did not support independence for ethnic minorities in republican states. And this interpretation was adopted by the United Nations and the Organization of African Unity (OAU). In 1964, for example, the OAU passed a resolution pledging "to respect the borders existing on their achievement of political independence."[24] This measure was subsequently used to deny recognition to the Biafrans, who attempted to secede from Nigeria in 1967, a move that helped doom the Biafrans to defeat.

Separatist movements throughout the postwar period may have hoped for superpower support, but superpower unwillingness to endorse separatist claims made it extremely difficult for them to secede from countries recognized by the United Nations as legitimate members of the new interstate system.

Still, despite the opposition of superpower states, domestic governments, and majority populations, separatist movements survived. They endured because they skillfully organized determined movements, because they were based in minority communities that continued to experience discriminatory government policies, which encouraged members of ethnic minorities to support or join separatist movements, and because they could often rely on financial and political support on émigré communities in neighboring or even distant states. The Eritrean émigré community in the United States published books, lobbied Congress, and raised money for the Eritreans in Ethiopia; Baltic communities based in

Chicago did the same, acting as surrogates for an independence movement that had almost entirely disappeared in the Baltic states after 1952. Emigrés from the Baltic states staffed tiny offices in Washington, D.C. and churned out press releases on behalf of their overseas brethren throughout this period.

Eventually, in 1991, separatist movements in Eritrea and the Baltic states were able to secure their independence. The Eritreans were able to do so for several reasons. First, they were extremely skilled at creating an effective coalition with other ethnic minorities in the region—Omoros, Tigreans, Muslim, and Christians. This greatly increased their social, political, and military weight in their long campaign against Haile Selassie's government (1961–72), and then against a Marxist military junta assisted by Cuban troops and Soviet aid (1972–91). Second, successive Ethiopian governments opposed to Eritrean secession and independence were extremely corrupt, relied on violence and not persuasion to stay in power, and depended heavily on superpower financial and military support (Selassie's government relied on the United States; the military junta on the Soviet Union) to conduct their war against the Eritreans. Finally, when the Soviet Union began withdrawing its support for the Ethiopian regime in the mid–1980s, the Ethiopian government was greatly weakened. Eritrean forces and their coalition partners seized key cities and advanced on the Ethiopian capital, Addis Ababa, capturing it on May 28, 1991.

Shifting Soviet policy in the late 1980s, which greatly assisted Eritrean separatists, also led to the reemergence of separatist movements in the Baltics. Faced with a comprehensive economic crisis when he came to power in 1985, Gorbachev decided to reform the Soviet economy by reducing military expenditures, which he accomplished by ending Soviet military support for governments in Afghanistan and Ethiopia. He did this to redirect military resources to the civilian economy. To obtain widespread political support for economic reforms called "perestroika," he simultaneously promoted political reforms, which he called a policy of "glasnost." These policies made it possible for movements in the Baltics to organize and campaign for greater autonomy and eventual independence.

In this context, they were able to do so for two reasons. First, they were extremely skillful at organizing within the Communist Parties in the Baltics and then organizing massive public demonstrations that remained peaceful despite violent provocations by Soviet forces. Second, they were able to use two historic events to their advantage: the annexation of their countries by the Soviet Union as a result of the disreputable Hitler-Stalin Pact of 1939, and the provision in the Soviet Union's own constitution

that gave its constituent republics the right to secede. The separatist movements used both events successfully, simultaneously demanding that they should be independent because they had been illegally annexed and because they had a right as Soviet republics to hold referendums that would allow people to vote on independence referendums (which they did, winning by huge majorities in the Baltic states).

In both Eritrea and the Baltics, changes in Soviet policy during the 1980s made it possible for separatist movements to secede from states that had previously incorporated them. And change associated with Soviet reform and democratization in Eastern Europe encouraged a second generation of separatist movements to emerge, first in Yugoslavia, then in the republics of the Soviet Union, and then in Czechoslovakia.

Democratization and Separatism

Although separatist movements in Yugoslavia, the Soviet Union, and Czechoslovakia broke away from these states in 1991–92, at the same time that Eritrean and Baltic movements secured their independence, they had only been active for a few years and were a product of much more recent developments. In the Soviet Union, for example, protests organized around secessionist issues first appeared only in 1987. During the late 1980s, only a fraction of the political demonstrations held in the Soviet Union were organized by separatist movements.[25] By the end of 1989, however, "secessionist nationalism had made its appearance in almost every non-Russian republic."[26] During the next two years, support for separatism grew rapidly. While a survey in September 1989 found that only 20.6 percent of people in Ukraine supported independence, "by December 1991, 90.3 percent of these same inhabitants of Ukraine voted in favor of Ukraine's August 24 declaration of independence," observed political scientist Mark Beissenger.[27]

Support for separatism in Yugoslavia and Czechoslovakia followed a similar trajectory, growing from a sentiment of a small minority to support by majorities in some regions in just a few years' time.

Like first-generation separatists, second-generation separatists organized to avert problems and redeem promises. But they did so in response to a different set of problems and promises. Generally they were responding to problems associated with democratization, not decolonization, and saw separatism as a way to promote both self-government and economic development.

When Gorbachev came to power in 1985, he introduced economic and

political reforms designed to reduce a stagnant economy. In his effort to redirect Soviet military spending, Gorbachev withdrew Soviet troops from Afghanistan and support for communist governments overseas, and began negotiating arms control agreements with the United States. In early 1989, he also announced that Soviet military forces would no longer intervene on behalf of communist governments in Eastern Europe if they faced popular uprisings, as the Soviet Union had done in East Germany (1953), Hungary (1956), and Czechoslovakia (1968). These initiatives were designed to reduce the burden of heavy military spending on the Soviet economy so that the civilian economy could produce houses and manufacture cars rather than build missiles and tanks. But they had far-reaching consequences for Eastern Europe and, eventually, for the Soviet Union itself, leading to democratization and, in many places, to separatism.

After Gorbachev announced the end of Soviet military support for communist regimes in Eastern Europe in the spring of 1989, "dissident" movements quickly organized to demand that communist parties relinquish power and adopt democratic political institutions and capitalist economic policies. And in the fall, Communist Parties were swept from power in Hungary, Poland, Czechoslovakia, Bulgaria, East Germany, and Romania, in most cases peacefully. In their place, civilian democratic parties assumed power. In Yugoslavia, events took a different turn, primarily because the communist regime there proved to be more resistant to change.

When Yugoslavia was invaded by Nazi Germany during World War II, communists led by Josip Broz Tito organized a partisan resistance movement that harassed German forces throughout the war. The Communist Party in Yugoslavia received considerable domestic public support for its wartime role. This popularity contrasted sharply with the unenthusiastic response that other Communist Parties received when they took power throughout the rest of Eastern Europe in the late 1940s. Because these other governments were installed by the Soviets, they claimed little domestic political support, largely because they played little or no role in the anti-Nazi resistance. The popularity of the Yugoslavian Communist Party, and Tito's determination to keep Yugoslavia independent from Soviet control in the postwar period, created a regime with considerable popular support. And unlike other communist regimes in Eastern Europe, the government experimented with various kind of neocapitalist economic policies, permitting some private ownership and encouraging participation in the government and the army by members of the country's many ethnic groups.

But after Tito died in 1980, political groups began to quarrel over the distribution of power and the direction of economic policy. When unpopular communist regimes in other Eastern European countries were swept from power in 1989, many people in Yugoslavia—particularly in Slovenia and Croatia—also demanded an end to communism and the adoption of democracy and capitalism. While communist regimes elsewhere surrendered power quickly, the Yugoslavian communists did not, largely because they could still rely on considerable support, particularly from the country's Serbian population, which was more closely identified with communist rule than other ethnic groups.

Although the context for power in post-Tito Yugoslavia initially began as a quarrel over the distribution of political power and the direction of economic policy, it increasingly became defined in ethnic terms. Movements in Slovenia and Croatia demanded a noncommunist political system and a fully capitalist economy, while movements in Serbia defended the political and economic institutions associated with the communist government. Serbian attempts to use economic pressure—embargoes and boycotts of goods from other regions—to obtain political concessions from other regions encouraged the development of separatist movements in Slovenia and Croatia and led to increased awareness of ethnic identities throughout the country. Movements in Slovenia and Croatia then held referendums, formed governments, and announced their independence from Yugoslavia on June 26, 1991. The Yugoslav government regarded the referendum process as invalid because only residents of Slovenia and Croatia participated in them, not residents in other "republics," and because Serbian minorities in these regions boycotted the elections. Because the Yugoslavian government based in Belgrade retained control of the army and received considerable support from the Serbian population based in Serbia but also living throughout the country, it briefly invaded the breakaway republics. It was rebuffed in heavy fighting, but a savage civil war followed, a war defined increasingly in ethnic terms.

Because communism was both more moderate and more popular than elsewhere in Eastern Europe, it proved more resistant to the changes associated with democratization. And this resistance contributed to the rise of separatism, conflict, and ethnic war, first in Croatia and then in Bosnia-Herzegovina. In both of these states, minority Serbian populations opposed independence for separatists supported by Croatian and Bosnian majorities in those regions. And Serbian minorities fought either to subdivide Croatia and Bosnia to create Serbian states of their own, or to reunite Serbian-controlled territories with Yugoslavia. Because they received substantial military and economic support from Yugoslavia, they have been

able to defeat Croatian and Bosnian armies and militias, besiege cities like Sarajevo, and drive non-Serbian populations out of the territories they control.

In Czechoslovakia, conflict over the distribution of political power and the direction of economic policy in the postcommunist era also contributed to the rise of separatism and breakup of the country in 1992. But in Czechoslovakia, partition did not lead to ethnic warfare, as it did in Yugoslavia.

After peaceful protests forced the communist government in Czechoslovakia to yield power in 1989, a large number of political parties organized to compete for power. (In the country's last nationwide election in 1992, forty-two different political parties fielded candidates for office.) The Civic Democratic Party (CDP) came to power in 1990 and its prime minister, Václav Klaus, took rapid steps to dismantle socialist economic policies and introduce a capitalist economy. Because this led to rising unemployment, particularly in Slovakia, where much of the country's heavy industry had been located by the communist regime, many people supported the go-slow economic policies of the Movement for a Democratic Slovakia (MDS), a separatist movement led by former communist Vladimir Meciar. In the June 1992 elections, Klaus's CDP won one-third of the vote, enough to outdistance all other parties, but not enough to form a government on its own. In efforts to form a government, the CDP began negotiations with the MDS, which had placed a distant second in the voting. Although a majority of voters throughout the country still supported a unified country, the CDP and MDS agreed to divide the country into two parts without putting partition to an electoral test. The CDP agreed to partition because it wanted to pursue its capitalist development program without obstruction from the go-slow separatist minority; the MDS wanted partition so that it could assume power on its own terms and slow the pace of economic change in Slovakia. And so the two parties agreed to a "velvet divorce."

The reforms initiated by Gorbachev had far-reaching consequences not only in Eastern Europe but also in the Soviet Union. Like ex-communist groups in Yugoslavia and Slovakia, some sections of Soviet society opposed reform and tried to slow the pace of economic and political change. On August 19, 1991, communist officials opposed to reform attempted to overthrow Gorbachev's government by force. But nonviolent resistance to the coup in Moscow and widespread opposition to its objectives by many military and civilian leaders led to its collapse in just three days. Unlike in Yugoslavia or China, where communist governments had been able to deflect or defeat proponents of change, the communist rear guard

in the Soviet Union could not reverse changes they had themselves initiated. The collapse of the coup discredited the Communist Party's residual authority, leading to demands for independence by government officials in virtually all the constituent republics. While only a few of them had been separatists by choice, all soon became separatists of necessity, using their regional power to address the economic problems that confronted them.

After decades of failure, separatist movements in 1991–92 achieved remarkable success, creating a score of new states in the Horn of Africa, Eastern Europe, and the Soviet Union. This stunning change in the political fortunes of separatist movements encouraged other ethnic groups to organize new separatist movements and revived long-dormant ones. In Asia, the Middle East, Africa, Europe, and North America, ethnic separatist movements initiated or renewed their demands for independence. Separatist movements even appeared in Latin America for the first time, with the emergence in 1993 of a movement demanding the creation of a "Republic of the Pampas" in three southern Brazilian states.[28]

Many other separatist movements now stand on the threshold of success. The Quebecois in Canada, the League of the North in Italy, the Palestine Liberation Organization in Israel's occupied territories, Kashmiris in India, and Kurds in Iraq have acquired important international recognition or gained enough popular support to contest for political power. It will not be easy for any of them to become independent, but their chances are better now than they have been for decades.

Separatist movements have even appeared in the United States, particularly in its islands: Puerto Rico, Hawaii, and Staten Island.

In Puerto Rico, which became a U.S. colony after it was taken from the Spanish empire during the Spanish-American war, a movement demanding independence first emerged when the island became a commonwealth of the United States in 1952. This status meant that inhabitants of Puerto Rico were U.S. citizens, could serve in the army and be tried in U.S. courts, but could not elect representatives to the U.S. Congress or vote for presidents. In recent years, islanders have debated whether to become an independent republic, join the United States as its fifty-first state, or remain a commonwealth. Although the independence movement represents a minority of voters, the issues they raise are the subject of intense debate in Puerto Rico and among the many Puerto Ricans living in the United States. A November 1993 referendum resulted in a majority voting to retain commonwealth status, what the *New York Times* called "their existing ambiguous relationship with the United States."[29]

In Hawaii, native Hawaiians have organized movements demanding

greater sovereignty, independence, even a return to monarchy, which was overthrown by American businessmen aided by U.S. marines in 1893. Hawaii was subsequently annexed and eventually made a state in 1959.[30] As in Puerto Rico, the state may hold a referendum on the issue of sovereignty in coming years.

On Staten Island, residents are debating whether the borough should secede from New York City. Although Staten Islanders would remain residents of New York State and citizens of the United States, the idea of municipal separatism is much the same as national separatism. As Chip Brown wrote in the *New York Times Magazine*,

> The fires of secession burn among the proud resentful Staten Islanders, just as they do among Azerbaijanis, Kurds, Quebecois and Californians. Like separatists elsewhere, Staten Islanders have made their own declarations of independence—issuing a challenge to the idea that the city is a whole greater than its parts.[31]

Like other separatists, they argue that self-government would give them power over their political affairs and the local economy that they cannot now obtain as residents of New York City's smallest borough.

Separatism and Social Problems

During the postwar period separatist movements emerged in response to the problems and promises associated with the rise of the new interstate system: decolonization and more recently democratization. But the success and proliferation of separatist movements after 1991–92 created new problems for divided states and the interstate system. And separatism raised important questions about the relation between majority and minority in democratic polities.

Where separatists were successful at dividing old states and creating new ones, three kinds of problems emerged: social dislocation, discrimination, and disputes over sovereignty.

The first problem became evident in Yugoslavia, where partition "uprooted an estimated three million people, 600,000 of whom have fled the Balkans altogether."[32] Many left ahead of the fighting, while many were forced from their homes by systematic ethnic cleansing campaigns designed to eliminate ethnic minorities in areas controlled by "majority" groups. And in the former Soviet republics of Armenia and Azerbaijan, "war has generated an estimated 500,000 refugees."[33]

Large-scale migrations have occurred wherever countries have been partitioned. People not only flee the new country, but many people also return to it from émigré and diaspora communities in neighboring and overseas countries. These forced and voluntary migrations have a disruptive social impact, affecting housing and job markets and creating enormous distress for families divided by new borders.

Second, the leaders of newly created states frequently adopted policies that discriminate against residual minority populations. In the Baltics, for example, Estonia denied citizenship to ethnic Russian residents, even those born in Estonia, unless they could pass an Estonian language test. Stringent citizenship requirements, which effectively discriminated against the Russian speaking minorities in Baltic states, have been criticized by Western human rights groups, which complained that Estonia "adopted steps to restrict citizenship and exclude Russian-speaking inhabitants."[34] And while Baltic governments discriminated against resident minorities, they granted "automatic" citizenship to Baltic peoples who were citizens of other countries, such as the United States.

Where minorities fear or experience discriminatory measures by newly created governments, they frequently organize separatist movements of their own, as the Serbian populations in Croatia and Bosnia did after these states declared their independence from Yugoslavia.

Third, governments on both sides of the new divide have contested the sovereignty of their new neighbors. They have argued about responsibility for repaying the national debt that existed prior to partition, disputed control of conventional and nuclear military forces—Ukraine and Russia argued over who would control the Black Sea fleet and who would control Soviet nuclear weapons based in Ukraine—and debated whether international treaties made before partition applied with equal force to newly divided states. In many cases, disputes over these and other issues have led to economic embargoes and retaliatory tariffs, which have spilled over into international diplomatic forums.

These partition-related problems have led in some, but not all, cases to war—civil and interstate wars now rage in Yugoslavia and the Soviet Union—and to subdivision. As a result of intense, protracted fighting in Bosnia, the United Nations is pressing for an agreement that would partition the newly created state into two parts (one Bosnian and the other Serbian), though at one time in 1993 they proposed dividing it into three parts (Bosnian, Serbian, and Croatian).

Of course, the problems associated with contemporary separatism have not led to conflict in all of the newly divided states. The partition into Czech and Slovak republics was amiable, and many Soviet successor states

have established friendly and even cordial relations with their neighbors and resident minority populations. But even where partition is peacefully accomplished, it raises several issues for individual states and the interstate system as a whole.

For individual states, the first issue is how to reach a decision to divide. In the Baltics, Slovenia, and Croatia, referendums were held and resident voters were asked to decide whether a declaration of independence should be issued. Although elections were openly held and resulted in large electoral majorities for independence, they left unresolved a number of questions. Who could participate in such an important vote? Just residents of these "republics" or residents of the entire republic (the Soviet Union, Yugoslavia)? Would the results be compromised if some resident groups refused to participate in such a referendum (Serbs in Croatia)? As Spanish Prime Minister Filipe Gonzalez Marquez asked, "Is self-determination up to the Lithuanians only, or is it also up to the Russians who live in Lithuania? Or the Poles who live in Lithuania. . . . "[35] And would the results of such a referendum be permanently binding? In Canada, the 1995 referendum on independence for Quebec was defeated by a majority of voters in Quebec itself. But separatists who lost have recently demanded another, saying they will keep holding elections until they win. The issue here is whether the results are binding for all or are binding only for separatists if they win.

The problem is that the partition process in recently divided countries has not resolved debate about these issues. And while partition in Czechoslovakia was peaceful, it was never put to a direct electoral test. Where issues about the process remain unresolved, the long-term legitimacy of the resulting partition may be undermined and subsequently challenged. As President Abraham Lincoln asked in his first inaugural address, "Why may not any portion of the confederacy a year or two hence arbitrarily secede again, precisely as portions of the present Union now secede from it?"[36]

Contemporary separatism also raises a number of issues for the interstate system as a whole. Since 1900, and particularly after 1945, the interstate system has encouraged and accommodated a vast expansion in the number of states in the world. The number of states has almost quadrupled, from fifty in 1900 to about one hundred ninety today. The proliferation of states has created difficult problems. Can the number of states be greatly increased to accommodate the hundreds or thousands of ethnic minority groups without considerable conflict? And if it could be done peacefully, would this make sense in a world that many people argue is becoming more global and interdependent? Some observers have argued

that regional and global economic and political institutions such as the European Union and United Nations, but also multinational corporations and transnational lobbies like OPEC, are "eroding national sovereignty and giving rise to new entities . . . that increasingly lack a meaningful national identity—that neither reflect nor respect nationhood as an organizing or regulative principle."[37]

In this context, the attempt to create new political boundaries may be irrelevant. As IBM executive Jacques G. Maisonrouge has argued, "For business purposes, the boundaries that separate one nation from another are no more real than the equator. They are merely convenient demarcations of ethnic, linguistic and cultural entities."[38]

While the rise of contemporary separatism has important consequences for individual states and the interstate system, it also has important implications for the meaning of democracy in nation-state republics.

When they developed political institutions to promote democracy, the founders of new republics in the United States and France argued that democracy should consist of majority rule, with protection for the rights of individuals and minorities (they had in mind dissenting "political" minorities, not so much ethnic or "religious" minorities). To prevent the rise of a "tyranny of the majority," they created institutions to check majority rule and allow minorities to themselves become majorities organizing political parties and coalitions with other groups. As Lincoln described it, "A majority held in restraint by constitutional checks and limitations, and always changing easily with the deliberate changes of popular opinion and sentiments, is the only true sovereign of a free people."[39] Lincoln's election was the product of one such shift, since the Republican Party grew from a political minority to a governing majority in the years just before the Civil War.

But the rise of the new interstate system, which is based in part on the principle of self-determination, and the proliferation of separatist movements in recent years, has tested the relation between majority and minority in nation-states. In many countries, the relation between majority and minority has become a contentious issue, particularly when these positions are closely identified with ethnic and religious identities. Because these social identities are relatively hard to change, it is difficult for the social composition of majority and minority to "change easily with the deliberate changes of popular opinion" so that political power can be shared with or acquired by others. Where people are unwilling or unable to become part of a majority and rule, at least for a time, they may begin to regard this system as unfair and undemocratic, as a tyranny of the majority. Under these circumstances, minorities may begin to look for

other ways to secure their own self-determination, often by seeking states of their own, where they can exercise power as a majority, not a minority. But when they do so, they may in turn create political institutions that prevent others, now a minority, from becoming part of a ruling majority. In this way, the relation between majority and minority is fundamentally altered. Under these circumstances, people with certain ethnic-religious identities become permanently assigned to majority or minority positions, a development that can compromise the meaning of democracy.

Two different solutions to this development have been proposed by political theorists in recent years. In her book *The Tyranny of the Majority*, the lawyer and African-American civil rights activist Lani Guinier argues that minorities be allowed to win on occasion so that they can meaningfully participate in the exercise of political power. Based on what she calls "the principle of taking turns," she suggests that different kinds of electoral procedures should be used so that the "minority gets to influence decision making and the majority rules more legitimately."[40] Procedures that can assist minorities in circumstances where "a fixed majority refuses to cooperate with the minority" include the following:

- The redrawing of electoral districts, often called "gerrymandering," so that ethnic or racial minority groups can become more of a majority in one district than a minority in many districts.
- Cumulative voting systems, where people are combined into a large district and given several votes, which they may cast for one person—a method that has given voters an opportunity to express the intensity of their political preferences.[41]

Guinier's proposals, and others like hers, assume that ethnic identities do not easily change, and that electoral systems are therefore needed to promote changing political relations between majority and minority.

But the assumption that ethnic identities are not easily changed is challenged by other theorists who argue that the attempt to use electoral systems based on ethnic identities itself contributes to the hardening of ethnic identities. As an alternative, they suggest that politicians and social movements work to change given social identities so that people can think of themselves and others in a different way. By changing people's identities, they hope to construct a new political majority. Dr. Martin Luther King Jr., for instance, argued that if poor blacks organized themselves only as blacks, they would remain a minority without substantial power.[42] But if they thought of themselves as "poor," a condition they shared with many other ethnic groups, they could create a wider, more powerful

political movement, one that might aspire to become a majoritarian movement. His "I have a dream" speech at the Lincoln Memorial in 1963 called for the social construction of a new identity that included people from other religious and ethnic groups, an identity that would enable African Americans and other groups to move out of their positions as "minorities" and into a position of "majority." But King's argument, which assumed that ethnic identities can change, has been difficult to realize in the United States. For the most part, ethnic-based movements have adopted the separatist view that they can become majorities only where they can rule on their own terms.

Notes

1. Gurr, Ted R. *Minorities at Risk: A Global View of Ethnopolitical Conflicts.* Washington, D.C.: U.S. Institute of Peace Press, 1993, pp. 5, 4.

2. Neilsson, Gunnar P. "States and 'Nation-Groups': A Global Taxonomy," in Edward A. Tiryakian and Ronald Rogowski, eds., *New Nationalisms of the Developed West: Toward Explanation.* Boston: Allen and Unwin, 1985, p. 30.

3. Brown, Michael E. "Causes and Implications of Ethnic Conflict," in Michael E. Brown, ed., *Ethnic Conflict and International Security.* Princeton: Princeton University Press, 1993, p. 6. Smith, Anthony D. *The Ethnic Revival.* Cambridge: Cambridge University Press, 1981, pp. 9–10.

4. *New York Times*, February 7, 1993. Barbara Crossette. "What Is a Nation," *New York Times*, December 26, 1994.

5. Schaeffer, Robert. *Warpaths: The Politics of Partition.* New York: Hill and Wang, 1990, pp. 73–86.

6. Ibid., passim.

7. Halperin, Morton H., Scheffer, David J., Small, Patricia L. *Self-Determination in the New World Order.* Washington, D.C.: Carnegie Endowment for International Peace, 1992, pp. 125–26.

8. Shtromas, Alexander. "The Baltic States," in Robert Conquest, ed., *The Last Empire: Nationality and the Soviet Future.* Stanford: Hoover Institution Press, 1986, pp. 188–89.

9. Ibid., p. 193.

10. Welsh, David. "Domestic Politics and Ethnic Conflict," in Michael E. Brown, 1993, p. 44.

11. Hobsbawm, Eric J. *Nations and Nationalism Since 1780: Programme, Myth, Reality.* Cambridge: Cambridge University Press, 1990, pp. 60–61.

12. Bohlen, Celestine. "Secession for Northern Italy Goes Forward, Symbolically," *New York Times*, August 22, 1996.

13. Rajah, Ananda. "Ethnicity, Nationalism, and the Nation-State: The Karen in Burma and Thailand," in Gehan Wijeyewardene, ed., *Ethnic Groups Across*

National Boundaries in Mainland Southeast Asia. Singapore: Institute of Southeast Asian Studies, 1990, pp. 111–12. Mirante, Edith. "Ethnic Minorities of the Burma Frontiers and Their Resistance Groups," *Cultural Survival,* 1987, p. 60.

14. Ibid.

15. Ibid., pp. 60–61.

16. Rajah, 1990, p. 111.

17. Schaeffer, 1990, pp. 43–44.

18. Knight, David B. "Geographical Perspectives on Self-Determination," in Peter Taylor and John House, eds., *Political Geography: Recent Advances and Future Directions.* London: Croom Helm, 1984, p. 180.

19. Personal interview, January 14, 1992.

20. *New York Times,* March 15, 1991. *New York Times,* June 5, 1991.

21. Horowitz, Donald L. "Ethnic and Nationalist Conflicts," in Michael T. Klare and Daniel C. Thomas, eds., *World Security: Trends and Challenges at Century's End.* New York: St. Martin's Press, 1991, p. 229.

22. Mayall, John. *Nationalism and International Security.* Cambridge: Cambridge University Press, 1990, p. 66.

23. Bonner, Raymond. *New York Times,* December 6, 1991.

24. Chipman, John. "Managing the Politics of Parochialism," in Michael E. Brown, 1993, p. 242. Asiwaju, A. I. *Partitioned Africans: Ethnic Relations Across Africa's International Boundaries, 1884–1984.* New York: St. Martin's Press, 1985, p. 2.

25. Beissinger, Mark R. "Demise of an Empire-State: Identity, Legitimacy and the Deconstruction of Soviet Politics," in Crawford Young, ed., *The Rising Tide of Cultural Pluralism: The Nation-State at Bay.* Madison: University of Wisconsin Press, 1993, pp. 104–5.

26. Ibid., p. 106.

27. Ibid.

28. Brooke, James. "White Flight in Brazil? Secession Caldron Boils," *New York Times,* May 12, 1993.

29. Rohter, Larry. "Puerto Rico Votes to Retain Status as Commonwealth," *New York Times,* November 15, 1993.

30. "Movement for Sovereignty is Bubbling Across Hawaii," *New York Times,* June 5, 1994.

31. Brown, Chip. "Separatism Surging," *New York Times Magazine,* January 30, 1994.

32. Brown in Michael E. Brown, 1993, p. 17.

33. Ibid.

34. Park, Andrus. "Ethnicity and Post-Soviet Transition: The Case of Estonia in Comparative Perspective," Global Forum Series. Durham, N.C.: Center for International Studies, Duke University, 1993, pp. 29–30.

35. Gardels, Nathan. "Dangers of Self-Determination: Interview with Prime Minister Filipe Gonzalez," *San Francisco Chronicle,* October 28, 1991.

36. Sandburg, Carl. *Abraham Lincoln: The War Years,* vol. 1. New York: Harcourt, Brace, 1939, pp. 131–32.

37. Barber, Benjamin. "Jihad vs McWorld," *The Atlantic*, March 1992, p. 53.

38. Narin, Tom. "Internationalism and the Second Coming," *Daedalus*, 1993, p. 157.

39. Sandburg, 1939, pp. 131–32.

40. Guinier, Lani. *The Tyranny of the Majority: Fundamental Fairness in Representative Democracy*. New York: The Free Press, 1994, p. 5.

41. Ibid.

42. King, Martin Luther, Jr. *A Testament of Hope: The Essential Writings of Martin Luther King Jr.*, ed. James M. Washington. San Francisco: Harper and Row, 1986, pp. 97, 219–20.

14

Mafias and the Global Drug Trade

In 1970, President Nixon announced the government's War on Drugs, the first of many contemporary antidrug campaigns. Since then, the U.S. government has spent nearly $70 billion on law enforcement and drug treatment programs, and now budgets about $12 billion annually for antidrug campaigns.[1] But despite massive government spending, heroin and cocaine supplies have grown, becoming cheaper, purer, and more readily available. And the foreign mafias that control the global trade in these drugs have become rich and powerful.

The expansion of the global drug trade in recent years has increased the power of foreign mafias, created social and environmental problems in countries where drugs are produced and consumed, and contributed to widespread violence and the spread of disease. To appreciate these developments, it is necessary first to outline a brief history of the regional mafias that seized control of the global drug trades in the 1970s and '80s.

Regional Mafias

The mafias that came to control the global drug trades in the 1970s and '80s grew out of regional crime gangs that emerged in Europe, the Americas, and Asia during the previous century. The Sicilian and Italian-American mafias, Chinese triads, Japanese yakuza, and Colombian bandidos had different organizational structures. But because they behaved in similar ways and engaged in similar criminal activities—providing "protection," operating "vice industries," and trafficking in illegal drugs—they can collectively be described as mafias.

The term "mafia" first appeared in Sicily during the 1860s, when republican revolutionaries successfully overthrew the island's Spanish mon-

archy and united it with other states on the peninsula, resulting in the creation of modern Italy.[2] Because the new Italian government did not exercise great power in Sicily after the Spanish rulers had retired, government authority declined just as landlords and peasants were trying to redefine their economic and political relations. Peasants, for example, had only recently been released from feudal obligations to aristocratic landlords, but new market relations between landowners and a free peasantry had not yet been established. The political vacuum and economic uncertainty gave soldiers who had fought in the war of independence a chance to take matters into their own hands. They offered to guarantee the informal and contractual obligations made by members of competing social groups, using force if necessary. In the absence of central government authority or fully functioning markets, landlords, merchants, and peasants all feared that they would be cheated or preyed upon by others. To prevent this, they relied on a powerful third party to ensure that obligations were met and injustices punished. As one Sicilian more recently explained, "When the butcher comes to me to buy an animal, he knows that I want to cheat him. But I [also] know that he wants to cheat me. There we need, say [a third party] to make us agree. And we both pay [the third party] a percentage of the deal."[3]

By offering to "protect" each party from the other, and to punish either party if they renege on the agreement made, the third-party "mafioso" came to play an important and lucrative role in Sicilian society after independence. As anthropologist Diego Gambetta explains, "Protection . . . can play a crucial role as a lubricant of economic exchange. In every transaction in which at least one party does not trust the other to comply with the rules, protection becomes desirable, even if it is a poor and costly substitute for trust."[4]

In Sicilian society during the late nineteenth and early twentieth centuries, the self-appointed providers of protection and guardians of public order became known as mafioso. As the anthropologist Henner Hess explained, "A mafioso is simply a courageous, brave fellow who won't stand any nonsense from anyone."[5]

According to the sociologist Pino Arlacci, anyone in Sicily could become a mafioso or a man of honor: "Men of honor were made, not born, and the pursuit of honor was a free competition, open to all."[6] But the prize went most often to the man who could act with greater "cunning, courage and ferocity" than others, a man "strong enough to avenge himself for any insult to his person, or any extension of it, *and* to offer any such insult . . . to his enemies."[7]

A person who should show that he could avenge insult and give insult,

what Arlacchi calls a "double moral system," and use the threat of violence to compel respect for this behavior by others, was seen by Sicilians as capable of providing the kind of protection they required.[8] And once they assumed this role, mafioso were feared, respected, and well paid.

According to the historian Eric Hobsbawm and the sociologist Arlacchi, there was never a "single secret society," or a "secret, hierarchical and centralized criminal organization called the mafia, its members bound to one another by sinister and solemn oaths of mutual loyalty and assistance."[9] Instead, mafioso formed small local gangs, usually composed of five or six blood relatives, family members and friends called *cosca* that operated independently.[10] Their sometimes murderous competition was sometimes tempered by informal associations that could assign monopolies and arbitrate disputes among competing mafias. It is these informal groups that are described by journalists as "the mafia," but they are more like a trade association composed of affiliated competitors than a corporation made up of members organized into a single hierarchy.

At the turn of the century, some mafioso immigrated to the United States along with the thousands of Sicilian peasants who could not find land or make a living on the island. In the United States mafioso offered protection in immigrant urban communities, trying to broker relations among local government officials, employers, and immigrant communities. In contrast with Sicilian mafias, U.S. mafia families recruited or admitted members of other ethnic groups—Jewish and Irish mafioso participated in U.S. gangs. They were also larger in size, with some five thousand members in the United States and perhaps fifty thousand close associates.[11]

In other countries, mafialike groups also emerged: triads in China, yakuza in Japan during the nineteenth century, bandidos in Colombia during the 1950s, and more recently "mafiyas" in the former Soviet Union.

In nineteenth-century China, young single men who could not rely on their families or communities to support or assist them formed what anthropologists called "fictive kinship" in "mutual-aid societies." Young men who joined these societies pledged to protect each other from feudal landlords, unscrupulous merchants, corrupt officials, predatory warlords, and the Manchu dynasty.[12] They frequently organized in secret to shield members from the state, which viewed them as a threat to its power and made membership in secret societies illegal. As a Chinese proverb explained, "Armies protect the emperor, secret societies protect the people."[13]

Like their Sicilian counterparts, "the line between protection and predation was always thin [in Chinese society]," and secret societies often

turned to "thievery, extortion, and the control of . . . gambling, robbery and prostitution enterprises in China and in Chinese overseas communities. . . . "[14] And like Sicilian mafias, they had a political dimension. Early Chinese secret societies or triads tried to overthrow the alien Manchu rulers, much as Sicilian mafias were originally rebels against Spanish Bourbon rule.[15] Indeed, triads first came to prominence during their role in the Taiping Rebellion (1851–64), at about the same time that mafias emerged during the rebellion in Sicily and the unification of Italy (1860–61).[16] After the Taiping Rebellion failed, many politically minded "Triad members became involved in . . . piracy and smuggling [and] some fled to America, where they established branches of the Triad Society known as the Chee kung Tong."[17] So, like their Sicilian counterparts, Chinese gangsters joined the migration to the United States and organized criminal enterprises in immigrant communities.

In China, triads became prominent in Shanghai, which became a notorious center of opium use and prostitution after the Chinese monarchy was overthrown by republican revolutionaries in 1911. And triad leaders worked closely with Chiang Kai-shek's nationalist government to administer the city and attack the growing communist movement in the 1920s.[18] After the long civil war between nationalists and communists, a contest that was interrupted by Japanese invasion and then renewed after World War II, triads fled China when the communists took power and established a new base in Hong Kong, then a British colony.

The arrival of numerous triads in postwar Hong Kong initially led to a fierce, murderous competition among triad groups for control of criminal activity in the city. In 1955, the 14K Triad, the largest group, attempted to amalgamate the colony's three hundred thousand triad members into a single criminal syndicate.[19] They nearly succeeded in consolidating triad power, but in 1956 they joined a popular demonstration against continued British rule in the colony, evidently hoping that the revolt would result in independence for the colony and even greater power for the triad. But the British crushed the revolt and deported much of the 14K leadership. This led to renewed competition among Hong Kong triads, but also to the creation of new triads by gangsters deported to Taiwan.[20]

Postwar triads based in Hong Kong and Taiwan differ in some important respects from Sicilian and Italian-American mafias. While Italian and American mafia groups are usually composed of family members and friends of the same ethnic groups, members of Chinese triads are not related by blood, but are joined in fictive kinships, where people adopt one another as brothers and embrace the gang as their family. Because they are based on fictive rather than real kinships, triads can admit more

members and grow larger than blood-related mafia groups. So, for example, the 14K Triad has some twenty-four thousand members and the Wo group has twenty-nine thousand.[21] Most Italian-American mafia families in the United States each have between fifty and two hundred members.[22]

Like Chinese triads, the yakuza in Japan are large criminal gangs based on fictive kinships. They also first emerged in the mid-nineteenth century, when Japan, like China and Sicily, was undergoing rapid political and economic change.

After 1854, when U.S. naval forces under Commodore Matthew C. Perry forced Japan to trade with the world, Japan's central government—the Tokugawa shogunate—began to collapse. The demise of the shogunate and the subsequent installation of the Meiji government in 1868 led to the end of feudalism, the rapid development of industry, and a rapid migration of rural peasants to the cities. Under these conditions, masterless samurai who had become gamblers (*bakuto*) and street peddlers (*tekiya*) began to provide "protection" to peasants who had seen old feudal obligations disappear and new, market-based contractual relations arise, a development that led, as it did in Sicily during the same period, to considerable mistrust and uncertainty.[23] The individuals and groups who enforced "obligations" in a situation where government laws and market relations were not fully functioning took the name "yakuza" from a traditional card game, in which the combination of 8 (*ya*), 9 (*ku*), and 3 (*sa*) was the worst possible hand.[24]

Yakuza in Japan were joined by a common ideology of *giri*, an obligation to show gratitude but also the duty to exact revenge, and *ninjo*, the obligation to be generous and compassionate for the weak and disadvantaged.[25] The ability to practice both giri and ninjo enabled Yakuza to claim a role in Japanese society as "protectors," people able to guarantee obligations between parties who could not trust each other and punish those who reneged on their duties. Like men of honor in Sicily, yakuza take great pride in the social role. They demonstrate this by covering their bodies with distinctive tattoos, an extremely painful process that serves as a test of endurance and courage, and by using kitchen knives or small swords to sever parts of their fingers (*yubitsume*) to demonstrate the sincerity of an apology for failing to fulfill their own obligations to others, usually duty to their gang.[26] Finger cutting is a visible symbol of the yakuza's ability to make and enforce obligations, a practice that gives credibility to their role as protector.

Yakuza gangs first became prominent in the 1920s. They grew from small local gangs to large national gangs during the U.S. occupation of Japan after World War II. By 1978, the Yamaguchi-gumi, the largest ya-

kuza gang, counted 10,382 members and police estimated that there were 108,266 yakuza in Japan.[27] Unlike their triad and mafia counterparts, the yakuza play a very public role in society. Yakuza members sport lapel badges indicating their membership and rank in particular gangs, operate local storefront offices that display their gang emblems, and publish newspapers: the Yamaguchi-gumi "publishes the monthly *Yamaguchi-Gumi Jiho* and sends it to all gang members."[28] They do this in part because Japanese society is more tolerant of their role and because yakuza operate many legitimate businesses alongside their illegal enterprises. Although the yakuza have historically trafficked in methamphetamine or "speed," they did not trade in heroin, largely because there is little demand for it in Japan (drug users prefer speed to heroin or cocaine).

It is more difficult to say much about the origins of the Colombian cartels that came to control the cocaine trade in the 1970s and '80s because little has been written about them. But some sociologists argue that bandidos and bandoleros first became numerous in Colombia during the 1950s, after the assassination of leftist leader Jorge Eliécer Gaitán in 1948 led to a decade of fractious fighting, martial law, civil war, and widespread political corruption. During this period, known in Colombia as *la violencia*, in which some two hundred thousand people were killed, groups of smugglers, bandits, and gunmen emerged. Although the fighting eventually ended and a functioning government was reestablished, many of these groups of armed men remained, engaging in criminal enterprises rather than conducting political warfare. "At the beginning of the 1970s," Arlacchi argues, "many members of this outlaw army became involved in international cocaine and marijuana smuggling, often meeting the needs of the Colombian mafia families."[29] These origins suggest many similarities with other mafialike groups around the world: the emergence of armed men who take charge of local affairs at a time when government authority is weak and normal economic relations are disrupted.

The Russian mafiyas have emerged in the same kind of setting, where government authority is weak and new economic relations are uncertain and problematic. While they have grown strong in Russia, it is not clear whether they will emerge as a powerful global mafia because they do not, as yet, control a major source of drugs—a prerequisite for entry into the global drug trade.

There are important differences between the mafias, triads, yakuza, bandidos, and mafiyas that emerged in different parts of the world. They emerged at different times: Sicilian mafias, Chinese triads, and Japanese yakuza in the mid-nineteenth century, Italian-American mafias in the 1920s, Colombian bandidos in the 1950s, and Russian mafiyas in the

1990s. Some of these mafias were based on blood-relations and family members, which kept them relatively small (Sicilian, Italian-American, and Colombian mafias), while Asian gangs were based on fictive kinships, which enabled them to become quite large.[30] But despite different social origins and organizational orientations, criminal groups in different regions behaved in much the same way, acting with both courtesy and cunning, demonstrating both compassion and revenge, and displaying great energy.

> These people have amazing vitality. They never stand still, they're never idle. One moment they are busy over some deal, later on they're having lunch with friends, then they are working on some other business affair, then they visit one of their lovers. Then some "situation" comes up which they have to "control". . . . They are always on the move, traveling from place to place in their cars. . . . Then it's off to the bar, to talk. They go see some relatives and discuss business again. . . . Lots of them are polygamous, they have several families and lots of children. They eat, they drink, they have a good time, they kill. The whole thing's done with feverish intensity: never an empty space, never a slack moment.[31]

More important, the different gangs engage in common criminal activities, what might be called the "protection" and "vice industries."

When they first emerged, regional mafias provided protection, acting to guarantee and enforce "obligations" between parties who could not trust one another because government laws and market relations were weak, ineffective, or incomplete. Members of ethnic communities—landowners, small businesses, peddlers, vendors, and shopkeepers—willingly or unwillingly paid mafias to provide protection and mediate relations among different groups. While protection activities provided their initial source of income, mafias soon turned to vice industries—gambling, prostitution, and drugs—to generate income.

In illegal vice markets, demand is relatively inelastic. This means that consumer demand remains high even if prices rise. (In legal markets, where need and compulsion are less strongly felt, consumer demand usually falls when prices rise, a relation that economists describe as elastic.) Mafias typically seek out activities where consumers are compulsive, where goods and services are illegal, because profits are higher than those obtained in legal and competitive markets. And by using violence or the threat of violence, mafias can discourage competition in these industries and obtain monopoly power, which enables them to reap even higher profits.

In the United States, for example, mafia families or firms have long

controlled the major vice industries. In major U.S. cities, mafias operated numbers lotteries, off-track betting on horseraces and backroom casinos, and they loaned money at high interest rates to gamblers and operators of these enterprises, a practice known as "loansharking." Before state governments started their own lotteries, poor and working people wagered small amounts of money on a combination of three numbers (1 to 999). Numbers runners collected bets and mafia firms paid winners in the daily lottery. To guarantee fairness, the winning number was selected from an external source that could generate random numbers—for example, the last three digits of the closing figures for the New York Stock Exchange.[32] Naturally, mafia firms collected more money in bets than they paid out in prizes, though this operation required considerable capital in the event that large amounts had been placed on winning numbers. Mafia entrepreneurs and bookies also collected bets on horseraces, an illegal form of gambling because state laws required that bets could only be made at the racetrack. Because many poor or working people could not attend the races, mafia firms collected their wagers and paid off winners. For gamblers who preferred games of chance, mafias operated backroom casinos, complete with roulette wheels and tables for blackjack, poker, or craps. Because they were vulnerable to discovery by police, mafia casinos typically moved frequently, often daily, from one location to another.

Of course, people who gamble need money to wager, and people who operate gambling businesses—often as a concession awarded by mafias to nonmafia members (there were too many outlets for mafioso to staff directly)—need capital to set up shop and pay out prizes. Because it is difficult for many people to borrow money for these purposes without collateral, mafias loaned money to gamblers and gaming operators at high interest rates, typically at 150 percent interest per year, but ranging as high as 1,000 percent per year.[33] Loan sharks also made loans to owners of small businesses or to people who could not obtain unsecured loans from banks or legitimate creditors. In Japan, for example, where it is extremely difficult for small businesses and consumers to obtain credit—before 1983, *legal* interest rates for consumer loans were as high as 110 percent annually—yakuza firms played a major role as creditors in Japan's forty-two thousand loansharking firms.[34]

In addition to gambling, mafia firms controlled prostitution and the trade in hard-core pornographic goods. Although mafias sometimes owned and operated brothels, prostitution was typically operated by others—brothel madams and streetwalker pimps—who ran their businesses as concessions and paid a percentage of their earnings to mafias for protection. By contrast, the pornographic industry in the United States—the

manufacture of hard-porn books, magazines, and films—was directly controlled by mafia firms. In Asia, triads and yakuza have organized the sex-tourist industries in the Philippines, Taiwan, and Thailand. In 1982, Thai police estimated that seven hundred thousand women and children were employed as prostitutes in Thailand, "nearly 10 percent of all Thai women between the ages of 15 and 30."[35]

Finally, U.S. mafias have long trafficked in illegal drugs, alcohol in the 1920s and early '30s, and heroin "as early as 1935," according to Gambetta.[36] Triads in China trafficked in opium during the nineteenth century and, after it was first synthesized in 1898, heroin. In Japan, the use of opiates is uncommon, but the use of speed became common during World War II when it was discovered that the drug could keep weary soldiers going.[37] After the war, the yakuza monopolized the illegal trade in amphetamines. Bandidos in Colombia began trafficking in marijuana during the 1960s and then cocaine in the '70s. But while illegal drug trades provided an important source of revenue for some mafias prior to the 1970s, most mafias around the world relied on protection and other vice industries to provide the bulk of their income. Income from illegal drugs remained relatively unimportant until recently because the demand for drugs was small, steady, and geographically confined. In the United States, heroin use was confined to large cities, located mostly on the East Coast and centered in New York City. The triads served the heroin market in Hong Kong, where the addict population was quite large, but not markets outside the colony. The yakuza dominated amphetamine markets in Japan, but there was little international trade in this drug. Colombian bandidos smuggled marijuana to U.S. markets, but cocaine use was confined primarily to consumers in the Andean region—in the 1960s it was too expensive for most consumers outside the region.

But the local character of regional mafias changed dramatically in the 1970s. The booming trade in illegal drugs after 1970 transformed regional mafias, turning them into global gangs.

Growing Drug Supplies, Rising Demand

In 1970, in the War on Drugs, Nixon consolidated federal drug control efforts, increased their budgets, expanded drug treatment programs, which promoted the use of methadone as an alternative to heroin, persuaded the governments of Turkey and Mexico to eradicate illegal opium fields in their countries, and passed laws that made it easier to prosecute mafias and protect witnesses from mob retribution.[38] Nixon's war on ille-

gal drugs was a response to mounting supplies of and to increased use of marijuana, heroin, and psychoactive drugs like LSD. Cocaine was also popular, but it was not yet widely used in 1970. Heroin was the chief target of Nixon's drug war because the number of heroin users had grown from perhaps 50,000 in 1960 to 500,000 in 1970, a tenfold increase.[39] The number of heroin addicts remained steady for five years and then dropped sharply to perhaps 200,000 addicts at the end of the 1970s. Heroin use increased slowly in the 1980s, reaching 500,000 again in 1985, and then grew to 700,000 by the end of the decade. During the 1990s, heroin use increased dramatically, perhaps doubling to 1.5 million users by 1995. The recent influx of cheap, pure, smokable heroin from the Golden Triangle may increase heroin use again, much as the advent of cheap, smokable "crack" dramatically increased cocaine use in the mid-1980s.

To understand these developments, it is necessary to look first at the rising supply of illegal drugs, focusing on heroin and cocaine, and then at the growing demand for illegal drugs in the United States.

Drug Supplies

Prior to 1970, most of the world's opium was grown in the Golden Crescent (Turkey, Iran, Afghanistan, Pakistan, and India). Some opium was also grown in the Golden Triangle (Burma, Laos, and Thailand), with a small amount harvested in Mexico.

Opium, the raw material for refined heroin, is grown in rugged and remote areas, where governments exercise little legal authority, either by fiercely independent mountain farmers (in the Golden Crescent and in Mexico) or by local warlords (in the Golden Triangle). In the Golden Triangle, nationalist Chinese army groups took refuge in Burma during the Chinese Civil War and raised opium to finance their remnant military forces.[40]

Coca leaf, the raw material for refined cocaine, is grown in the White Mountains (Peru, Bolivia, and Colombia). Independent peasant farmers grow about 90 percent of the world coca crop in just one country: Peru.

The opium and coca grown in all three regions are refined, processed, and transported to global drug markets by mafias. Historically, opium from the Golden Crescent has been controlled by Sicilian, French, and Italian-American mafias; opium from the Golden Triangle has been dominated by Chinese triads based in Hong Kong and Taiwan; and, more recently, coca from the White Mountains has been refined and transported by Colombian bandidos who, during the 1970s, organized the cartels based in Medellin and Cali.

It is important to note that mafias do not grow the raw materials or sell the refined drugs on the street. Instead, they monopolize the refining and transport sectors, what might be called the manufacturing and wholesale business. They let independent peasants or local warlords produce the raw material and let local street gangs retail the drugs, both fiercely competitive sectors where the risk of discovery and arrest are high. Mafias thus concentrate on the most profitable and least risky part of the business.

According to *The Economist*, farmers in Peru grow coca leaf, which sells for $2.10 per kilogram; local entrepreneurs then treat it with chemicals to produce a crude paste, which they can sell to the cartels for $875 per kilo. The cartels then refine it into a base and then into pure cocaine, which in 1980 sold for $60,000 per kilo and in 1990 for $10,000.[41] The cocaine is then sold to street-level retailers, usually gangs, who dilute or "cut" the cocaine, which they sold for $150,000 per kilo in 1980 and about $90,000 per kilo in 1990.[42]

The process of growing, refining, transporting, and selling heroin is almost identical.[43] Farmers make substantial profits, much more than can be made growing any other crop. And if they process opium or coca leaf crudely, they can increase their investment 400 percent. Mafias that refine and transport the drugs can realize profits of 6,000 percent at 1980 prices, perhaps only 1,200 percent at 1990 prices, while street gang retailers mark up their goods between 100 and 800 percent. Although everyone earns substantial profits from the drug trade, mafia firms make the greatest gains, while taking the smallest risks.[44]

When we examine the supply of illegal drugs since World War II, three important developments stand out. First, the global supplies of opium-heroin and coca-cocaine have grown dramatically. In 1950, about 500 tons of heroin were produced, most of it from the Golden Crescent. In 1970, about 1,000 tons were produced, much of the increase coming from the Golden Triangle. Global heroin production remained fairly steady during the 1970s, then increased again during the 1980s, so that more than 3,500 tons were produced in 1990, a more than threefold increase, due primarily to increased production in the Golden Triangle. Between 1950 and 1990, world heroin production increased sevenfold.[45]

Accurate estimates of illegal cocaine production prior to 1980 are difficult to obtain, but in 1980, some 220,000 acres of coca leaf were grown, producing 40 to 48 tons of cocaine. In 1989, 520,000 acres of coca were grown and 350 to 400 tons of cocaine were produced, a tenfold increase.[46]

Second, the center of cultivation shifted from the Golden Crescent to

the Golden Triangle during the 1970s and '80s, a development that greatly affected the mafia refiners connected to opium growers in each region.

In 1970, Turkey was the world's largest opium producer, growing as much as 80 percent of the world total.[47] But Nixon persuaded the Turkish government to launch a successful poppy eradication campaign that effectively ended its role as the world's premier supplier, and he persuaded India and Mexico to do the same, though Mexico was then only a minor producer.[48] As a result, opium cultivation shifted to other regions in the Golden Crescent, with Afghanistan becoming a major producer along with Iran and Pakistan during the 1970s. But during the 1980s, a number of developments would shift the center of opium cultivation east to the Golden Triangle.

In 1979, the Islamic Revolution in Iran led to the overthrow of Reza Shah Pahlavi's government and a ban on opium production and heroin use. In the same year, the Soviet Union invaded Afghanistan to support the communist government there. Revolution curtailed opium production in Iran and invasion curtailed it somewhat in Afghanistan, though mujahadeen rebels fighting the Soviet invaders allowed farmers to continue growing opium in regions under their control so that the proceeds of opium sales could be used to finance arms purchases and assist the war effort. As opium production in the Golden Crescent slowed, the number of drug users in Afghanistan, Iran, and Pakistan grew dramatically. Pakistan's 670,000 to one million heroin users now consume more opium than that country produces, and Iran's 200,000 registered addicts (with as many as 800,000 not registered) consume large quantities. As a result, there was less opium available to export, perhaps as little as 15 percent of the total by 1990.[49]

With opium producers in the Golden Crescent facing these difficulties, Golden Triangle producers stepped into the breech. Opium production and heroin processing in the Golden Triangle had increased dramatically in the 1960s and early 1970s, principally to supply a growing population of user-addicts in Vietnam: U.S. soldiers fighting in the war and Vietnamese civilians. But by 1975, U.S. troops had been withdrawn, and the communist government that came to power banned the import and use of opium and heroin. This meant that opium growers and heroin refiners had surplus supplies—as much as 50 percent of their supply was available for export. So they turned their attention to U.S. drug markets. In 1980, only 5 percent of the heroin sold in New York City originated in the Golden Triangle. But by 1990, triad importers of Golden Triangle heroin had captured 90 percent of the New York City market.[50]

Third, rising drug supplies led to falling street prices and increasing

purity, which made it economical to develop cheap kinds of drugs that can expand consumer demand in new ways. This process occurred first with cocaine, more recently with heroin.

During the 1980s, world cocaine supplies grew rapidly, from 40 to 48 tons in 1980 to 350 to 400 tons in 1989. As supplies grew, the price dropped and the purity increased. Cocaine sold on the street increased from about 12 percent pure in 1980 to 60 to 80 percent in 1989. By 1985, it became economical to process cocaine one step further, creating a smokable, crystalline form of cocaine called "crack."[51]

The widespread availability of inexpensive crack opened new consumer markets and stimulated demand for the drug, particularly in low-income neighborhoods where cocaine had been prohibitively expensive. Because smokable crack is psychologically more addictive than powdered cocaine, and because it is cheap—"a single dose might cost only $10 or $15"— mafias were assured of steady repeat sales among relatively poor consumers.[52] Since 1985, the number of cocaine users has nearly quadrupled, from 500,000 to 1.8 million.[53]

While the demand for cocaine and then crack equaled and then surpassed that of heroin in the mid-1980s, the demand for heroin is again on the rise, largely as a result of similar developments.

During the 1980s and early 1990s, heroin production increased dramatically, particularly in the Golden Triangle, where supplies increased from about 1,000 tons in 1980 to between 2,400 and 3,950 tons in 1990. Mounting global heroin supplies led to falling prices and increased purity of drugs sold on the street. By 1991, the street price of a single dose of heroin had dropped from $10 to $3. "They're lowering the price of a single dose and over time more people are going to get hooked," said Richard Calkins, a drug abuse official at the Michigan Department of Health.[54] In 1979, for example, the heroin packets sold to user-addicts contained only 3.6 percent heroin. the rest consisted of additives. But by 1990, the purity had increased to 40 to 60 percent, and by 1994 it had increased to nearly 90 percent.[55] Lower prices and increasing purity made it possible to introduce and sell a new, smokable form of heroin. (In the previous century, people smoked raw opium, not processed heroin.)

Like crack, smokable heroin may stimulate consumer demand and open new markets for the drug. Unlike crack, smokable heroin is less addictive than heroin that is injected. And because it can be consumed without using needles, it reduces the risks of contracting AIDS and other diseases like hepatitis.[56] Because it is perceived as less addictive and safer, smokable heroin may become popular among populations that had previously shunned or avoided the drug. "When a drug like heroin becomes

more available and more potent, you attract the swing market of 'garbage heads' who take whatever drugs they can find until they get hooked on something," observed Pete Pinto.[57]

There is some evidence that this has already occurred. The number of people treated in hospital emergency rooms for heroin use has tripled from 10,561 visits in 1985 to 30,800 visits in 1993.[58] Based on evidence that the heroin addict population numbered 500,000 in 1985, and that 10,000 users sought emergency treatment, the increase in hospital admissions would indicate that the user population had grown to as many as 1.5 million by 1993. But because the purity of the drug also increased in this period, the growing number of hospital admissions may be due to the fact that users more frequently took overdoses with increasingly "rich" heroin. If that is the case, the number of heroin users may not be as large as emergency admissions would suggest. Still, the fact that heroin supplies are growing, prices falling, purity increasing, and demand growing for smokable heroin suggests that the demand for heroin is likely to increase rapidly in coming years.

Consumer Demand

Although consumer demand for illegal drugs is extremely hard to measure with certainty, it is clear that drug use in the United States and other countries has fluctuated during this century. In the United States, where some attempt has been made to estimate demand, the use of illegal drugs generally declined during the first half of the century and rose during the second half.

In 1900, when heroin could be purchased legally, there were perhaps two hundred fifty thousand heroin user-addicts in the United States.[59] Government restrictions and then prohibition of heroin and cocaine sales in the 1920s (and marijuana in the 1930s), and introduced drug treatment programs, effectively reduced the supply and increased the price of these drugs, and the addict population steadily declined during the 1920s and '30s. Heroin use nearly vanished in the 1940s when the war prevented drug supplies from reaching consumers, resulting in what some writers describe as a "drug famine" in the United States and Europe.[60]

It is not entirely clear why drug use declined so dramatically during these decades, though the rising cost of heroin and cocaine, coupled with falling incomes for most people during the Depression, and the availability of treatment programs may have discouraged users from seeking the drug and forced them to consume cheaper drugs like alcohol and tobacco.

After World War II, heroin once again became available and the number of heroin users grew to perhaps 20,000 in 1950 and then to 50,000 in 1960. In the next decade, the number of heroin users grew by leaps and bounds, to about 250,000 in 1970 and 500,000 by 1975, a tenfold increase.[61]

The number of users actually fell by more than half during the late 1970s, from 500,000 to about 200,000 between 1976 and 1979.[62] This sharp decline, what some experts have called a "heroin drought," was probably due to two developments. First, successful opium eradication campaigns in Turkey, India, and Mexico reduced supplies from traditional sources and increased the cost of heroin in the United States. Second, it fell because addicts made use of widely available federal drug treatment programs and heroin substitutes, particularly methadone.[63]

But the number of heroin users began to climb again in the 1980s, returning to the 1975 level of 500,000 by 1985, and then continued to grow to 700,000 in 1990 and perhaps as many as 1.5 million by 1994.

Just as it is not clear why heroin use declined between 1900 and 1945, it is not clear why demand for the drug increased after the war. Nor is it clear why it increased so dramatically in the United States and *not* in other first world countries. As sociologist Elliott Curry notes,

> Most Americans do not realize how atypical we are . . . that the United States leads the world in drug abuse. . . . More people died in 1989 of the effects of cocaine abuse alone in Los Angeles than died of *all* drug-related causes in Holland, with 15 times the population. . . . The American drug problem continues to tower above those of the rest of the industrial world, and it does so despite an extraordinary experiment in punitive control.[64]

Maybe the demand for heroin and other drugs is more sensitive to the supply-price-purity of drugs than previously thought. Because many analysts assume that because heroin is addictive, they argue that the demand for the drug is inelastic or unresponsive to changes in availability, price, or purity. But it may not be as addictive as many people have assumed. In 1988, U.S. Surgeon General C. Everett Koop said that nicotine was *as* addictive as heroin.[65] And the National Institute of Drug Abuse reported that nicotine is "as addictive as heroin and 5 to 10 times more potent than cocaine or morphine in producing effects on mood or behavior."[66] This is interesting because many tobacco smokers quit even though nicotine is an addictive drug. This suggests that heroin users may be able to quit more easily than many analysts have previously assumed. For example, among patients who were given heroin/morphine to treat painful illnesses, only a small percentage of them became addicted, and researchers re-

ported that "there is a growing literature showing that [narcotics] can be used by patients for a long time, with few side effects, and that addiction and abuse are not a problem."[67]

If heroin use is both less addictive and more sensitive to supply-price-purity than many analysts have long assumed, then demand for the drug may have increased dramatically during the postwar period because heroin supplies have increased and prices have fallen. The big increase in demand for heroin, during the 1960s and again during the 1980s, came at times when heroin supplies increased rapidly, tripling in the 1960s and nearly quadrupling in the 1980s. And demand for heroin actually fell during the late 1970s, when the availability of heroin from traditional sources in Turkey and Mexico declined. Much the same is true of cocaine. Cocaine use expanded dramatically as the supply of the drug increased and prices fell during the 1980s. This suggests that demand in the United States expanded in large part *because* heroin and cocaine became cheaper and more widely available, and these drugs became more plentiful because drug producers and mafia refiners increased supplies and made determined efforts to sell their drugs in U.S. markets, where they could get higher prices than they could by selling drugs to relatively poor domestic consumers in the Golden Crescent, Golden Triangle, and White Mountains. Their efforts to produce, refine, and transport drugs to U.S. markets may explain why drug use is more widespread in the United States than in other first world countries. Mafias may have flooded the U.S. market to increase demand among consumers able to pay relatively high prices. They can and do sell drugs to domestic consumers, but the price they can get is lower than what even poor U.S. consumers can pay.

While a comprehensive explanation of the changing relation between the supply of and demand for illegal drugs is difficult to make, there is no doubt that both drug supplies and drug use have increased. And these developments had important consequences for countries where drugs are produced, for mafias that refine and transport drugs, and for countries where drugs are consumed.

Social Consequences of the Drug Trade

The emergence of a global drug trade has created a variety of social problems for different groups in different settings. In drug-producing countries, opium and coca production has led to rising domestic drug use, environmental destruction, widespread corruption, and outright civil war between governments and mafias. For mafias that refine and trade drugs,

the rise of Golden Triangle heroin controlled by Chinese triads and of White Mountain cocaine by Colombian cartels has contributed to the decline of the Italian-American mafia, which had been weakened by changing government policies and new social developments in the 1970s and '80s. And widespread drug use in countries like the United States has led to the spread of crime and disease, murderous competition among street gangs for control of the retail trade, and rising economic costs associated with prosecuting and imprisoning drug users and dealers.

In drug-producing regions, the cultivation and processing of opium and coca have created three kinds of problems. First, the increasing availability of drugs in raw, semiprocessed, and refined forms has stimulated consumption by domestic users. Although people in the Golden Crescent and Golden Triangle have long used opium, and peasants in the White Mountains have long chewed coca leaf, the number of users consuming semiprocessed drugs like *basuco* (a smokable cocaine paste) has grown substantially in recent years.[68] There are now between 200,000 and 800,000 heroin addicts in Iran, and between 670,000 and one million in Pakistan, and heroin use has grown significantly in Thailand and even in China along the Myanmar border, where heroin use for many years had disappeared.[69] The U.S. State Department reported in 1985 that "40,000 to 50,000 Bolivians, 150,000 Peruvians, and more than 600,000 Colombians have 'serious' addiction problems."[70]

Second, the cultivation of drugs in some settings has contributed to environmental destruction. In Peru, for example, coca cultivation is centered in the upper Huallaga River valley, a mountainous rain forest region. Growers there have cleared 1.7 million acres of fragile rain forests for the crop, which is hard on the soil and contributes to soil erosion.[71] Farmers dump the chemical used to process coca leaf into coca paste into the valley's rivers. A Peruvian forest engineer estimated in 1987 that coca growers annually dump "15 million gallons of kerosene, 8 million gallons of sulphuric acid, 1.6 million gallons of acetone, 1.6 million gallons of the solvent toluene, 16,000 tons of lime and 3,200 tons of carbide" into the watershed.[72]

Drug-producing countries have also experienced a third problem: corruption, conflict, and civil war. These problems have been most evident in Colombia. After Colombia's President Virgilio Barco Vargas moved to seize mafioso property and permit the extradition of Colombian cartel leaders to the United States for trial, the mafias based in Medellin declared war on the government on August 25, 1989:

> We declare absolute and total war on the government, on the industrial and political oligarchy, on the journalists that have attacked and ravaged us, on

the judges that have sold out to the government, on the extraditing magis-
trates, on the presidents of the unions and all those who persecuted and
attacked us."[73]

The "Extraditables," led by Pablo Escobar, also warned that they would
"not respect the families of those who have not respected our families."[74]

Prior to 1989, Colombian cartels had assassinated ministers of justices,
police chiefs, attorney generals, political candidates, union organizers, and
political leaders. Nearly three thousand died in cartel-directed violence in
1988 alone.[75] But their declaration of war in 1989 escalated the conflict
between mafias and government officials and led to mafia kidnappings
and assassinations of journalists and others. After twenty-two journalists
were assassinated, many newspapers shut their offices and reporters fled
into exile.[76] And after Escobar offered a bounty for the murder of policemen, some three hundred policemen were killed.[77]

Although the government managed to trap and kill Escobar on a roof-
top in December 1993, the mafias remained intact under new leadership,
based now in Cali, and they had forced the government to retreat from
its promise to extradite mafioso to the United States, which had been
their chief demand at the outset of the conflict.[78]

For mafias that refine and trade in drugs, the emergence of the Golden
Triangle and the White Mountains as centers of global drug production
has had important consequences, particularly in the United States. As the
center of opium production shifted from the Golden Crescent to the
Golden Triangle in the 1980s, and as the White Mountains became the
center of coca production, the triad and cartel mafias that refined and
transported heroin and cocaine from these two regions prospered, while
the Sicilian and Italian-American mafias that traded heroin from the
Golden Crescent suffered. The decline of the Golden Crescent contributed to the decline of the U.S.-based mafia, which had been weakened by
a series of other legal and social developments in the 1970s and '80s. By
1990, the Italian-American mafia based in the United States had been
eclipsed by foreign triads and cartels.

The decline of domestic U.S. mafias can be attributed to three legal,
social, and economic developments in the 1970s and '80s.

First, state governments and private entrepreneurs began taking over
the vice industries, which had long been the domestic mafia's main source
of revenue. Recall that mafias relied on income from gambling and sex. In
1964, New Hampshire opened the country's first state-run lottery. And
since then, states have legalized many forms of gambling to raise revenues
without raising taxes. By 1992, thirty-seven states ran lotteries, which dis-

placed the old, mafia-run numbers lotteries. Many states now permit casino gambling, and Indian tribes operate casinos on reservations in states that do not otherwise permit them. Several states operate off-track betting parlors for racing fans: New York went into the bookmaking business in 1971.[79]

As a result of the widespread legalization of gambling, a development that began slowly in the 1970s and accelerated in the 1980s, "gambling is now squarely in the American mainstream," argues gambling industry consultant Eugene Christiansen.[80] "When the British legalized casinos in 1968, the purpose was to control organized crime," argues Jerome Skolnick.[81] In the United States the purpose was to raise revenue, but the result was much the same. In 1992, Americans wagered $329.9 billion, and state and local governments collected $29.9 billion in revenues, three times as much as they had in 1982, a figure "more than six times what people spent on movie tickets."[82]

With the growing public enthusiasm for legal and state-run gambling, interest in illegal mafia-run gambling has waned, and numbers lotteries, bookies, and backroom casinos have virtually disappeared.

Just as state governments and private corporations have taken over the gaming sector of the vice industry, private entrepreneurs have taken over much of the sex industry. During the 1970s, when the Supreme Court eased obscenity laws and state and local governments decriminalized some sexual acts between consenting adults, private entrepreneurs began producing sexually oriented magazines, books, and increasingly, videotapes that consumers could purchase and watch at home.[83] Independent female sex workers abandoned pimps and mafia-run brothels and began providing sexual services to consumers directly through underground newspapers and advertisements in the Yellow Pages. Sex workers even began organizing prostitutes' unions like COYOTE (Cast Off Your Old, Tired Ethics) that lobbied for decriminalization and greater protection for sex industry workers.[84] The rise of widespread pornography and independent female sex workers eroded the role previously played by madams, pimps, and mafias, a development that greatly reduced mafia income from the sex industry.

Second, while legalization and decriminalization of traditional vice industries eroded the mafia's income base, the federal government adopted laws and programs that helped it prosecute mafias successfully. The cornerstone of the government's antimafia policy was the passage in 1970 of the Racketeer-Influenced and Corrupt Organizations Act (RICO). This law allows federal attorneys to prosecute criminal organizations (not just individuals) and seize money, businesses, and property acquired through criminal activity.[85]

The government also began a witness protection program designed to protect informants and witnesses from mafia retribution. It took some years before attorneys were able to make use of the law, but in the 1980s, aggressive federal attorneys like Rudolph Giuliani (later mayor of New York) used the statute to prosecute New York mafia families successfully.[86] Aggressive application of the law, and timely defections by key mafioso who agreed to become witnesses against other mafioso, enabled federal prosecutors to convict dozens of leading mafioso in the "Mob Commission," "Pizza Connection," and "Gambino Crime Family" trials, effectively decapitating U.S. mafia firms. As Guiliani claimed in 1987, "I do not believe that the Mafia, or La Cosa Nostra, will be an organization that means anything to anyone a decade from now . . . it is something that will be part of our history. . . . "[87]

By 1992, police investigators in Los Angeles described Italian-American gangsters as the "Mickey Mouse Mafia," saying that the mob was so weak that "illegal book makers refuse to pay it for the right to operate."[88] In New Jersey, the head of the state police described local mafioso as the "Geritol Gang" because they had become so aged and ineffective.[89]

For the U.S. mafia, the problems associated with the transformation of the vice industries and aggressive government prosecution were compounded, in the 1980s, by a third problem: decreased heroin supplies from the Golden Crescent because the 1979 revolution in Iran and the Soviet invasion of Afghanistan had disrupted its traditional sources of opium. And while U.S. and Sicilian mafias scrambled for secure supplies, they faced increasing competition from triads selling heroin and cartels peddling cocaine in U.S. markets.

In this intermafia competition, foreign mafias possessed important advantages over domestic U.S. mafias. Foreign mafias were based close to drug supplies but far from U.S. government prosecutors. This meant they were better placed to obtain drugs and evade the law, particularly since government authority was weak in their host countries. And they were able to establish connections with young, aggressive street gangs based in U.S. immigrant communities: Vietnamese, Russian, Israeli, Jamaican, Hispanic. When triads entered the New York heroin market in the 1980s, they used Chinese street gangs to retail the drug.[90] It was difficult for undercover New York City police to prosecute these organizations because few officers spoke Chinese dialects. So while foreign mafias could draw recruits from new immigrant communities, domestic mafias found it increasingly difficult to recruit from Italian neighborhoods, which were disappearing as a result of migration to the suburbs.[91]

These advantages, coupled with new, lower-priced drugs (a product of

expanding drug cultivation), enabled foreign mafias to wrest control of lucrative U.S. drug markets from weakened domestic mafias. As the *New York Times* reported in 1991, "New York's five mafia families . . . have deteriorated in recent months to the point that three are virtually out of business and two are crumbling."[92] The state's task force on organized crime predicted that the families would be "reduced to the level of street gangs within a decade."[93]

Although no one bemoans the disappearance of domestic U.S. mafias, the rise of foreign mafias means that law enforcement efforts will be less effective in coming years than they were in the 1980s.

The growing consumption of illegal drugs has contributed to three kinds of problems in the United States. First, illegal drug use contributes to crime and the spread of disease. Although the price of heroin and cocaine fell during the 1980s, they were still relatively expensive, which meant that many users and addicts committed crimes to raise money to purchase drugs. A 1972 Ford Foundation study found that prostitution provided 30.8 percent, shoplifting 22.6 percent, and burglary 19 percent of the funds raised by heroin addicts to purchase drugs, though the author noted that male addicts often sold heroin to defray costs and female addicts relied most heavily on prostitution to earn the money they needed.[94] Another Ford Foundation study estimated that "up to 50 percent of property crimes in the major metropolitan areas with a serious heroin problem are committed by addicts."[95] As a result, rising drug use helped drive up crime rates in the past thirty years.

Heroin use also contributed to the spread of disease in the 1980s. Because some heroin addicts work as prostitutes and/or share the needles used to inject the drug, the AIDS virus spread rapidly among heroin users, prostitutes, and their customers during the 1980s. In New York City, 4 to 7 percent of intravenous drug users contract AIDS every year, which means that between forty thousand and seventy thousand have contracted AIDS in the 1980s.[96]

Second, street gangs have engaged in a murderous competition for control of the retail drug trade. The violence grew dramatically during the late 1980s as street gangs vied for control of the newly opening crack trade. In Washington, D.C., more than 80 percent of all homicides in 1989 were drug-related, and residents of that city were more likely to be killed than people living in Northern Ireland, the Punjab, Lebanon, or El Salvador, places where civil wars then raged.[97] Although the violence has abated somewhat, it has become so common among street gangs that they refer to young street dealers as "Dixie Cups, because they are so disposable," says New York District Attorney Walter Arsenault.[98]

Third, crime and violence associated with the consumption and trade in illegal drugs have created a variety of problems for federal, state, and local government officials. As officials intensified antidrug campaigns, they passed stiffer laws that led to more arrests. Between 1980 and 1989, drug arrests increased 105 percent.[99] But drug-related arrests clogged the courts and prisons. In California, the prison population quintupled from "20,000 in 1979 to over 100,000 in early 1991—roughly the number behind bars in Great Britain and West Germany combined . . . [and] more men are now in prison for drug offenses than were behind bars for all [other] crimes in 1980."[100] Some people estimate that by 1995, nearly 70 percent of federal inmates will be drug offenders.[101]

Growing prison populations have led to increased prison construction, an expensive undertaking. Federal spending on the drug war grew to $13 billion in 1993, and states spent an additional $18 billion on enforcement and $20 billion for new prisons.[102]

Assessing the War on Drugs

Frustrated by these developments, some government officials have argued that drug use should be decriminalized or legalized under controlled circumstances. In 1993, U.S. Surgeon General Joycelyn Elders recommended that the government should study the idea of legalizing drugs because, she said, "I do feel that we would markedly reduce our crime rate if drugs were legalized."[103] Some federal judges have also called for the legalization of marijuana, heroin, and crack, arguing that the war on illicit drugs was "bankrupt" and was overwhelming the courts and prison system.[104] This view has been supported by some mayors and former government officials. But most U.S. government officials oppose legalization, a view that has wide public support. As an alternative, some officials have urged the expansion of drug treatment, methadone maintenance, and needle-swap programs.[105]

Historically, a number of policies have been effective against mafias, though not necessarily drug use. The legalization of alcohol greatly reduced the power of mafias who prospered from the illegal trade. The government's restrictions on machine-gun ownership took the dangerous .45-caliber Browning submachine gun out of circulation for many years, until the advent of new small-caliber, assault-rifle technologies put dangerous weapons back into circulation. The takeover of the vice industries—gambling by state governments and private corporations, pornography and prostitution by independent entrepreneurs and female

sex workers—reduced mafia income sources. And the adoption of RICO and witness protection programs proved to be effective legal tools against domestic mafia firms. Overseas, the opium eradication campaigns in Turkey and Mexico were relatively successful, though production shifted to other regions, and antidrug campaigns in some countries have sometimes been effective, though their success depended on fairly draconian measures by revolutionary governments in Iran, China, and Vietnam.

But while these measures have undermined mafias and reduced the crime and violence associated with mafias and the vice industry, they did not greatly reduce *drug use*. Indeed, alcohol consumption increased after Prohibition, though alcohol consumption is now lower on average than it was at the beginning of the century. Marijuana is a good example of how decriminalization can curb mafia violence but also increase use.

In the 1960s, most of the marijuana consumed in the United States was cultivated in Mexico, Colombia, Jamaica, and Thailand, and imported by foreign mafias, principally Mexican. Unlike heroin or cocaine, marijuana was not processed by mafia importers. Indeed, marijuana sold on U.S. streets contained seeds and stems that had to be cleaned out by consumers. During the 1970s, U.S. consumers began cultivating and hybridizing marijuana using seeds obtained from foreign imports. Growers in northern California developed new, more potent hybrid varieties, called "sensimilla" because they were "without seeds," that quickly captured a growing share of the U.S. market.

The widespread cultivation of hybrid marijuana by independent U.S. growers and the sale of the drug through networks of small-scale dealers—a development made possible by the decriminalization of marijuana possession and use in many states during the 1970s—greatly reduced demand for foreign marijuana and diminished the role of mafias in the trade. Consequently, there is little of the crime and violence associated with the cultivation, trade, and use of marijuana that is seen with illegal drugs.

But while there is little crime or violence, there is extensive marijuana use. Marijuana use rose in the 1960s and 1970s, declined somewhat in the mid-to-late 1980s, and then rose again in 1993.[106] What's more, the drug consumed by smokers today is much more potent, and more expensive, than the cheap, weak imports consumed in the 1960s. According to one federal study, the amount of THC (tetrahydrocannabinol, the active ingredient in marijuana) in the average joint increased every year after 1973, from 0.2 percent in 1972 to 3.6 percent in 1988.[107] If a joint of marijuana had the potency of a can of beer in the 1960s, it has the potency of whisky today.

To a large extent, governments face two related problems. If they want

to curb drug use by making it illegal, they create a role for mafia firms, which contributes to crime and violence. If they want to curb the role of mafias and reduce the crime and violence associated with the illegal drug trade, they may contribute to increased drug use, though determined public education and drug treatment programs can sometimes reduce drug use over a long period of time.

Both strategies have important social costs. On the one hand, laws criminalizing drug use have led, in the 1970s and '80s, to the emergence of powerful, violent, and wealthy global mafias. U.N. Secretary General Boutros Boutros-Ghali warned in 1994,

> Organized crime has become a world phenomenon. In Europe, in Asia, in Africa and in America, the forces of darkness are at work and no society is spared. Transnational crime undermines the very foundations of the international democratic order. It poisons the business climate, corrupts political leaders and undermines human rights.[108]

On the other hand, the continued or increased use of powerful drugs would have important consequences for consumers and societies. Drug users risk death and disease, and addictions can adversely affect individual behavior. The cost of treating or addressing the medical and social consequences of individual addiction can be high, as society has discovered with widespread alcohol and tobacco use.

The problem for government officials in coming years is to address both problems simultaneously, keeping in mind that efforts to address one problem may contribute to the other.

Notes

1. Treaster, Joseph B. "20 Years of War on Drugs, and No Victory Yet," *New York Times*, June 14, 1992.

2. Hobsbawm, Eric. *Primitive Rebels: Studies in Archaic Forms of Social Movement in the 19th and 20th Centuries*. New York: Frederick A. Praeger, 1963, pp. 36–37. Gambetta, Diego. *The Sicilian Mafia: The Business of Private Protection*. Cambridge: Harvard University Press, 1993, p. 136.

3. Gambetta, 1993, p. 1.

4. Ibid., p. 2.

5. Hess, Henner. *Mafia and Mafiosi: The Structure of Power*. Lexington, Mass.: Lexington Books, 1973, p. 1.

6. Arlacci, Pino. *Mafia Business: The Mafia Ethic and the Spirit of Capitalism*. London: Verso, 1986, p. 9.

7. Ibid., pp. 3, 4.

8. Ibid., pp. 3, 4, 5.

9. Hobsbawm, 1963, p. 33. Arlacci, 1986, p. 44.

10. Hobsbawm, 1963, pp. 33–34. Arlacci, 1986, pp. 44, 138.

11. Anderson, Annelise G. *The Business of Organized Crime: A Cosa Nostra Family*. Stanford: Hoover Institution Press, 1979, p. 12. Stark, David H. *The Yakuza: Japanese Crime Incorporated*. Ph.D. Dissertation, University of Michigan. Ann Arbor: University Microfilms, 1981, p. 237.

12. Ownby, David, and Somers, Mary. *Secret Societies Reconsidered: Perspectives on the Social History of Modern South China and Southeast Asia*. Armonk, N.Y.: Sharpe, 1993, p. 4.

13. Posner, Gerald L. *Warlords of Crime: Chinese Secret Societies—The New Mafia*. New York: McGraw-Hill, 1988, p. 31.

14. Murray, Dian. "Migration, Protection and Racketeering: The Spread of the Tiandihui within China," in David Ownsby and Mary Somers, 1993, p. 181. Bresler, Fenton. *The Chinese Mafia*. New York: Stein and Day, 1981, p. 29.

15. Ibid., pp. 27–28.

16. Ibid., p. 30.

17. Ibid.

18. Posner, 1988, p. 34.

19. Ibid., p. 40.

20. Ibid., pp. 40–41.

21. Kaplan, David E., and Dubro, Alec. *Yakuza: The Explosive Account of Japan's Criminal Underworld*. Reading, Mass.: Addison-Wesley, 1986, p. 214.

22. Kaplan and Dubro, 1986, p. 141.

23. Ibid., p. 18.

24. Ibid., p. 24. Stark, 1981, p. 27.

25. Kaplan and Dubro, 1986, pp. 28–29.

26. Stark, 1981, pp. 110–11.

27. Ibid., pp. 35–36.

28. Ibid., pp. 56, 232–33. Kaplan and Dubro, 1986, pp. 6, 146.

29. Arlacci, 1986, p. 222.

30. Ibid., p. 219.

31. Ibid., p. 131.

32. Ibid., p. 56.

33. Anderson, 1979, p. 65.

34. Kaplan and Dubro, 1986, pp. 167–68.

35. Ibid., p. 203.

36. Gambetta, 1993, p. 234.

37. Posner, 1988, p. 76.

38. Musto, David F. *The American Disease: Origins of Narcotic Control*. New York: Oxford University Press, 1987, pp. 254–58.

39. Ibid., p. 254.

40. Richburg, Keith B. "From Fighting Mao to Tending Opium Gardens," *Washington Post*, June 13, 1988.

41. Andreas, Peter, and Youngers, Coletta. "U.S. Drug Policy and the Andean Cocaine Industry," *World Policy Journal*, Summer 1989, p. 535. Falco, Mathea.

"Foreign Drugs, Foreign Wars," in *Political Pharmacology: Thinking About Drugs, Daedalus*, 121, 3, Summer 1992, p. 4.

42. "The Kickback from Cocaine," *The Economist*, July 21, 1990, p. 40. Falco, 1992, p. 8.

43. Holahan, John F. "The Economics of Heroin," in Patricia Wald and Peter Hutt, eds., *Dealing with Drug Abuse: A Report to the Ford Foundation*. New York: Praeger, 1972, pp. 261, 270. Arlacci, 1986, p. 194.

44. Holahan in Patricia Wald and Peter Hutt, 1986, p. 272.

45. Posner, 1988, pp. 26, 72, 74, 77. Lintner, Peter. "A Fix in the Making," *Far Eastern Economic Review*, June 28, 1990, p. 20. Sciolino, Elaine. "U.S. Finds Output of Drugs in World Growing Slowly," *New York Times*, March 2, 1988. Sciolino, Elaine. "World Drug Crop Up Sharply in 1989 Despite U.S. Effort," *New York Times*, March 2, 1990. Arlacci, 1986, pp. 187–88, 215–16. Winslow, George. "Credibility A Casualty in the War on Drugs," *In These Times*, May 12–23, 1989, p. 19. McCoy, Alfred W. *The Politics of Heroin in Southeast Asia*. New York: Harper & Ros, 1972, pp. 78, 1, 354. Holahan in Patricia Wald and Peter Hutt, 1972, p. 259. Bresler, Fenton. *The Chinese Mafia*. New York: Stein & Day, 1981, pp. 2–3.

46. Gorriti, Gustavo A. "How to Fight the Drug War," *Atlantic Monthly*, July 1989, p. 70.

47. Holahan in Patricia Wald and Peter Hutt, 1972, pp. 256–57, 258, 262.

48. Ibid., p. 265.

49. Falco, 1992, p. 10. Sciolino, 1988. "The Quality of Mercy," *The Economist*, July 22, 1989, p. 43. Ghazi, Katayon. "Drug Trafficking Is Thriving in Iran," *New York Times*, December 4, 1991.

50. Erlanger, Steven. "Burma's Unrest and Weather Help Opium Flourish," *New York Times*, December 11, 1988.

51. Riding, Alan. "Colombian Cocaine Dealers Tap European Market," *New York Times*, April 29, 1989. Musto, 1987, p. 274. Berke, Richard L. "After Studying for War on Drugs, Bennett Wants More Troops," *New York Times*, August 6, 1989.

52. Skolnick, Jerome H. "Rethinking the Drug Problem," in Jerome H. Skolnick and Elliott Currie, *Crisis in American Institutions*. New York: HarperCollins, 1994, p. 444. Musto, 1987, p. 274.

53. MacDonald, Scott B. *Dancing On a Volcano: The Latin American Drug Trade*. New York: Praeger, 1988, p. 3. "Drugs: How to Beat Them," *The Economist*, August 12, 1989, p. 20.

54. Treaster, Joseph B. "A More Potent Heroin Makes a Comeback in a New, Needleless Form," *New York Times*, April 28, 1991.

55. Ibid.

56. Treaster, Joseph B. "To Avoid AIDS, Users of Heroin Shift from Injecting It to Inhaling It," *New York Times*, November 17, 1991.

57. Treaster, April 28, 1991.

58. Gabriel, Trip. "Heroin Finds a New Market Along Cutting Edge of Style," *New York Times*, May 8, 1994.

59. Musto, 1987, p. 5.

60. McCoy, 1972, pp. 6, 24, 16, 87.

61. Wald and Hutt, 1972, p. 4.

62. Falco, 1992, p. 2.

63. Reuter, Peter. "Can Domestic Sources Substitute for Imported Drugs?" in Peter H. Smith, ed., *Drug Policy in the Americas*. Boulder, Colo.: Westview, 1992, p. 168.

64. Currie, Elliott. *Reckoning: Drugs, the Cities and the American Future*. New York: Hill and Wang, 1993, pp. 10, 12, 33.

65. Henneberger, Melinda. " 'Pot' Surges Back, But It's, Like, A Whole New World," *New York Times*, February 6, 1994.

66. "Addiction by Design," *New York Times*, March 6, 1994.

67. Rosenthal, Elisabeth. "Patients in Pain Find Relief, Not Addiction, in Narcotics," *New York Times*, March 28, 1992.

68. MacDonald, 1988, p. 4.

69. Kristof, Nicholas D. "Heroin Use Spreads in China Among the Curious or Bored," *New York Times*, March 20, 1991.

70. MacDonald, 1988, p. 4.

71. Brooke, James. "Peruvian Farmers Razing Rainforest to Sow Drug Crops," *New York Times*, August 13, 1989.

72. Ibid. Scott, Peter Dale, and Marshall, Jonathan. *Cocaine Politics: Drugs, Armies and the CIA in Central America*. Berkeley: University of California Press, 1991, p. 74. Alvarez, Elena. "Coca Production in Peru," in Peter H. Smith, 1992, p. 83.

73. Kristof, 1991.

74. Brooke, James. "Drug Traffickers in Colombia Start a Counterattack," *New York Times*, August 25, 1989.

75. Andreas and Youngers, 1989, p. 538. Brooke, James. "Drugs and Terror Linked in Colombia," *New York Times*, April 6, 1989. Guillermoprieto, Alma. "Exit El Patron," *The New Yorker*, October 25, 1993, p. 79.

76. Brooke, James. "Colombian Kidnappings are Gagging the Press," *New York Times*, January 28, 1991. Brooke, James. "Colombian Abductions a Sign of Continuing Drug War," *New York Times*, September 23, 1990.

77. Brooke, James. "Vigilantes Cut Murder Rate in Colombian Cocaine Center," *New York Times*, February 15, 1992.

78. Smith, 1992, p. 1. MacGregor, Felipe E. *Coca and Cocaine: An Andean Perspective*. Westport, Conn.: Greenwood, 1993, p. 46. Gutkin, Steven. "Colombia Called 'Narco-Democracy,' " *San Francisco Chronicle*, October 1, 1994.

79. Tierney, John. "For New York City's OTB, A Sure Bet Ends Up a Loser," *New York Times*, November 14, 1994. Clines, Francis X. "Gambling, Pariah No More, Is Booming Across America," *New York Times*, December 5, 1993.

80. Ibid.

81. Skolnick and Currie, 1994, p. 442.

82. Kleinfield, N. R. "Legal Gambling Faces Higher Odds," *New York Times*, August 29, 1993.

83. Jenness, Valerie. *Making It Work: The Prostitutes' Rights Movement in Perspective.* New York: Aldine de Gruyter, 1993, pp. 24–25. Sandza, Richard. "Going After a Porn Czar," *Newsweek,* August 8, 1988.

84. Jenness, 1993, pp. 2–6, 18–19.

85. Holahan in Patricia Wald and Peter Hutt, 1972, p. 182.

86. Davis, John H. *Mafia Dynasty: The Rise and Fall of the Gambino Crime Family.* New York: HarperCollins, 1993, p. 183.

87. Oreskes, Michael. "Guiliani Says Mafia is Dying Under Prosecution," *New York Times,* March 3, 1987. Blumenthal, Ralph. "Verdict Is Termed a Blow to the Mafia," *New York Times,* November 20, 1986.

88. "Mafia Prosecutors Quitting As Strike Forces Disband," *New York Times,* January 4, 1990.

89. Ibid.

90. Kifner, John. "New Immigrant Wave from Asia Gives the Underworld New Faces," *New York Times,* January 5, 1991.

91. Arlacci, 1986, p. 227.

92. *New York Times,* January 4, 1990.

93. Ibid.

94. Holahan in Patricia Wald and Peter Hutt, 1972, pp. 289–90, 292.

95. Wald and Hutt, 1972, p. 6.

96. Lee, Felicia R. "Data Show Needle Exchange Curbs HIV Among Addicts," *New York Times,* November 26, 1994.

97. Berke, Richard L. "Capitol Offers Unlimited Turf to Drug Dealers," *New York Times,* March 28, 1989. "Uncivil Wars," *The Economist,* October 7, 1989, p. 38.

98. "Ganging Up on the Gangs," *The New Yorker,* October 10, 1994, p. 44.

99. Currie, 1993, pp. 14–15. Husch, Jerri A. "Culture and U.S. Drug Policy: Toward a New Conceptual Framework," in *Daedalus,* 1992, p. 268.

100. Currie, 1993, p. 16.

101. Blansfield, James M. "What Legalizing Drugs Would Mean," *New York Times,* December 28, 1993.

102. Moberg, David. "Codependence," *In These Times,* December 27, 1993, p. 24.

103. Labaton, Stephen. "Surgeon General Suggests Study of Legalizing Drugs," *New York Times,* December 8, 1993.

104. Labaton, Stephen. "Federal Judge Urges Legalization of Crack, Heroin and Other Drugs," *New York Times,* December 13, 1989. Weinstein, Jack B. "The War on Drugs Is Self-Defeating," *New York Times,* July 8, 1993.

105. Massing, Michael. "Help Addicts? Sure. We Promise. Really!" *New York Times,* October 22, 1993. Altman, Lawrence K. "U.S. to Ease Methadone Rules in Bid to Curb AIDS in Addicts," *New York Times,* March 3, 1989. Holmes, Steven A. "Treasury Imposes New Regulations on Some Shotguns," *New York Times,* March 1, 1994. Lee, 1994.

106. Henneberger, 1994.

107. Reuter in Peter H. Smith, 1992, pp. 172–73.

108. Rosenthal, 1992.

Index

About the Author

For many years, Robert Schaeffer worked as a journalist and an editor for Friends of the Earth, *Nuclear Times*, and *Greenpeace Magazine*. He now teaches global sociology and environmental studies at San Jose State University, where he is a member of the sociology department. He participates in Pugwash Conferences on Science and World Affairs, which in 1995 won the Nobel Peace Prize. And he is the editor of *War in the World-System* (1990), and author of *Warpaths: The Politics of Partition* (1990) and *Power to the People: Democratization Around the World* (1997).